No. 205—$27.85

CONTENTS

Modern Aviation Library
BLUE RIDGE SUMMIT, PA. 17214

THE COMPLETE GUIDE TO
SINGLE-ENGINE
CESSNAS —3RD EDITION

BY JOE CHRISTY

Copyright © 1979 by TAB BOOKS

Library of Congress Cataloging in Publication Data

Christy, Joe.
    The complete guide to single-engine Cessnas.

    Published in 1971 under title: The single-engine cessnas.
    Includes index.
    1. Cessna (Airplanes) I. Title.
TL686.C4C46   1979   629.133'343   79-14328
ISBN 0-8306-9800-0
ISBN 0-8306-2268-3

CONTENTS

ACKNOWLEDGMENT

The author is grateful to Cessna's Larry Wiggins, Photo Editor, for his cheerful help during the preparation of this book.

J.C.

FOREWORD

Clyde Vernon Cessna was a 31 year-old automobile mechanic in 1910 when he saw a trio of magnificent men perform in their flying machines at Oklahoma City. Clyde made detailed sketches of the Bleroit monoplane possessed by one of the birdmen and, a year later, had built a passable replica which he flew — after twelve attempts and eleven crashes — from the Salt Plains near Jet, Oklahoma. Clyde thereupon forsook the horseless carriage business and embarked upon an aerial exhibition tour of the county fair circuit. His first appearance was at Cherokee, Oklahoma, for which he received $300 for simply taking-off and circling the pasture. Such an accomplishment, in 1911, was unquestionably worth every cent of it.

During the next six years, until WW-I intervened, Cessna became a highly successful exhibition pilot (the *only* way there was to make a living with an airplane in those days), and he built an improved craft each winter at the family farm near Rago, Kansas. By 1917, his *Comet* monoplane averaged 124.62 mph in a flight between Wichita, Kansas and Blackwell, Oklahoma.

Clyde was 37 years old when America entered WW-I and was not accepted for military service. He farmed until 1919, then returned to the air. Late in 1924 he was still barnstorming (though by then using a Laird Swallow — sold to him by a Swallow salesman named Walter Herschel Beech) when Walter Beech and another Swallow employee, Lloyd Carlton Stearman, talked Cessna into joining them in the formation of a new airplane manufacturing business. With $10,000 in capital put up by Beech and Cessna, and Stearman's drawings of a three-place biplane, the Travel Air Company began operation with six employees in a small shop behind the Broadview Hotel in downtown Wichita.

But three chiefs in a single tepee made at least two too many. Though Travel Air grew rapidly, Stearman pulled out in 1926 to form his own company (later absorbed by Boeing), and Cessna

7

Dwane Wallace and his uncle, Clyde Cessna.
Photo taken shortly before Cessna's death in 1954.

The company's first production aircraft were called the "A" series.

sold out the following year to found the Cessna Aircraft Company (after several months as the Cessna-Roos Aircraft Corporation in partnership with Victor H. Roos, a former associate of Giuseppe M. Bellanca). Beech continued successfully with Travel Air, which was merged into the (then) giant Curtiss-Wright complex in 1929.

Meanwhile, Cessna steadily built his company. In 1929, he purchased 80 acres at Cessna's present main plant site and constructed five buildings. He had 80 employees, and his products were the Cessna Model A series; clean, four-place cantilever monoplanes powered with a variety of engines, the most popular of which was the Model AW, fitted with a 125-hp Warner or a 200-hp Wright Whirlwind. These Cessnas were Clyde's own designs, and were so basically sound one can still see some Model AW in single-engine Cessnas today. Between 1931 and 1936, Cessnas won the Detroit News "World's Most Efficient Airplane" trophy three times to gain permanent possession of that famed award.

The Great Depression halted production at Cessna in 1932, and one can only speculate as to what may have happened to the company (Clyde was nearing retirement age, and other airframe makers were being liquidated almost daily as the economic disaster worsened) had not Clyde given an airplane ride to his 12 year-old nephew, Dwane L. Wallace, back in 1923. From that time forward, young Wallace knew that his future would be in aviation. He soloed an OX-5 Travel Air in 1932, and graduated from Wichita State University in 1933 with a bachelor's degree in aeronautical engineering.

Since Cessna was closed down, Dwane worked briefly for Walter Beech (who had started Beech Aircraft Corporation in 1932, offering the Model 17 "Staggerwing"), then Dwane persuaded his uncle to reorganize the Cessna Aircraft Company and re-open the plant, producing a new four-to-five-place monoplane of outstanding performance. The resulting Cessna Airmaster kept the company alive and is regarded as a classic design today.

Clyde retired to his farm in 1936 (he died in 1954), and Dwane Wallace — at age 25 — became president of the company, as well as part-time janitor, test pilot, engineer and chief salesman. In fact, prize money won by Wallace racing the new C-34 Airmaster usually went to meet the company's modest payroll. Production averaged less than 30 units per year for 1934 through 1938.

The coming aircraft production demands of WW-II signaled an abrupt change in Cessna's fortunes. The company's first twin-engine plane, the T-50, appeared in 1939 and was bought first by the RCAF, then by the USAAF. More than 5,400 of these craft were built during WW-II as the AT-8, AT-17 and UC-78. The British and Canadians called it the "Crane;" the USAAF designation was "Bobcat." But to the cadets who transitioned in this twin-engine trainer it was affectionately (if irreverently) known as the "Useless-78," "Bamboo Bomber" or "Rhapsody in Glue."

Also during WW-II, Cessna produced troop-carrying gliders, and sub-assemblies for Boeing and Douglas — with, of course, greatly expanded factory facilities.

When the war ended, the company again turned to the commercial aircraft business. After a five-month conversion, Cessna introduced its first post-war models, the two-place 120 and 140. Production of these neat little craft reached 30 units per day in the summer of 1946, and that year's sales totaled nearly 4,000 airplanes.

Cessna broadened its market in 1947 with introduction of the four-place 190 and 195 — essentially, all-metal Airmasters. And the following year production was started on the new four-place Model 170.

10

C-165 Airmaster; from 1935's C-34 until 1941's C-165D 185 were constructed

The L-19 Bird Dog (later designated O-1 by the Army) appeared in 1949, then the Korean War claimed a large portion of Cessna's production capacity with sub-assemblies for Boeing, Lockheed and Republic. But in 1954, along with the T-37 jet trainer, the five-place twin-engine Model 310 was introduced to the public. The tricycle-gear Models 172 and 182 came out in 1955, and then, when the two-place tri-gear Model 150 was added in 1959, the basic Cessna line of single-engine aircraft was established for years to come.

That was the year that Cessna expanded into the electronics business with acquisition of Aircraft Radio Corporation (ARC), and the year that total company sales for the first time passed the $100 million mark. In 1969 total sales were $282.9 million. And it is probably worth remarking that, in 1939 when Dwane Wallace closed the deal with Canada for the first 180 Cranes, there was exactly $5.03 in the company's bank account. As this is written, Dwane is still top man at Cessna as board chairman — and it's safe to say the company's bank account is somewhat larger these days.

CHAPTER 1: CESSNA 120 AND 140

During the fall of 1970, we checked with a number of aircraft dealers in Texas, Oklahoma and Kansas to get some impressions of the used plane market. We knew of course that new lightplane sales were down at the time, along with everything else in the aerospace industry, but we suspected that "experienced" lightplanes were still finding plenty of buyers.

This seemed to be the case. Every dealer we talked with said he could sell more used airplanes if he had them — and the two-place Cessna 140 and four-place Cessna 170 were the craft most often mentioned as desirable merchandise from both sellers' and buyers' points of view.

This meant that the fabric-wing 140, which sold for a maximum of $3,495 new (1946-1949), was bringing from $2,000 to $2,400 almost 25 years later. And a good metal-wing 140A (or a 140 with metalized wing), which had an original list price of $3,695, was commanding up to $2,750 in the 1970 market.

Simple inflation was largely responsible for the apparently negligible depreciation of low-priced lightplanes during these years. For example, shortly before we left the airport business in mid-1963, among the planes we sold were a clean little 140, for $2,100, and an equally good 170 for $4,700. Those same airplanes (in the same condition) would have brought at least that much seven years later.

But in addition to inflation, the basic soundness of the early post-war Cessnas has also contributed to their high re-sale value. The 120/140 is a trim little ship with honest flying characteristics and performance matching or exceeding that of the later 150.

The 120 and 140 are basically the same airplane; the 120 being the economy version without electrical system, starter or flaps, and possessing a minimum of instruments. Both aircraft are powered with the C-85 Continental engine — except for the 521 metal-winged 140A's produced at the factory. The 140A is fitted with a Continental C-90. Since many fabric-wing 140's were later converted to metal-wingers, these will probably still be equipped with the 85-hp engine and therefore are not 140A's. As originally delivered from

The Cessna 140 of 1946 had fabric-covered wing, 85-hp engine. Maximum list price was $3,495.

Cessna, all 120's and 140's were unpainted, except of course for silver dope finish on the fabric wings. In recent years, however, many have been given modern paint schemes.

Some 120's have been fitted with the Continental C-85-12 (the 140 engine, which has starter and generator) and a complete electrical system; and though such a craft may be called a "140," it really isn't — unless it has also been given the 140 wings with flaps and the 140's plusher cabin and extra instruments. But it does come close, because the 140's flaps are not the big "para-lift" barn-door airfoils found on later Cessnas, and do not help much, if any, on short take-offs, and though useful for landings, will seem anemic if you've been flying, say, a 150.

At the end of the sixties, there were about 1,200 120's and 3,500 140's still around.

Entering the 140 will at first seem an awkward and ungraceful exercise to those unaccustomed to the older tail-draggers, but it's no worse than a T-Craft, Luscombe or Aeronca, and certainly beats boarding a J-3 Cub. The seats are comfortable, but the cabin is small and becomes cramped for two (sitting side-by-side) if both are over 175 pounds.

Starter, throttle, parking brake, carburetor heat and mixture control are at bottom center of the instrument panel, with electrical switches immediately beneath. Elevator trim, flap control and fuel selector switch are between the seats. The fuel selector switch is three-position, for either of the two 12½-gallon wing tanks, or "Off." Fuel gauges are of the direct-reading type and located in each wing root inside the cabin. Fuel to the engine is gravity-fed via the selector-switch junction, then through a strainer on the firewall to the carburetor.

These little Continental engines are easy to start (when properly maintained), though on a cold day three or four strokes of the primer are required. Since this is a tail-wheel airplane, taxi in an S-pattern to clear the blind spot over the nose. During the pre-take-off check, test mags at 1,800 rpms; set carb heat at "Cold," turn elevator trim wheel to "Take-Off;" determine that flaps are up and locked, and of course be sure your fuel selector is turned to the fullest tank. This is also when you are supposed to lock the door and windows, although we can't guarantee that they'll stay that way on some 140's after all these years.

Average take-off roll with the 140 at full gross load (1,450 lbs) is between 600 and 750 feet in a no-wind condition, depending upon ground elevation and temperature. Holding the tail a little below horizontal, she breaks ground at slightly over 40 mph. Then, climb-out should be made at between 80 and 90 mph for good engine cooling. This will give you a rate-of-climb of about 600 feet per minute initially; and on a normal day, somewhere between 300 and 400 fpm at 7,000 ft.

Sure, this is less than fighter airplane performance; but you are aviating with 85 horsepower and burning only 5 gallons of gasoline per hour. At the 140's normal cruising speed of 105 mph, that's more than 20 miles per gallon — which is far better than your car (any car) can do. Full Throttle (2,575 rpms) will up your speed to between 115 and 120 mph and raise gas consumption to about 6 gallons per hour.

Stalls are gentle in the 120 and 140. We once read a "pilot's report" in an aviation magazine wherein the writer said the 140 "stalls without warning." He just wasn't payin' attention. This craft does have a marked buffett preceding the stall. The nose falls through at about 47 mph, power off and clean. With flaps and power off, the break comes at about 43 or 44 mph. Flaps down and power on, she quits flying at about 38 mph. Recovery is quick, and there is some aileron control into the stall, although the 140's ailerons — like those on other single-engine Cessnas — are a bit too soft to suit some pilots.

Landing the 140, use carburetor heat and set the mixture control at "Full Rich." Sixty-five to seventy mph is a good gliding speed, with some nose-up trim cranked into lighten the control pressure. Flaps will steepen your glide without a build-up in airspeed, and do help to sink through the ground cushion after flareout. The 120, which has no flaps, seems to want to float a little at this point. But both 120 and 140 are fairly easy to land, and each has a relatively wide tread for planes of this configuration (the first of the Cessna steel-spring landing gears), and therefore are surefooted on the ground.

In sum, it's hard to imagine how anyone could get into the air with his own airplane for much less money than with a 120 or 140 — assuming that you find one that has been well maintained and isn't on the brink of expensive refurbishing. The only FAA Bulletin

The 1949 Cessna 140A had metal wing, single strut, and 90-hp engine; sold for $3,695. Cruising speed, 105 mph. Still popular on the used plane market.

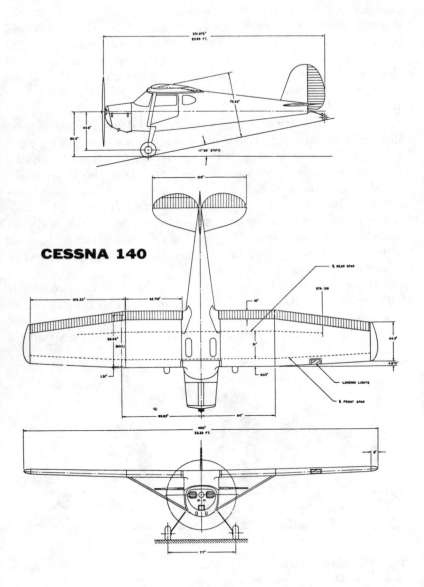

CESSNA 140

(AD Note) of consequence ever issued on these planes was AD-50-31-1, which calls for a reinforcement to the vertical fin spar. So, if you're thinking of buying such a plane, check the airframe log to make sure this has been complied with.

You'll also want to make a close inspection for corrosion and determine the condition of the wing fabric among other things. But let's face it, there is really only one reasonably safe way to select a used airplane of any kind: hire an experienced A&P (airframe & powerplant) mechanic — one who has no interest in the deal one way on another — to thoroughly inspect a plane before you buy it. This will cost you about $50.

Yes, it hurts a little to ante up $50; particularly if you go home without that airplane you had your heart set on. But it's better than buying a machine that spends much of its time in the shop running up repair bills.

SPECIFICATIONS, CESSNA 120 & 140

Engine	Continental C-85 or C-90
Wingspan	33 ft 4 in
Length	21 ft 6 in
Height	6 ft 3 in
Wing Area	159.3 sq ft
Wing Loading	9.1 lbs sq ft
Power Loading	17.1 lbs per hp
Empty Weight	120, 770; 140, 890 lb
Gross Weight	1,450 lbs
Useful Load	120, 680; 140, 560 lb
Fuel Capacity	25 gal
Oil Capacity	5 qts

PERFORMANCE, CESSNA 120 & 140*

Take-Off Distance	500 ft
Rate-of-Climb (Initial)	680 ft per min
Service Ceiling	15,500 ft
Top Speed	125 mph
Cruising Speed	105 mph
Range (with reserve)	450 mi
Stall Speed (without power; flaps up)	49 mph
Stall Speed (without power; flaps down)	45 mph
Landing roll (without brakes)	230 ft

*Original factory figures computed at full gross load and standard atmosphere (sea level; 59 degrees F).

CHAPTER 2: CESSNA 190 AND 195

Our description of the Cessna 190 and 195 will undoubtedly be a little biased, but it's not our fault. We don't *start* feuds with airplanes or other inanimate (?) objects. But "Shakey Jake" clearly disliked us from the beginning. Shakey was a 195 who belonged to a flying club. He got his name from his Jacobs engine, and he was brought to us for sundry maintenance and repairs. That is, he was brought to our shops when we were in the FBO business several years ago.*

Shakey was in and out of our place for many months, during which time he humiliated this writer on many occasions, dripped oil on our clean floors and obviously would have done us bodily harm had he ever got the chance. He had a crosswind landing gear, and everytime he saw us approach him he'd splay his wheels in different directions and dare us to move him. Everyone else around there could roll Shakey to or from the hangars and he'd go quietly. But not for this reporter; he hated us.

Shakey got the best of us in the end. His owners brought him in for a new windshield and, innocently, we gave an estimate and agreed to do the job. Well, please be advised, friends, such a request should be regarded in law as sufficient provocation for justifiable homicide. At least, when it involves an airplane with Shakey's delinquent social tendencies.

As it happened, our AI was away on a ferry flight, our number one A&P was on vacation, and there was no one in the shops except a young A&P just out of vo-tech school. And it quickly became apparent that replacing a 195 windshield was a job for two skilled airframe mechanics. But, naturally, Shakey would not have needed a windshield had our experienced men been on hand. Also, as you would expect, this happened in the middle of an Oklahoma summer. So, we sat in Shakey's cabin — where the temperature approximated that of Death Valley — for a couple of days, and tried to guess which of the roughly 4,000 locknuts we were supposed to hold while the young A&P tightened from the outside and the suspicion grew that our replacement windshield was really for a DC-3 or something else. Anyway, our AI returned at the end of the

*The author is not an aircraft mechanic. As part-owner of this flight operation, his principal duties, it seems, were often those of line boy, mechanics' helper and rest room cleaner.

week, looked at the job in amazement, and did it all over again. We probably only lost a few hundred dollars on the deal.

With this as background, you'll understand if we are less than enthusiastic about the 195. As we said at the start, it clearly isn't our fault. Any pilot will agree that some airplanes just naturally dislike some people.

The first 190 appeared in 1947 and was powered with the Continental R-670-23 engine of 240 hp. The 195 quickly followed, and was offered with a choice of three Jacobs powerplants: the 245-hp R-755-9; the 275-hp R-755-B2 and the 300-hp R-755-A2.

A total of 204 190's were built, 1947-1953 inclusive; and 890 195's were produced, 1947-1957 inclusive. In addition, 83 of the 300-hp 195's were built for the military as the LC-126, 1950-1952, with 15 going to the Air Force, 5 to the Air National Guard and 63 to the Army (our nemesis, Shakey, was actually an Army surplus LC-126).

The Cessna 195

Prices ranged from $12,750 for early models up to $24,700 for the last 300-hp 195's. About 450 Cessna 195's were still on the FAA's "active" list in 1970; and some could be found on the used airplane market for $6,000 to $7,000 in "average" condition. It should be noted, however, that this craft possesses an impressive number of staunch friends, enough to form an International 195 Club, and these owners, flying mint-conidtion 195's, do not of course place "average" prices on them — if and when they are willing to sell at all. Thus, there were some like-new (or better-than-new) 195's around valued from $10,000 upwards at the beginning of the seventies.

Most 195's have a retracting step that extends when the cabin door is opened; on some this step may be permanently fixed. The cabin is roomy — positively spacious by lightplane standards — with a pair of individual adjustable seats in front and a solid-cushion type seat in back that accommodates three. As is obvious from the outside, forward visibility over the nose, from the pilots' seats, is very limited when this airplane is in three-point attitude. While on the ground, an acre or two of instrument panel seems to block out most of the world, so taxiing must be done in an S-pattern if you want a clue as to what you're about to run in to.

Fuel from the 40-gallon tank in each wing (total: 80 gal.) is gravity-fed to the Continental engine in the 190; but a fuel pump is used in the 195 because of its higher horsepower. In case of fuel-pump failure, a by-pass line will keep the Jacobs supplied with sufficient fuel by gravity alone to maintain normal cruise. The Jacobs must be primed on every start; two or three strokes of the primer on warm days, and five to seven strokes on cold days.

Starting the Jacobs, fuel mixture of course is set at "Full Rich;" carburetor heat at "Cold," but the propeller is set at "Low RPM" to prevent taking too much oil from the engine at this point. With the master switch "On," the engine primed and throttle cracked, turn the key ignition to "Battery Start" position, make sure your prop is clear and then press the starter button. As soon as the engine fires, turn the key ignition to "Both Run." The engine may require another shot or two of prime to keep it running at first.

By this time, the roomy transport-type cabin, generous expanse of instrument panel and that big radial barking defiance at the world, may combine to give you the air of Captain Sternjaw, departing upon his regular run to Kalamazoo. If so, okay, because there are times when this airplane needs full attention and a bit of

More than 120 members of the International 195 Club met at Wichita in 1970, flying in a total of 41 Cessna 195's for the three-day party.

professionalism in flying technique, especially after landing flare-out in a cross-wind, when it has a strong tendency to weathercock.

During the take-off run, visibility over the nose improves as the tail comes up. Full right rudder trim will compensate for much of the torque, and the 195 will fly off at about 60 mph — with an average take-off roll of about 900 feet — in a slightly tail-low attitude.

Full throttle is allowable for one minute, and this will give you an initial climb-rate of about 1,000 fpm at 2,200 rpms and 85 mph. But the recommended climb/cruise configuration is 2,000 rpms at 23 inches of manifold pressure with about 100 knots or 115 mph showing. This produces, usually, around 500 to 600 fpm, and the 195 will hold this, with very little drop in the rate-of-climb, through 4,000 feet.

Although a lot of people have described the 195 as a "good instrument airplane," we'd have to disagree. True, good turns (without altitude loss or gain) are easier on instruments until one learns where the horizon should be with relation to the top of the instrument panel, or whatever you finally pick as a reference for eyeball turns; and since aileron response is slow there's naturally less over-controlling with a set of "white knuckles" on the wheel during instrument flight. The 195 does have a big airplane feel, which alone must induce a certain feeling of security. But it needs to be flown. In cruise configuration, no matter how carefully you trim it, the plane will, left to itself, slowly porpoise, alternately gaining and losing up to 75 feet or even more.

Stall behavior is neither good nor bad. The 195 has plenty of aileron into the stall, and you'll use it. Power off and clean, the stall comes at about 65 mph. With power off and flaps, the break is a bit sharper at about 62 mph. With power on and flaps down, the pay-off registers at about 56-58 mph. These figures are average, for a moderate day and at near full gross load.

This airplane is easy to land — if the wind is straight down the runway. In a cross-wind some artful rudder work is required and, as far as we were ever able to discover, a certain amount of good luck.

This trait undoubtedly prompted installation of a cross-wind landing gear on some 195's (and 170's). And we'll say this for the cross-wind gear: it does exactly what it's supposed to do. That is, it keeps you rolling straight down the runway while the airplane

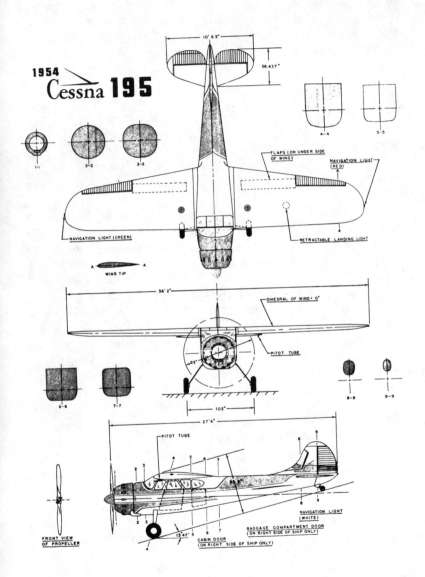

1954
Cessna **195**

10' 6.5"

56.437"

4-4

5-5

1-1   2-2   3-3

FLAPS (ON UNDER SIDE
OF WING)

NAVIGATION LIGHT
(RED)

NAVIGATION LIGHT (GREEN)

RETRACTABLE LANDING LIGHT

A — WING TIP — A

36' 2"

DIHEDRAL OF WING= 0°

PITOT TUBE

.93"

6-6   7-7

8-8   9-9

102"

27' 4"

PITOT TUBE

NAVIGATION LIGHT
(WHITE)

FRONT VIEW
OF PROPELLER

13' 47' 5"

CABIN DOOR
(ON RIGHT SIDE OF SHIP ONLY)

BAGGAGE COMPARTMENT DOOR
(ON RIGHT SIDE OF SHIP ONLY)

points in another direction. But it does take a modicum of faith to use it at first. Every nerve in your being will rebel at the prospect of actually touching-down while still crabbing 15 degrees or so into the wind. After a few landings, however, you'll probably feel it's the only practical gear for the 195. That is, until you have to wrestle the stubborn thing in and out of the hangar a few times.

Depending upon its condition, the 195 should give you a true air speed of 165-170 mph at 7,000 feet where about 70% of its power is available. Fuel consumption is about 16 gallons per hour with the 300-hp Jacobs.

Like we said in the beginning, this isn't a very objective report — maybe even a little unfair. But if an airplane ever gets it in for you, the way Shakey did for us, you'll understand.

SPECIFICATIONS, CESSNA 195

Engine	Jacobs R-755
Propeller	Hamilton Standard Constant Speed
Wing Span	36 ft 2 in
Length	27 ft 4 in
Height	7 ft 2 in
Wing Loading	15.36 lbs per sq ft
Power Loading	11.16 lbs per hp
Empty Weight	2,100 lbs
Gross Weight	3,350 lbs
Useful Load	1,250 lbs
Baggage Capacity	220 lbs
Fuel Capacity (usable)	75 gal
Oil Capacity	5 gal

PERFORMANCE, CESSNA 195

Take-Off Distance	800 ft
Take-Off over 50-ft Obstacle	1,600 ft
Landing Distance	700 ft
Landing over 50-ft Obstacle	1,600 ft
Rate of Climb, Maximum Initial	1,200 ft per min
Service Ceiling	18,300 ft
Maximum Speed	185 mph
Cruise Speed (70% Power)	170 mph
Range at 70% Power	800 mi
Stall Speed, Power Off, Flaps 45 Degrees	62 mph

The first (1948) Cessna 170 had two wing struts on each side, fabric-covered wing and a scaled-up 140 tail. Price was $7,245.

CHAPTER 3: CESSNA 170

The Cessna 170 series airplanes are still much in demand on the used market more than 20 years after this design first appeared. Good ones, late in 1970, were bringing 75% of their original purchase price. New prices ranged from $7,245 to $8,295 during production (1948-1955 inclusive), and a 170A or 170B in good condition would quickly find a buyer willing to pay up to $5,000 for it in 1970.

As with the used 140's, a portion of this relatively-high figure could be attributed to inflation. But again, as with the 140's, the Cessna 170 series compare very favorably, performance-wise, with the posher and sleeker tri-cycle gear models that replaced them. A comparison with the 1971 Model 172 (basic price, $13,425), will show what we mean:

	170B (1952)	172 (1971)
Top Speed	140 mph	139 mph
Cruising Speed	120 mph	131 mph
	(65% power)	(75% power)
Initial Climb Rate	690 fpm	645 fpm
Useful Load	995 lbs	1,050 lbs
Range	540 mi	615 mi

To be fair, we must point out that the above figures do not reflect the 172's added comfort, quieter cabin, easier landing and ground handling, 360-degree vision and a number of other little niceties, including a rakishly-swept rudder (which adds nothing except looks, and probably even costs a couple of mph in speed). And considering the additional fact that the 172 is brand new, while the 170B probably has at least 4,000 hours on its aging frame, there's little doubt but that the new 172 is a better buy at perhaps three times the price (including avionics) — if one has the money and/or a sound financial reason for operating a plane in this class.

But for the pilot who wants a four-placer primarily for pleasure, and cannot or does not wish to invest more than $4,000-$5,000 in such a machine, a well-maintained 170 may well be his best choice. There is also the possibility of a used 172, and we'll discuss that series in a following chapter.

The original 170 had a fabric-covered wing, two wing struts on each side and a 140-type rudder. The 170A, which appeared in 1949, had a metal-covered wing and new dorsal fin, plus a single lift strut on each side. The 170B, similar to the 170A but with L-19 type flaps added, was introduced in 1952. Officially, production ceased with the 1955 Model 170B; but 72 were built in 1956 (alongside the new 172), and 36 were produced in 1957, according to Cessna records. Altogether, 5,136 of the 170 series were built, and about 2,800 remained on the FAA's active list at the end of 1970.

The 170 is fairly easy to board for a tail-wheel airplane, and visibility over the nose is good. Noise-level in flight is about what you'd expect in an older airplane. This craft does want to weathercock on the ground in a good wind, and that can be a problem on a big airport when you have a long way to taxi. Having said that, it's hard to find any other fault with the 170. Its flying characteristics are all good; it's a pleasure to fly.

Cessna 170B of 1952 was all metal and had performance matching or surpassing the Model 172 which descended from it. Priced at $8,295 when production stopped in 1955, this model, in good condition, would bring 3/4ths of that in the used market in 1971.

The venerable L-19 Bird Dog (0-1), kissin' cousin to the 170, has maximum speed of 116 mph at 5,000 ft. Cessna produced 3,431 Bird Dogs from 1950 through 1969 inclusive.

Following standard pre-take-off procedures, the 170B will normally become airborne in about 700-800 feet, depending upon all-up weight and air density, indicating around 55 mph. Initial climb will be in the neighborhood of 700 fpm; up to 1,000 fpm if you are light.

This is a stable airplane in all axes, and requires reasonable coordination between wheel and rudder pedals for good turns. The 170's 145-hp Continental engine delivers 65% power at 5,000 feet pressure altitude turning 2,450 rpms, and produces 120 mph TAS with 8 gph fuel consumption at this setting. Since later model Cessnas using a quite similar engine cruise it at 2,700 rpms, the 170's recommended cruise rpms should result in fewer mechanical problems.

Stalls are gentle in this craft, and there is no wing drop except

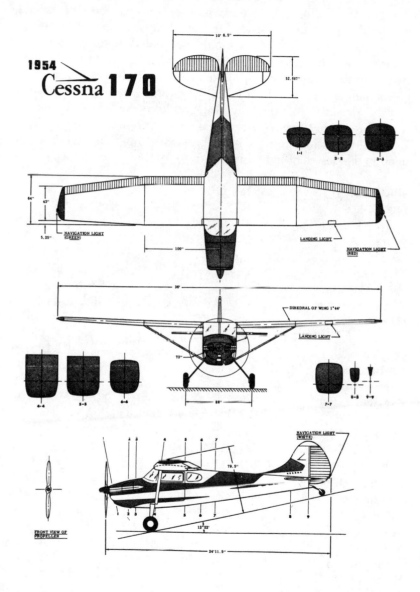

1954
Cessna 170

NAVIGATION LIGHT (GREEN)

LANDING LIGHT

NAVIGATION LIGHT (RED)

DIHEDRAL OF WING 1°44'

LANDING LIGHT

NAVIGATION LIGHT (WHITE)

FRONT VIEW OF PROPELLER

in full-power stalls. In all cases, this machine recovers from the stall very quickly. We also regard the 170 as easy to land for a tail-dragger. It will float if you're carrying only a little too much speed; it was designed for full-stall landings. Still, the old pros tell us that's the way all lightplanes should be landed, nose wheel or not.

Summing up: The 170 is a simple and straightforward machine that is economical to operate and maintain. Its systems remind us of something we once heard Bill Lear say: "You'll never have to replace, repair or maintain anything you leave out." That was Lear's way of re-stating the engineers' hallowed axiom of "KISS" ("Keep It Simple, Stupid"), and a principle that's especially sensible applied to the design of light airplanes.

SPECIFICATIONS, CESSNA 170

Engine	Continental C-145
Propeller	McCauley IA170 or Sensenich 73BR-50
Wing Span	36 ft
Length	24 ft 11½ in
Wing Area	175 sq ft
Wing Loading	12.6 lbs per sq ft
Power Loading	15.2 lbs per hp
Height	6 ft 7½ in
Empty Weight	1,205 lbs
Gross Weight	2,200 lbs
Useful Load	995 lbs
Fuel Capacity	42 gal
Baggage Capacity	120 lbs

PERFORMANCE, CESSNA 170

Take-Off Distance	700 ft
Take-Off Distance Over 50 ft Obstacle	1,500 ft
Landing Distance	500 ft
Landing Distance Over 50 ft Obstacle	1,100 ft
Rate of Climb, Maximum Initial	690 ft per min
Service Ceiling	15,500 ft
Maximum Speed	140 mph
Cruise Speed (65% Power)	120 mph
Range at 65% Power	540 mi
Stall, Power Off, No Flaps	58 mph
Stall, Power Off, Flaps Down	52 mph

CHAPTER 4: CESSNA 180 AND 185

When the Cessna 180 was first introduced in 1953, it was enthusiastically received by businessmen pilots of that time, and by operators who needed a flying machine in this class with more flexibility than the 170: a nimble load-carrier with a cruise above 150 mph capable of flying from all kinds of fields, including those at high altitudes. Also a good instrument airplane, it was, in short, the flying machine that put the "U" in utility.

The early 180's grossed only 15% (350 lbs) more than the 170, but possessed almost 40% more horsepower (225-hp vs. 145-hp), and this resulted in a quick-footed craft.

The 180 lost its businessmen buyers, however, when Cessna decided, in 1956, to bring out the 182 (essentially, a 180 with an idiot landing gear). Nevertheless, the 180 continued in production because a lot of operators in the back-country still found it ideally suited to their requirements and, at the beginning of the seventies, it probably was the most widely used ranch and bush airplane in the world. This is why those of us whose activities take us from one paved runway to another in the "Lower 48," don't see many 180's; they're mostly working in Latin America, Alaska and the American West. More than 5,000 had been built at the end of the sixties.

The 180 hasn't changed an awful lot over the years. It received five extra horsepower (to 230-hp) in 1956 and its gross weight had grown to 2,800 lbs by 1970, along with increased range (bigger fuel tanks), and an extra window on each side. The 180's nose cowling was re-designed in 1959 for better cooling and additional ram-air pressure to the intake, and the gear legs have been re-shaped to obtain a wider track. In 1970, the plane appeared with new conical-cambered wingtips and a few fresh pretties in the cabin. By that time the price — pushed by inflation — was up to $19,725. In 1953, the first 180 had a list price of $12,950.

Since the 180 is a working airplane, its cabin is austere; no fancy upholstery, and its basic interior configuration includes only the pilot's seat. Removable seats for five more passengers are extra-cost items. Flaps are manually operated, and the stabilizer trim wheel and fuel selector switch are located between the seats. It is, in short, an airplane of few surprises — except in the performance

department. If you've been flying its citified counterpart (the 182), you'll find that the 180 out-performs the tri-gear dude in all areas except top speed.

Tail-wheel airplanes *do* require extra skill and experience on the ground and in cross-wind landings, and we fail to understand why some av-writers have claimed otherwise. But if you learned

1976 Cessna Skywagon 180

to fly in a tail-dragger, or have some experience in one, you are bound to like the 180. At anything less than full gross load, it'll climb out at 1,000 fpm or better, and its ceiling of almost 20,000 feet promises that it'll take you anywhere and be content with the merest excuse for a landing patch.

The 180 has excellent slow-flight characteristics with a solid control-feel, particularly rudder, and refuses to fully stall with power off and only one or two aboard. It merely shakes a little and bobs its nose seeking a flyable angle-of-attack while determinedly resisting a clean break. She will of course break from power stalls, or even if you are carrying enough weight, power or no power. Even then, this airplane is almost immediately flying again as soon as you relax back-pressure on the wheel.

Summing up: a delightful craft if you are one who prefers to fly the airplane rather than have the airplane fly you.

The Cessna 185 Skywagon is, essentially, a beefed-up 180 with more power. Externally, the airframe may appear to be the same as the 180's, but internally the 185 has additional bracing and a re-designed wing for extra strength. It also has a big dorsal fin which quickly distinguishes it from the 180. The 185 was added to the Cessna utility fleet in 1961. It was fitted with the 260-hp Continental IO-470-F engine through the 185E model of 1966. In that year, Cessna offered the E Model with the IO-520D 300-hp Continental, and in 1967 dropped the 260-hp 180 altogether. From 1966 through 1970, Cessna called the 300-hp model the A185E Skywagon.

Skywagon it is. With room for six big people, a useful load of 1,775 lbs (1,620-1,730 lbs for earlier models), and a cruising speed of 169 mph, the 185 sort of picks up where the 180 leaves off — like going from a half ton to a three-quarter ton pickup, or perhaps more to the point, from a Chevy station wagon to a Buick wagon. It had good performance in 1961, and ten years later (unlike most airplanes) it had not taken on a lot of weight which would subtract from that performance. When the 40 extra horsepower was added, gross weight went up only 150 lbs to 3,350; and empty weight was increased but 15 lbs. Therefore, that extra power was available to do some useful work, and not wasted on a heavier airframe. To put it another way, the 185, which weighs only 30 lbs more than the 180 (empty), carries 520 lbs more load at about the same speed, 169 vs. 170 mph.

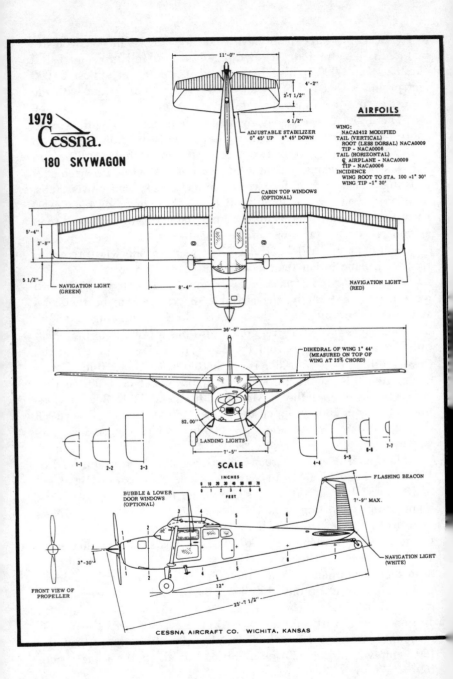

1979

Cessna.

180 SKYWAGON

11'-0"

4'-2"

2'-7 1/2"

6 1/2"

ADJUSTABLE STABILIZER
0° 45' UP   8° 45' DOWN

AIRFOILS

WING:
  NACA2412 MODIFIED
TAIL (VERTICAL)
  ROOT (LESS DORSAL) NACA0009
  TIP - NACA0006
TAIL (HORIZONTAL)
  $\mathcal{C}$ AIRPLANE - NACA0009
  TIP - NACA0006
INCIDENCE
  WING ROOT TO STA. 100 +1° 30'
  WING TIP -1° 30'

CABIN TOP WINDOWS
(OPTIONAL)

5'-4"

3'-8"

5 1/2"

NAVIGATION LIGHT
(GREEN)

8'-4"

NAVIGATION LIGHT
(RED)

36'-0"

DIHEDRAL OF WING 1° 44'
(MEASURED ON TOP OF
WING AT 25% CHORD)

82.00"

LANDING LIGHTS

7'-5"

1-1   2-2   3-3

4-4   5-5   6-6   7-7

SCALE

INCHES
0 10 20 30 40 50 60 70

FEET
0   1   2   3   4   5   6

FLASHING BEACON

BUBBLE & LOWER
DOOR WINDOWS
(OPTIONAL)

7'-9" MAX.

NAVIGATION LIGHT
(WHITE)

3°-30'

FRONT VIEW OF
PROPELLER

12°

25'-7 1/2"

CESSNA AIRCRAFT CO.   WICHITA, KANSAS

34

Between 1971 and 1976, the Cessna 180 accumulated a number of detail and dress-up changes; but the only significant air-frame change was the "new wing" introduced with the 1973 model. This airfoil is still a modified NACA 2412, but does provide improved handling, especially in the rolling moment, at low air-speeds.

For 1976, improvements included new fifth and sixth seats which fold flush and need not be removed when converting to cargo configuration, along with a new flap-extension speed (maximum) upped to 140 mph (120 kts). Factory list price for 1976: $30,150.

1979 CESSNA 185 SKYWAGON PERFORMANCE AND SPECIFICATIONS*

	LANDPLANE		SKIPLANE	
SPEED:				
Maximum at Sea Level	148 knots**	274 kph	129 knots	239 kph
Cruise, 75% power at 8000 feet	142 knots**	263 kph	124 knots	230 kph
CRUISE, Recommended lean mixture with fuel allowance for engine start, taxi, takeoff, climb and 45 minutes reserve at 45% power				
75% power at 8000 feet with 84 gallons usable fuel	825 nm 5.9 hr	1528 km 5.9 hr	720 nm 5.9 hr	1333 km 5.9 hr
Maximum range at 10,000 feet with 84 gallons usable fuel	1010 nm 9.2 hr	1871 km 9.2 hr	820 nm 8.4 hr	1519 km 8.4 hr
RATE OF CLIMB AT SEA LEVEL	1100 fpm	335 mpm	910 fpm	277 mpm
SERVICE CEILING	17,700 ft	5395 m	14,700 ft	4480 m
TAKEOFF PERFORMANCE:				
Ground roll	625 ft	191 m	----	----
Total distance over 50 ft obstacle	1205 ft	367 m	----	----
LANDING PERFORMANCE:				
Ground roll	480 ft	146 m	----	----
Total distance over 50 ft obstacle	1365 ft	416 m	----	----
STALL SPEED, CAS				
Flaps up, power off	53 knots	98 kph	53 knots	98 kph
Flaps down, power off	48 knots	89 kph	48 knots	89 kph
MAXIMUM WEIGHT:				
Ramp	2810 lb	1275 kg	2800 lb	1270 kg
Takeoff or landing	2800 lb	1270 kg	2800 lb	1270 kg
STANDARD EMPTY WEIGHT:				
Standard 180	1643 lb	745 kg	1785 lb	810 kg
II Configuration	1694 lb	769 kg	----	----
MAXIMUM USEFUL LOAD:				
Standard 180	1167 lb	530 kg	1015 lb	460 kg
II Configuration	1116 lb	506 kg	----	----
BAGGAGE ALLOWANCE	170 lb	77 kg	170 lb	77 kg
WING LOADING	16.1 lb/sq ft	78.6 kg/sq m	16.1 lb/sq ft	78.6 kg/sq m
POWER LOADING	12.2 lb/hp	5.5 kg/hp	12.2 lb/hp	5.5 kg/hp
WING SPAN	35 ft, 10 in	10.92 m	35 ft, 10 in	10.92 m
WING AREA	174 sq ft	16.2 sq m	174 sq ft	16.2 sq m
LENGTH	25 ft, 7 1/2 in	7.81 m	27, 9 1/2 in	8.47 m
HEIGHT	7 ft, 9 in	2.36 m	7 ft, 9 in	2.36 m
FUEL CAPACITY, Total	88 gal	333 liters	88 gal	333 liters
OIL CAPACITY	12 qt	11.4 liters	12 qt	11.4 liters

ENGINE: Teledyne Continental 0-470-U engine; 230 bhp at 2400 rpm

PROPELLER: Constant speed, 2 blades, 82 inch diameter (2.08 m)

NOTE: Weight of the optional Nav-Pac is: 16 lb   7 kg

*Subject to change without notice
**These speeds are one knot higher with optional speed fairings installed

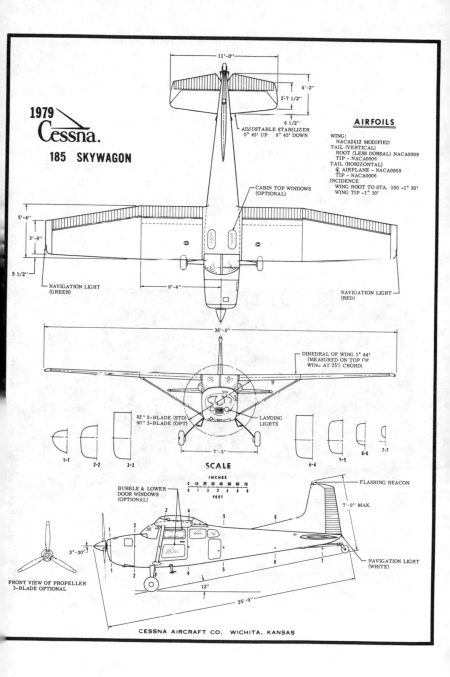

1979

Cessna.

185 SKYWAGON

11'-0''

4'-2''

2'-7 1/2''

6 1/2''

ADJUSTABLE STABILIZER
0° 45' UP   8° 45' DOWN

CABIN TOP WINDOWS
(OPTIONAL)

5'-4''

3'-8''

5 1/2''

NAVIGATION LIGHT
(GREEN)

8'-4''

NAVIGATION LIGHT
(RED)

AIRFOILS

WING:
    NACA2412 MODIFIED
TAIL (VERTICAL)
    ROOT (LESS DORSAL) NACA0009
    TIP - NACA0006
TAIL (HORIZONTAL)
    C_L AIRPLANE - NACA0009
    TIP - NACA0006
INCIDENCE
    WING ROOT TO STA. 100 +1° 30'
    WING TIP -1° 30'

36'-0''

DIHEDRAL OF WING 1° 44'
(MEASURED ON TOP OF
WING AT 25% CHORD)

82'' 2-BLADE (STD)
80'' 3-BLADE (OPT)

LANDING
LIGHTS

7'-5''

1-1   2-2   3-3

4-4   5-5   6-6   7-7

SCALE

INCHES
0 10 20 30 40 50 60 70
0   1   2   3   4   5   6
FEET

BUBBLE & LOWER
DOOR WINDOWS
(OPTIONAL)

FLASHING BEACON

7'-9'' MAX.

3°-30'

NAVIGATION LIGHT
(WHITE)

FRONT VIEW OF PROPELLER
3-BLADE OPTIONAL

12''

25'-9''

CESSNA AIRCRAFT CO.   WICHITA, KANSAS

37

The Cessna 185 Skywagon received a number of detail changes between 1971 and 1976, along with the "camber-lift" airfoil modification for improved slow-flight handling, and an increased maximum allowable flap-extension speed. Most of the changes were for added comfort and convenience.

There's always a different paint scheme each year, of course, and ol' debbil inflation keeps inching-up the basic list price—$35,550 for the 1976 model. Meanwhile, Cessna claims increased efficiency; but performance figures for the 1976 model are almost identical to those of, say, the 1970 185 Skywagon. During these five years, this aircraft gained about 100 lbs empty weight, with a corresponding loss in useful load. Clearly, you pay for the frills two ways.

1979 Cessna 185 Skywagon

1979 CESSNA 180 SKYWAGON PERFORMANCE AND SPECIFICATIONS*

	LANDPLANE		SKIPLANE	
SPEED:				
Maximum at Sea Level	155 knots**	287 kph	136 knots	252 kph
Cruise, 75% power at 7500 feet	145 knots**	269 kph	132 knots	244 kph

CRUISE, Recommended lean mixture with fuel allowance for engine start, taxi, takeoff, climb and 45 minutes reserve at 45% power

	LANDPLANE		SKIPLANE	
75% power at 7500 feet with	680 nm	1259 km	610 nm	1130 km
84 gallons usable fuel	4.7 hr	4.7 hr	4.7 hr	4.7 hr
Maximum range at 10,000 feet with	835 nm	1546 km	715 nm	1324 km
84 gallons usable fuel	7.4 hr	7.4 hr	6.7 hr	6.7 hr
RATE OF CLIMB AT SEA LEVEL	1010 fpm	308 mpm	810 fpm	247 mpm
SERVICE CEILING	17,150 ft	5227 m	13,300 ft	4054 m
TAKEOFF PERFORMANCE:				
Ground roll	770 ft	235 m	----	----
Total distance over 50 ft obstacle	1365 ft	4.6 m	----	----
LANDING PERFORMANCE:				
Ground roll	480 ft	146 m	----	----
Total distance over 50 ft obstacle	1400 ft	427 m	----	----
STALL SPEED, CAS:				
Flaps up, power off	56 knots	104 kph	56 knots	104 kph
Flaps down, power off	49 knots	91 kph	49 knots	91 kph
MAXIMUM WEIGHT:				
Ramp	3362 lb	1525 kg	3350 lb	1520 kg
Takeoff or landing	3350 lb	1520 kg	3350 lb	1520 kg
STANDARD EMPTY WEIGHT:				
Standard 185	1681 lb	762 kg	1823 lb	827 kg
II Configuration	1731 lb	785 kg	----	----
MAXIMUM USEFUL LOAD:				
Standard 185	1681 lb	763 kg	1527 lb	693 kg
II Configuration	1631 lb	740 kg	----	----
BAGGAGE ALLOWANCE	170 lb	77 kg	170 lb	77 kg
WING LOADING	19.3 lb/sq ft	94.2 kg/sq m	19.3 lb/sq ft	94.2 kg/sq m
POWER LOADING	11.2 lb/hp	5.1 kg/hp	11.2 lb/hp	5.1 kg/hp
WING SPAN	35 ft, 10 in	10.92 m	35 ft, 10 in	10.92 m
WING AREA	174 sq ft	16.2 sq m	174 sq ft	16.2 sq m
LENGTH	25 ft, 7 1/2 in	7.81 m	27 ft, 9 1/2 in	8.47 m
HEIGHT	7 ft, 9 in	2.36 m	7 ft, 9 in	2.36 m
FUEL CAPACITY, Total	88 gal	333 liters	88 gal	333 liters
OIL CAPACITY:	12 qt	11.4 liters	12 qt	11.4 liters

ENGINE: Teledyne Continental IO-520-D Fuel Injection Engine
300 bhp at 2850 rpm (takeoff)
285 bhp at 2700 rpm (maximum continuous)

PROPELLER:*** Constant speed, 2 blades, 82 inch diameter (2.08 m)

NOTE: Weight of the optional Nav-Pac is: 21 lb   10 kg

*Subject to change without notice
**These speeds are one knot higher with optional speed fairings installed
*Performance with the optional 3-bladed propeller (80 inch diameter, 2.03 m) is esentially the same as the 2-bladed propeller

The 1958 Model 172 was the third of this series and still much resembled a 170B with tricycle gear and 180-type rudder. The first 172 was the 1956 Model. Performance has changed little over the years.

CHAPTER 5: CESSNA 172/SKYHAWK AND 175/SKYLARK

The Cessna 172 and Skyhawk owner — who represents at least 10% of general aviation — has largely been misunderstood by the old hands in this business whose lives have always revolved around airplanes. Those of us who never wanted to be anything but a "pilot" from the time we were nine years old (and forty years ago that seemed to us a lofty ambition indeed), have been puzzled by all these bright young men ("newcomers") who buy and fly modern lightplanes merely for the sake of convenience.

It's the Generation Gap, Dad. The Travel Air 4000 and the grass landing patches we remember with such fondness possess no more relevance for today's young man on the way up than did the horse and buggy for us. The average Skyhawk owner probably never heard of a Gee Bee Racer; and what's more, he hasn't time to listen while we tell him about it with a faraway look in our eye. The horrible truth is, he's not interested.

Cessna recognized the emergence of this new breed and correctly assessed its attitude back in the mid-fifties. Clearly, there was a big and growing market for a four-place business/pleasure aircraft that did not demand professional-type skills and experience for its safe operation. A practical machine to serve the man who regarded a personal airplane as a kind of super-car. Cessna's super-car is the 172/Skyhawk.

The 172 was introduced in 1956, and it was, in effect, a 170 with tricycle landing gear and 180 tail. This happy combination was squarely on target; and though it has submitted to a number of changes over the year — mostly to make it prettier — the 1971 Model 172 and Skyhawk is still pretty close to the original, performance-wise, as a look at the model comparison charts (following Chapter 10) will reveal.

A brief flight evaluation of a 1957 Model 172, followed by checks of a 1962 Skyhawk and a 1968 Skyhawk should provide good representative coverage of this series. The Skyhawk, as you undoubtedly know, is simply the deluxe version of the 172, the principal differences being that the Skyhawk has a full gyro panel activated by an internal vacuum system, full paint job and speed fairings on the wheels.

The 1957 Model 172 was in excellent condition and as neat inside as TLC (Tender Loving Care) could keep it after thirteen years. Our only beef was that the flight instruments were not well grouped, but had apparently been stuck in the panel at random. An aging mechanic insisted that this was Cessna's standard arrangement for that airplane. Maybe so; we couldn't remember.

This craft sits a little higher off the ground than later models; and the old starter pull-knob is right beside the parking brake, making it easy to grab the wrong one. Otherwise, you feel right at home in this plane if you've flown later Cessnas. Firing up the engine and taxiing is standard Cessna; it rolls easily with the merest hint of power. The nosewheel's steerability is fairly limited via the rudder pedals, but it will swivel through an arc of about 30-degrees by applying full rudder and toe-brake for tight turns on the ground.

Take-off was the same now-famous "drive 'er down the runway and into the air" of later Cessnas. Then, with three aboard and full tanks (about 230 lbs below gross of 2,200 lbs), the '57 Model showed an initial climb of 500 fpm at 78 mph on a warmish day. At 6,500 ft with 2,400 rpms, which we judged to be 65% power, the IAS (Indicated Air Speed) was 106 mph. Corrected for temperature and altitude, this worked out to slightly over 120 mph TAS (True Air Speed). This latter figure was determined courtesy of Mr. Dalton's E-6B Computer; but we must confess to an attachment for the ancient (a la Travel Air days) method of arriving at this number by simply adding 2% per thousand feet of altitude to the IAS. It's not precise, but usually close enough for lightplane VFR when lapse rates are normal.

Stall characteristics of Cessna's 1957 Model Super-Car are also "Standard Cessna," which is to say you have to work at it to force this airplane into full-stall with power off. It prefers to just sit there and mush along with the stall warning horn assaulting your ears and the airspeed indicator bumping at 50 mph. It's easier to make the plane break from a stall with power on, but the air speed falls clear down to 40 mph on the dial. Some aileron control remains even at these indicated speeds, but it's probably wiser to level the wings with the rudder, especially if the flaps are down, and even more especially if you're at or near gross load. We're not sure whether it would happen with a Cessna, but we do know that sudden aileron movement in or near the stall will add just enough drag on the down-aileron side to stall-out that wing and induce a quick spin on some airplanes.

The owner of this airplane demonstrated landings holding a final approach speed of 70 mph. He touched-down on the main wheels in a full-stall from the flare, and allowed the nosewheel to come down immediately. This is the "drive it back on the ground" method and seems to work very well for a lot of people, although many instructors used to recommend holding the nosewheel off until it eased down of its own accord. With the nosewheel on the pavement, one does have much easier and better control, however. Also, the Cessna nose-wheel is attached to the airframe rather than the engine mount, and for short-field landings the Owner's Manual advises that the nose-wheel be put down immediately after touch-down.

The 1962 Skyhawk we checked was also well-equipped and in top condition. Except for its paint scheme, differently shaped speed fairings on the wheels and lack of a rear window, it closely resembled its newer sisters. Inside, the instrument panel held the six flight instruments in two rows directly in front of the pilot (airspeed, directional gyro and attitude gyro across the top; altimeter, turn/bank and rate-of-limb across the bottom). Engine controls were grouped at bottom-center of panel, of course, along with the fuel sump drain knob. It's a matter of opinion, but in our view there are a few things necessary to a happy flight that should be checked *visually* and positively, like fuel tanks, oil level, tires, etc., and we just don't trust that painless (and blind) sump-drain operation from inside the cabin.

Fuel is gravity-fed to the 145-hp Continental 0-300-D engine via the fuel selector switch located between the front seats. Its

1971 Cessna Skyhawk

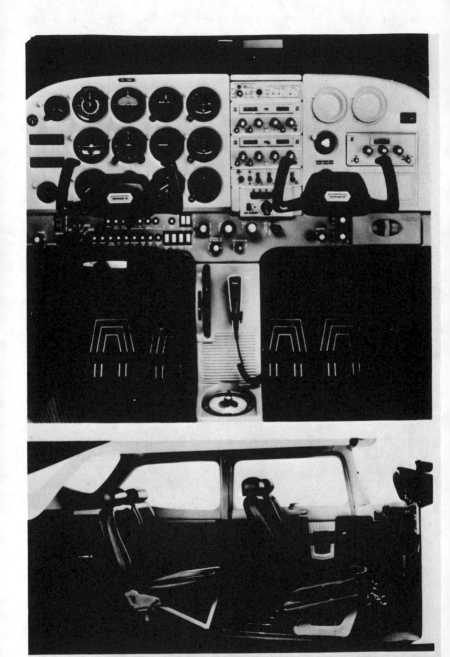

1976 Cessna Skyhawk

positions are *Off, Left, Right* and *Both,* although we get the impression that few pilots ever use fuel from the left or right wing-tank individually. Total fuel is 42 gallons, with slightly less than 41 usable.

Engine starting procedure is standard: Battery switch, "ON;" mixture set at "Full Rich," throttle slightly cracked, a couple of squirts of primer and turn ignition key past "Both" to start. We note that this owner checks his mags at 1,700 rpms, pivots his Skyhawk in a complete 360-degree circle so he can get a look at the entire pattern around this uncontrolled field, then drives down the runway and into the air, lifting off at about 60 mph without flaps. It is a cool day, about 50 degrees F at field elevation of 1,180 ft. The take-off run is estimated at 750 feet, with two of us aboard and full tanks (340 lbs below gross).

Initial climb registers 900+ fpm with maximum power and 70 mph. This drops back to 500 fpm as we lower the nose and increase speed to 100 mph with 2,500 rpms. Our host tells us that the 1962 Skyhawk's best cruising speed comes at 7,000 feet, where 2,500 rpms produces about 134 mph TAS for him. However, we stayed at 3,500 where 116 mph IAS translated into 124 mph TAS at 38 degrees F. Our friend told us that his 2,500 rpm cruise consumed 8½ gallons of fuel per hour.

Returning to his home field, our host drove his Skyhawk onto the runway holding 70 mph over the fence and let his nose-wheel come down almost immediately after the main wheels touched. He then raised his flaps and held a little back-pressure on the control wheel during roll-out. He braked sparingly into a 3-5 mph wind and used an estimated 600 feet of runway.

The 1968 Skyhawk had recently had a thorough work out at the hands of our colleague, Miss Page Shamburger. Page has about 5,000 hours in her logbook and now owns a Bonanza; but she started out in Cessnas (140's and 170's), and says she "feels right at home with these fellers." Since she spent considerable time in Skyhawk N83314L, we asked her for her impressions.

"Beginning with this 1968 Model, the 172/Skyhawk has the 150-hp 'Blue Streak' Lycoming engine," Page said, "but I really can't see where it adds anything, except maybe a little dab of useful load. This is because the 1968 Model is 40 pounds lighter than the '67 Model. Gross remains at 2,300 pounds, where it has been since 1963.

"Inside, instruments are T-grouped, and dry vacuum pumps have replaced the plumbing and oil-lubricated pumps for gyro instruments. Electrically operated flaps are standard on both the 172 and Skyhawk. The rear-vision mirror, by the way, costs $20 extra, and I found it useless, at least for rear-visioning.

"Normal engine-start procedures awaken the Lycoming's hundred and-fifty horses, and I thought this airplane seemed markedly quieter inside, probably because the twin exhaust stacks of the Continental-powered Skyhawks and 172's have been changed to a single and longer stack on the Lycoming-engined craft.

"Since this airplane was a factory demonstrator, it was loaded with avionics and extras, bringing its empty weight up to 1,407 pounds. However, I had left 893 pounds useful, which seemed enough for 'most anything. Checking my notes, I'm reminded that, taxiing out, the shorter nose-strut, introduced in 1967 to reduce in-flight drag, also allows you to see the concrete very close ahead.

"With 297 pounds of people (two hundred for Cessna's John Gallaher; ninety-seven for me), and full tanks, I was 340 pounds under gross. And according to my notes, I lifted-off in less than 800 feet at 65 mph (elevation, 1,370 ft), and remarked on the secure feeling of the Skyhawk even during those early, crucial seconds of flight. I felt that I had stability to spare. I climbed at 85 mph showing 750 fpm.

"Leveling off at 10,500 feet, I found my TAS by using the handy computer on the airspeed indicator. This is a rotating bezel mounted on the periphery of that instrument. You rotate it to set pressure ailtitude opposite outside air temperature (OAT), then read true air speed directly below the indicator needle. With an OAT of 22 degrees, I had 134 mph true at 65% power.

"During let-down for Oklahoma City, I tried some stalls and was intrigued with the pre-stall warning given by the reeds inside the wing that cry at an increasingly-higher pitch as the wing gets nearer the stall. This simple system works from air pressure flowing over the reeds, and no exterior sensor vane — so vulnerable to accidental bending — is needed. Straight ahead, with flaps up and power off, the nose sticks 'way up in the air, where the controls get heavy enough to prompt you to crank in some elevator trim (via the control located on the center console). Then this airplane broke clean at 50 mph indicated — 57 mph corrected — shaking and whistling frantically at me for mistreating it so. Flaps lower the stall to 41 IAS (49 mph corrected), and the nose-up angle is strictly unreal.

"Landings? Well, it's a Cessna; just no problem. I did the first one holding 80 mph, and flaring at that speed produced some 'ballooning.' Second time around, with half-flaps and indicating 73 mph, I put it where I wanted it and it stayed there."

The 1971 Skyhawk/172 possessed a few improvements over previous models, the main one being a switch to the Cardinal-proved tubular landing gear legs. These tapered tubular struts, encased in streamlined housings, are superior to the "slab steel" struts because they absorb shocks fore-and-aft as well as up-and-down. In our view, this is the most practical, versatile and trouble-free landing gear offered on any light airplane. We first encountered this gear back in November, 1967, when it was introduced on the original Cardinal/177. We were sold on it then. We still are. If you think the Skyhawk/172 has been easy to land in the past, this gear is, surely, the meringue on that piece of pie.

The 1971 Model also had re-styled wheel fairings. Cessna apparently re-shapes these things more for model identification than anything else. The latest ones may *look* racy, but they are undoubtedly less efficient aerodynamically than the old fashioned tear-drop shape.

Other new features for 1971 included a re-designed nose cap to eliminate propeller "slap" noise in the cabin and nose-mounted landing light. Optional, were new overhead windows, wingtip

Cessna SKYLARK

strobe lights (white), a hands-off boom microphone and full paint job on the 172 version. The fully-articulating seats, introduced on the 1970 Model, may be adjusted to any position from fully reclined to full forward, and through a wide range of heights. The '71 Model, for the first time, offered gen-u-wine leather upholstery as an option with the Skyhawk. Most impressive of all, perhaps, was the welcome news in 1971 that the 150-hp Lycoming engine had a recommended time between overhaul of 2,000 hours. When Cessna switched to this engine in 1968, recommended TBO was 1,500 hours. It was 1,200 hours for the 0-300 Continental in earlier Skyhawk/172's.

For total utility, the re-designed instrument panel of the 1971 Model offers plenty of space for magical black boxes, including 300 Nav-O-Matic autopilot, 300 Transceiver, 90 and 360-channel Nav/ Coms, ADF, Marker Beacon, Glideslope Receiver, the 300 Transponder with a reply code capability of up to 4,096 with Modes A and AC, and the ARC (Cessna) DME.

Performance of the 1971 Models were not much changed, as a check of the Model Comparison Tables at the back of this book will confirm. List price of the basic 172 for 1971 was $13,425, and the '71 Skyhawk list was $14,995.

The Army and Air Force Cessna T-41 is the military version of the 172, and Cessna records showed that about 500 T-41's had been delivered as of October 1, 1970.

The Cessna 175/Skylark was brought out in 1958 and, for a couple of years, sold almost as well as the 172/Skyhawk (the Skyhawk version of the 172 first appeared in 1959); but the 175 slipped badly in sales in 1961, and production ended in 1963, at which time Cessna briefly called this airplane the "172 Powermatic."

The 175/Skylark and Powermatic is basically a 172 airframe fitted with the Continental GO-300-E engine of 175 hp, and constant speed propeller. The GO-300-E is a geared mill which produces its maximum power at 2,400 propeller rpms while the crankshaft rpms register 3,200, a ratio of .75:1. Since the propeller reduction-gear box is located above the drive shaft on the front of the engine, the same 84-inch propeller as used on the 145-hp engines gains a couple of inches in ground clearance. And since this is the same engine as the 145-hp 0-300-D employed by Skyhawks of this period — except for the gearing — it's obvious that the additional 30 horse-power results from the higher crankshaft speed, and *that* clearly can't *add* anything to engine life or reliability.

This model has an extra knob in the cockpit: the prop pitch control. It is also a push-pull type and changes the setting of the propeller governor to control engine speed. This control may be moved through its full range by depressing a locking button in the center of the knob, while minor adjustments are made by releasing the locking button and rotating the knob — clockwise to increase rpms and counter-clockwise to decrease rpms.

For all ground operations and take-off, the propeller control should be full in (high rpms). After take-off, reduce throttle first, then reduce rpms. Since a small control movement will produce a considerable rpm change, you should set up climb and cruise rpms by screwing the knob in or out.

This airplane also has cowl flaps which are not found on comparable models of the 172. These of course merely control the flow of air over the engine for greater efficiency under varying conditions. Opening the cowl flaps on the ground and during steep climbs, for example, improves engine cooling. In flight, closing the flaps reduces the cooling air to the engine and reduces drag. This control is a double-button type with a friction lock.

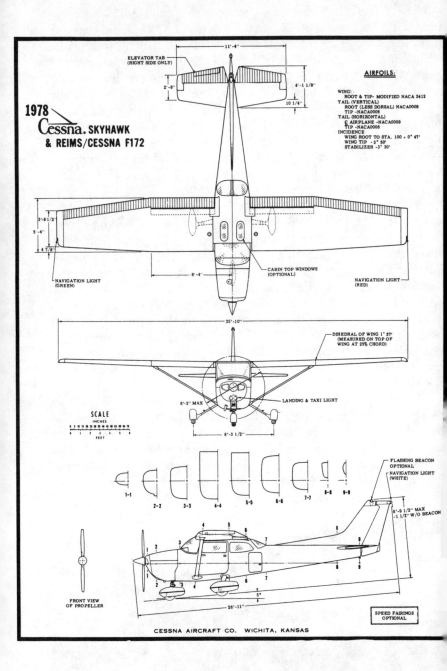

AIRFOILS:

WING:
ROOT & TIP- MODIFIED NACA 2412
TAIL (VERTICAL)
ROOT (LESS DORSAL) NACA0009
TIP -NACA0006
TAIL (HORIZONTAL)
$\mathcal{C}$ AIRPLANE -NACA0009
TIP -NACA0006
INCIDENCE
WING ROOT TO STA. 100 + 0° 47'
WING TIP -2° 50'
STABILIZER -3° 30'

1978
Cessna. SKYHAWK
& REIMS/CESSNA F172

ELEVATOR TAB
(RIGHT SIDE ONLY)

11'-4"

2'-8"

4'-1 1/8"

10 1/4"

3'-8 1/2"

5'-4"

4 7/8"

NAVIGATION LIGHT
(GREEN)

CABIN TOP WINDOWS
(OPTIONAL)

8'-4"

NAVIGATION LIGHT
(RED)

35'-10"

DIHEDRAL OF WING 1° 37'
(MEASURED ON TOP OF
WING AT 25% CHORD)

6'-3" MAX

LANDING & TAXI LIGHT

8'-3 1/2"

SCALE
INCHES
FEET

1-1   2-2   3-3   4-4   5-5   6-6   7-7   8-8   9-9

FLASHING BEACON
OPTIONAL
NAVIGATION LIGHT
(WHITE)

8'-9 1/2" MAX
-1 1/2" W/O BEACON

FRONT VIEW
OF PROPELLER

5°

26'-11"

SPEED FAIRINGS
OPTIONAL

CESSNA AIRCRAFT CO. WICHITA, KANSAS

50

These planes use the same fuel system as that of the 172/Sky-hawk, except that capacity is 10 gallons greater.

This series of course has improved performance compared to the standard 172's, but the difference was probably not great enough to warrant the extra cost. The 1958 Cessna 175 had a basic list of $10,995 vs. $8,995 for the 172. By 1963, the "Powermatic 172" was priced at $13,275 vs. $10,245 for the 172, while the 1963 "Skyhawk Powermatic" sold for $14,650 vs. $11,995 for the 1963 145-hp Skyhawk.

Cessna 175/Skylark and Powermatic specifications and performance figures follow at the end of this chapter.

SPECIFICATIONS, CESSNA 175/SKYLARK AND POWERMATIC

	175 (1958)	Powermatic (1963)
Engine	Continental GO-300-E	Continental GO-300-E
Wingspan	36 ft 2 in	36 ft 2 in
Length	25 ft	26 ft 6 in
Height	8 ft 6 in	8 ft 11 in
Wing Area	174 sq ft	174 sq ft
Gross Weight	2,350 lbs	2,500 lbs
Wing Loading	13.5 lbs sq ft	14.4 lbs sq ft
Power Loading	13.4 lbs/hp	14.3 lbs/hp
Useful Load	945 lbs	1,140 lbs
Fuel Capacity	52 gals	52 gals

PERFORMANCE, CESSNA 175/SKYLARK AND POWERMATIC

	175 (1958)	Powermatic (1963)
Take-Off	640 ft	000 ft
clear 50 ft	1,340 ft	1,205 ft
Landing	600 ft	610 ft
clear 50 ft	1,155 ft	1,200 ft
Climb, Initial	850 fpm	830 fpm
Service Ceiling	17,800 ft	17,000 ft
Maximum Speed	147 mph	146 mph
Cruise (75%)	140 mph	138 mph
Range (@75%)	585 mi	540 mi
Stall (no flaps)	58 mph	64 mph
Stall (flaps 40-deg)	50 mph	55 mph

1978 CESSNA SKYHAWK PERFORMANCE AND SPECIFICATIONS*

	LANDPLANE		FLOATPLANE	
SPEED:				
Maximum at Sea Level	125 knots	231 kph	96 knots	178 kph
Cruise, 75% power at 8000 feet**	122 knots	226 kph	95 knots	176 kph

CRUISE, Recommended lean mixture with fuel allowance for engine start, taxi, takeoff, climb and 45 minutes reserve at 45% power

	LANDPLANE		FLOATPLANE	
75% power at 8000 feet** with 40 gallons usable fuel	485 nm / 4.1 hr	898 km / 4.1 hr	385 nm / 4.1 hr	713 km / 4.1 hr
75% power at 8000 feet** with 50 gallons usable fuel	630 nm / 5.3 hr	1167 km / 5.3 hr	500 nm / 5.3 hr	926 km / 5.3 hr
Maximum range at 10,000 feet with 40 gallons usable fuel	575 nm / 5.7 hr	1065 km / 5.7 hr	435 nm / 5.3 hr	806 km / 5.3 hr
Maximum range at 10,000 feet with 50 gallons usable fuel	750 nm / 7.4 hr	1389 km / 7.4 hr	570 nm / 6.9 hr	1056 km / 6.9 hr
RATE OF CLIMB AT SEA LEVEL	770 fpm	235 mpm	740 fpm	226 mpm
SERVICE CEILING	14,200 ft	4328 m	15,000 ft	4572 m
TAKEOFF PERFORMANCE:				
Ground roll (or water run)	805 ft	245 m	1400 ft	427 m
Total distance over 50 ft. obstacle	1440 ft	439 m	2160 ft	658 m
LANDING PERFORMANCE:				
Ground roll (or water run)	520 ft	159 m	590 ft	180 m
Total distance over 50 ft. obstacle	1250 ft	381 m	1345 ft	410 m
STALL SPEED, CAS:				
Flaps up, power off	50 knots	93 kph	48 knots	89 kph
Flaps down, power off	44 knots	81 kph	44 knots	81 kph
MAXIMUM WEIGHT	2300 lb	1043 kg	2220 lb	1007 kg
STANDARD EMPTY WEIGHT:				
Skyhawk	1393 lb	632 kg	1569 lb	712 kg
Skyhawk II	1419 lb	644 kg	----	----
MAXIMUM USEFUL LOAD:				
Skyhawk	907 lb	411 kg	651 lb	295 kg
Skyhawk II	881 lb	399 kg	----	----
BAGGAGE ALLOWANCE	120 lb	54 kg	120 lb	54 kg
WING LOADING	13.2 lb/sq ft	64 kg/sq m	12.7 lb/sq ft	62 kg/sq m
POWER LOADING	14.4 lb/hp	6.5 kg/hp	13.9 lb/hp	6.3 kg/hp
WING SPAN	35 ft, 10 in	10.92 m	35 ft, 10 in	10.92 m
WING AREA	174 sq ft	16.16 sq m	174 sq ft	16.16 sq m
LENGTH	26 ft, 11 in	8.20 m	26 ft, 8 in	8.13 m
HEIGHT	8 ft, 9 1/2 in	2.68 m	11 ft, 11 in	3.63 m
FUEL CAPACITY, Total:				
Standard Tanks	43 gal	163 liters	43 gal	163 liters
Long Range Tanks	54 gal	204 liters	54 gal	204 liters
OIL CAPACITY	6 qt	5.7 liters	6 qt	5.7 liters
ENGINE	Lycoming O-320-H2AD Engine; 160 bhp at 2700 rpm			
PROPELLER	Fixed Pitch 75 inch diameter (1.91 m)		Fixed Pitch 80 inch diameter (2.03 m)	

*Subject to change without notice
**Cruise performance at 75% power is at 4000 feet for the floatplane

1978 CESSNA HAWK XP PERFORMANCE AND SPECIFICATIONS*

SPEED:

Maximum at Sea Level	133 knots	246 kph
Cruise, 80% power at 6000 feet	130 knots	241 kph

CRUISE, Recommended lean mixture with fuel allowance for engine start, taxi, takeoff climb and 45 minutes reserve at 45% power

80% power at 6000 feet with 49 gallons usable fuel	480 nm 3.7 hr	889 km 3.7 hr
Maximum range at 10,000 feet with 49 gallons usable fuel	575 nm 6.1 hr	1065 km 6.1 hr

RATE OF CLIMB AT SEA LEVEL	870 fpm	265 mpm
SERVICE CEILING	17,000 ft	5182 m

TAKEOFF PERFORMANCE:

Ground roll	800 ft	244 m
Total distance over 50 ft. obstacle	1360 ft	415 m

LANDING PERFORMANCE:

Ground roll	620 ft	189 m
Total distance over 50 ft. obstacle	1270 ft	387 m

STALL SPEED, CAS:

Flaps up, power off	53 knots	98 kph
Flaps down, power off	46 knots	85 kph

MAXIMUM WEIGHT	2550 lb	1157 kg

STANDARD EMPTY WEIGHT:

Hawk XP	1531 lb	695 kg
Hawk XP II	1557 lb	706 kg

MAXIMUM USEFUL LOAD:

Hawk XP	1019 lb	462 kg
Hawk XP II	993 lb	451 kg

BAGGAGE ALLOWANCE	200 lb	91 kg
WING LOADING	14.7 lb/sq ft	71.6 kg/sq m
POWER LOADING	13.1 lb/hp	5.9 kg/hp
WING SPAN	35 ft, 10 in	10.92 m
WING AREA	174 sq ft	16.16 sq m
LENGTH	27 ft, 2 in	8.28 m
HEIGHT	8 ft, 9 1/2 in	2.68 m
FUEL CAPACITY, Total	52 gal	197 liters
OIL CAPACITY	8 qt	7.6 liters

ENGINE: Teledyne-Continental IO-360-K fuel injection engine; 195 bhp at 2600 rpm

PROPELLER: Constant speed, 76 inch diameter (1.93 m)

*Subject to change without notice

CHAPTER 6: THE CESSNA 177/CARDINAL

When the first 177 and Cardinal was introduced in November, 1967, with a swinging party for dealers and av-writers at Cessna's Wichita Delivery Center, we were there for a serious look at this all-new design. While most of our colleagues were swapping lies, enjoying the Dixieland band and stuffing themselves with bar-b-que, we slipped off with a company check-pilot for an afternoon of air work in 2207Y, one of the first Cardinals built (1968 Model).

We liked that airplane, and found almost nothing to pick at. However, owners soon discovered to their horror that it didn't fly or land exactly like a strutless Skyhawk, and some heavy-handed Super-Car drivers managed to smash the Cardinal tail into the pavement on landing, knock-off a few nose-wheels, etc. (apparently, this was possible if one closed his eyes, used full back-pressure on the wheel at the flare and then sat rigidly waiting for the crashing noises to subside).

Cessna accepted the blame gracefully. That was proper because, after all, they had lulled a generation of Cessna pilots into near-effortless flying with the extremely-forgiving 172 series, and it probably wasn't ethical to suddenly offer, to many of those same customers, a Cessna that didn't handle exactly like a Cessna. The company therefore picked up the tab for a list of modifications that gentled the Cardinal and returned the smiles to the faces of dealers and customers.

The principal modification made to the first Cardinals was installation of inverted slots near the leading edge of the stabilator, because it was discovered that, in a full nose-up attitude, the stabilator was stalling out. This was Cessna's first application of a horizontal stabilator (which replaces the more conventional horizontal stabilizer and elevators), and it was chosen for the Cardinal because, with the wing placed so far back for improved pilot visibility and better balance, tail surfaces would have had to be considerably enlarged or the fuselage lengthened to achieve adequate control using a stabilizer and elevator system. The stabilator is more effective for its size and saves both weight and drag.

When the Cardinal first appeared, a Cessna engineer told us that it represented an engineering attempt to design the airplane of the seventies; a plane that would set the trend at Cessna for the coming decade. That was in the fall of 1967; and two years later, when the 1970 Model was announced, we believed that the Cardinal had evolved into that very thing. The 1969 Model went to 180-hp (from the original 150-hp); then the 1970 Model added a constant-speed propeller to efficiently employ those 30 extra horses, and *also* received an all new wing (a new airfoil shape), a wing that at last made the sleek Cardinal "fly like a Cessna."

Then, obviously feeling that they had combined all the right things in a single airframe, Cessna coasted with the 1971 Model Cardinal and 177, offering no other significant changes except a re-designed nose-plate containing the landing light, plus some minor interior pretties.

About 1,000 of the original 1968 Models (150-hp) were built, and slightly over 400 of the 180-hp 1969 Cardinals followed. The real story of the Cardinal, however, will be told during the early seventies, with the new wing, constant-speed propeller and tamed stabilator control combining a "Cessna ride" with increased performance — and offered in an expanding market (following the recession of 1970).

Going back to the tapes we made when we were introduced to the first Cardinal, we're reminded that that caper was a magazine assignment and, looking for a fresh angle to interest the reader, we invited a 20 year-old girl pilot, Miss Saundra Nix, to go along and do most of the flying so she could give her impressions. Sandy was a sophomore at Oklahoma State University at the time, but the holder of a Flight Instructor's Rating. She had soloed at 16 and obtained her Commercial License at 18.

Sandy had been instructing in 150's, and was enchanted with the Cardinal's sports car look, wide wheel-tread and its soft ground ride (this was Cessna's first use of the shot-peened vanadium-steel tubular gear legs). The plane's cabin was "huge" in Sandy's estimation, and so comfortable it was "unreal."

With Sandy flying and the check-pilot in the right-front seat, we had the spacious back seat to ourselves. So, we kept the tape recorder going and took notes on instrument readings in all flight regimes. Lift-off was normal, requiring eleven seconds and about 900 feet. We had a 3-5 knot south wind, ground temp of 80 degrees F, and were approximately 300 lbs under allowable gross. Sandy stayed low until we were clear of the McConnell AFB jet pattern, then climbed at 90 mph which resulted in 800 fpm, dropping to about 700 fpm as we passed through 4,000 feet. There, she tried some stalls, which the Cardinal resisted with a noticable buffet, sort of like a V-tail Bonanza, but recovery was quick and sure and our pilot (pilotess?) reported that the airplane "felt good" throughout the stall. She also remarked that the variation between indicated air speed and calibrated air speed at high angles-of-attack seemed very small. This machine was supposed to stall at 64 mph without power and no flaps, and that's about what it indicated instead of 55 or other low figure.

Cruise, at 75% power at 9,000 feet, was listed in the pilot's

1971 Cessna

manual at 134 mph, and Zero Seven Yankee gave us 135 mph TAS under those conditions. Sandy remarked upon the effectiveness of the stabilator and fiddled with the trim, adding that this airplane "doesn't feel much like a 172."

At this point, we were approaching Eldorado, Kansas, so we went down to try some landings. Sandy was over the fence indicating 85 mph and she got a fair bounce at touch-down. She looked at the check-pilot as if he'd betrayed her. "I *never* bounce a Cessna with that old slab-steel gear on it," she accused.

"You over-controlled a little," he replied. "Most people do until they get used to the new stabilator."

"Yecch!" Sandy said, sticking out her tongue. She fed-in power and went around for another try.

After her third landing — by then coming over the fence with 80 mph indicated — Sandy was putting the Cardinal down very nicely, so she abandoned the concrete runway and began shooting landings cross-wind in the grass. The Cardinal's low profile proved very useful as well as pretty in this activity, and our pilot reported that it handled a side-wind almost as well as a low-winger. And it was during the landings and take-offs on the sod that we decided that Cessna should go to the new tubular-steel landing gear on all their airplanes. That ground was anything but smooth; but we got a smooth ground roll nevertheless, while the gear legs danced frantically in all directions. Truly, that new Cessna gear is the greatest thing since varnished propellers.

It was almost dark when we returned to Cessna Field, and

by then Sandy was much taken with the Cardinal. Climbing into her little Cessna 150, she looked back at the shiny, low-slung Cardinal and sighed, "Now I know how Cinderella felt when her lovely coach turned back into a pumpkin."

In our view, the original Cardinal wasn't as unforgiving as some have claimed. If you were paying attention and flew it by feel instead of by rote, it behaved exactly as it was supposed to. What it failed to do was respond perfectly to Skyhawk technique, because it simply was not just a strutless Skyhawk. We know a fellow out in Amarillo, Texas who owns an early Cardinal and likes it. He says he's at a loss to explain why its original owner sold it at a bargain. We think the explanation may lie in the fact that our Texas friend had not been flying a Cessna when he bought his Cardinal.

Anyway, the 1970 and 1971 models of the Cardinal and 177 (the latter being the economy version of the Cardinal) have that new wing and a domesticated stabilator (modified linkage to the control wheel), and these changes, along with the extra power and constant-speed prop, do make this a different airplane — as Cessna says, a good airplane made great.

The 1971 model is a slightly fancied-up version of the '70 model with no significant aerodynamic change. The interior was re-styled and padding added to door posts, front seat backs and lower instrument panel. The wheel pants were re-shaped again, which appears to be Cessna's way of keeping up with Detroit, and the nose-plate re-designed to contain the landing light. All the good things were kept from previous models, of course, including the

1976 Cessna Cardinal

58

four-foot-wide doors which provide the easiest cabin entry and exit in the industry, and the 115 cubic-foot cabin remains the biggest in its class, offering posh surroundings for four adults and two children, or four people and lots of luggage. The 1971 Cardinal had a list of $17,995 while the Model 177 was priced at $16,795 fly-away-factory, Wichita.

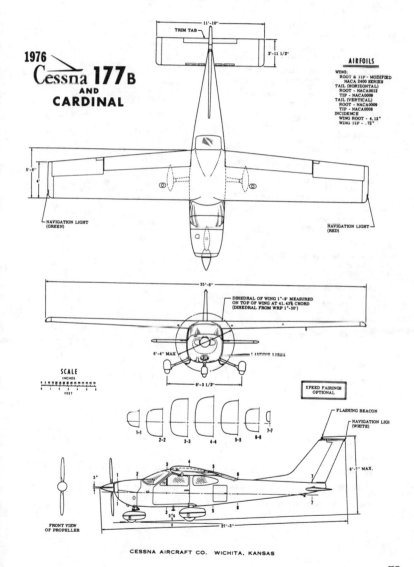

1976 Cessna 177B AND CARDINAL

AIRFOILS

WING:
ROOT & TIP - MODIFIED
NACA 2400 SERIES
TAIL (HORIZONTAL)
ROOT - NACA0012
TIP - NACA0009
TAIL (VERTICAL)
ROOT - NACA0009
TIP - NACA0008
INCIDENCE
WING ROOT - 4.12°
WING TIP - .72°

TRIM TAB

11'-10"

2'-11 1/2"

NAVIGATION LIGHT (GREEN)

NAVIGATION LIGHT (RED)

5'-6"

4"

35'-6"

DIHEDRAL OF WING 1°-9' MEASURED ON TOP OF WING AT 41.43% CHORD (DIHEDRAL FROM WRP 1°-30')

6'-4" MAX

8'-3 1/2"

SCALE
INCHES
FEET

SPEED FAIRINGS OPTIONAL

1-1   2-2   3-3   4-4   5-5   6-6   7-7

FLASHING BEACON

NAVIGATION LIGHT (WHITE)

8'-7" MAX.

FRONT VIEW OF PROPELLER

3"

3'4"

27'-3"

CESSNA AIRCRAFT CO.   WICHITA, KANSAS

59

1976 Cardinal/Cardinal II Performance and Specifications*

SPEED:
Maximum at Sea Level	139 knots	257 kph
Cruise, 75% power at 10,000 feet	130 knots	241 kph

CRUISE, Recommended Lean Mixture with fuel allowance for engine start, taxi, takeoff, climb and 45 minutes reserve at 45% power

75% power at 10,000 feet with 49 gallons usable fuel	535 nm 4.2 hr	991 km 4.2 hr
75% power at 10,000 feet with 60 gallons usable fuel	675 nm 5.3 hr	1250 km 5.3 hr
Maximum range at 10,000 feet with 49 gallons usable fuel	615 nm 6.1 hr	1139 km 6.1 hr
Maximum range at 10,000 feet with 60 gallons usable fuel	780 nm 7.7 hr	1445 km 7.7 hr
RATE OF CLIMB AT SEA LEVEL	840 fpm	256 mpm
SERVICE CEILING	14,600 ft	4450 m
TAKEOFF PERFORMANCE:		
Ground roll	750 ft	229 m
Total distance over 50 ft. obstacle	1400 ft	427 m
LANDING PERFORMANCE:		
Ground roll	600 ft	183 m
Total distance over 50 ft. obstacle	1220 ft	372 m
STALL SPEED, IAS		
Flaps up, power off	52 knots	96 kph
Flaps down, power off	40 knots	74 kph
MAXIMUM WEIGHT	2500 lb	1134 kg
STANDARD EMPTY WEIGHT		
Cardinal	1533 lb	695 kg
Cardinal II	1560 lb	708 kg
MAXIMUM USEFUL LOAD:		
Cardinal	967 lb	439 kg
Cardinal II	940 lb	426 kg
BAGGAGE ALLOWANCE	120 lb	54 kg
WING LOADING	14.4 lb/sq ft	70.2 kg/sq m
POWER LOADING	13.9 lb/hp	6.3 kg/hp
WING SPAN	35 ft, 6 in	10.82 m
WING AREA	174 sq ft	16.16 sq m
LENGTH	27 ft, 3 in	8.31 m
HEIGHT	8 ft, 7 in	2.62 m
FUEL CAPACITY, Total:		
Standard tanks	50 gal	189 liters
Long range tanks	61 gal	231 liters
OIL CAPACITY	9 qt	8.5 liters
ENGINE	Lycoming O-360-A1F6D engine; 180 bhp at 2700 rpm	
PROPELLER	Constant speed, 76 inch diameter (1.93 m)	

*Subject to change without notice

The 1972 Cardinal possessed detail changes only, and few of those. The 1973 model appeared with a recontoured engine cowl and new model of the 180-hp Lycoming 0-360 engine which featured an improved oil filter system and a few pounds less weight. Maximum (optional) fuel capacity was upped to 61 gallons.

In 1974, the principal improvement to the Cardinal appears to have been a larger coathanger in the baggage compartment. However, factory list price was held at the 1972 level.

By 1975, increased use of bonded construction in the doors and engine cowling, along with improved streamlining of the landing gear, had added a little speed.

The 1976 Cardinal could boast an even dozen changes—if you want to count such details as chrome plated seat adjustment handles and stronger vent-window frame. And, yes, Cessna still employs that maniac who gets his jollies by switching things around on the instrument panel every year or so. This is listed as an "improvement" on the 1976 Cardinal.

Factory prices for 1976: $27,250 as it rolls from the paint shop; $29,850 for the Cardinal II with basic avionics, and $33,550 for the Cardinal II with "Nav Pac," which may be described as a complete navigation/communications system and includes strobe lights, heated pitot, and an alternate static source.

The Cardinal RG is discussed in Chapter 11.

CESSNA **150**

CHAPTER 7: CESSNA 150 AND 150 AEROBAT

On February 23, 1951 the last Cessna 140A left the assembly line in Wichita, and for seven years Cessna did not offer a two-place airplane. By 1958, however, a good volume-production two-place trainer was so much in demand that flight operators were paying more for 7-year-old 140's than those craft sold for new. True, there were a couple of good fabric-covered two-placers in the market, but the economical all-metal 140A had spoiled a lot of flight operators (and customers); nothing less than a 140 follow-on would do.

Happily, Cessna listened to those voices from the aeronautical wilderness — and produced a 140 follow-on. They called it the Cessna 150.

The first 150 appeared late in 1958, and it did not pretend to improve upon the 140's performance figures, but instead used its ten extra horsepower to do much the same with greater ease and comfort without significantly increasing cost of operation. In short, it was a scaled-down 172, and except for the pleasant fact that the new 150 had a slightly quicker control-response — seemed a bit more "lighthearted" — it inherited all of the 172's amiable characteristics. It came close to being the ideal sport/trainer, as its apparently ageless popularity has attested ever since.

Now, before we go any further we must acknowledge that a lot of people may protest the above statement. Some will maintain that the ideal sport/trainer is the Cherokeke 140; others will say it's the Musketeer Sport or the Citabria, etc. Therefore, we've got to hedge by admitting that it all depends upon who's talking. It isn't possible to (honestly) say that one airplane is "better" than another, because *every* aircraft design is a compromise; to get something, you have to give something. If you want speed, for example, you must pay for it with other desirable traits, including economy of operation. So, the most anyone can do is decide which airplane is best for him; and that, clearly, is determined by each individual's preferences, prejudices and, perhaps, the personal weaknesses most of us possess. But we can allow our "ideal" statement to stand if we add "for the most people," because the Cessna 150 has far out-sold all other planes in its class.

In 1969, 61% of all flight-training hours were flown in Cessnas, primarily the 150. Of the 6,800,000 flight-training hours flown that year in the U.S. by all types of aircraft, 3,100,000 flight-training hours were accounted for by the Cessna 150. So, who can argue with success of that magnitude?

The 150, like most airplanes, has grown a little heavier as the years pass, and has paid for it with a little bit of performance. This seems inevitable, because customers want ever more comfort and convenience, and appear willing to give up a little range/speed/climb-rate to pamper the flesh. A look at the Model Comparison Tables following Chapter 10 will show this trend, which Cessna successfully curbed after 1966. The 1962 and 1963 Models (Commuter version) had low empty weights, and slightly better performance. The big rear window was added in 1964; doors were enlarged and squared-off and the swept-rudder added in 1966. The conical-camber wingtips came with the 1970 Model, and in 1971 the 150 received that lovely tubular-steel landing gear, new noseplate with landing light and extended prop shaft, plus new dorsal fin — and of course, re-shaped wheel pants (called "speed fairings" by Cessna advertising men, though they add little speed).

The conical wingtips, which improve turn and slow-flight

1971 Cessna Model 150

stability, are about the only significant aerodynamic changes in the 150 design since its inception. All the other many improvements have made it quieter, easier to handle on the ground, handier to operate in the air, better to see out of and prettier to look at. Come to think of it, that's about all Detroit has done for cars during the past thirty years.

The first 150, the 1959 Model, is still a nice little flying machine if it has been properly maintained (we probably should speak of all Cessna models in present tense, since all — back through the pre-WW-II Airmaster — are still flying in surprising numbers). The 1959 Model has the pull-starter (since replaced by the key ignition type), and a cabin more closely resembling the 140 than that of later 150's; but it flies just like its fancier off-spring of later years.

One of these early ones, say, 1959-1963, which may be found in the used plane market at prices ranging from $4,000 to $6,000, is probably a much better buy than the cheaper, fabric-covered used planes for the median-income pilot who flies mostly for fun. The 150 will not depreciate much, and its maintenance will be less costly, particularly if one is faced with a re-cover job on the rag-winger. Also, the 150 is always good merchandise in the used market when one is ready to trade or sell. During the late sixties, it was not at all uncommon for a man to buy a used 150, fly it for a couple of years, then sell it for as much as he paid for it in the first place. His cost of ownership was represented by whatever it cost him to keep it in top condition. And since the average 150 (all models) will burn only 5 to 6 gallons of fuel per hour (at 115-120 mph) it gives compact-car gas milage.

But "practical" reasons aside, the 150 also has a sort of friendly air about it that just naturally attracts people. In contrast to the rather ominous stance of the bigger, faster and more powerful craft that seems to *challenge* you to flight, the saucy little 150 *invites* you with a twinkle, as if to say, "C'mon, let's go have some fun!"

This characteristic implies, of course, that it won't place any great demands upon you. And it doesn't. We taped a demonstration ride in a 1966 Model — that was the year the swept rudder and bigger doors were added, along with larger tire size (same as 172) — and this airplane, with a little over 1,100 hours on its recording tach, still looked new late in 1970.

We were surprised to discover that the old pull-type starter lever was still used in the 150 as late as 1966, and the flap indicator, above the left window, was awkward to read; but electric flaps began with this model and the old "axe handle" flap lever disappeared from between the seats in favor of a switch on the panel. Stabilizer trim is on a console just below the throttle.

To start the engine, mixture is set at "Rich," fuel selector switch, "On" (there are no Left and Right positions for individual fuel tanks), crack throttle 1/4th of an inch, a couple of shots of "prime," clear the prop and firmly pull the starter T-handle.

As the oil pressure comes up, we ask Ground Control at Lawton (Oklahoma) Municipal for taxi instructions and then move out. She rolls easily, the 100-hp Continental muttering happily under its

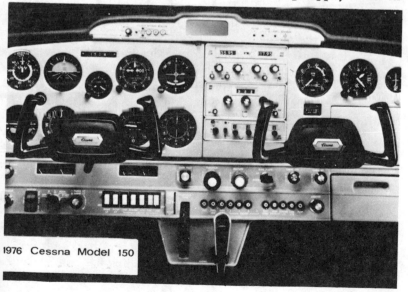

1976 Cessna Model 150

breath. Nose-wheel steering with the rudder pedals is quick and positive. On the taxi strip, we set altimeter (field elevation, 1,108 ft), and determine that we are about 170 lbs below our allowable gross weight.

Prior to take-off, the magneto checks are made at 1,700 rpms. The Owner's Manual discourages full-power run-ups unless a malfunction is suspected. Besides, with plenty of runway available, the full-power check is more practical during the early part of the take-off run, because there's plenty of room to shut-down everything and stop if a problem is suspected. Completing our pre-take-off check, we make sure the doors are latched; all flight controls free; adjust stabilizer trim to "Take-Off;" check operation of carburetor heat (leaving it at "Cold"), and check flaps in "Up" position. Then, with tower's blessing, we feed-in power and accelerate down the runway centerline.

As the air speed passes 40 mph, we begin to ease back on the control wheel, and a few seconds later, as the airspeed needle passes 50 mph, the 150 "slips the surly bonds of earth" and returns to its natural habitat. We leave the engine at full power and adjust the speed at 85 mph with the control wheel. This results in an initial climb-rate of 650 feet per minute (fpm) with an OAT of 64 degrees F. A steeper angle, which brings the airspeed needle back to 75 mph, gives us 740 fpm. We leave the pattern, and continue upward on a westerly heading to get away from military and airline traffic in the area.

We lean mixture as we climb in order to maintain best rpms, and level off at 5,000 feet, which puts us well above the haze layer in clear air. A check on cruising speeds at this altitude shows 121 mph TAS turning 2,750 rpms. It drops back to about 108 mph TAS at 2,500 rpms. This latter setting should lower fuel consumption to about 5 gph (from more than 6 gph) and increase range by approximately 75 miles. It is also, of course, easier on the engine. Optimum cruise at 2,650 rpms produces 115 mph true at this height.

We try some stalls, and with power off, no flaps, the 150 mushes along, control wheel back, wings level at 48 mph IAS. With flaps down and power off, there is a more definite break at about 42 mph IAS, preceded by some buffeting, but again wings remain level and the airplane is flying almost as soon as back-pressure on the wheel is relaxed. It's a little more fun stalling out of a 30-degree bank with flaps. The break is quite clean from this attitude and the

1076 Cessna Model 150

buffeting pronounced, while the pay-off comes at about 58 mph. However, the down-wing comes up at once and recovery is swift.

The only surprise one is likely to encounter doing stalls in the later model Cessnas (beginning with the 1966 Model 150), is the wierd sound (our colleague Don Downie likened it to the "dying gasp of a collapsing bag pipe") of the Cessna pneumatic reed stall-warning device. This system, maintenance-free and non-electrical, admits the relative wind through a 3/4-inch opening in the wing's leading edge which flows through the reed device to produce an increasingly eerie sound as one aproaches the stall. It really raises the hair on the back of your neck, and should be the most effective stall-warner in the business, next to a short-tempered flight instructor.

Landings are typical Cessna landings. You can make the 150 float and porpoise coming in with too much speed and a high flare; but it'll eventually mush onto the runway and land itself anyway. Or, you can drag over the fence at 60 mph and plop it down firmly on all three wheels. It won't complain. But if you're willing to work at your landings a little, this airplane will really make you look good in the maneuver that has traditionally been the primary measuring stick of pilot proficiency.

From the time the first 150 appeared late in 1958, it has been offered in three versions, the Standard, Trainer and Commuter. The 150 Aerobat was added in 1970, and about 300 were sold during its first year in production (Still another version is the French-built F150, sold throughout Europe since 1966.)

The 1971 Model 150's were announced in September, 1970, and the most significant improvement (in our opinion) was the switch to the Cardinal-type hollow, tubular-steel gear legs. This system gives the 150 an even wider track — nearly 8 ft — and a ground ride that surely can't be bettered short of the hovercraft principle. If that isn't enough, Cessna says that this gear has four to five times the service life of previous landing gears.

Interiors were again poshed-up for '71, and the contoured cabin ceiling of easy-to-clean, rip-resistant Ensolite (a 1970 innovation) added 2½ inches to headroom. A new level of quietness resulted from the propeller extention and new cowling. There was also a new safety belt system.

List prices for the 1971 Model 150's were: Standard, $8,895; Trainer, $10,775; Commuter, $11,995 and Aerobat $10,995.

The Cessna 150 Aerobat is the versatile one. It is a trainer, cross-country personal/business plane, and a fun machine approved for all the aerobatic maneuvers most private pilots are likely to master. It is certified for barrel rolls, aileron rolls, single snap rolls, loops, Immelmann turns, spins, Cuban-8's and vertical reversements. It is stressed for six G's positive and three G's negative flight loads. Special equipment includes quick-release door mechanisms, seats with removable bottom and back cushions to accommodate either back or seat-pack parachutes, quick-release lap belts and shoulder

68

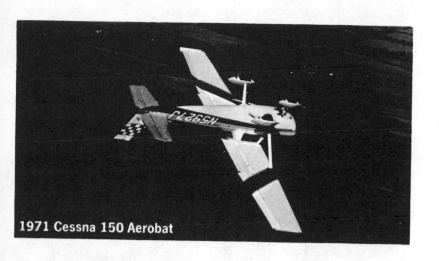

1971 Cessna 150 Aerobat

1971 Cessna 150 Aerobat

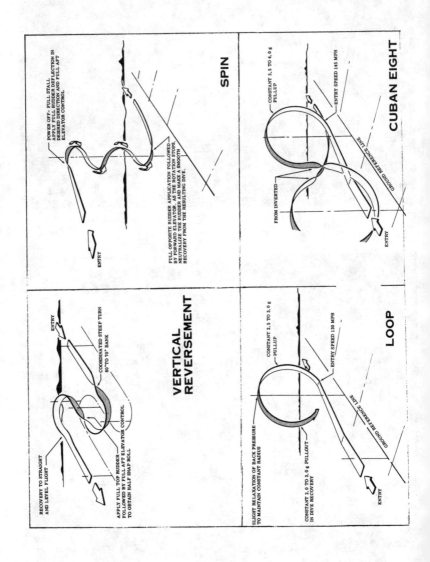

SPIN

POWER OFF- FULL STALL
APPLY FULL RUDDER DEFLECTION IN
DESIRED DIRECTION AND FULL AFT
ELEVATOR CONTROL

FULL OPPOSITE RUDDER APPLICATION FOLLOWED
BY FORWARD ELEVATOR. AS THE ROTATION STOPS,
NEUTRALIZE THE RUDDER AND MAKE A SMOOTH
RECOVERY FROM THE RESULTING DIVE.

ENTRY

CUBAN EIGHT

CONSTANT 3.5 TO 4.0 g
PULLUP

ENTRY SPEED 145 MPH

GROUND REFERENCE LINE

FROM INVERTED

ENTRY

VERTICAL REVERSEMENT

ENTRY

RECOVERY TO STRAIGHT
AND LEVEL FLIGHT

COORDINATED STEEP TURN
60° TO 70° BANK

APPLY FULL TOP RUDDER
FOLLOWED BY FULL AFT ELEVATOR CONTROL
TO OBTAIN HALF SNAP ROLL

LOOP

SLIGHT RELAXATION OF BACK PRESSURE
TO MAINTAIN CONSTANT RADIUS

CONSTANT 2.5 TO 3.0 g
PULLUP

ENTRY SPEED 130 MPH

GROUND REFERENCE LINE

CONSTANT 2.0 TO 3.0 g PULLOUT
IN DIVE RECOVERY

ENTRY

70

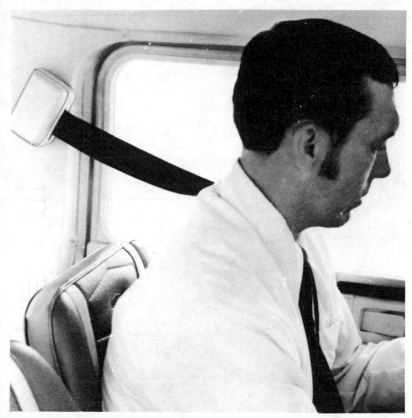

Inertia Reel Combination Shoulder Harness and Lap Belt Restraint System— Cessna Model 150

harness, tinted ceiling skylights, and G-meter—plus the distinctive paint job.

We used to visit the late akro champ Hal Krier whenever we were in Wichita, because aerobatics had fascinated us ever since those long ago days when we dared a loop or two with the Spartan C-3 bipe in which we got our first bootleg stick-time (with a 40-hour newly-minted private pilot acting as our instructor). And when the 150 Aerobat appeared, we hoped we'd be lucky enough to get Krier to fly with us and put it through its paces.

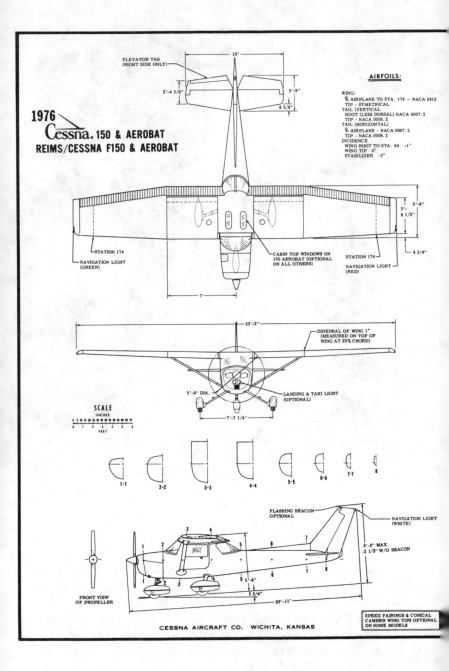

ELEVATOR TAB
(RIGHT SIDE ONLY)

10'

2'-4 3/8"

3'-8"

9 5/8"

1976
Cessna. 150 & AEROBAT
REIMS/CESSNA F150 & AEROBAT

5'-4"

3'-
8 1/2"

4 3/4"

STATION 174

NAVIGATION LIGHT
(GREEN)

CABIN TOP WINDOWS ON
150 AEROBAT (OPTIONAL
ON ALL OTHERS)

STATION 174

NAVIGATION LIGHT
(RED)

7'

33'-2"

DIHEDRAL OF WING 1°
(MEASURED ON TOP OF
WING AT 25% CHORD)

5'-9" DIA.

LANDING & TAXI LIGHT
(OPTIONAL)

7'-7 1/4"

SCALE
INCHES
FEET

1-1   2-2   3-3   4-4   5-5   6-6   7-7   8

FLASHING BEACON
OPTIONAL

NAVIGATION LIGHT
(WHITE)

8'-6" MAX.
-2 1/2" W/O BEACON

5'-9"

3 3/4°

23'-11"

FRONT VIEW
OF PROPELLER

SPEED FAIRINGS & CONICAL
CAMBER WING TIPS OPTIONAL
ON SOME MODELS

CESSNA AIRCRAFT CO.   WICHITA, KANSAS

We weren't *that* lucky, but we were fortunate enough to be in Wichita the day Harold Krier (three-time Men's National Champion Aerobatic Pilot)evaluated the prototype 150 Aerobat back in June, 1969. We had dinner with Harold that evening (well, actually, hamburgers and malts at a drive-in), and he was enthusiastic over the new Aerobat.

Harold told us that, in his opinion, this craft represented an excellent blending of desirable traits in a sport/trainer: it was capable of all the fancy didos the average private pilot has any business performing; yet it retained all the forgiving and gentle qualities of its non-checkered sisters. In fact, it *was* the same as other 150's, with just a little beefing-up here and there.

Harold said he had performed snap rolls; snaps from wingovers, slow rolls, 4-point rolls (without power), Immelmanns, loops, loops with snaps, Cuban-8's, spins and a number of inverted maneuvers that the airplane would not be certified for. He said the rudder was inadequate for some maneuvers, but explained that that is true of almost any production craft not designed exclusively for aerobatics.

Harold did surprise us when he said he hoped Cessna kept the 100-hp engine in the Aerobat; we had always had the impression that the tumble types wanted power to spare. But Krier said, "I think the 150 is a very nice little package as it stands, and I don't think Cessna should tamper with it. Give it a bigger engine and you have to modify the airframe. It gets bigger and heavier and more expensive and you no longer have a 150, but something else entirely."

By 1972, the Cessna 150 alone accounted for 15% of all flying done. It's hard to add much to a recommendation of that caliber. It's even harder to significantly improve upon a machine that satisfies its market so well. The 1973 Model 150 appeared with lower seats for more headroom, and a redesigned instrument panel along with new control wheels.

The 1974 Cessna 150's gained little but cosmetic changes such as re-shaped wheel fairings and of course a different paint scheme. The 1974 Aerobat was fitted with a propeller possessing a Clark Y airfoil section, and this increased cruising and top speeds to 119 and 124 mph respectively, while raising service ceiling to 14,000 ft.

The 1975 models of the 150 series received increased fin and rudder area for better crosswind handling by adding six inches to the height of the rudder. The extra rudder is especially useful to the Aerobat model because, as any aerobatic pilot will tell you, no production airplane ever has enough rudder for precision aerobatics.

The Clark Y propeller, proven on the '74 Aerobat, was installed on all 150 models in 1975.

The new prop, along with the improved wheel and brake fairings, did add performance—up to 130 mph top speed with full throttle and the tach 200 rpms over redline. Actually, we got 119 mph TAS at a more practical 2,650 rpms.

The 1976 models of the 150 series offered little improvement over the previous year—chromed door handles, slight amount of new soundproofing, and seats ground-adjustable for height.

1976 factory suggested prices: $12,650 for the Standard 150; $16,350 for the 150 Commuter; $18,750 for the Commuter II with complete avionics, and $15,250 for the Aerobat.

1976 Models 150/A150 Performance and Specifications*

	COMMUTER		AEROBAT	
SPEED:				
Maximum at Sea Level	109 knots	202 kph	108 knots	200 kph
Cruise, 75% power at 7000 feet	106 knots	196 kph	105 knots	194 kph
CRUISE, Recommended Lean Mixture with fuel allowance for engine start, taxi, takeoff, climb and 45 minutes reserve at 45% power:				
75% power at 7000 feet with	340 nm	630 km	335 nm	620 km
22.5 gallons usable fuel	3.3 hr	3.3 hr	3.3 hr	3.3 hr
75% power at 7000 feet with	580 nm	1074 km	570 nm	1086 km
35 gallons usable fuel	5.5 hr	5.5 hr	5.5 hr	5.5 hr
Maximum range at 10,000 feet with	420 nm	778 km	415 nm	769 km
22.5 gallons usable fuel	4.9 hr	4.9 hr	4.9 hr	4.9 hr
Maximum range at 10,000 feet with	735 nm	1361 km	725 nm	1343 km
35 gallons usable fuel	8.5 hr	8.5 hr	8.5 hr	8.5 hr
RATE OF CLIMB AT SEA LEVEL	670 fpm	204 mpm	670 fpm	204 mpm
SERVICE CEILING	14,000 ft	4267 m	14,000 ft	4267 m
TAKEOFF PERFORMANCE:				
Ground Roll	735 ft	224 m	735 ft	224 m
Total Distance Over 50 ft. Obstacle	1385 ft	422 m	1385 ft	422 m
LANDING PERFORMANCE:				
Ground Roll	445 ft	136 m	445 ft	136 m
Total Distance Over 50 ft. Obstacle	1075 ft	328 m	1075 ft	328 m
STALL SPEED, IAS				
Flaps up, power off	46 knots	85 kph	49 knots	91 kph
Flaps down, power off	42 knots	78 kph	44 knots	82 kph
MAXIMUM WEIGHT	1600 lbs	726 kg	1600 lb	726 kg
STANDARD EMPTY WEIGHT:				
Commuter/Aerobat	1104 lb	501 kg	1076 lb	488 kg
Commuter II	1122 lb	509 kg	---	---
MAXIMUM USEFUL LOAD				
Commuter/Aerobat	496 lb	225 kg	524 lb	238 kg
Commuter II	478 lb	217 kg	---	---
BAGGAGE ALLOWANCE	120 lb	54 kg	120 lb	54 kg
WING LOADING	10.0 lb/sq ft	48.9 kg/sq m	10.2 lb/sq ft	49.8 kg/sq m
POWER LOADING	16.0 lb/hp	7.3 kg/hp	16.0 lb/hp	7.3 kg/hp
WING SPAN	32 ft, 9 in	10.11 m	32 ft, 8 1/2 in	9.97 m
WING AREA	159.5 sq ft	14.8 sq m	157 sq ft	14.6 sq m
LENGTH	23 ft, 11 in	7.29 m	23 ft, 11 in	7.29 m
HEIGHT	8 ft, 6 in	2.59 m	8 ft, 6 in	2.59 m
FUEL CAPACITY, Total:				
Standard Tanks	26 gal	98 liters	26 gal	98 liters
Long Range Tanks	38 gal	144 liters	38 gal	144 liters
OIL CAPACITY	6 qt	5.7 liters	6 qt	5.7 liters
ENGINE	Teledyne Continental O-200-A Engine; 100 bhp at 2750 rpm			
PROPELLER	Fixed Pitch, 69 inch diameter (1.75 m)			

*Subject to change without notice

NOTE: All performance figures include the effect of speed fairings which improve the speeds by approximately 2 knots Speed fairings are standard equipment on the Commuter and Commuter II and are optional equipment on the Aerobat.

1978 MODEL 152 PERFORMANCE AND SPECIFICATIONS*

		Model 152		Aerobat	
SPEED**					
Maximum at Sea Level		110 knots	204 kph	109 knots	202 kph
Cruise, 75% power at 8000 feet		107 knots	198 kph	106 knots	196 kph

CRUISE, Recommended Lean Mixture with fuel allowance for engine start, taxi, takeoff, climb and 45 minutes reserve at 45% power

		Model 152		Aerobat	
75% power at 8000 feet with	Range	350 nm	648 km	345 nm	639 km
24.5 Gallons Usable Fuel	Time	3.4 hr	3.4 hr	3.4 hr	3.4 hr
75% power at 8000 feet with	Range	580 nm	1074 km	575 nm	1065 km
37.5 Gallons Usable Fuel	Time	5.5 hr	5.5 hr	5.5 hr	5.5 hr
Maximum Range at 10,000 feet with	Range	415 nm	769 km	410 nm	759 km
24.5 Gallons Usable Fuel	Time	5.2 hr	5.2 hr	5.2 hr	5.2 hr
Maximum Range at 10,000 feet with	Range	690 nm	1278 km	685 nm	1269 km
37.5 Gallons Usable Fuel	Time	8.7 hr	8.7 hr	8.7 hr	8.7 hr
RATE OF CLIMB AT SEA LEVEL		715 fpm	218 mpm	715 fpm	218 mpm
SERVICE CEILING		14,700 ft	4480 m	14,700 ft	4480 m
TAKEOFF PERFORMANCE:					
Ground Roll		725 ft	221 m	725 ft	221 m
Total Distance Over 50 ft. Obstacle		1340 ft	408 m	1340 ft	408 m
LANDING PERFORMANCE:					
Ground Roll		475 ft	145 m	475 ft	145 m
Total Distance Over 50 ft Obstacle		1200 ft	366 m	1200 ft	366 m
STALL SPEED, CAS					
Flaps up, power off		48 knots	89 kph	48 knots	89 kph
Flaps down, power off		43 knots	80 kph	43 knots	80 kph
MAXIMUM WEIGHT		1670 lb	757 kg	1670 lb	757 kg
STANDARD EMPTY WEIGHT:					
Standard Airplane		1081 lb	490 kg	1125 lb	510 kg
152 II		1118 lb	507 kg		
MAXIMUM USEFUL LOAD:					
Standard Airplane		589 lb	267 kg	545 lb	247 kg
152 II		552 lb	250 kg		
BAGGAGE ALLOWANCE		120 lb	54 kg	120 lb	54 kg
WING LOADING		10.5 lb/sq ft	51.1 kg/sq m		
POWER LOADING		15.2 lb/hp	6.9 kg/hp		
WING SPAN***		33 ft, 2 in	10.11 m		
WING AREA***		159.5 sq ft	14.8 sq m		
LENGTH		24 ft, 1 in	7.34 m		
HEIGHT		8 ft, 6 in	2.59 m		
FUEL CAPACITY, Total					
Standard Tanks		26 gal	98 liters	26 gal	98 liters
Long Range Tanks		39 gal	148 liters	39 gal	148 liters
OIL CAPACITY		6 qt	5.7 liters	6 qt	5.7 liters
ENGINE		Avco Lycoming O-235-L2C engine; 110 bhp at 2550 rpm			
PROPELLER		Fixed Pitch, 69 inch diameter (1.75 m)			

*Subject to change without notice
**Speed performance is shown for an airplane equipped with optional speed fairings, which increase the speeds by approximately 2 knots. There is a corresponding difference in range, while all other performance figures are unchanged when speed fairings are installed.
***Wing area and wing span are shown for an airplane equipped with modified conical wing tips which are optiona
With standard wing tips, the wing area is 157 sq ft (14.6 sq m) and the wing span is 32 ft, 8.5 inches (9.9

CHAPTER 8: CESSNA 182/SKYLANE, 205 AND SUPER SKYLANE

The Cessna 182 first appeared in 1956. It was a Model 180 with tricycle landing gear. Except for "styling" differences since that time, the same could be said for the 182's and Skylanes (the Skylane is the posh version of the 182) built through 1071. The 182/Skylane represents a substantial step upward from the 172/Skyhawk series, and the transition is not lightly made, because the Skylane does not fly or land like a Skyhawk. It's five hundred pounds more airplane, with more power (efficiently applied via a constant-speed prop), and it insists that its new owner stops grinning and starts thinking. It's not a student airplane; it's for serious cross-country transportation — any kind of country.

Since we didn't have a 1971 Model Skylane handy, we took a demonstration ride in a '69 Model, because there was little change in this craft during these three years, except for a slight weight increase (we were surprised that the '71 did not switch to tubular-steel gear legs). However, even that didn't turn out very well because we were up-tight for time and had only a couple of hours to go on a raw November day. That was decidedly unfair to an airplane that likes to get up high and go far. Our veteran Cessna man at Lawton (Oklahoma) Municipal, Ray Johnson, says that no one can really appreciate the Skylane until he's taken it on a long cross-country flight, preferably, to California or Oregon and back with some stops at high-altitude airports in the West.

As we said, the first (1956) 182 was a 180 with tricycle landing gear. In 1957, the gear legs were shortened, and a year later the Skylane version appeared. The swept tail was added in 1960; in '61 came an additional window on each side, and in 1962 the big rear window for 360-degree vision, plus electric flaps and a wider cabin. A lot of interior improvements followed during the next five years, then the 1969 Model again had its main gear legs shortened and the space between the wheels expanded. But since the nose-wheel could not be lowered (due to the need for prop clearance with the ground), this resulted in a slightly nose-high stance for the 182/Skylane, a situation that makes for easier entry and exit from the cabin, perhaps better rough-field handling and a lower profile to better handle cross-wind landings. But it doesn't do anything for the pilot transitioning from the 172, because, if he drives the 182 down to land like some people do the Super Car, he's liable to bend the firewall a little. The 182/Skylane must be brought in for a nose-high touch-down on the main wheels.

Of course, the 182 pilots will be quick to point out that that's the way we *should* have been landing the 172 and 150 (experienced flyers are like reformed sinners; they have small tolerance for those of us who are doing things the way *they* used to).

Anyway, the point is, the 182/Skylane is not going to cover up for you or shrug off indifferent control handling. She steps higher than the 172 and requires a tighter rein.

This is not to say that the Skylane is hard to fly or tricky. It isn't. It's still a Cessna. But the controls are heavier and you know you're flying more airplane. The principal differences for the pilot stepping up from the 150 or 172 will probably be in landings and power management. That "extra throttle" — prop control — gives fresh significance to the tachometer and adds a manifold pressure gauge.

1971 Cessna Skylane

Engine starting procedure is much like that of the 172 except that you have cowl flaps to open and prop pitch control to push in for "High RPMs." The pre-take-off run-up is done at the usual 1,700 rpms (with prop in high rpms), and in addition, you'll "exercise" the prop a couple of times — pull out the knob changing pitch from high to low rpms — to insure oil circulation that activates pitch change. Then, leaving the prop in high rpms, feed-in full throttle for take-off.

You'll notice the extra power, and 60 mph will come quickly. You'll also notice that it requires a firmer pressure to lift the nose-wheel off if you've been flying a Skyhawk.

Maximum power for the take-off climb should be limited to that absolutely necessary for safety, according to the Skylane Owner's Manual, so we reduce power to the recommended 23 inches of manifold pressure and 2,450 rpms (about 75% power) for climb-out at 100 mph. This gives us 1,300 fpm with the OAT registering 44 degrees F. We are almost 50 lbs light, however. The book says we can get 1,700 fpm at this loading with full power and an IAS of 85 mph.

The Skylane gives quite a bit of flexibility in cruise and range at various altitudes. Fully loaded, at 2,500 feet, turning 2,450 with 23 inches, TAS is 156 mph and range (with 60 gal) is 660 miles. This can be stretched to 865 miles at this inefficient altitude if you cut rpms to 2,000 and manifold pressure to 17 inches with a TAS of 100 mph. But you aren't likely to ever go anywhere at that altitude in a Skylane. Seventy-five hundred feet is much better; 10,000 is probably best, and you can go to 15,000 if you have oxygen. At 15,000, 2,450 rpms and 16 inches will give you 145 mph TAS and a range of 835 miles.

For a given throttle setting, select the lowest rpms (with the prop control) in the green arc range that will give smooth engine operation. Cowl flaps should be adjusted to maintain cylinder head temperature at approximately 2/3 of the normal operating range (green arc); and to lean the mixture for the best range, pull out the mixture control until the engine becomes rough, then push it back in just far enough to smooth out the engine again. Any change in altitude, power setting or carburetor heat will require a change in the lean mixture setting.

It's possible to land the Skylane without use of trim, but that's doing it the hard way. And although the book says to bring it in power-off with 40-degrees of flap at 69 mph for short-field landings, this produces a fairly high sink rate and you've got to be right on top of it to make your flare just right or you'll touch-down pretty hard. Seems to us the best way is to hold a little power and flatten-out the final, gradually backing-off the throttle and closing it just a little before flare. Then hold the wheel well back to insure that you touch-down on the main gear. It's best to hold the nose-wheel off for the first couple of hundred feet of the roll-out, unless you have a cross-wind to contend with.

The 1970 Model 182/Skylane adopted the conical cambered wingtips and new elevator control system to lower elevator stick forces. Basic list price of the 182 was $19,795. The Skylane was priced at $20,895. Used prices range all the way down to about $6,000 for an early Model 182.

The Cessna 205 was produced 1962-1964 inclusive. It has been described as a stretched Skylane with an additional 30-hp and fuel injection. It was also called, at the time it appeared, a Cessna 210 with fixed landing gear. Anyway, less than 600 were built during those three years before it was replaced by — or evolved into — the Super Skylane.

The Super Skylane and Turbo Super Skylane would be easier for Cessna watchers to fit into their proper categories if Cessna would only call them "Super 206's" instead of Skylanes because, it seems to us, these craft aren't really Skylanes, but a definite step upward — in power, size and weight — to another class. They are

1964 CESSNA 205

in fact up-town versions of the 206 Skywagon. For the extra conveniences, snootier name and different paint scheme, you pay $1,400 ($25,995 for the '70 Skywagon 206 vs. $27,450 for the '70 Super Skylane), and this would seem to lend weight to our long-standing suspicion that Cessna dealers need only to ask, "How much money have you got?" in order to roll out an airplane and match that figure almost to the dollar. (We can just picture the scene: "But I've only got $27,400.09," the customer says. "That's all right, sir," the dealer replies and, picking up the phone asks for his service department. "Okay, Mac, take a seat out of that new Super Skylane. A gentleman here wants a five-placer.")

Seriously, Cessna *does* effectively cover the gen-av market in gradual steps, from the 150 to the Citation 500 Fan Jet.

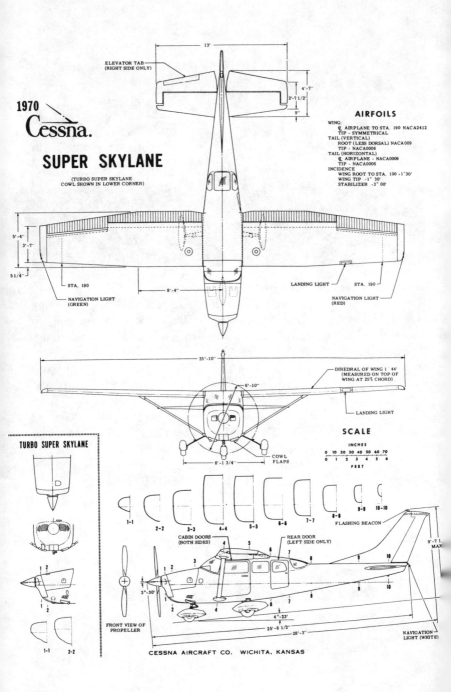

SUPER SKYLANE

1970 Cessna.

(TURBO SUPER SKYLANE COWL SHOWN IN LOWER CORNER)

ELEVATOR TAB (RIGHT SIDE ONLY)

13'
4'-7"
2'-7 1/2"
9"

AIRFOILS

WING:
  ℄ AIRPLANE TO STA. 190 NACA2412
  TIP - SYMMETRICAL
TAIL (VERTICAL)
  ROOT (LESS DORSAL) NACA009
  TIP - NACA0006
TAIL (HORIZONTAL)
  ℄ AIRPLANE - NACA0009
  TIP - NACA0006
INCIDENCE
  WING ROOT TO STA. 100 +1°30'
  WING TIP -1° 30'
  STABILIZER -3° 00'

5'-4"
3'-7"
5 1/4"

STA. 190
NAVIGATION LIGHT (GREEN)
8'-4"
LANDING LIGHT
STA. 190
NAVIGATION LIGHT (RED)

35'-10"
6'-10"
DIHEDRAL OF WING 1 44' (MEASURED ON TOP OF WING AT 25% CHORD)
LANDING LIGHT
8'-1 3/4"
COWL FLAPS

SCALE

INCHES
0 10 20 30 40 50 60 70
0 1 2 3 4 5 6
FEET

TURBO SUPER SKYLANE

1-1 2-2 3-3 4-4 5-5 6-6 7-7 8-8 9-9 10-10

FLASHING BEACON

CABIN DOORS (BOTH SIDES)
REAR DOOR (LEFT SIDE ONLY)

9'-7 1" MAX

3°-30'
FRONT VIEW OF PROPELLER
4'-23'
25'-8 1/2"
28'-3'
NAVIGATION LIGHT (WHITE)

1-1 2-2

CESSNA AIRCRAFT CO.   WICHITA, KANSAS

1970 Cessna Super Skylane

The Super Skylane was introduced late in 1964 (1965 Model), and was intended for the charter and air taxi operators. It would comfortably seat six adults (with plenty of leg room) and then take-off with full tanks and nearly 200 lbs of luggage. At optimum altitude, it would haul this load nearly 600 miles (with reserve fuel) at 160 mph or better, and it would do so economically, its fuel-injected 285-hp Continental 10-520-A engine consuming about 15 gallons of gas per hour.

By 1970, the Super Skylane had gained 300 lbs at gross weight and had an increased useful load of 250 lbs — at the cost of a slight amount of speed/range/initial climb. It seemed an excellent airplane for its task, but its future appeared uncertain because the Cessna 207 — for very little more money — could do even more with the same engine.

The Turbo Super Skylane, introduced in 1966, is equipped with a turbo supercharger. It has less useful load than its un-boosted sister, but will get up high and go fast.

The supercharger helps the engine breathe more efficiently when the temperature is hot and the density altitude is high. It provides 32.5 inches of manifold pressure up to 19,000 ft. Above that, it keeps working like an extra set of lungs compressing the thin air into a richer source of oxygen for the engine. As a result, the Turbo Super Skylane can effectively operate off the highest airfields in the world fully loaded.

This airplane will climb out at 1,030 fpm initially, and has a minimum loss of horsepower as altitude is gained. The turbo system continues to deliver cruise power up to 24,000 ft. There are no continuous control or throttle adjustments during climb, and no additional gauges to watch. The fuel-injected, 285-hp Continental engine (TS10-520-C) is specially adapted for turbocharging, and the turbine is automatically regulated by an absolute pressure controller and overboost control valve.

A two-to-three hour oxygen system is standard equipment on the Turbo Super Skylane. This installation includes an overhead console with capacity gauge and system control, six individual ports, control wheel microphone switch, external filler valve, and a 76-cubic-inch oxygen bottle.

Suggested list price of the Super Skylane for 1970 was $27,450. The Turbo Super Skylane for 1970 was priced at $31,950.°

The two models of the Super Skylane were discontinued after 1971; but since 649 were built, almost all of which are still flying, we should include them here.

The 182 and Skylane, of course, continues in production; indeed, ranking third in sales behind the Skyhawk and 150 models.

The Skylane appeared with the new tubular steel landing gear and "Camber-Lift" wing in 1972, resulting in a softer ground ride and better slow flight characteristics. The wing leading-edge was bonded, and this began the aerodynamic clean-up that, added to bonded doors and upper cowl in '73, new air scoops in '73, new engine baffles and Clark Y propeller section in '74, along with improved wheel and strut fairings and smoothed edges on fin and rudder in 1976, pay off in increased efficiency. Along the way were a host of detail comfort/convenience changes as well.

1976 factory prices: $32,150 for the basic Skylane; $38,550 for the Skylane II with factory installed avionics, and $41,450 for the Skylane II with Nav Pac.

°We do not attempt to discuss the various avionics installations available for Cessna airplanes due to space limitations in this book. For a complete rundown on light aircraft avionics and their uses, see the Modern Aircraft Series book, "NAV/COM GUIDE FOR PILOTS," by Don Downie.

1970 Super Skylane Performance and Specifications

)SS WEIGHT	3600 lbs., 1633 kg
ED: Best Power Mixture	
Top Speed at Sea Level	174 mph, 280 kph
Cruise, 75% Power at 6000 ft.	163 mph, 262 kph
GE: Normal Lean Mixture	
Cruise, 75% Power at 6000 ft.	650 miles, 1045 km
63 Gallons, No Reserve	4.0 hours
	162 mph, 261 kph
Cruise, 75% Power at 6000 ft.	830 miles, 1335 km
80 Usable Gallons, No Reserve	5.1 hours
	162 mph, 261 kph
Optimum Range at 10,000 ft.	1020 miles, 1640 km
80 Usable Gallons, No Reserve	7.6 hours
	134 mph, 216 kph
E-OF-CLIMB AT SEA LEVEL	920 fpm, 280 mpm
VICE CEILING	14,800 ft., 4511 m
EOFF:	
Ground Run	910 ft., 277 m
Total Distance Over 50-ft. Obstacle	1810 ft., 552 m
DING:	
Ground Roll	735 ft., 224 m
Total Distance Over 50-ft. Obstacle	1395 ft., 425 m
L SPEED:	
Flaps Up, Power Off	70 mph, 113 kph
Flaps Down, Power Off	61 mph, 98 kph
Y WEIGHT: (Approx.)	1835 lbs., 832 kg
L LOAD	1765 lbs., 801 kg
LOADING	20.7 lbs./ft.^{2}, 100.8 kg/m^2
R LOADING	12.6 lbs./hp, 5.7 kg/hp
CAPACITY: Total	
Standard Tanks	65 gallons, 246 liters
Optional Long-Range Tanks	84 gallons, 318 liters
CAPACITY: Total	12 quarts, 11.4 liters
R	Six-Cylinder, Fuel-Injection Engine, 285 Rated HP at 2700 RPM
ELLER:	
*Two-Bladed, Constant-Speed - Diameter	82 inches, 2.08 m
AREA	174 ft.^{2}, 16.2 m^2
TH	28 ft. 3 in., 8.61 m
HT: (With Depressed Nose Strut)	9 ft. 7-1/2 in., 2.93 m

rformance for optional three-bladed propeller is essentially the same as above.

1970 Turbo Super Skylane Performance and Specifications

GROSS WEIGHT — 3600 lbs., 1633 kg

SPEED: Best Power Mixture
- Top Speed at 19,000 ft. — 200 mph, 322 kph
- Cruise, 75% Power at 24,000 ft. — 184 mph, 296 kph
- Cruise, 75% Power at 10,000 ft. — 170 mph, 274 kph

RANGE: Normal Lean Mixture
- Cruise, 75% Power at 24,000 ft. / 63 Usable Gallons, No Reserve — 700 miles, 1127 km / 3.8 hours / 182 mph, 293 kph
- Cruise, 75% Power at 10,000 ft. / 63 Usable Gallons, No Reserve — 645 miles, 1038 km / 3.8 hours / 168 mph, 270 kph
- Cruise, 75% Power at 24,000 ft. / 80 Usable Gallons, No Reserve — 890 miles, 1432 km / 4.9 hours / 182 mph, 293 kph
- Cruise, 75% Power at 10,000 ft. / 80 Usable Gallons, No Reserve — 820 miles, 1320 km / 4.9 hours / 168 mph, 270 kph
- Optimum Range at 15,000 ft. / 80 Usable Gallons, No Reserve — 1050 miles, 1690 km / 7.6 hours / 139 mph, 224 kph

RATE-OF-CLIMB AT SEA LEVEL — 1030 fpm, 314 mpm

SERVICE CEILING — 26,300 ft., 8020 m

TAKEOFF:
- Ground Run — 910 ft., 277 m
- Total Distance Over 50-ft. Obstacle — 1810 ft., 552 m

LANDING:
- Ground Roll — 735 ft., 224 m
- Total Distance Over 50-ft. Obstacle — 1395 ft., 425 m

STALL SPEED:
- Flaps Up, Power Off — 70 mph, 113 kph
- Flaps Down, Power Off — 61 mph, 98 kph

EMPTY WEIGHT: (Approx.) — 1935 lbs., 878 kg

USEFUL LOAD — 1665 lbs., 755 kg

WING LOADING — 20.7 lbs./ft.^{2}, 100.8 kg/m^2

POWER LOADING — 12.6 lbs./hp, 5.7 kg/hp

FUEL CAPACITY: Total
- Standard Tanks — 65 gallons, 246 liters
- Optional Long-Range Tanks — 84 gallons, 318 liters

OIL CAPACITY: Total — 13 quarts, 12.3 liters

POWER — Six-Cylinder, Turbosupercharged, Fuel-Injection Engine, 285 Rated HP at 2700 RPM

PROPELLER:
- *Two-Bladed, Constant-Speed - Diameter — 82 inches, 2.08 m

WING SPAN — 35 ft. 10 in., 10.92 m

WING AREA — 174 ft.^{2}, 16.2 m^2

LENGTH — 28 ft. 3. in., 8.61 m

HEIGHT: (With Depressed Nose Strut) — 9 ft. 7-1/2 in., 2.93 m

*Performance for optional three-bladed propeller is essentially the same as above.

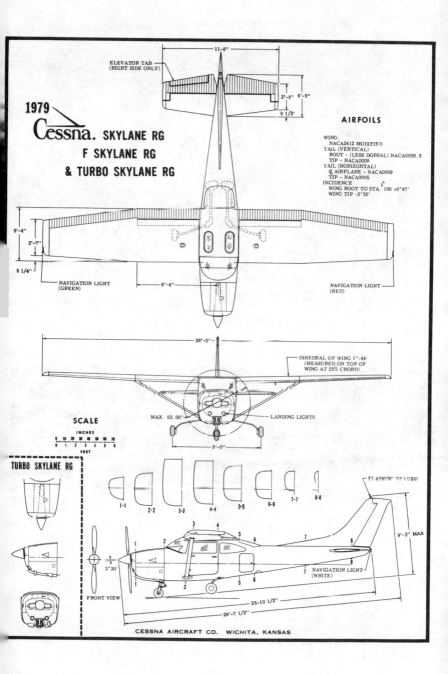

1979 Cessna. SKYLANE RG
F SKYLANE RG
& TURBO SKYLANE RG

ELEVATOR TAB
(RIGHT SIDE ONLY)

11'-8''
2'-8'' 4'-5''
9 1/2''

AIRFOILS

WING:
NACA2412 MODIFIED
TAIL (VERTICAL)
ROOT - (LESS DORSAL) NACA0009.5
TIP - NACA0008
TAIL (HORIZONTAL)
₵ AIRPLANE - NACA0009
TIP - NACA0005
INCIDENCE
WING ROOT TO STA. 100 +0°47'
WING TIP -2°50'

5'-4''
3'-7''
5 1/4''

NAVIGATION LIGHT
(GREEN)

8'-4''

NAVIGATION LIGHT
(RED)

36'-0''

DIHEDRAL OF WING 1°-44'
(MEASURED ON TOP OF
WING AT 25% CHORD)

SCALE

INCHES
0 10 20 30 40 50 60 70
0 1 2 3 4 5 6
FEET

MAX. 82.00''

LANDING LIGHTS

9'-0''

TURBO SKYLANE RG

3°30'

FRONT VIEW

1-1 2-2 3-3 4-4 5-5 6-6 7-7 8-8

FLASHING BEACON

9'-3'' MAX

NAVIGATION LIGHT
(WHITE)

25-10 1/2''

28'-7 1/2''

CESSNA AIRCRAFT CO. WICHITA, KANSAS

87

1979 Cessna Skylane RG

1976 Cessna Skylane II

1976 Skylane Performance and Specifications*

SPEED
  Maximum at Sea Level   148 knots   274 kph
  Cruise, 75% power at 7000 feet   144 knots   267 kph

CRUISE, Recommended Lean Mixture with fuel allowance for engine start, taxi, takeoff, climb and 45 minutes reserve at 45% power

75% power at 6500 ft. with 56 gal. usable fuel	475 nm 3.4 hr	880 km 3.4 hr
75% power at 6500 ft. with 75 gal. usable fuel	670 nm 4.7 hr	1241 km 4.7 hr
Maximum range at 10,000 ft. with 56 gal. usable fuel	565 nm 5.1 hr	1046 km 5.1 hr
Maximum range at 10,000 ft. with 75 gal. usable fuel	810 nm 7.3 hr	1500 km 7.3 hr

RATE OF CLIMB AT SEA LEVEL	890 fpm	271 mpm
SERVICE CEILING	17,700 ft	5395 m
TAKEOFF PERFORMANCE:		
Ground Roll	705 ft	215 m
Total distance over 50 ft. obstacle	1350 ft	411 m
LANDING PERFORMANCE		
Ground roll	590 ft	180 m
Total distance over 50 ft. obstacle	1350 ft	411 m
STALL SPEED, CAS		
Flaps up, power off	56 knots	104 kph
Flaps down, power off	50 knots	93 kph
MAXIMUM WEIGHT	2950 lb	1338 kg
STANDARD EMPTY WEIGHT		
Skylane	1707 lb	774 kg
Skylane II	1771 lb	803 kg
MAXIMUM USEFUL LOAD		
Skylane	1243 lb	564 kg
Skylane II	1179 lb	535 kg
BAGGAGE ALLOWANCE	200 lb	91 kg
WING LOADING	16.9 lb/sq ft	82.6 kg/sq m
POWER LOADING	12.8 lb/hp	5.8 kg/hp
WING SPAN	35 ft, 10 in	10.92 m
WING AREA	174 sq ft	16.2 sq m
LENGTH	28 ft, 2 in	8.59 m
HEIGHT	9 ft, 1 1/2 in	2.78 m
FUEL CAPACITY, Total		
Standard Tanks	61 gal	231 liters
Long Range Tanks	80 gal	303 liters
OIL CAPACITY	12 qt	11.4 liters

ENGINE: Teledyne Continental O-470-S Engine; 230 bhp at 2600 rpm

PROPELLER: Constant speed, 2 blades, 82 inch diameter (2.08 m)

*Subject to change without notice

1976 Cessna Stationair II

CHAPTER 9: THE CESSNA SKYWAGONS, MODELS 206 AND 207 AND STATIONAIR

The first Cessna 206 was the 1965 Model, at first called the "Super Skywagon." It was direcly descended from the Model 205 which had been produced 1962-1964 inclusive. The 206 in fact was built around the same basic airframe as the 205, though the fuselage was beefed-up to permit heavy floor lads and allow a 3½-ft double cargo door. It used the Model 210D Centurion wing (introduced on the 1964 Model 210) with 18.9 feet of flap and Frise type ailerons of increased chord. Its tail group was a slightly-modified version of the 210 empennage.

In 1966 the Turbo Super Skywagon was added to Cessna's "Utiline" series making a total of four single-engine utility craft These were the Models 180, 185 Skywagon, Super Skywagon and Turbo Super Skywagon. These latter two aircraft became, respectively, the Skywagon 206 and the Turbo Skywagon 206 in 1970 because the Model 207 was in the market by then and it would have had to be, presumably, the "Super Duper Skywagon" had the smaller craft kept the name "Super Skywagon."

If you find all this confusing (as we do), it's clearly because Cessna (as well as Cessna's competitors) has some allegedly-bright young men — with sideburns and loud neckties — who are well paid to mis-name things. Unfortunately, their often ill-invented and not-necessarily-descriptive terms also include many component parts of Cessna airplanes. We say, "unfortunately" because we think this

1970 Cessna Turbo Skywagon 206

cheapens a good product. A "Utiline" fitted with a "Quick-Scan" panel of "Space Age gray" featuring "Accru-Measure" fuel gauges, sounds like something dreamed up in Detroit rather than in Wichita. After all, the man who can write you a check for thirty thousand iron men in payment for a flying machine, presumably possesses a smattering of sophistication and a smidgen of savvy. We doubt that he's much impressed with Madison Avenue verbiage.

And we'll apologize to Cessna for voicing this pet peeve just as soon as we hear a Cessna owner refer to his "Broad Span" elevators or his "Sure-Grip" control knobs as such.

The Skywagon 206 was discontinued in 1971 after 1,578 had been built. The last ones were priced at $25,995 and $30,495, the latter being the Turbo version.

The Cessna Stationair was introduced in 1971, obviously replacing the 206 Skywagon—or perhaps, more accurately, a simple re-naming of the 206. In any case, the two are essentially the same airplane. Same airframe; same engine; new detail pretties, and a $3,000 price increase.

For 1972 the Stationair received the new Cessna wing with a slightly modified airfoil for improved slow flight handling, and a new nose cap containing the landing and taxi lights. After that, there were only detail changes through the 1976 model, by which time prices

1970 Cessna Skywagon 207

were up to $41,850 for the standard Stationair; $47,850 for the Turbo Stationair, and ranging upward to $52,150 for the Stationair II with complete avionics, and $58,200 for the Turbo Stationair II similarly equipped.

The Cessna Skywagon 207, introduced in 1969, is the real minibus of the industry. With a 14-ft cabin, the 207 provides 156 cubic feet inside that comfortably hauls seven any-sized adults and, apparently, all their worldly goods. In addition to luggage space in the aft cabin and a 300-lb-capacity optional cargo pod slung beneath the fuselage, the 207 also has a 120-lb. capacity forward luggage compartment in its stretched nose between the firewall and cabin. And since this working airplane has an economical cruise that consumes as little as 10 gallons of fuel per hour, any air taxi operator that doesn't make money with it, just ain't tryin'.

Actually, this may be slightly over-stating the case for the 207. It has a useful load of 1,920 lbs (which is 40 lbs more than its empty dry weight), but this is without seats, avionics and fuel. Full tanks and all necessary equipment will leave about 1,400 lbs for people and baggage; but even that transposes into seven 170-pounders and 200 lbs of luggage. The loading limits of this craft are such that one may distribute this (approximate) 1,400 lbs pretty much as he pleases, although the plane does fly better with some load well aft.

93

1976 Cessna Skywagon 207

Both 207 Models have the tubular-steel gear legs and the resulting luxury ground-ride.

The Turbo Skywagon 207 can operate easily from high altitude airports and can handle non-standard days with an extra margin of safety. At its 3,800-lb gross weight, it climbs 885 fpm at sea level and has a 24,500-ft service ceiling. The Turbo 207 can reach a top speed of 189 mph and a cruise speed of 176 mph at 75% power at 20,000 feet. Range is 725 miles (with reserve fuel remaining) at 20,000 and 75%.

Our evaluation of the Turbo 207 came on a damp and overcast November day when we were joined by two newspaper reporters and three others, plus the Cessna pilot, for a purely local flight.

Since the turbo system best reveals its muscle on hot days and/or in the high places, this wasn't a very good demonstration of the difference it makes. However, we did have seven people aboard, and with a good deal of optional equipment installed and about 50 gallons of fuel, we were within 150-175 lbs of the plane's maximum allowable weight. Ground temperature was 39 degrees F, wind was 3-5 mph down the runway and airport elevation 1,108 ft.

Engine-start procedure is simple. With electrical switches off and cowl flaps open, turn on the master switch and set parking brake. Then, mixture "Full Rich," prop in "High RPMs;" with throttle closed, punch the "Lo" side of the auxiliary fuel pump switch, turn ignition key to "Start," and slowly advance the throttle. With the engine idling satisfactorily, turn off the aux fuel pump (which acts as an automatic primer when cranking the engine), turn on radios and electrics.

The auxiliary fuel pump, which comes with fuel-injected engines, plus the constant speed prop, cowl flaps and rudder trim, are the new controls to get used to if you're transitioning from the smaller or older Cessnas.

With the 13-item pre-take-off check completed, our demo pilot dropped 10 degrees of flap and applied full power. He came back on the control column as we reached 70 mph and we were air-borne. Seconds later, the rate-of-climb needle settled on 900 fpm as our pilot cut back to 75% power and adjusted the climb with the wheel at a shade under 100 mph IAS. He leaned the mixture slightly as we climbed, but nothing else changed—except a slowly-increasing air speed—and we were still showing 900 fpm, at 100 mph, when we leveled off at 5,000. This of course represented a gain in TAS, with no loss in climb rate, at that altitude.

Our density altitude was a bit lower than that showing on the altimeter, and in cruise TAS worked out to 160 mph turning 2,500 rpms with 25 inches of manifold pressure, while the fuel flow meter registered 16 gallons per hour fuel consumption.

We weren't shown any stalls, because three of our passengers were new to "little" airplanes and our pilot—wisely—wanted to give them a smooth, confidence-building ride. He told us that 207 stalls are sedate, almost leisurely, and contain no surprises. Since we were impressed with his deliberate and conservative handling of the airplane, we decided his assessment would be accurate.

He showed us two landings (the second one evidently to prove that his "grease job" on the first wasn't an accident), and the way he did it, it sure looked easy. His approach was at 95 mph, slowing to 85 mph on final with full flaps. Then an unhurried, graceful flare, with throttle closed, brought touchdown on the main wheels at 65 mph. Roll-out required about 500 feet.

Suggested price of the 1976 Skywagon 207, f.a.f. $43,950 and $50,450 for the Turbo Skywagon 207.

1979 Cessna Stationair 6

1976 Cessna Stationair II

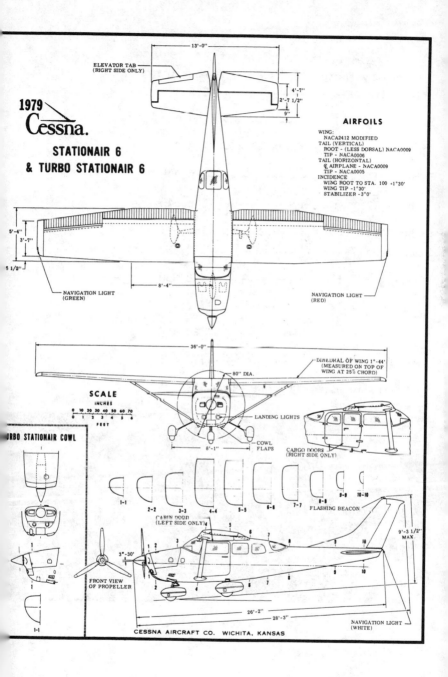

1979 Cessna.

STATIONAIR 6 & TURBO STATIONAIR 6

AIRFOILS

WING:
 NACA2412 MODIFIED
TAIL (VERTICAL)
 ROOT - (LESS DORSAL) NACA0009
 TIP - NACA0006
TAIL (HORIZONTAL)
 ℄ AIRPLANE - NACA0009
 TIP - NACA0005
INCIDENCE
 WING ROOT TO STA. 100 +1°30'
 WING TIP -1°30'
 STABILIZER -3°0'

ELEVATOR TAB
(RIGHT SIDE ONLY)

13'-0"
4'-7"
2'-7 1/2"
9"

5'-4"
3'-7"
5 1/2"

NAVIGATION LIGHT
(GREEN)

8'-4"

NAVIGATION LIGHT
(RED)

36'-0"

DIHEDRAL OF WING 1°-44'
(MEASURED ON TOP OF
WING AT 25% CHORD)

80" DIA.

SCALE
INCHES
0 10 20 30 40 50 60 70
0 1 2 3 4 5 6
FEET

LANDING LIGHTS

8'-1"

COWL
FLAPS

CARGO DOORS
(RIGHT SIDE ONLY)

TURBO STATIONAIR COWL

1-1 2-2 3-3 4-4 5-5 6-6 7-7 8-8 9-9 10-10

FLASHING BEACON

CABIN DOOR
(LEFT SIDE ONLY)

3°-30'

FRONT VIEW
OF PROPELLER

9'-3 1/2"
MAX

26'-2"
28'-3"

NAVIGATION LIGHT
(WHITE)

1-1

CESSNA AIRCRAFT CO. WICHITA, KANSAS

97

Prices of the airplanes f.a.f.
(fly away factory), Wichita, Kansas are:

Stationair 6----------------------$52,350

Stationair 6 II-------------------$59,985

Stationair 6 II w/Nav-Pac--------$63,235

Turbo Stationair 6---------------$58,995

Turbo Stationair 6 II------------$66,645

Turbo Stationair 6 II w/Nav Pac--$69,895

Stationair 7----------------------$60,550

Stationair 7 II-------------------$68,850

Stationair 7 II w/Nav-Pac--------$72,100

Turbo Stationair 7---------------$67,450

Turbo Stationair 7 II------------$75,825

Turbo Stationair 7 II w/Nav-Pac--$79,075

1976 Cessna Stationair II

1979 CESSNA STATIONAIR 6 PERFORMANCE AND SPECIFICATIONS*

	LANDPLANE		FLOATPLANE	
SPEED:				
Maximum at Sea Level	156 knots	289 kph	138 knots	256 kph
Cruise, 75% power at 6500 feet	147 knots	272 kph	132 knots	244 kph

CRUISE, Recommended lean mixture with fuel allowance for engine start, taxi, takeoff, climb and 45 minutes reserve at 45% power

	LANDPLANE		FLOATPLANE	
75% power at 6500 feet with	725 nm	1343 km	650 nm	1204 km
88 gallons usable fuel	5.0 hr	5.0 hr	5.0 hr	5.0 hr
Maximum range at 10,000 feet with	900 nm	1667 km	770 nm	1426 km
88 gallons usable fuel	7.8 hr	7.8 hr	7.7 hr	7.7 hr
RATE OF CLIMB AT SEA LEVEL	920 fpm	280 mpm	925 fpm	282 mpm
SERVICE CEILING	14,800 ft	4511 m	13,900 ft	4237 m
TAKEOFF PERFORMANCE:				
Ground roll (or water run)	900 ft	274 m	1835 ft	559 m
Total distance over 50 ft obstacle	1780 ft	543 m	2820 ft	860 m
LANDING PERFORMANCE:				
Ground roll (or water run)	735 ft	224 m	780 ft	238 m
Total distance over 50 ft obstacle	1395 ft	425 m	1675 ft	511 m
STALL SPEED, CAS:				
Flaps up, power off	62 knots	115 kph	56 knots	104 kph
Flaps down, power off	54 knots	100 kph	51 knots	94 kph
MAXIMUM WEIGHT:				
Ramp	3612 lb	1638 kg	3500 lb	1588 kg
Takeoff or landing	3600 lb	1633 kg	3500 lb	1588 kg
STANDARD EMPTY WEIGHT:				
Stationair 6	1919 lb	870 kg	2261 lb	1026 kg
Stationair 6 II	1980 lb	898 kg	2321 lb	1053 kg
Utility Stationair 6 - 1 seat	1817 lb	824 kg	2178 lb	988 kg
Utility Stationair Six II - 1 seat	1877 lb	851 kg	2238 lb	1015 kg
MAXIMUM USEFUL LOAD:				
Stationair 6	1693 lb	768 kg	1239 lb	562 kg
Stationair 6 II	1632 lb	740 kg	1179 lb	535 kg
Utility Stationair 6 - 1 seat	1795 lb	814 kg	1322 lb	600 kg
Utility Stationair 6 II - 1 seat	1735 lb	787 kg	1262 lb	573 kg
BAGGAGE ALLOWANCE	180 lb	82 kg	180 lb	82 kg
WING LOADING	20.7 lb/sq ft	101 kg/sq m	20.1 lb/sq ft	98.1 kg/sq m
POWER LOADING	12.0 lb/hp	5.4 kg/hp	11.7 lb/hp	5.3 kg/hp
WING SPAN	35 ft, 10 in	10.92 m	35 ft, 10 in	10.92 m
WING AREA	174 sq ft	16.2 sq m	174 sq ft	16.2 sq m
LENGTH	28 ft, 3 in	8.61 m	29 ft, 8 in	9.04 m
HEIGHT	9 ft, 3 1/2 in	2.83 m	14 ft, 1 1/2 in	4.31 m
FUEL CAPACITY, Total	92 gal	348 liters	92 gal	348 liters
OIL CAPACITY	12 qt	11.4 liters	12 qt	11.4 liters

ENGINE   Teledyne Continental IO-520-F Fuel Injection Engine:
300 bhp at 2850 rpm (takeoff)
285 bhp at 2700 rpm (maximum continuous)

PROPELLER: Constant speed, 3 blades, 80 inch diameter (2.03 m)

NOTE: Weight of the optional Nav-Pac is: 15 lb   7 kg

*Subject to change without notice

1979 CESSNA TURBO STATIONAIR 6 PERFORMANCE AND SPECIFICATIONS*

SPEED:

Maximum at 17,000 feet	174 knots	322 kph
Cruise, 80% power at 20,000 feet	167 knots	309 kph
Cruise, 80% power at 10,000 feet	152 knots	282 kph

CRUISE, Recommended lean mixture with fuel allowance for engine start taxi, takeoff, climb and 45 minutes reserve at 45% power

80% power at 20,000 feet with 88 gallons usable fuel	690 nm 4.4 hr	1278 km 4.4 hr
80% power at 10,000 feet with 88 gallons usable fuel	655 nm 4.4 hr	1213 km 4.4 hr
Maximum range at 20,000 feet with 88 gallons usable fuel	785 nm 6.4 hr	1454 km 6.4 hr
Maximum range at 10,000 feet with 88 gallons usable fuel	805 nm 7.3 hr	1491 km 7.3 hr

RATE OF CLIMB AT SEA LEVEL	1010 fpm	308 mpm
SERVICE CEILING	27,000 ft	8230 m

TAKEOFF PERFORMANCE:

Ground roll	835 ft	255 m
Total distance over 50 ft obstacle	1640 ft	500 m

LANDING PERFORMANCE:

Ground roll	735 ft	224 m
Total distance over 50 ft obstacle	1395 ft	425 m

STALL SPEED, CAS:

Flaps up, power off	62 knots	115 kph
Flaps down, power off	54 knots	100 kph

MAXIMUM WEIGHT:

Ramp	3616 lb	1640 kg
Takeoff or landing	3600 lb	1633 kg

STANDARD EMPTY WEIGHT:

Turbo Stationair 6	1984 lb	900 kg
Turbo Stationair 6 II	2044 lb	927 kg
Turbo Utility Stationair 6 - 1 seat	1881 lb	853 kg
Turbo Utility Stationair 6 II - 1 seat	1942 lb	881 kg

MAXIMUM USEFUL LOAD:

Turbo Stationair 6	1632 lb	740 kg
Turbo Stationair 6 II	1572 lb	713 kg
Turbo Utility Stationair 6 - 1 seat	1735 lb	787 kg
Turbo Utility Stationair 6 II - 1 seat	1674 lb	759 kg

BAGGAGE ALLOWANCE	180 lb	82 kg
WING LOADING	20.7 lb/sq ft	101 kg/sq m
POWER LOADING	11.6 lb/hp	5.3 kg/hp
WING SPAN	35 ft, 10 in	10.92 m
WING AREA	174 sq ft	16.2 sq m
LENGTH	28 ft, 3 in	8.61 m
HEIGHT	9 ft, 3 1/2 in	2.83 m
FUEL CAPACITY, Total	92 gal	348 liters
OIL CAPACITY	13 qt	12.3 liters

ENGINE: Teledyne Continental TSIO-520-M, Turbocharged Fuel Injection Engine:
310 bhp at 2700 rpm (takeoff)
285 bhp at 2600 rpm (maximum continuous)

PROPELLER: Constant speed, 3 blades, 80 inch diameter (2.03 m)

NOTE: Weight of optional Nav-Pac is: 15 lb   7 kg

*Subject to change without notice

1979 Cessna Stationair 7

1976 Cessna Skywagon 207

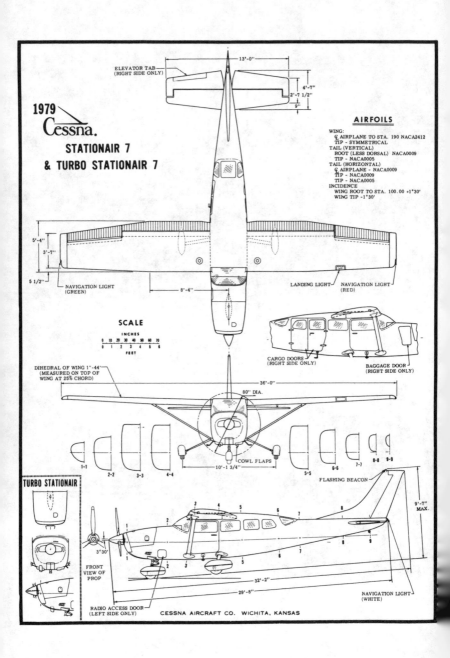

AIRFOILS

WING:
    Ç AIRPLANE TO STA. 190 NACA2412
    TIP - SYMMETRICAL
TAIL (VERTICAL)
    ROOT (LESS DORSAL) NACA0009
    TIP - NACA0005
TAIL (HORIZONTAL)
    Ç AIRPLANE - NACA0009
    TIP - NACA0009
    TIP - NACA0005
INCIDENCE
    WING ROOT TO STA. 100.00 +1°30'
    WING TIP -1°30'

1979
Cessna.

STATIONAIR 7
& TURBO STATIONAIR 7

ELEVATOR TAB
(RIGHT SIDE ONLY)

13'-0''

4'-7''
2'-7 1/2''
9''

5'-4''
3'-7''
5 1/2''

NAVIGATION LIGHT
(GREEN)

8'-4''

LANDING LIGHT — NAVIGATION LIGHT
(RED)

SCALE

INCHES
0 10 20 30 40 50 60 70
0 1 2 3 4 5 6
FEET

CARGO DOORS
(RIGHT SIDE ONLY)

BAGGAGE DOOR
(RIGHT SIDE ONLY)

DIHEDRAL OF WING 1°-44'
(MEASURED ON TOP OF
WING AT 25% CHORD)

36'-0''

80'' DIA.

1-1   2-2   3-3   4-4

COWL FLAPS

10'-1 3/4''

5-5   6-6   7-7   8-8   9-9

FLASHING BEACON

9'-7''
MAX.

TURBO STATIONAIR

D

3°30'

FRONT
VIEW OF
PROP

RADIO ACCESS DOOR
(LEFT SIDE ONLY)

32'-2''

29'-8''

NAVIGATION LIGHT
(WHITE)

CESSNA AIRCRAFT CO.   WICHITA, KANSAS

1979 CESSNA STATIONAIR 7 PERFORMANCE AND SPECIFICATIONS*

SPEED**
Maximum at Sea Level	150 knots	278 kph
Cruise, 75% power at 6500 feet	143 knots	265 kph

CRUISE, Recommended lean mixture with fuel allowance for engine start, taxi, takeoff, climb and 45 minutes reserve at 45 % power

75% power at 6500 feet with	390 nm	722 km
54 gallons usable fuel	2.8 hr	2.8 hr
75% power at 6500 feet with	565 nm	1046 km
73 gallons usable fuel	4.0 hr	4.0 hr
Maximum range at 10,000 feet with	470 nm	870 km
54 gallons usable fuel	4.2 hr	4.2 hr
Maximum range at 10,000 feet with	690 nm	1278 km
73 gallons usable fuel	6.2 hr	6.2 hr

RATE OF CLIMB AT SEA LEVEL	810 fpm	247 mpm
SERVICE CEILING	13,300 ft	4054 m

TAKEOFF PERFORMANCE:
Ground roll	1100 ft	335 m
Total distance over 50 ft obstacle	1970 ft	600 m

LANDING PERFORMANCE:
Ground roll	765 ft	233 m
Total distance over 50 ft obstacle	1500 ft	457 m

STALL SPEED, CAS:
Flaps up, power off	65 knots	120 kph
Flaps down, power off	58 knots	107 kph

MAXIMUM WEIGHT:
Ramp	3812 lb	1729 kg
Takeoff and landing	3800 lb	1724 kg

STANDARD EMPTY WEIGHT:
Stationair 7	2076 lb	942 kg
Stationair 7 II	2145	973 kg
Utility Stationair 7 - 1 seat	1971 lb	894 kg
Utility Stationair 7 II - 1 seat	2040 lb	925 kg

MAXIMUM USEFUL LOAD:
Stationair 7	1736 lb	787 kg
Stationair 7 II	1667 lb	756 kg
Utility Stationair 7 - 1 seat	1841 lb	835 kg
Utility Stationair 7 II - 1 seat	1772 lb	804 kg

BAGGAGE ALLOWANCE	300 lb	136 kg
WING LOADING	21.8 lb/sq ft	107 kg/sq m
POWER LOADING	12.7 lb/hp	5.7 kg/hp
WING SPAN	35 ft, 10 in	10.92 m
WING AREA	174 sq ft	16.2 sq m
LENGTH	32 ft, 2 in	9.80 m
HEIGHT	9 ft, 7 in	2.92 m

FUEL CAPACITY, Total:
Standard tanks	61 gal	231 liters
Long range tanks	80 gal	303 liters

OIL CAPACITY	12 qt	11.4 liters

ENGINE: Teledyne Continental IO-520-F Fuel Injection Engine:
300 bhp at 2850 rpm (takeoff)
285 bhp at 2700 rpm (maximum continuous)

PROPELLER: Constant speed, 3 blades, 80 inch diameter (2.03 m)

NOTE: Weight of optional Nav-Pac is: 16 lb   7 kg

*Subject to change without notice
**Speed performance is shown for an airplane equipped with optional speed fairings which increase the speed by 3 to 4 knots. There is a corresponding difference in range while all other performance figures are unchanged when speed fairings are installed.

1979 CESSNA TURBO STATIONAIR 7 PERFORMANCE AND SPECIFICATIONS*

SPEED:**
Maximum at 17,000 feet	170 knots	315 kph
Cruise, 80% power at 20,000 feet	161 knots	298 kph
Cruise, 80% power at 10,000 feet	148 knots	274 kph

CRUISE, Recommended lean mixture with fuel allowance for engine start, taxi, takeoff, climb and 45 minutes reserve at 45% power

80% power at 20,000 feet with 54 gallons usable fuel	350 nm 2.4 hr	648 km 2.4 hr
80% power at 10,000 feet with 54 gallons usable fuel	345 nm 2.4 hr	639 km 2.4 hr
80% power at 20,000 feet with 73 gallons usable fuel	525 nm 3.5 hr	972 km 3.5 hr
80% power at 10,000 feet with 73 gallons usable fuel	510 nm 3.5 hr	945 km 3.5 hr
Maximum range at 20,000 feet with 54 gallons usable fuel	385 nm 3.3 hr	713 km 3.3 hr
Maximum range at 10,000 feet with 54 gallons usable fuel	415 nm 3.6 hr	769 km 3.6 hr
Maximum range at 20,000 feet with 73 gallons usable fuel	585 nm 5.0 hr	1083 km 5.0 hr
Maximum range at 10,000 feet with 73 gallons usable fuel	610 nm 5.3 hr	1130 km 5.3 hr

RATE OF CLIMB AT SEA LEVEL	885 fpm	270 mpm
SERVICE CEILING	26,000 ft	7925 m

TAKEOFF PERFORMANCE:
Ground roll	1030 ft	314 m
Total distance over 50 ft. obstacle	1860 ft	567 m

LANDING PERFORMANCE
Ground roll	765 ft	233 m
Total distance over 50 ft obstacle	1500 ft	457 m

STALL SPEED, CAS:
Flaps up, power off	65 knots	120 kph
Flaps down, power off	58 knots	107 kph

MAXIMUM WEIGHT:
Ramp	3816 lb	1731 kg
Takeoff or Landing	3800 lb	1764 kg

STANDARD EMPTY WEIGHT:
Turbo Stationair 7	2157 lb	978 kg
Turbo Stationair 7 II	2226 lb	1010 kg
Utility Turbo Stationair 7 - 1 seat	2052 lb	931 kg
Utility Turbo Stationair 7 II - 1 seat	2121 lb	962 kg

MAXIMUM USEFUL LOAD:
Turbo Stationair 7	1659 lb	753 kg
Turbo Stationair 7 II	1590 lb	721 kg
Utility Turbo Stationair 7 - 1 seat	1764 lb	800 kg
Utility Turbo Stationair 7 II - 1 seat	1695 lb	769 kg

BAGGAGE ALLOWANCE	300 lb	136 kg
WING LOADING	21.8 lb/sq ft	107 kg/sq m
POWER LOADING	12.3 lb/hp	5.6 kg/hp
WING SPAN	35 ft, 10 in	10.92 m
WING AREA	174 sq ft	16.2 sq m
LENGTH	32 ft, 2 in	9.80 m
HEIGHT	9 ft, 7 in	2.92 m

FUEL CAPACITY, Total:
Standard Tanks	61 gal	231 liters
Long range tanks	80 gal	303 liters

OIL CAPACITY	13 qt	12.3 liters

ENGINE: Teledyne Continental TSIO-520-M Turbocharged, Fuel Injection Engine:
310 bhp at 2700 rpm (takeoff)
285 bhp at 2600 rpm (maximum continuous)

PROPELLER: Constant speed, 3 blades, 80 inch diameter (2.03 m)

NOTE: Weight of the optional Nav-Pac is: 16 lb   7 kg

*Subject to change without notice
**Speed performance is shown for an airplane equipped with optional speed fairings which increase the speed by 3 to 4 knots. There is a corresponding difference in range while all other performance figures are unchanged when speed fairings are installed.

104

CHAPTER 10: CESSNA 210/CENTURION

The first Cessna 210 was the 1960 Model, announced late in 1959. At that time, many of us tended to think of it as a slicked-up 182 with a crazy retract gear and bigger engine (IO-470E fuel-injected Continental of 260-hp), but it wasn't. It was an all-new design aimed at the Bonanza/Comanche market. It had a top speed of 199 mph, a cruise (75% @ 7,000) of 190 mph and should have been right on target; but customer acceptance was slow. Ten years later, sales of this craft still lagged behind Cessna's expectations and the explanation remained obscure, probably clouded by an un-voiced (and un-reasoned) customer prejudice — perhaps something some people didn't like about the plane and were ashamed or reluctant to admit.

We're guessing about this, because we don't know why Cessna's top performer in the single-engine class has not taken a bigger share of that market. From the beginning, it has performed just as Cessna claimed, and has never been accused of possessing any vicious traits.

Anyway, beginning with the 1969 Model, the question — if it remains — will have to come from the other side of our mouth, because the new Centurions (nee 210) are different airplanes and demand fresh evaluations.

Known as the "210" during its first four years of production, this design became the "Centurion" in 1964 when it received a re-designed wing with more flap area, four additional inches on the tail surfaces and the IO-520A 285-hp engine (turtle deck with back windows was added in 1962, along with four extra inches of cabin width). In 1967, the Centurion appeared with a full-cantilever wing; and in 1968 de-icing and anti-icing systems for prop, wing and tail were offered.

But the strutless Centurions of 1967-68, though structurally sound, apparently didn't look that way to many because of their pronounced (three degrees) dihedral. At least, that was Cessna's conclusion. Therefore, the cantilever wing was flattened-out on the 1969 Model, with only one degree of dihedral remaining, and the

1979 Cessna Pressurized Centurion

1970 Cessna Turbo Centurion

1976 Cessna Turbo Centurion II

ailerons inter-connected with the rudder via a spring load to keep good stability.

Then, in 1970, the Centurion received a 25% bigger cabin to make it a full six-place airplane, with new side windows extending almost half the length of the cabin sans posts. Also in 1970, the Centurion went to the tubular-steel main-gear legs for softer landings and a wider stance (the nose-wheel strut was shortened on the 1969 Model, and the "chin" housing eliminated).

The new gear retracts completely into the fuselage within a few seconds at the touch of a control on the pedestal. The system has a fluid reservoir and is under pressure only during the time the gear is being activated. This improves reliability and should reduce service costs.

The cabin is accessible through a yard-wide door on each side, and offers a full assortment of convenience items such as individual air vents, ash trays, cigarette lighter and magazine pockets — all close at hand. Other standard cabin accessories include sun visors, map pockets, arm rests, an integrally-mounted overhead light console for the pilot's area and individual lights above the passenger seats.

Some of the purists may complain about the inter-connected roll and yaw controls, but this objection won't be as "pure" as the gung-ho crowd will have you believe, because this principle was employed by the Wright brothers on the world's first successful airplane. It seems to us that the only pilots who have a valid objection to inter-connected controls are the aerobatic types; and Cessna clearly didn't intend that anyone should slow-roll the Centurion across country at 200 miles per. However, you can over-ride the spring-load inter-connect anytime you want or need to.

If you've been flying a Super Skylane or anything of comparable muscle, transition to the Centurion will be easy. But if you're accustomed to smaller and slower craft, you really should have at least three hours of dual (and a minimum of 150 hours in your logbook) before sashaying off to far away places in this — or any other — high performance retractable. It is a big airplane, and a sudden one. Cruising at 185-190 mph requires that you think more than one check-point ahead in matters of fuel management, efficient let-downs and weather evaluation. In short, it's a lot more airplane than a Skyhawk, and it demands a higher level of competence to safely operate it.

1976 Cessna Turbo Centurion II

We don't mean by this that the Centurion is physically hard to fly. It is not. It is very stable, with a solid, big-airplane feel, as a long-legged personal transport should be. What we mean by "higher level of competence" is that, as aircraft weight and speed goes up, so does the penalty for error.

The Turbo Centurion is of course the high-altitude performer, and the one that makes a "standard day" out of a hot and humid one. The turbo system assures maximum horsepower up to 19,000 feet, and beyond that keeps working to compress the thin air into a richer source of oxygen for the engine. This system adds no extra controls to adjust or gauges to monitor, and no constant adjusting of the throttle is required during the climb to 19,000. The turbine is automatically regulated by an absolute pressure controller and an over-boost control valve which automatically bleeds off excessive compressor discharge pressure. And all this is housed in a (wouldn't you just know it?) "Jet-Flow" cowling.

The Turbo Centurion comes with a 74-cubic-foot capacity oxygen system as standard equipment. This system includes an overhead oxygen console with a capacity gauge system control, control wheel microphone switch and automatic regulator.

Suggested list price of the 1976 Centurion was $55,950 while the Turbo Centurion was priced at $61,950.

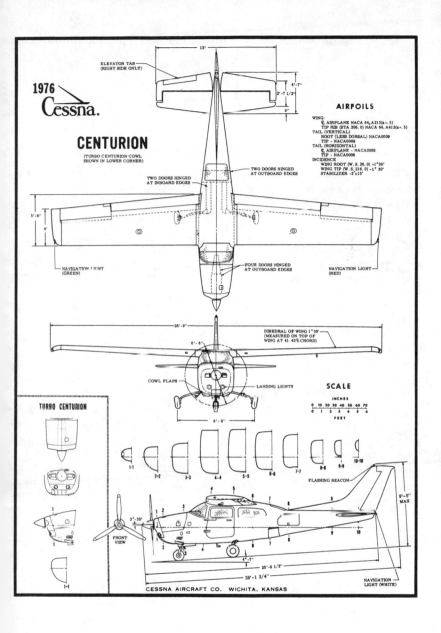

1976 Cessna.

CENTURION

(TURBO CENTURION COWL
SHOWN IN LOWER CORNER)

ELEVATOR TAB
(RIGHT SIDE ONLY)

13'

4'-7"
2'-7 1/2"

TWO DOORS HINGED
AT INBOARD EDGES

TWO DOORS HINGED
AT OUTBOARD EDGES

5'-6"
4"

NAVIGATION LIGHT
(GREEN)

FOUR DOORS HINGED
AT OUTBOARD EDGES

NAVIGATION LIGHT
(RED)

AIRFOILS

WING:
  ℄ AIRPLANE NACA 64₁A215(a=.5)
  TIP RIB (STA 206.0) NACA 64₁A412(a=.5)
TAIL (VERTICAL)
  ROOT (LESS DORSAL) NACA0009
  TIP - NACA0008
TAIL (HORIZONTAL)
  ℄ AIRPLANE - NACA0009
  TIP - NACA0006
INCIDENCE
  WING ROOT (W.S. 26.0) +1°30'
  WING TIP (W.S. 216.0) -1° 30'
  STABILIZER -3°±15'

36'-9"

DIHEDRAL OF WING 1°30'
(MEASURED ON TOP OF
WING AT 41.43% CHORD)

6'-8"

COWL FLAPS

LANDING LIGHTS

SCALE

INCHES
0 10 20 30 40 50 60 70
0 1 2 3 4 5 6
FEET

8'-8"

1-1
7-7
3-3
4-4
5-5
6-6
7-7
8-8
9-9
10-10

FLASHING BEACON

TURBO CENTURION

9'-5"
MAX

3°-30'

FRONT
VIEW

1-1

4'-7"

25'-8 1/2"

28'-1 3/4"

NAVIGATION
LIGHT (WHITE)

CESSNA AIRCRAFT CO. WICHITA, KANSAS

109

1976 Cessna Model 210 Performance and Specifications

SPEED:
  Maximum at Sea Level .... 175 knots .... 324 kph
  Cruise, 75% power at 6500 ft .... 171 knots .... 317 kph

CRUISE, Recommended Lean Mixture with fuel allowance for engine start, taxi, takeoff, climb and 45 minutes
    reserve at 45% power

  75% power at 6500 feet with 534 lbs usable fuel ..... 855 nm 5.1 hr .... 1583 km 5.1 hr

  Maximum range at 10,000 ft with 534 lbs usable fuel .. 1060 nm 7.8 hr .... 1963 km 7.8 hr

RATE OF CLIMB AT SEA LEVEL .... 860 fpm .... 262 mpm

SERVICE CEILING .... 15,500 ft .... 4755 m

TAKEOFF PERFORMANCE:
  Ground roll .... 1250 ft .... 381 m
  Total distance over 50 ft. obstacle .... 2030 ft .... 619 m

LANDING PERFORMANCE:
  Ground roll .... 765 ft .... 233 m
  Total distance over 50 ft. obstacle .... 1500 ft .... 457 m

STALL SPEED, CAS
  Flaps up, power off .... 65 knots .... 120 kph
  Flaps down, power off .... 56 knots .... 104 kph

MAXIMUM WEIGHT .... 3800 lb .... 1724 kg

STANDARD EMPTY WEIGHT:
  Centurion .... 2170 lb .... 984 kg
  Centurion II .... 2244 lb .... 1018 kg

MAXIMUM USEFUL LOAD:
  Centurion .... 1630 lb .... 740 kg
  Centurion II .... 1556 lb .... 706 kg

BAGGAGE ALLOWANCE: Maximum with 4 people .... 240 lb .... 109 kg

WING LOADING .... 21.7 lb/sq ft .... 106 kg/sq m

POWER LOADING .... 12.7 lb/hp .... 5.7 kg/hp

WING SPAN .... 36 ft, 9 in .... 11.2 m

WING AREA .... 175 sq ft .... 16.26 sq m

LENGTH .... 28 ft, 3 in .... 8.61 m

HEIGHT .... 9 ft, 8 in .... 2.95 m

FUEL CAPACITY, Total .... 90 gal .... 341 liters

OIL CAPACITY .... 10 qt .... 9.5 liters

ENGINE: Teledyne Continental IO-520-L, Fuel Injection engine: 300 bhp at 2850 rpm (takeoff)
                                                               285 bhp at 2700 rpm (maximum continuous)
PROPELLER: Constant speed, 3 blades, 80 inch diameter (2.03 m)

*Subject to change without notice

110

1976 Cessna Model T210 Performance and Specifications

:ED:
aximum at 19,000 feet   205 knots   380 kph
ruise, 75% power at 24,000 feet   202 knots   374 kph
ruise, 75% power at 10,000 feet   179 knots   332 kph

:SE, Recommended Lean Mixture with fuel allowance for engine start, taxi, takeoff, climb and 45 minutes reserve at 45% power

5% power at 20,000 feet with 534 lbs usable fuel	860 nm 4.7 hr	1593 km 4.7 hr
5% power at 10,000 feet with 534 lbs usable fuel	830 nm 4.8 hr	1537 km 4.8 hr
aximum range at 20,000 feet with 534 lbs usable fuel	1005 nm 7.0 hr	1861 km 7.0 hr
ximum range at 10,000 feet with 534 lbs usable fuel	1020 nm 7.4 hr	1889 km 7.4 hr

: OF CLIMB AT SEA LEVEL   930 fpm   283 mpm

'ICE CEILING   28,500 ft   8687 m

OFF PERFORMANCE:
ound Roll   1170 ft   357 m
tal Distance Over 50 ft. obstacle   2030 ft   619 m

ING PERFORMANCE:
ound Roll   765 ft   233 m
tal Distance over 50 ft. obstacle   1500 ft   457 m

L SPEED, CAS
aps up, power off   65 knots   120 kph
aps down, power off   56 knots   104 kph

MUM WEIGHT   3800 lb   1724 kg

OARD EMPTY WEIGHT:
rbo Centurion   2293 lb   1040 kg
rbo Centurion II   2366 lb   1073 kg

MUM USEFUL LOAD
rbo Centurion   1507 lb   684 kg
rbo Centurion II   1434 lb   651 kg

GE ALLOWANCE: Maximum with 4 people   240 lb   109 kg

LOADING   21.7 lb/sq ft   106 kg/sq m

LOADING   13.3 lb/hp   6.0 kg/hp

SPAN   36 ft, 9 in   11.2 m

AREA   175 sq ft   16.26 sq m

H   28 ft, 3 in   8.61 m

T   9 ft, 8 in   2.95 m

CAPACITY, Total   90 gal   341 liters

APACITY   11 qt   10.4 liters

E: Teledyne Continental TSIO-520-H, Turbocharged, fuel injection engine: 285 bhp at 2700 rpm

LLER: Constant speed, 3 blades, 80 inch diameter (2.03 m)

ect to change without notice

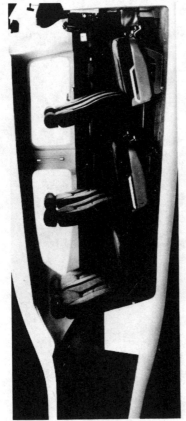

1976 Cessna Turbo Centurion II

CHAPTER 11: CESSNA CARDINAL RG

The Cardinal RG, with retractable landing gear, was introduced in 1971 as Cessna's answer to the Piper Cherokee Arrow 200 and the Beechcraft Sierra. All use the same engine (different "dash-numbers"), and on paper, at least, specs and performance figures for all three are so close together they are almost interchangeable. Basic list price of the Cardinal RG in 1976, at $35,550, was $900 below basic list of the Sierra and about $2,000 above the Arrow's base price.

These three airplanes do handle differently. The Cardinal RG has the gentlest stall, mushing straight ahead with the wheel full back. The Sierra's ailerons are sharper; but soft ailerons have always been a Cessna trait. Cardinal RG pitch control is a bit heavier compared to both low-wingers; rudder seems about the same. Nothing to pick at on any of the three, really. So in the end it comes down to a matter of personal preferences. We like the Cardinal because its wing is on top. In hot weather that makes a big difference; and in rainy weather it makes a big difference. And since the wing is positioned largely behind the pilot, one doesn't give away all that much in upward visibility.

In 1972, the Cardinal RG received a redesigned propeller which added a little to its performance in both speed and rate-of-climb. In 1973, ten gallons were added to its fuel capacity for a total of 61 gallons; and the front seats were made vertically adjustable. The following year, the Cardinal RG was given a new cabin heating and ventilation system; and in 1976, strengthened wheels and brakes, along with a redesigned instrument panel and a dozen minor detail improvements.

In addition to the basic RG, priced at $35,550 in 1976, also offered is the Cardinal RG II, $42,250, and the Cardinal RG II with Nav Pac, $45,050.

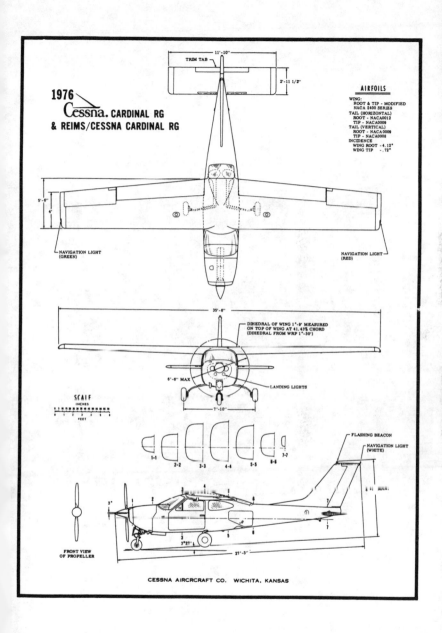

1976
Cessna. CARDINAL RG
& REIMS/CESSNA CARDINAL RG

11'-10"

TRIM TAB

2'-11 1/2"

AIRFOILS

WING:
  ROOT & TIP - MODIFIED
  NACA 2400 SERIES
TAIL (HORIZONTAL)
  ROOT - NACA0012
  TIP - NACA0009
TAIL (VERTICAL)
  ROOT - NACA0009
  TIP - NACA0008
INCIDENCE
  WING ROOT -4.12°
  WING TIP -.72°

5'-6"

4'

NAVIGATION LIGHT
(GREEN)

NAVIGATION LIGHT
(RED)

35'-6"

DIHEDRAL OF WING 1°-9' MEASURED
ON TOP OF WING AT 41.43% CHORD
(DIHEDRAL FROM WRP 1°-30')

6'-8" MAX

LANDING LIGHTS

7'-10"

SCALE
INCHES
FEET

1-1 2-2 3-3 4-4 5-5 6-6 7-7

FLASHING BEACON

NAVIGATION LIGHT
(WHITE)

3"

3°27'

27'-3"

FRONT VIEW
OF PROPELLER

CESSNA AIRCRCRAFT CO. WICHITA, KANSAS

115

1976 Cessna Cardinal RG II

1976 Model 177RG Performance and Specifications

SPEED:
  Maximum at Sea Level   156 knots   289 kph
  Cruise, 75% power at 7000 feet   148 knots   274 kph

CRUISE, Recommended Lean Mixture with fuel allowance for engine start, taxi, take-off, climb and 45 minutes reserve at 45% power

  75% power at 7000 feet with 60 gal. usable fuel   715 nm 4.9 hr   1324 km 4.9 hr

  Maximum Range at 10,000 ft with 60 gal. usable fuel   895 nm 7.5 hr   1658 km 7.5 hr

RATE OF CLIMB AT SEA LEVEL   925 fpm   282 mpm

SERVICE CEILING   17,100 ft   5210 m

TAKEOFF PERFORMANCE:
  Ground Roll   890 ft   271 m
  Total Distance over 50 ft. obstacle   1585 ft   483 m

LANDING PERFORMANCE:
  Ground Roll   730 ft   223 m
  Total Distance over 50 ft. obstacle   1350 ft   411 m

STALL SPEED, CAS
  Flaps up, power off   57 knots   106 kph
  Flaps down, power off   50 knots   93 kph

MAXIMUM WEIGHT   2800 lb   1270 kg

STANDARD EMPTY WEIGHT:
  Cardinal RG   1707 lb   774 kg
  Cardinal RG II   1768 lb   802 kg

MAXIMUM USEFUL LOAD
  Cardinal RG   1093 lb   496 kg
  Cardinal RG II   1032 lb   468 kg

BAGGAGE ALLOWANCE   120 lb   54 kg

WING LOADING   16.1 lb/sq ft   78.6 kg/sq m

POWER LOADING   14.0 lb/hp   6.4 kg/hp

WING SPAN   35 ft, 6 in   10.82 m

WING AREA   174 sq ft   16.2 sq m

LENGTH   27 ft, 3 in   8.31 m

HEIGHT   8 ft, 7 in   2.62 m

FUEL CAPACITY, Total   61 gal   231 liters

OIL CAPACITY   9 qt   8.5 liters

ENGINE: Avco Lycoming IO-360-A1B6D Engine; 200 bhp at 2700 rpm

PROPELLER: Constant speed, 2 blades, 78 inch diameter (1.98 m)

*Subject to change without notice

1976 Cessna Cardinal RG II

CHAPTER 12: CESSNA AGwagon, AGtruck, and AGcarryall

Cessna entered the agricultural aircraft field in 1966 with its AGwagon, and within five years dominated the market, offering the AGwagon with a choice of 230 or 300-hp. In 1972, three additional ag-craft were added: the AGtruck, AGcarryall, and AGpickup. The 230-hp AGpickup was the economy model, and was discontinued in 1976.

All low-wing models featured the new "Camber-Lift" wing in 1972; and the high-wing AGcarryall was fitted with it in 1973. Translated, "Camber-Lift" means that Cessna aerodynamicists slightly re-shaped the time-proven NACA 2412 airfoil to produce tighter turns and improved slow-flight characteristics without penalty to other performance. It was a good move, despite the stupid name. *Camber* lift, indeed. Is there any other kind?

Cessna's AG-craft were so well conceived in the beginning that experience has revealed nothing of significance that required changing in airframes or engines. Most of the improvements since 1972 have been in the aircrafts' dispersal systems. The detail changes have encompassed such things as new voltage regulator ('76), better cabin ventilation ('75), air intake on fin to pressurize tailcone and keep out chemicals ('75), new strut fairings ('73), etc.

Cessna built 553 AG-craft during its 1975 fiscal year; and the agricultural aircraft market continues to grow. Innovative and adaptive use of aerial application presents far-reaching possibilities for a worldwide increase in production of food and fiber products. Nowadays, double-cropping, accomplished by aerial seeding of a second crop into stands of existing ones, tend to extend the growing year and allow the farmer to get two crops from the same land. Fertilization, seeding, weed control, insect control, defoliation, desiccation and land clearing are established practices currently performed by air which contribute markedly to increased agricultural output.

Chemical stimulation of growing crops, and range fire control are new uses for agricultural aircraft that are now showing good results.

The AGwagon and AGtruck employ the same airframe and same 300-hp engine with constant speed propellers. The AGcarryall, with a hopper capacity of 151 gals (as opposed to 200 gals for the AGwagon, and 280 gals for the AGtruck), is designed as an all-purpose ag-plane. The AGcarryall comes equipped with a liquid dispersal system, and optional equipment includes seating for up to six adults.

With its center-mounted dispersal controls, the AGcarryall is an excellent student trainer and general purpose craft for aerial application operators. It is a good ag-craft for a wide range of liquid dispersal tasks. With spray booms removed, the AGcarryall may be quickly converted to a six-place inter-city transport or an efficient cargo hauler. The AGcarryall has a factory list price of $36,075.

The AGwagon and the AGtruck, both of which may be equipped with a night operations package, are priced at $32,825 and $36,950 respectively.

1976 Cessna AGwagon

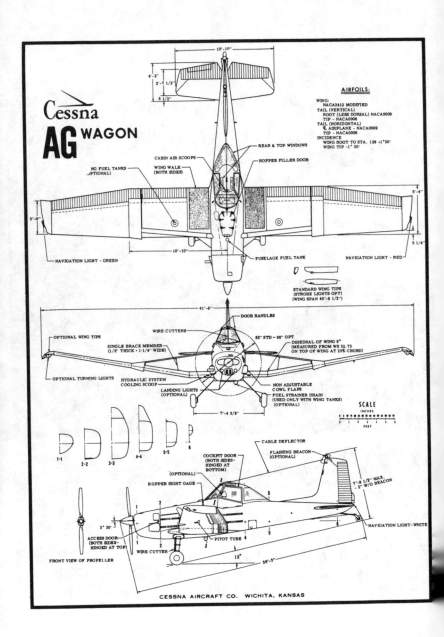

Cessna
AG WAGON

AIRFOILS:
WING:
  NACA2412 MODIFIED
TAIL (VERTICAL)
  ROOT (LESS DORSAL) NACA0009
  TIP - NACA0006
TAIL (HORIZONTAL)
  ⅊ AIRPLANE - NACA0009
  TIP - NACA0006
INCIDENCE
  WING ROOT TO STA. 129 +1°30'
  WING TIP -1° 30'

10'-10"
4'-2"
2'-7 1/2"
6 1/2"

REAR & TOP WINDOWS
CABIN AIR SCOOPS
HOPPER FILLER DOOR
NG FUEL TANKS (OPTIONAL)
WING WALK (BOTH SIDES)
5'-4"
3'-8"
5 1/4"
10'-10"
NAVIGATION LIGHT - GREEN
FUSELAGE FUEL TANK
NAVIGATION LIGHT - RED

STANDARD WING TIPS
(STROBE LIGHTS OPT)
(WING SPAN 40'-8 1/2")

41'-8"
DOOR HANDLES
WIRE CUTTERS
82" STD - 86" OPT
OPTIONAL WING TIPS
SINGLE BRACE MEMBER
(1/2" THICK • 1-1/4" WIDE)
DIHEDRAL OF WING 9°
(MEASURED FROM WS 52.75
ON TOP OF WING AT 25% CHORD)
OPTIONAL TURNING LIGHTS
HYDRAULIC SYSTEM
COOLING SCOOP
LANDING LIGHTS
(OPTIONAL)
NON ADJUSTABLE
COWL FLAPS
FUEL STRAINER DRAIN
(USED ONLY WITH WING TANKS)
(OPTIONAL)
7'-4 3/8"

SCALE
INCHES
FEET

1-1
2-2
3-3
4-4
5-5
6

CABLE DEFLECTOR
COCKPIT DOOR
(BOTH SIDES-
HINGED AT
BOTTOM)
FLASHING BEACON
(OPTIONAL)
(OPTIONAL)
HOPPER SIGHT GAGE
7'-8 1/2" MAX.
- 2" W/O BEACON
NAVIGATION LIGHT - WHITE
3° 30'
ACCESS DOOR-
(BOTH SIDES-
HINGED AT TOP)
WIRE CUTTER
PITOT TUBE
FRONT VIEW OF PROPELLER
12°
26'-3"

CESSNA AIRCRAFT CO. WICHITA, KANSAS

1976 AGwagon AGtruck
Permance and Specifications*

	NO DISPERSAL EQUIPMENT		WITH LIQUID DISPERSAL EQUIPMENT INSTALLED	
SPEED:				
Maximum at Sea Level	151 mph	240 kph	121 mph	195 kph
Cruise, 75% power at 6500 ft	140 mph	225 kph	113 mph	182 kph
CRUISE, Recommended Lean Mixture with fuel allowance for engine start, taxi, take-off, climb and 45 minutes reserve at 45% power				
75% power at 6500 feet with Range	230 mi	370 km	180 mi	290 km
36.5 Gallons Usable Fuel Time	1.7 hr	1.7 hr	1.7 hr	1.7 hr
75% power at 6500 feet with Range	370 mi	595 km	295 mi	475 km
52 Gallons Usable Fuel** Time	2.7 hr	2.7 hr	2.6 hr	2.6 hr
RATE OF CLIMB AT SEA LEVEL	940 fpm	285 mpm	690 fpm	210 mpm
SERVICE CEILING	15,700 ft	4785 m	11,100 ft	3383 m
TAKE-OFF PERFORMANCE:				
Ground Roll	610 ft	186 m	680 ft	207 m
Total Distance Over 50 ft. Obstacle	970 ft	296 m	1090 ft	332 m
LANDING PERFORMANCE:				
Ground Roll	420 ft	128 m	420 ft	128 m
Total Distance Over 50 ft. Obstacle	1265 ft	386 m	1265 ft	386 m
STALL SPEED, CAS				
Flaps up, power off	61 mph	98 kph	61 mph	98 kph
Flaps down, power off	57 mph	92 kph	57 mph	92 kph

	AGWAGON		AGTRUCK	
MAXIMUM WEIGHT: Normal Category	3300 lb	1497 kg	3300 lb	1497 kg
Restricted Category	4000 lb	1814 kg	4200 lb	1905 kg
STANDARD EMPTY WEIGHT: With no dispersal equipment	1985 lb	900 kg	2059 lb	934 kg
With liquid dispersal system	2140 lb	971 kg	2214 lb	1004 kg
HOPPER CAPACITY	200 gal	757 liters	280 gal	1060 liters
	27 cu ft	0.75 cu m	37.4 cu ft	1.06 cu m
WING LOADING: 3300 lbs	16.3 lb/sq ft	79.8 kg/sq m	16.1 lb/sq ft	78.8 kg/sq m
POWER LOADING: 3300 lbs	11.0 lb/hp	5.0 kg/hp	11.0 lb/hp	5.0 kg/hp
WING SPAN	40 ft, 8 1/2 in	12.4 m	41 ft, 8 in	12.7 m
WING AREA	202 sq ft	18.8 sq m	205 sq ft	19.0 sq m
LENGTH	26 ft, 3 in	8.0 m	26 ft, 3 in	8.0 m
HEIGHT	8 ft	2.44 m	8 ft	2.44 m
FUEL CAPACITY, Total				
Standard Tanks	37 gal	140 liters	54 gal	204 liters
Optional Tank	54 gal	204 liters	--	--
OIL CAPACITY	12 qt	11.4 liters	12 qt	11.4 liters
ENGINE	Teledyne Continental IO-520-D Fuel Injection Engine 300 bhp at 2850 rpm (take-off) 285 bhp at 2700 rpm (max. cont.)			
PROPELLER	Constant Speed, 2 blades, 82-inch diameter (2.08 m)			

*Subject to change without notice
**Standard on AGtruck, optional on AGwagon

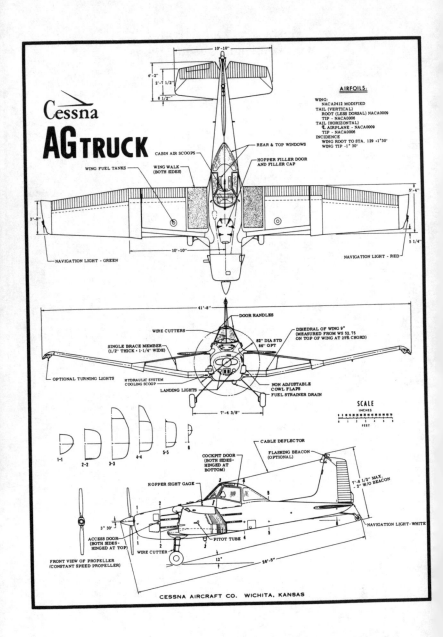

Cessna

AG TRUCK

1976 Cessna AGtruck

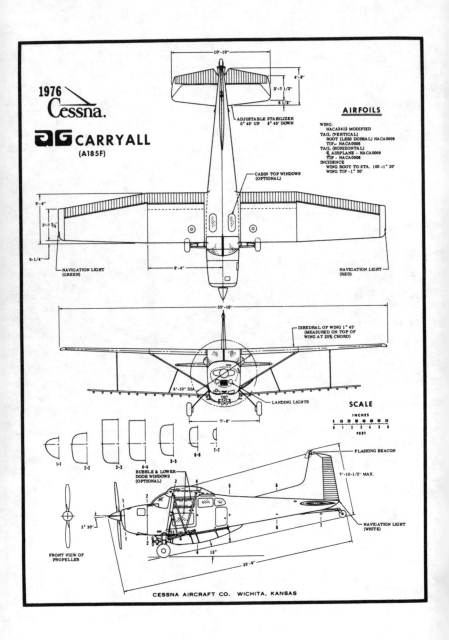

1976 Cessna.

aG CARRYALL
(A185F)

AIRFOILS

WING:
 NACA2412 MODIFIED
TAIL (VERTICAL)
 ROOT (LESS DORSAL) NACA0009
 TIP— NACA0006
TAIL (HORIZONTAL)
 ℄ AIRPLANE - NACA0009
 TIP - NACA0006
INCIDENCE
 WING ROOT TO STA. 100 +1° 30'
 WING TIP -1° 30'

10'-10"
4'-2"
3'-7 1/2"
6 1/2"

ADJUSTABLE STABILIZER
0° 45' UP   8° 45' DOWN

CABIN TOP WINDOWS
(OPTIONAL)

5'-4"
3'-7 3/4"
5-1/4"

NAVIGATION LIGHT
(GREEN)

8'-4"

NAVIGATION LIGHT
(RED)

35'-10"

DIHEDRAL OF WING 1° 45'
(MEASURED ON TOP OF
WING AT 25% CHORD)

6'-10" DIA

LANDING LIGHTS

SCALE

INCHES
0 10 20 30 40 50 60 70
0 1 2 3 4 5 6
FEET

7'-8"

1-1 2-2 3-3 4-4 5-5 6-6 7-7

BUBBLE & LOWER
DOOR WINDOWS
(OPTIONAL)

FLASHING BEACON

7'-10-1/2" MAX.

3° 30'

NAVIGATION LIGHT
(WHITE)

FRONT VIEW OF
PROPELLER

12°

25'-9"

CESSNA AIRCRAFT CO. WICHITA, KANSAS

1976 Cessna AGcarryall

1976 AGcarryall Specifications & Performance
with Sorenson Spray System*

SPEED:
**Maximum at Sea Level		148 mph	238 kph
**Cruise, 75% power at 7500 feet		140 mph	225 kph

CRUISE, Recommended Lean Mixture with fuel allowance for engine start, taxi, take-off, climb and 45 minutes reserve at 45% power

75% power at 7500 feet with	Range	395 mi	636 km
55 gallons usable fuel	Time	2.9 hr	2.9 hr
75% power at 7500 feet with	Range	565 mi	909 km
74 gallons usable fuel	Time	4.1 hr	4.1 hr

RATE OF CLIMB AT SEA LEVEL	845 fpm	257 mpm
SERVICE CEILING	13,400 ft	4085 m

TAKE-OFF PERFORMANCE
Ground Roll	885 ft	270 m
Total Distance over 50 ft. obstacle	1450 ft	442 m

LANDING PERFORMANCE
Ground Roll	480 ft	146 m
Total Distance over 50 ft. obstacle	1400 ft	427 m

STALL SPEED, CAS
Flaps up, power off	65 mph	105 kph
Flaps down, power off	56 mph	90 kph

MAXIMUM WEIGHT
Normal Category	3350 lb	1519 kg
Restricted Category	3350 lb	1519 kg

STANDARD EMPTY WEIGHT	1902 lb	863 kg
SPRAY TANK CAPACITY	151 gal	572 liters
WING LOADING	19.3 lb/sq ft	94.2 kg/sq m
POWER LOADING	11.2 lb/hp	5.1 kg/hp
WING SPAN	35 ft, 10 in	10.92 m
WING AREA	174 sq ft	16.2 sq m
LENGTH	25 ft, 9 in	7.85 m
HEIGHT	7 ft, 9 in	2.36 m

FUEL CAPACITY, Total
Standard Tanks	61 gal	231 liters
Long Range Tanks	80 gal	303 liters

OIL CAPACITY	12 qt	11.4 liters

ENGINE: Teledyne Continental IO-520-D Fuel Injection Engine
300 bhp at 2850 rpm (take-off) 285 bhp at 2700 rpm (maximum continuous)

PROPELLER: Constant speed, 2 blades, 82-inch diameter (2.08m)

*Subject to change without notice
**With spray booms removed, top speed and cruise speed are increased by 10 mph

How To Fly Helicopters

How To Fly
Helicopters
by Larry Collier

Copyright © 1979 by TAB BOOKS

Library of Congress Cataloging in Publication Data

Collier, Larry.
    How to fly helicopters.

    Includes index.
    1. Helicopters—Piloting. 1. Title.
TL716.5.C64   629.132"525   78-21015
ISBN 0-8306-9840-X
ISBN 0-8306-2264-0

CONTENTS

1

WHERE IT ALL BEGAN

The history of rotary-wing is a long and complex one. Its beginning is colored with uncertainty. Which came first, fixed-wing craft or rotorcraft? That question is as controversial as asking, "Which came first, the chicken or the egg?"

According to myth and legend , as far back as 3000 B.C., a Persian monarch harnessed a flock of trained eagles as a means of becoming airborne.

Early Greek mythology tells how an architect, Daedalus, and his son, Icarus, attempted to escape from the island of Crete by the use of wax wings. On jumping from a high mountain, Icarus was so struck by the beauty of flight that he forgot about escape and soared higher and higher. He ultimately soared too high, and the sun's rays melted the wax, causing the first known case of aerial structural failure from material fatigue.

For the first known document concerning rotary-wing flight, look to the great Taoist and Alchemist Ko Hung in the Fourth Century A.D. In the *Pao Phu Tau*, Ko Hung said that some had made "flying cars" from wood of the inner parts of the jujube tree. And, they used ox-leather fastened to returning blades so as to set the machine in motion. There's little doubt that this first plan for flight is the helicopter top, later known as the "Chinese Top."

The Chinese Top, dating back to the Fourth Century A.D.

Leonardo da Vinci spent some years trying to develop flying machines in Italy around 1485 A.D. He contributed to man's attempt to fly by sketching the most advanced plans of the period for an aircraft. He called it the "Aerial Screw," which was, in fact, a helicopter. Da Vinci's theory for "compressing" the air to obtain lift was similiar to that for today's rotorcraft.

Two Frenchmen, Launoy and Bienvenu, in 1784, demonstrated a scientific toy helicopter at the World's Fair in Paris. The toy helicopter, employing turkey feathers for rotor blades, rose to a height of about 70 feet. The machine created a startling amount of interest from representatives of various nations, who sent reports back to their respective countries. Inventors reasoned that if a man-made toy could be so developed, it should certainly be possible to build a larger model flying device capable of carrying men. If anything, it fired their imagination.

The famous English inventor, Sir George Cayley, demonstrated a helicopter in 1843 which featured lateral twin booms, each mounted with one set of rotors to provide lift. A small steam engine was housed in the fuselage and delivered power to the rotor system and twin, four-bladed propellers for horizontal propulsion. The twin-boom helicopter developed too little or no lift, however, it also served to stimulate the imagination of other inventors.

An Italian engineer Enrico Forlanini, constructed a steam-powered, contra-rotating, coaxial helicopter in the late 1870s. Its steam engine developed a total of 1/5 hp and weighed a hefty 6½ pounds. Reports say this machine climbed about 40 feet, remaining aloft for approximately 20 minutes.

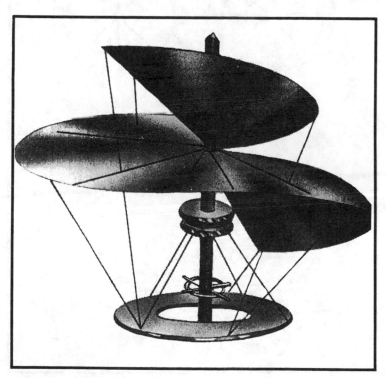

In about 1490, Leonardo da Vinci described a helicopter, based on the principle of the "Archimedian Screw."

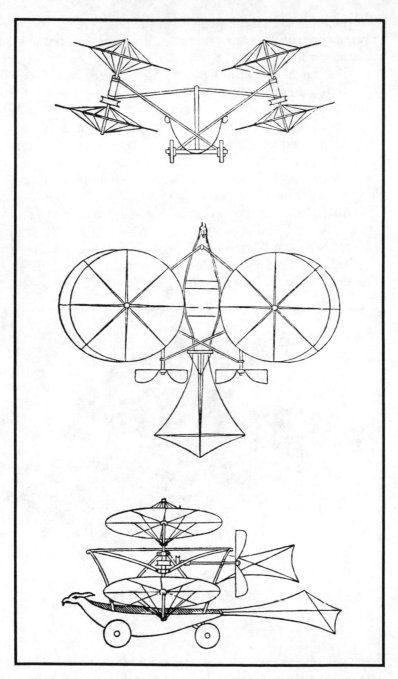

Sir George Cayley's three-view of his helicopter which was demonstrated in 1843. It was driven by a small steam engine.

By the beginning of the 20th Century, interest in rotary wing was stirring in such advanced countries as England, France, Germany, Italy, Spain, Russia and the United States. However, lacking an efficient powerplant, early inventors were limited. Another fact seemed fairly obvious: The turning of a single, overhead rotor system created forces that made the fuselage act erratic and, sometimes, uncontrollable. Early pioneers used either a coaxial, contra-rotating design or a twin rotor in which the rotors turned in opposite directions.

With the appearance of the internal combustion engine (gasoline), a major breakthrough was found for an efficient powerplant. It was the forerunner of successful flight with a high degree of efficiency (weight vs. horsepower). Engineers have since developed internal combustion engines that weigh less than one pound per horsepower.

In 1907, Paul Cornu, a Frenchman, constructed the first helicopter which showed signs of success. Cornu's copter had dual rotors, each about 20 feet in diameter, located fore and aft, and was powered by a 24-hp engine. Tilted vanes were used below the rotors for control purposes. Wide belts extended upward from the engine and outward to the rotors. These belts slipped considerably, but Cornu succeeded in rising vertically from the ground to a height of a few feet, thus becoming the first man to actually rise in true helicopter flight, even though his flight only lasted a matter of seconds.

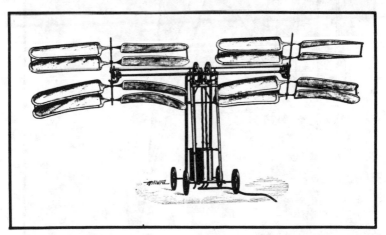

Enrico Forlanini's 1/5-hp, contra-rotating, coaxial helicopter of the late 1870s.

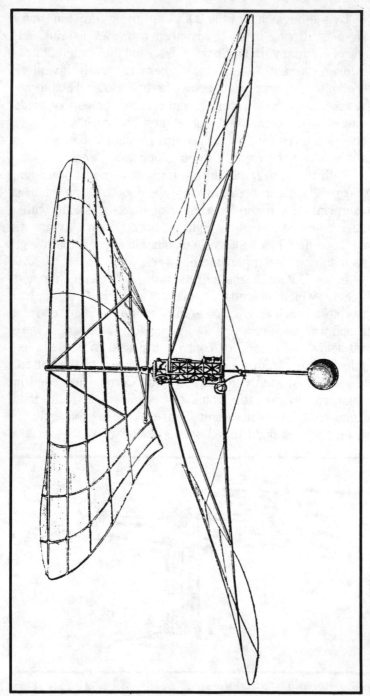

Castel Helicopter (1878).

Also in 1907, Louis Charles Brequet, another Frenchman, introduced a new design of the direct-lift aircraft, which he called a "helicoplane." It utilized four rotors and was a rather large machine. Each rotor consisted of four biplane blades. This copter attracted much attention. The Brequet-Richet No. 1 could become airborne, but had to be steadied by men holding it at all four corners. However, in 1908, the Brequet-Richet No. 2 flew skyward to a height of about 15 feet and forward some 60 feet. The second craft had only two rotors, mounted on fixed wings. The rotors had a fixed forward tilt. Although this machine was completely unstable and later crashed, it produced stimulation for fellow inventors.

Igor I. Sikorsky, later to become an outstanding figure in the industry, built two basic helicopter models: One in 1909 and the second in 1910. Although neither were considered successful, the second one was capable of lifting its own weight.

In 1916, following Sikorsky's experiments, Lt. Petroczy and Professor von Karmon of Austria constructed a con-

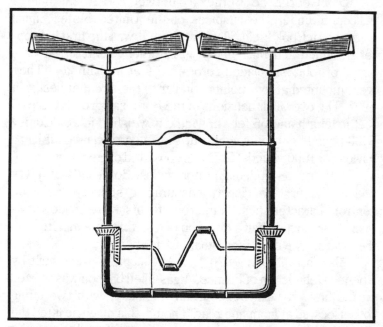

This machine was invented by Richard Owen in 1885. It provided for the pilot, and lifting screws were worked by foot-power.

trarotating, coaxial helicopter with three 40-hp engines that drove 20-foot rotors. This craft was used to serve as an observation platform. Three cables were attached to the craft in such a way that they would unreel from a ground control unit as the craft climbed vertically. Mounted above the rotating blades, a tub-type structure served as the observer's compartment. Before the cables were sufficiently taut on takeoff, the machine proved to have considerable instability. However, a number of flights were made to a satisfactory altitude for a duration of nearly an hour.

Henry Berliner, son of a Washington inventor, Emile, built and tested two entirely different helicopters in 1920-22. The first utilized a twin-rotor arrangement, with a 13-foot rotor diameter and vanes in the slipstream for flight control. His second copter was a dual-rotor design, powered by an 80-hp engine. Mounted on booms, the rotors extended from each side of the aircraft. Both of Berliner's machines were very unstable, but each flew several minutes on different occasions.

Dr. George de Bothezat, between 1920-23, built a helicopter under the auspices of the United States Signal Corps at McCook Field, Dayton, Ohio. It was the first helicopter designed and built under government contract. It consisted of four, six-bladed rotors, 25 feet in diameter. They were mounted at four points, similar to the Brequet design in 1907. The overall dimensions of the Bothezat aircraft were 65 feet in length and 65 feet in width. It weighed in at a clumsy 3400-pounds empty weight, but the inventor claimed it had a payload of 1000 pounds. Controls consisted of auxiliary propellers and variable-pitch main rotor blades. Bothezat's craft was one of the first to display encouraging stability and good control characteristics. Numerous flights were made, however these sorties had a duration of less than one minute, and the craft never rose more than six feet.

Also in the early 1920s, two helicopters were built by Etienne Dehmichen of France. A gas-filled balloon was utilized on the first. It was mounted longitudinally, with two lifting rotors located at front and rear. Though this machine lifted the weight of the machine and operator, it was found to be very unstable and uncontrollable. Four main rotors were used in

Curtiss-Bleeker.

15

the second Dehmichen craft that measured 21-25 feet in diameter. In addition, five small, horizontal props were incorporated. Two propellers for propulsion and one for steering were also used. Powered by a 120-hp engine, the craft incorporated 13 separate transmission systems. Even though more than 1000 flights of several minute durations were made in this helicopter, the complexity of the structure made it impractical.

Marquis de Pescara, a Spaniard, built several different man-carrying helicopters that performed well during the early and mid-1920s. The most successful one, a streamlined fuselage that resembled the body of a modern racing automobile. A coaxial, contra-rotating rotor system of a biplane-type was used, having a diameter of 21 feet. It was composed of six pairs of strutted blades, and the two rotor systems were arranged with one above the other. Horizontal flight was achieved by changing the pitch of the rotor blades during the cycle of rotation. Powered by a 120-hp Hispano-Suiza engine, this craft is reported to have demonstrated noteworthy flight characteristics.

A young, fixed-wing inventor, Juan de la Cierva, also a Spaniard, turned to exploring the rotary-wing field, wanting to develop a craft which could land at a low speed for maximum safety. Combining the features of the conventional airplane with that of the freely rotating, overhead rotor system, he developed a craft that was the forerunner of today's autogyro. Employing a conventional propeller in the nose of the aircraft, the autogyro used a large, overhead rotor system in lieu of fixed-wings to produce lift. Engine power driving the propeller created a forward thrust, with the resultant forward motion of the machine creating a favorable reaction on the rotor blades, causing them to "windmill," thus creating lift. A forward speed of about 30 mph would cause enough air to flow over the rotor blades to turn them at a sufficiently high rpm to support the aircraft in flight. This reaction is known "autorotation."

De la Cierva flew the English Channel in an autogyro in 1928. He took off from England and landed at Le Bourget Field, Paris, with an average speed of 100 mph. Much publicity was accorded this epic flight, because the machine proved

Langdon Helicopter.

extremely safe and foolproof, in that it could land at a low airspeed in a small area.

In 1930 the first helicopter incorporating a single, main rotor and a vertical tail rotor to compensate for torque was built by a Dutchman named von Baunhauer. A 200-hp engine drove the main rotor, and a separate 80-hp engine powered the tail rotor as a separate entity. Although this particular helicopter did fly, it was damaged before satisfactory tests could be completed.

Louis Charles Brequet, designer of the earlier and original four-rotor configuration, reappeared on the scene in 1935 with a coaxial-rotored aircraft, powered by a 350-hp engine. This new craft's arrangement demonstrated some promising characteristics, notably control and stability. However, it was extremely heavy, and there was a possibility of trouble from interference of the two rotors.

Many prominent, rotary-wing enthusiasts thought that the Brequet craft was the first successful helicopter ever built, although it was damaged beyond repair before the actual test data could be finished.

Germany's foremost designer of fighter aircraft during World War II, Heinrich Focke, in 1937, developed the Focke-Achgelis helicopter. Two large rotors were mounted on lateral booms, with each boom supporting its own rotor system. The main rotors, turning in opposite directions to compensate for torque were powered by a 160-hp, radial engine. This engine was cooled by a small, wooden prop, mounted on the nose-section of the engine. The machine weighed in at 2400 pounds and was controlled by changing the rotor-blade pitch.

Hanna Rasche, a woman test pilot, demonstrated its unique characteristics in the Deutschland Halle in Berlin. This auditorium was relatively small, measuring but 250 feet in length and only 100 feet wide. Retsch demonstrated hovering, 360-degree hovering turns, backward and sideward flight and remaining stationary over a fixed point.

The Focke FW-61 broke all existing international records in 1937 and 1939 and became recognized as the first practical, successful helicopter in the world. Some of its records were:

Pitcairn Autogyro.

Duration—1:20:49
Distance—143.069 miles in straight flight
Altitude—11,243 feet
Speed—76 mph

Resuming his study of rotary-winged craft, which he had started in 1909, Igor Sikorsky, in 1939, turned his efforts toward a single, main rotor and tail-rotor design. This new development called for coaxial rotor systems, with rotors turning in opposite directions to compensate for torque. The Sikorsky VS-300, on May 6, 1941, broke the world endurance record previously held by the Focke FW-61, by remaining aloft for 1:32:26, almost 12 minutes better than Focke's craft.

Design of the VS-300 included one main rotor, one tail rotor and two horizontal rotors mounted on booms extending laterally from the tail section. The main rotor produced lift, the tail rotor compensated for torque, and the horizontal rotors were used for directional control.

In 1941 the Flettner 282 made its flying debut. Like many of its predecessors, it had side-by-side, intermeshing rotors. Interesting features were the automatic control of rotor rpm by blade pitch changes and the automatic change to autorotative pitch in the event of engine failure. Anton Flettner could claim considerable success with his helicopters. The F1 was used operationally the next year.

During the period that Sikorsky was perfecting and leading the way with his helicopters, Arthur Young designed a copter for the Bell Aircraft Corporation, designated H-13. This machine had a semi-rigid rotor head, a two-bladed main rotor with stabilizer bar and a two-bladed tail rotor. It was a two-place, side-by-side craft, with a four-wheel landing gear. It was powered by a 178-hp Franklin engine.

A later model, the H-13D, incorporated a tail-skid, was powered by a 200-hp Franklin and mounted with suitable supports for two external litters. The H-13 was used for Army reconnaissance, artillery spotting, wire-laying and transportation. It made Army history with numerous, rapid evacuations of wounded troops from the battle fields in Korea.

Frank Piasecki first started his helicopter career with a small, one-place copter in 1943. It had a single, main rotor and

Louis Charles Brequet reappeared on the scene in 1935 with this coaxial-rotored craft, powered by a 350-hp engine.

21

an anti-torque tail rotor. Although it was only an experimental model, it did actually fly and launched Piasecki into his more famed models of tandem, dual design. These craft incorporated two, large, horizontal rotors, one mounted on the front and the other on the rear of the fuselage. Turning in opposite directions, the rotors thus eliminated torque reaction.

The tandem rotor design has a definite advantage in that the center of gravity (CG) travel load is not critical, since lifting rotors are mounted on the longitudinal axis of the fuselage at each end. Should a tendency toward a nose-heavy or tail-heavy condition develop, the rotor at that end would simply do more work, thus correcting the condition.

Piasecki's HRP-1 and HRP-2 were designed and developed in 1946. The HRP-2 had a stronger structure, but, otherwise, they were the same. Powered by a 600-hp Pratt & Whitney engine, the HRP-2 was a 10-placer, while the HRP-1 was powered by a 525-hp Continental and a 4-7 seater.

Later models by Piasecki were giants of the industry. Such models as the YH-16 and YH-21. The YH-21 was a 16-22 place, tandem rotored, single-engine rescue and utility craft, 20-feet-long and powered by a 1425-hp Wright engine. It had a 697-mile range, useful load of 2720 pounds, max forward speed of 120 mph and a 15,700-foot service ceiling. The YH-16 utilized a twin-engine, twin-rotor combination. The rotors, arranged in tandem, overlapping configuration, scribed overlapping arcs. An engine was located under each rotor and either engine could drive both rotors by means of an interconnected shaft. With rotors at each end of the 77-foot fuselage, this design permitted full use of the center portion of the fuselage for cargo or passengers and eliminated the balance problem encountered with single rotor-types. Cabin space available was 2250 cu. ft. for a disposable load of up to 40 persons, or 6000-8000 pounds. It was capable of flying 300 miles and returning to its point of origin with a crew of four and 27 passengers.

Stanley Hiller Jr. first entered the rotorcraft scene at the same time as Sikorsky and Bell, but his first, small, single-seated, coaxial craft, designated the XH-44, lacked stability. Engineering and production design for the Hiller 360 was completed in 1949. This model incorporated a "rotomatic"

Igor Sikorsky test hopping an early design.

Early model Hiller.

device, an airfoil surface with which the pilot aerodynamically controlled the main rotor system. Powered by a 178-hp engine, it was capable of carrying three people side-by-side and was, ultimately, accepted by the armed forces in 1951. Since this early-day craft, Hiller, like Sikorsky and Bell, has become a major success in the rotary-wing field.

Sikorsky Skycrane.

25

Still in wide use today is the Kaman K-1, with two, intermeshing rotors.

Also during 1950, the McDonnell Corporation, then of St. Louis, built a 10-passenger, dual-rotor, side-by-side, twin-engined machine. Entered in the Arctic Rescue Contest in that year, it proved to be a very worthy craft. McDonnell was the first to develop a small, single-place, jet helicopter designated the H-20, but better known as the "Little Henry."

During this period the Kaman Aircraft Corporation in Connecticut developed the HTK-1 helicopter. This machine was demonstrated, showing encouraging flight characteristics and employed servo flaps to tilt the rotor system, instead of control plates. Powered by a 240-hp, Lycoming engine, the craft had two, intermeshing rotors, each 40 feet in diameter. These rotors were located on lateral booms, giving it a max speed of 70 knots.

The rigid rotor Cheyenne takes off and lands vertically like a helicopter but flies with a speed of more than 250 mph.

The McCulloch MC-4 is a tandem aircraft, taking full advantage of the tandem configuration for a craft its size. The cockpit arrangement is for side-by-side, dual controls. It is 32 feet five inches long, with a height of nine feet three inches. It has a rotor diameter of 23 feet, max gross weight of 2300 pounds and a typical loading would be pilot, copilot and a passenger. It has a range of 200 miles at 75 mph, with 170 pounds of baggage or cargo. A 200-hp, six cylinder, air cooled engine is mounted horizontally to effect a horizontal output shaft. Equipped with a tricycle-type fixed gear, a full swiveling cantilever-type nose wheel is provided at the forward end of the craft.

The MC-4 is capable of a high speed at sea level of 100 mph, has a service ceiling of 10,000 feet, empty weight of 1600 pounds, a useful load of 700 pounds and a maximum rate of climb at sea level of 1000 fpm.

The Doman LZ-5 is a third generation model and features such key applications as a hingeless, four-bladed, oil lubricated rotor system that gives a minimum of vibration in the fuselage and controls. Body layout of the craft emphasizes an empty weight of 2860 pounds, useful load of 1559 pounds for a max gross of 4419. Service-wise, it's slanted for evacuation missions, frontline air observations and reconnaissance, wire-laying, supply and survey work. The machine is powered by a 400-hp Lycoming.

The Kellett Aircraft Corporation developed a large and powerful helicopter for the United States Air Force, designated XH-10. It has a twin, three-bladed, counter-rotating and intermeshing rotor. This type of rotor system eliminates the necessity for an anti-drag device, such as a tail rotor, leaving more power for direct lift. The configuration was first developed on the German Flettner craft, discussed earlier.

The XH-10 has a streamlined fuselage with tricycle gear, plexiglass-bubble nose and a horizontal stabilizer utilizing three vertical fins. A large cargo space inside the all-metal, semi-monocoque fuselage permits a wide range of uses. It has a large cargo door, with a hydraulic hoist in the cargo compartment to facilitate ground loading and airborne rescue.

This helicopter's 65-foot rotors are driven by two, 525-hp Continenta engines. It features such modernizations

The roll-out and first official flight of the armed version of the U.S. Army CH-47A Chinook helicopter in November 1965. The Chinook is a product of Boeing aircraft, Vertol Division.

29

as parking brakes, taxi brakes, full panel flight instruments, radio installation and a heating system. It can lift a gross weight of over 15,000 pounds while at a hover and cruise at a forward speed in excess of 120 mph. It can fly on one engine, at normal gross weight, at altitudes up to 4600 feet and has good autorotational characteristics.

Since World War II, development of the helicopter followed a predictable route, although frustratingly slow for those already convinced of the craft's potential. It was really the Korean Conflict that proved the helicopter to doubters: That it was an indispensable, multi-purpose tool, taking up where the fixed-wing airplane left off.

However, it was the Vietnam conflict that really started helicopters moving and firmly implanted them into our aviation society. For it was there in Vietnam that not only did the rotorcraft perform in an outstanding mode, likened to Korea, but carried it much further as those who flew the gunships can attest.

Hughes, Hiller, Enstrome, Bell, Sikorsky and many others are still paving the way, experimenting and making practical such items as fiberglass, polyresin coated rotor blades, Turbojets, etc., letting the rotorcraft mix well in a fixed-wing world.

2

AERODYNAMICS

Anything that flies; whether rotor, fixed wing, motorized or glider, does so through the use of airfoils. With them, an aircraft is able to get off the ground, maneuver through the air and land. Without them, flying would simply be an impossibility. Being so basic to flight, then, just what is an airfoil?

Airfoil

An airfoil is any device capable of producing lift. Almost everything is capable of producing lift to a certain degree, however, so almost everything can be called an airfoil. Take the ordinary, garden variety rock, for example. It can produce lift to a certain extent when moved fast enough through the air or the air moved fast enough over the rock.

Speaking specifically of aviation, an airfoil is described as, "any surface aerodynamically designed to produce a minimum of drag and a maximum of lift when air passes over it." Applied to fixed-wing aircraft, a common airfoil would be wing shaped. Applied to helicopters, it would be shaped like a rotor blade.

There are three main parts to an airfoil: leading edge, trailing edge and the camber. There is an imaginary straight line running from the leading edge to the trailing edge called the "chord line." The curve of the airfoil's surface above this chord line is called the "Upper Camber," and the lower curvature is the "Lower Camber."

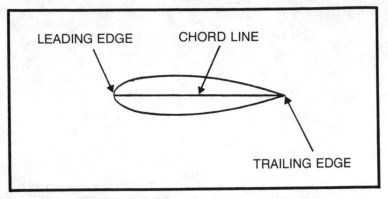

The chord line of an airfoil is the imaginary line joining the leading and trailing edges.

You'll find airfoils that are fat, thin, long, and short, but two that are basic to aviation are the "symmetrical" and "unsymmetrical." Most airplane wings are unsymmetrical, meaning the upper camber has more curvature than the lower camber. Currently, most helicopter rotor blades are symmetrical, in that the upper and lower cambers are of equal curvature.

Relative Wind

Before getting into such things as lift, weight, thrust and drag, take a look at a few things that affect the helicopter's blade; namely air movement, relative wind, pitch angle and angle of attack.

"Relative wind" is described as the direction of airflow in regards to the airfoil. Confusing? Not really. If the airfoil moves forward horizontally, the relative wind moves parallel to but in the opposite direction of that traveled by the airfoil. If the airfoil moves forward and upward, the relative wind moves parallel to, backward and downward. The relative wind always moves parallel to, but in the opposite direction of the airfoil's flight path.

In regards to helicopter rotor blades, relative wind is determined by three factors: rotation of the rotor blades through the air, flapping of the rotor blades (up and down movement) and the horizontal movement of the helicopter as a whole.

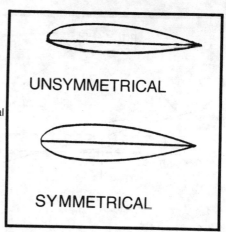

Symmetrical and unsymmetrical airfoils.

UNSYMMETRICAL

SYMMETRICAL

Blade Pitch Angle:

Using the horizontal plane of the main rotor hub as a base line, the blade's pitch angle is measured from the blade's chord line to the hub's base line. This angle is important, because it can be changed from inside the cockpit through the use of cyclic pitch control and the collective pitch control; two controls used to vary flight characteristics.

Even though the copter's body can turn on a horizontal plane, the blade's pitch angle will remain constant until changed manually by the pilot from inside the cockpit.

Angle of Attack

Similar to the pitch angle, in that angle of attack is also measured from the blade's chord line, it's different, in that it's measured not to the rotor hub line but to the relative wind plane. The angle of attack is determined also by the flight path of the helicopter, since relative wind runs parallel to it.

The angle of attack can be more than, equal to or less than the pitch angle. If you change the pitch angle of the blades, you

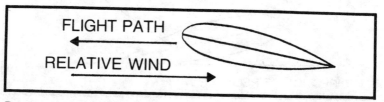

FLIGHT PATH

RELATIVE WIND

Relative wind is always parallel to and in the opposite direction to the flight path.

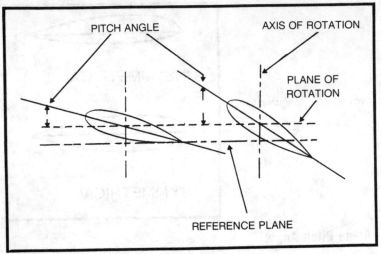

The pitch angle is the angle between the chord line and reference plane determined by the rotor hub or the plane of rotation.

also change the angle of attack, since you would be changing the blade's chord line in reference to the relative wind. However, the opposite isn't true; by changing the angle of attack, you're not necessarily changing the pitch angle of the blade. Remember, angle of attack is dependent on relative wind, and pitch angle is dependent on the rotor hub.

Lift

The values of pitch angle, angle of attack, relative wind, upper and lower cambers and chord lines combine to give you, among other things, varying degrees of "lift." How is lift derived from, and its relationship to, the above parts?

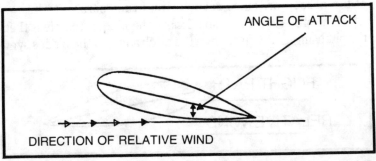

The angle of attack is the angle between the relative wind and the chord line.

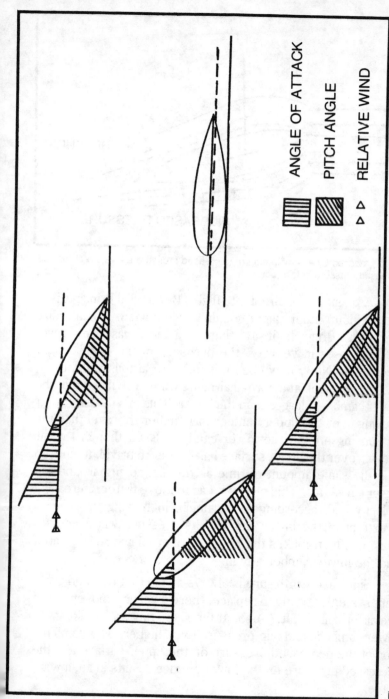

ANGLE OF ATTACK

PITCH ANGLE

△ ▷ RELATIVE WIND

The relationship between angle of attack and drag. As the angle of attack increases, lift and drag also increase.

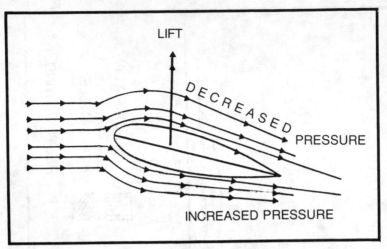

LIFT

DECREASED PRESSURE

INCREASED PRESSURE

Lift is produced by a combination of decreased pressure above the airfoil and increased pressure below (bottom).

As basic as the airfoil is to flight, Bernoulli's Principle is to lift. Without either, flight couldn't be obtained. To capsulize Bernoulli's Principle, it says that as a liquid or gas (in our case, air) increases in velocity, the pressure of the liquid or gas decreases. Now, how does this apply to airfoils and lift?

Take a look at a normal airplane wing. You'll see that the upper camber is larger than the lower. This means that the air moving over the upper camber has farther to travel than the air moving around the lower camber. Even though the air moving over the upper surface has farther to travel, it must do it in the same amount of time as the air moving around the lower curvature. This means it has to move faster, increasing velocity and, according to Bernoulli, increasing its velocity over that of the lower camber, its pressure will decrease. This, in effect, makes the upper camber a low pressure area and the lower camber a high.

Since a low pressure is always a void that the high pressure system is trying to replace, there's vertical movement of the airfoil called "lift." Also, at the same time, air striking the lower camber builds up pressure even higher. The combination of the decreased pressure on the upper surface and the increased pressure on the lower surface results in an upward force.

If you increase the blade's pitch angle, the relative wind will strike the blade's leading edge lower down, thus giving the wind still farther to travel over the upper camber. And, having farther to travel, it must increase speed even more, causing an even lower pressure, which will, of course, result in more lift. So, by increasing the blade's pitch angle, you create lift.

It's true that a symmetrical airfoil produces symmetical airflow patterns above and below the airfoil at a zero angle of attack, and therefore zero lift. But at any positive angle of attack the airflow above the airfoil creates the familiar low pressure area as it does with asymmetrical airfoils.

Air Density & Lift

Although it can't be controlled as other factors, air density plays a great part in total lift. Take a look at the makeup of

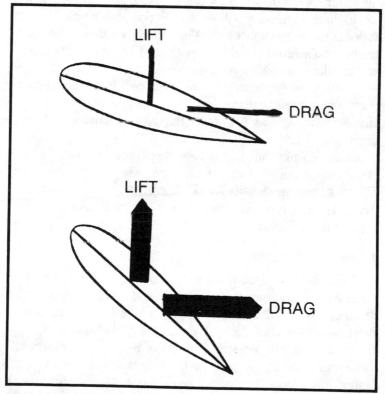

The relationship between angle of attack and drag. As the angle of attack increases, lift and drag also increase.

air density: temperature, humidity and pressure. Ideally, you would want a low temperature, low humidity and a high pressure. A combination of all three would give an airfoil its best lift.

With a "low temperature" the air is thick and compact. The lower the temperature, the more compact the air for creating lift. Just the reverse is true with high temperatures. The higher the temperature the thinner the air. Air that is heated expands. The higher the temperature the more the expansion, and the less air there is for creating lift. Remember, the lower the temperature, the more compact the air and the more air there is to move across the blade's surface to create lift.

"Dry" air is more dense than wet (humid) air. Therefore, the dryer it is the more compact, and the more air there is to move across the blade for increased lift. Water droplets in the air displace it, making it less dense. So, as humidity (water vapor in the atmosphere) goes up, lift comes down. Unfortunately, you seldom find dry air without it being hot; but again, we're talking about an ideal situation.

With a "high pressure," the air is compressed and compact, giving great volume to the air passing over the blade. However, with a low pressure, the air is expanded and thin, decreasing lift.

Capsulizing, thus far we have discussed two main factors in the creation of lift: blade pitch angle, which increases angle of attack, and air density, which increases the air's volume. There is, however, another very important item that also creates lift...Thrust.

Thrust

The faster a blade moves through the air, the higher the volume of air that moves over its surface. And, the higher the volume, like air density, the more lift produced. Although most helicopter pilots like to fly at a steady blade or rotor rpm, they can change its velocity, thus increasing or decreasing lift as desired. Just like in your automobile when you want to go faster, you simply "put your foot on the gas." It's similar with helicopters. If you want to increase blade rpm, you simply give it a little more go.

Another item not to be forgotten, since it has to do with rpm, is the blade's thickness. Using the same principle as with the air moving over the blade, you can readily see where the thicker the airfoil or blade, the more lift is obtained because the farther the air has to travel up and over.

Normally, you'll see larger helicopters, such as those used for heavy transport, using thick rotor blades. Thin bladed craft use a higher rpm than thick bladed ones.

Drag

At the same time the blade is producing lift, it's also creating another force called "drag." Drag is the term used for the force that opposes or resists the blade's movement through the air; you probably know it as the retarding force of inertia or "wind resistance."

Drag acts parallel to, but in the opposite direction of the blade's flight path. Also, you can say that it runs parallel to, and in the same direction as relative wind. It's this force that causes a reduction in rpm when changing to a higher pitch angle and/or a higher angle of attack. An increase in pitch angle or angle of attack not only produces an increase in lift but also an increase in drag.

Ever wonder why when you increase the power in your car, you increase in speed only to a certain extent, and to go any faster you have to again increase the power?

What you have is drag overcoming thrust. As your car accelerates so does drag. However, drag increases slower than thrust initially, then increases faster, until power or thrust is stalemated by resistances (drag).

Stall

When the blade's angle of attack increases to a certain point, the air can no longer flow smoothly over the top surface because of the required change in direction. At this point, where the air is breaking away from the upper camber, it's said to "burble." It's also at this point that lift is partially destroyed, and any farther increase in the angle of attack decreases the amount of lift proportionately. This loss of streamlined air flow results in a swirling, turbulent airflow and a large increase in the amount of drag. It's also at this point that the blade is said to be in a stalled condition.

If a stall is incurred, lift must be restored to the blades. This can be done is two ways or a combination of the two: increasing the rotor rpm, thus forcing the air to move back over the blade, destroying the burble and the stall; or the angle of attack must be decreased, enough so that the air will once again move over the blade. Since most pilots like to run at a steady rpm, it's only natural to correct a stalled condition by reducing the angle of attack with the cyclic stick, since changing the blade's pitch angle with the collective would also change the rpm setting.

Weight

The total weight of a helicopter (gross weight) is the first force that must be overcome if flight is to be obtained. Weight is overcome by the lift created by the main rotor blades. It's the force of gravity that works on a helicopter, acting downward toward the earth's center, regardless of the machine's flight path or attitude.

In a small craft, the thing to be most concerned with is not to exceed its maximum gross weight limitation. However, with the larger, more complex machines, another item must be reckoned with; that of balance. Not only must you keep the total weight at or below that specified, but you must also balance all of that weight within certain limits: Center of Gravity (c.g.). Too much weight concentrated in the front of the cabin area could cause drastic flight characteristics, as would too much in the rear area.

On some of the smaller helicopters, with side-by-side seating, even flight with one person creates an odd balancing situation when hovering. As you're taught to fly with an instructor, you get used to that weight balancing-out yours. However, when you solo for the first time, you might feel uncomfortable, because then the 165 pounds or so of the instructor are no longer present, causing a minor balancing problem.

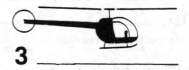

3

AERODYNAMICS OF FLIGHT

The basic ingredients of flight have been discussed in the preceding chapter. Now, put them together with different helicopter components and see how the craft aerodynamically lifts off, hovers, flys and lands.

Hovering Flight

In a no-wind condition hover, the helicopter's blade tip path is horizontal to, or parallel to the ground. Lift and thrust act straight up, and weight and drag act straight down. In other words, the sum of the lift and thrust forces equal and cancel out the forces of weight and drag. To hover, however, the craft must first get off the ground.

Vertical Flight

Vertical flight during a no-wind condition plays on the same basic forces as the hover. Lift and thrust forces act vertically upward, while weight and drag both act vertically downward. With vertical flight, however, the two groups are unequal. When lift and thrust equal weight and drag, the helicopter hovers. When lift and thrust are more than weight and drag, the machine rises vertically. If lift and thrust are less than weight and drag, the craft descends vertically.

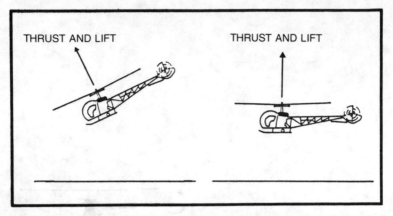

THRUST AND LIFT   THRUST AND LIFT

The total lift-thrust force acts perpendicular to the rotor disc or tip-path plane.

Forward Flight

Forward flight is accomplished when the rotor's tip path plane is tilted forward. The forward tilting motion thus tilts the total lift/thrust force forward of the vertical. The results of this motion divides the lift/thrust component into two forces: lift acting vertically upward and thrust acting horizontally in the direction of flight. The results of this combination is a lifting force which splits the two, called "resultant" lift.

In addition to the lift and thrust forces, there are again, weight and drag forces, plus any wind condition that's present. In straight-and-level, unaccelerated, forward flight, lift equals weight and thrust equals drag. If lift exceeds the weight component, the helicopter climbs in the forward flight attitude. If, on the other hand, lift is less than weight, the craft descends in the forward flight attitude. You can also say that if thrust is greater than drag, the machine will accelerate in the forward flight attitude. And, if thrust is less than drag, the helicopter decelerates or loses speed in the forward flight attitude.

Sideward Flight

Sideward flight is obtained by tilting the rotor head. This is accomplished through cyclic pitch control movement. Tilting the rotor head causes the total lift/thrust component to tilt sideways, this the vertical lift factor is still straight up, weight straight down, thrust moves sideward horizontally and drag acts in the opposite direction. Resultant lift; the splitting of lift/thrust forces, moves the helicopter to the side.

It can be readily seen that by tilting the rotor, flight can be made forward, sideward, rearward or in any direction you

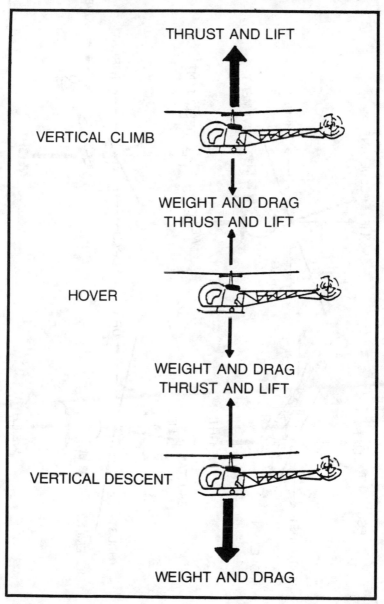

Forces acting on a helicopter during vertical climb, hover and vertical descent.

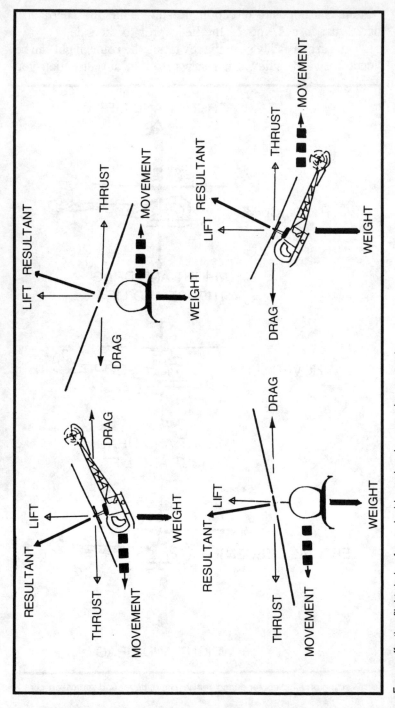

Forces effecting flight during forward, sideward and rearward movement.

44

desire to travel. As will be discussed in more detail later, this rotor head or hub tilting is accomplished by the pilot from inside the cockpit.

Torque

Another factor to be reckoned with and corrected for is "torque." Newton's Third Law Of Motion states, "To every action there is an equal and opposite reaction." Applied to helicopters, this simply means that the main rotor blades turn in one direction, normally counterclockwise, the helicopter fuselage tends to turn in the opposite direction, normally clockwise.

Since torque is the direct result of engine power supplied to the rotor blades, with the fuselage turning as a result of the engine's power, torque effect corresponds to engine power changes. If you add power, the torque factor increases; if you decrease power, the torque factor decreases.

Auxiliary Rotor(s)

If uncorrected, torque would cause an uncontrollable situation. It's most apparent at slow speed with high power output, such as in a hover, lift-off and during transitional flight. A force that compensates for torque and keeps the fuselage from turning in the direction of the rotor blade motion when powerless (autorotation) is produced from an auxiliary rotor,

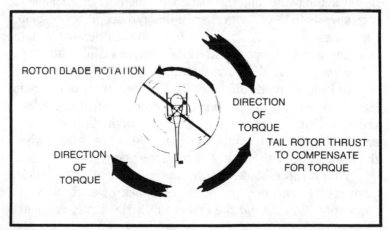

Tail (antitorque) rotor thrust compensates for the torque effect of the main rotor.

also known as a tail rotor or antitorque rotor, located at the end of the tail boom. It's simply placed vertically on the rear of the craft and produces thrust in the opposite direction of torque. Foot pedals (rudders) placed in the cockpit act with the similar action as rudders on fixed-wing aircraft, only controlling the auxiliary rotor's thrust, thus the pilot has a means of cancelling torque.

Gyroscopic Precession

The spinning main rotor of a helicopter acts like a gyroscope, in that is has the properties of gyroscopic action, one of which is precession. Gyroscopic precession is the resultant action (or deflection) of a spinning object when a force is applied to it. This action occurs approximately 90 degrees in the direction of rotation from the point where the force (deflection) is applied. It's through the use of this principle that the tip-path of the main rotors may be tilted from the horizontal.

By moving the cyclic pitch control in a two-bladed rotor system, the angle of attack of one rotor blade is increased, resulting in a greater lifting force being applied at this point in the horizontal plane of rotation. This same applied force simultaneously decreases the angle of attack on the other blade a like amount, thus decreasing the second blade's lifting force.

The blade with the increased angle of attack tends to rise higher in the plane, and the blade with the decreased angle of attack tends to lower. Because of the gyroscopic precession, the blades don't raise or lower to maximum deflection until reaching a point approximately 90 degrees after the initial deflection point in the horizontal plane of rotation.

In simplification, the retreating blade's angle of attack is increased and the advancing blade's angle of attack is decreased. This results in a tipping forward of the tip-path plane, since maximum deflection takes place 90 degrees later when the blades are at the rear and front respectively.

With a three-bladed rotor, the movement of the cyclic pitch control changes the angle of attack of each blade an appropriate amount, so the end result is the same: A tipping forward of the tip-path plane, when the maximum change in angle of attack is made, as each blade passes the same points at which the maximum increase and decrease are made for the two-bladed rotor.

As each of the three blades pass the 90 degree position on the left, the maximum increase in angle of attack occurs. As each blade passes the 90 degree position to the right, the maximum decreases in angle of attack occurs. Maximum deflection takes place 90 degrees later: Maximum upward deflection at the rear and maximum downward deflection at the front. The tip-path plane tips forward.

Dissymmetry of Lift

The area within the tip-path plane of the main rotor is known as the "disc area" or "rotor disc." When hovering in a no-wind condition, lift created by the rotor blades at all corresponding positions around the rotor disc is said to be equal. "Dissymmetry of lift," is created by horizontal flight or by wind during hovering flight and is the difference in lift that exists between the advancing blade of the disc area and the retreating blade arc half.

In a no-wind hovering situation, say the blade tips traveling the horizontal plane are moving at 400 mph. The speed of the relative wind at the blade tips can be said to be the same throughout the tip-path plane; or uniformly 400 mph throughout the complete circle. The speed of the relative wind at any specific point along the rotor blade will be the same throughout the tip-path plane. However, the speed is reduced as this point moves closer to the rotor hub, because the closer the point to the hub, the less speed is required to stay up with the blade tips.

As the helicopter moves into forward flight, the relative wind moving over each rotor blade becomes a combination of the rotational speed of the rotor and the forward movement of the craft. Looking down on the blade-path plane, at the 90 degree position on the right side, the advancing blade has a combined speed of the blade velocity, plus the speed of the helicopter. At the 90 degree position on the left side, the retreating blade speed is the blade velocity, less the speed of the helicopter. In other words, the relative wind is at a maximum at the 90 degree position on the right side and at a minimum at the 90 degree position on the left side.

Blade Flapping

Earlier, under "angle of attack" in Chapter Two, it was stated that for any given angle of attack, lift increases as the velocity of the airflow over the airfoil increases. It should be apparent that lift over the advancing half of the rotor disc will be greater than lift over the retreating half during horizontal flight or when hovering in a wind, unless some compensation is made. Equally apparent is the fact that the helicopter will roll to the left, unless some compensation is made.

With a three-bladed rotor system, the rotor blades are attached to the rotor hub by a horizontal hinge which permits the blades to move in a vertical plane, flapping up or down, as they rotate. In forward flight, assuming that the blade-pitch angle remains constant, the increased lift on the advancing blade will cause the blade to flap up, thus decreasing the angle of attack, because the relative wind will change from a horizontal direction to a more downward direction, thus decreasing some of its lift. At the same time, the decreased lift on the retreating blade will cause the blade to flap down, increasing the angle of attack, because the relative wind changes from a horizontal direction to more of an upward direction, thus increasing its lift component.

This combination of decreased angle of attack on the advancing blade and an increased angle of attack on the retreating blade, through this blade flapping motion, tends to equalize the lift over the two halves of the rotor disc.

In a two-bladed system, the blades flap as a unit. As the advancing blade flaps up, due to increased lift, the retreating blade flaps down, due to the decreased lift. Changes in the angle of attack on each blade by this flapping action tends to equalize lift over the two halves of the rotor disc.

Coning

Before takeoff, the rotor blades rotate in a plane nearly pependicular to the rotor mast. Centrifugal force is the major force acting on the blades. As a vertical takeoff is made, the additional force of lift takes place, acting upward and parallel to the mast. The result of these two forces makes the blades assume a conical path, instead of remaining in the plane perpendicular to the mast.

Coning, then, is the upward bending of the blades, caused by the combined forces of lift and centrifugal force. It results in blade bending in a semirigid rotor. In the case of an articulated rotor, the blades assume an upward angle throughout, by movement about "flapping hinges."

Axis of Rotation

There's an imaginary line about which the rotor rotates called the "axis of rotation." This axis is represented by an imaginary line drawn through the center of, and perpendicular to, the tip-path plane, and shouldn't be confused with the rotor mast. The only time the rotor axis and rotor mast coincide is when the axis of rotation is perpendicular to the rotor mast.

Coriolis Effect

In a three-bladed rotor system, when the rotor blades flap upward, the distance of the center of mass of the blades from their axis of rotation decreases. The distance of the center of mass from the axis of rotation (measured perpendicular to

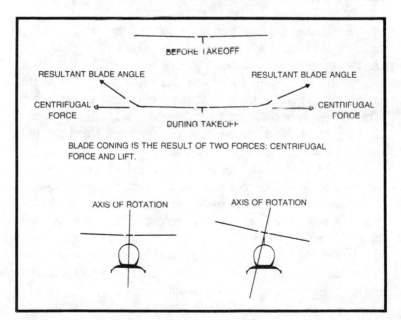

The "axis of rotation" is an imaginary line, perpendicular to the tip-path plane, around which the rotor moves.

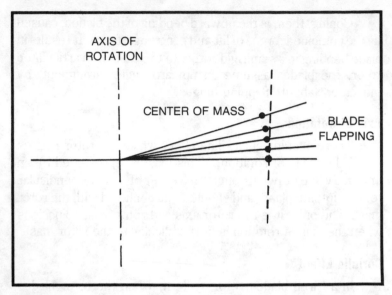

Coriolis effect takes place to compensate for the change in distance of the center of mass from the axis of rotation as the blades flap, changing blade speed.

the axis of rotation) times the rotational speed must always remain the same for a given rotor rpm.

Since this distance becomes shorter as the blades flap upward, the rotational speed must increase for the product of the two to remain the same. Conversely, when the blade flaps downward, the blade rotation must slow down, since the center of the mass is moved farther from the axis of rotation. This change in blade velocity in the plane of rotation causes a hunting action about the vertical (drag) hinge. This tendency of the blade to increase/decrease its speed is known as Coriolis Effect. The acceleration/deceleration is absorbed by dampers or the blade structure itself, depending on its design.

You might compare Coriolis Effect to a spinning ice skater. When the skater spins with arms extended, rotation slows down, because the center of mass moves farther from the axis of rotation. When the skater spins with arms held close to the body, the rotation speeds up, because the center of mass moves closer to the axis of rotation.

Two-bladed rotor systems aren't normally subject to Coriolis Effect to the degree of the three-bladed system, since the blades are generally "underslung" with respect to the rotor hub. The change in distance of the center of mass from the axis of rotation is small. What hunting action is present is absorbed through blade bending.

Translating Tendency (drift)

The entire helicopter has a tendency to move in the direction of tail rotor thrust, which would be to the right, when in a hover. This movement is often referred to as "drift." To counteract this drifting movement, the rotor mast in some helicopters is rigged slightly to the left side, so that the tip-path plane has a built-in tilt to the left, thus producing a small, sideward thrust. In other helicopters, drift is overcome by rigging the cyclic pitch system to give the required amount of tilt to the tip-path plane.

Ground Effect

When hovering close to the ground, a helicopter's rotor blades will be displacing air downward (pulling it through and shoving it down) through the disc area faster than it can escape from beneath the craft. This builds up a cushion of denser (more compact) air between the ground and the helicopter.

This cushion of compact air, referred to as "ground effect," aids in supporting the helicopter while in a hover. Ground effect is usually only effective at a height of ½ the diameter of the rotor disc. And, if the machine moves forward,

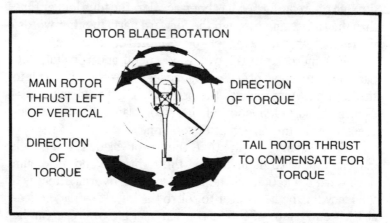

Tail rotor thrust causes drift and is compensated for by rigging the cyclic pitch system or mast to have a built-in tilt of the tip-path plane to the left.

normally faster than three to five mph, this effect is lost. Therefore, since the cushion is lost on helicopter movement, additional lift is required to keep from unexpectedly sinking back to terra firma.

Translational Lift

Another form of lift that enhances helicopter performance is created by its movement in any direction, except vertical. Sure, lift is lost when the copter moves out of its ground effect, but once it reaches approximately 15 mph in horizontal flight its rotor blades become more efficient, acting much as a fixed wing. The additional lift created at this speed and beyond is referred to as "effective translational lift" and is easily recognized by a sudden or marked increase in the craft's performance.

Since translational lift depends on airspeed rather than ground speed, the craft doesn't have to be moving to be affected. Translational lift will be present in a hover, if there's enough wind present (15 mph).

Transverse Airflow

With a helicopter in forward flight, air passing through the rear portion of the rotor arc has a higher downwash velocity than air passing through the forward portion. This increased downwash speed is caused primarily because the air passing through the rear portion has been accelerated for a longer time than the air passing through the forward part. In other words, the relative wind has a higher speed at the rear than the front.

This increase in relative wind speed and resultant lift, plus the gyroscopic precession, causes the rotor disc to tilt to the left side. According to the principle of gyroscopic precession, maximum deflection of the rotor blades occurs 90 degrees later in the direction of rotation.

This means simply that the rotor blades will reach maximum upward deflection on the right side and maximum downward deflection on the left side. The overall effect is a tendency for the helicopter to roll to the left. It's most noticeable on entry into effective translational lift where it can be accompanied by vibration.

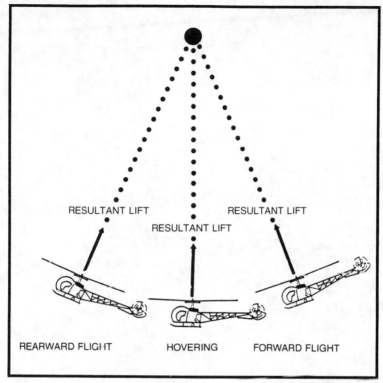

RESULTANT LIFT RESULTANT LIFT

RESULTANT LIFT

REARWARD FLIGHT HOVERING FORWARD FLIGHT

A helicopter acts much like a pendulum, since it's suspended from the rotor mast head; like a weight on the end of a string.

Pendular Action

Since the fuselage of the helicopter is suspended from a single point and has considerable mass, it acts much like a ball suspended from the end of a string. It's free to oscillate either longitudinally or laterally in the same way as the ball on the end of the string.

This pendular action can be exaggerated by over-controlling. Control forces (stick movement), therefore, should be decidedly moderate.

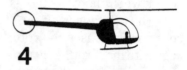

4

FLIGHT CONTROLS

There are basically four controls in a helicopter that you use during flight: Cyclic Pitch, Collective Pitch, Throttle and Antitorque.

With the use of these four controls, you can lift off, hover, transition, fly to your destination and land. By taking a look at their individual roles, as well as their integration into the total system, controls and the overall helicopter concept can better be understood.

Collective Pitch Control

The collective pitch lever, simply called the "Collective," is located on the left side of the pilot's seat in most models and is operated by the pilot's left hand. The collective moves up and down, with one end connected at the rear and, through a series of mechanical linkages, changes the pitch angle of the main rotor blades when moved up or down.

As collective is raised, there's a simultaneous, and equal, increase in the pitch angle of all the main rotor blades. And, as it's lowered, there's a simultaneous, and equal, decrease in main rotor blades pitch angle. The amount of lever movement determines the extent of pitch angle change.

As the rotor blades pitch angle changes, the angle of attack of each blade will also change. This change in the angle of attack will affect the blade's lift characteristics. As the angle of attack increases, drag and lift increase, however, rotor rpm decreases. As the angle of attack decreases, lift and drag decrease, but rotor rpm increases.

Since it's essential that rotor rpm remain constant, there must be some means of making a proportionate change in the power to compensate for the change in drag/rpm. This coordination of power with blade pitch angle is controlled through the collective's control cam linkage which automatically increases power when the collective is raised and decreases power when the collective is lowered.

The collective is the *primary* altitude control. Raising the collective increases the rotor's lift and, through the cam linkage with the throttle, increases engine power. The collective also is, therefore, the primary manifold pressure control.

Throttle Control

The throttle, often thought of as synonomous with the collective, is mounted on the forward end of the collective lever in the form of a twist-type grip on most helicopter models. The primary function of the throttle is to regulate rotor rpm directly and engine rpm indirectly.

In many smaller choppers there isn't any automatic syncronization of collective and rpm, or during an emergency with the more sophisticated, so it has to be done manually by twisting the throttle grip. Also, you may want to adjust or fine tune the rpm. Twisting the motorcycle-type grip outboard (clockwise) will increase rpm, and twisting inboard (counterclockwise) will decrease rpm.

The collective and throttle attachment work together, giving you the right blade pitch angle, manifold pressure (power) and rotor rpm. Since the collective is considered the primary control for manifold pressure and the throttle is considered the primary control for rotor rpm, they must work harmoniously together.

Remember, the collective also influences rotor rpm and the throttle also influences manifold pressure; each is considered to be a secondary control for each other's function. You must analyze both the tachometer (rpm indicator) as well as the manifold pressure gauge, which are usually housed in the

Collective and throttle (far left); Cyclic (center); and Antitorque (rudder) pedals (center left and left).

57

same unit for convenience. As a simplification, take a look at some sample problems that are common with this system and their solutions:

Problem: Manifold pressure low, rotor rpm low.
Solution: Increasing throttle will increase manifold pressure, and a higher rotor rpm will result.

Problem: Manifold pressure high, rotor rpm low.
Solution: Decreasing collective will reduce manifold pressure, decrease drag on the rotor, and a higher rpm will result.

Problem: Manifold pressure high, rotor rpm high.
Solution: Decreasing throttle reduces manifold pressure and results in a reduction of rotor rpm.

Problem: Manifold pressure low, rotor rpm high.
Solution: Increasing collective will increase manifold pressure, increase rotor drag, and a lower rotor rpm will result.

Flying a helicopter has often been compared to flying a heavy airplane at slow speeds. It takes time for corrections to be made; time between input of corrective measures on the controls and the time to helicopter response. It could possibly take as much as two seconds or more for the craft to respond to control input. This is one reason to avoid large adjustments. All corrections need to be accomplished through smooth pressure on the controls. Don't get anxious at not having a quick response and increase the input or put in another correction altogether.

Antitorque (rudder) Pedals

Thrust produced by the auxiliary (tail) rotor is governed by the position of the antitorque pedals. These pedals are linked to a pitch change mechanism in the tail rotor gear box and permits the pilot to increase or decrease the pitch of the tail rotor blades. The primary purpose of the tail rotor and its controls is to counteract the torque effect of the main rotor.

The tail rotor and its controls not only enable you to counteract the torque of the main rotor, but also to control the heading of the helicopter during a hover, hovering turns and

Collective and throttle are operated normally with pilot's left hand. Twist-grip type throttle and collective lever (lower).

hovering patterns. Understand that in forward flight, the rudder pedals are not used to control the heading of the craft, except during portions of crosswind takeoffs and approaches. They are, rather, used to compensate for torque; to put the helicopter in longitudinal trim so that coordination can be maintained. The cyclic control is used to change heading by making a coordinated turn to the desired direction.

For being so relatively simple, the development of an antitorque device puzzled the masters for many years. In any case, it takes no genius to understand the simplicity with which it works.

With the right pedal moved forward, the tail rotor either has a negative pitch angle or a small positive pitch angle. The farther forward the right pedal is pushed, the larger the negative pitch angle. The nearer the right pedal is to the neutral position, the more positive pitch angle the tail rotor will have. Somewhere in between, the tail rotor will have a zero pitch angle. As the left pedal is moved forward of the neutral position, the positive pitch angle of the tail rotor increases, until it becomes maximum with full forward displacement of the left pedal.

With a negative pitch angle, the tail rotor thrust is working in the same direction as torque reaction of the main rotor, and with a small positive pitch angle, the tail rotor doesn't produce enough thrust to overcome the torque effect of the main rotor during cruising flight. Therefore, if the right pedal is displaced forward of neutral during cruising flight, the tail rotor thrust will not overcome the torque effect, and the nose will yaw to the right.

The tail rotor will usually have a medium, positive pitch angle with the pedals in the neutral position. In medium positive pitch, the tail rotor thrust approximately equals the torque of the main rotor during cruising flight, so the helicopter is rigged to maintain a constant heading in level cruise flight.

With the left pedal in forward position, the tail rotor is in a high positive pitch position. In a high positive pitch position, tail rotor thrust exceeds that needed to overcome torque effect during cruising flight, so the helicopter's nose will yaw to the left.

This explanation is based on cruising power and airspeed. Since the amount of torque is dependent on the amount of engine power being supplied to the main rotor, the relative position of the pedals required to counteract torque will depend on the amount of power being used at any time. In general, the less power being used, the greater the forward displacement of the right pedal; the greater the power being used, the greater the forward displacement of the left pedal.

The maximum, positive pitch angle of the tail rotor is generally greater than the maximum negative pitch angle available. This is because the primary purpose of the tail rotor

Hughes 500 series antitorque (rotor) system.

Cyclic pitch control between pilot's legs normally, and manipulated with pilot's right hand.

is to counteract the torque of the main rotor. The capability for tail rotors to produce thrust to the left (negative pitch angle) is necessary, because during autorotation, the drag of the transmission tends to yaw the nose to the left in the same direction that the main rotor is turning.

Cyclic Pitch Control

As discussed earlier, the at rest lift/thrust force is always perpendicular to the tip-path plane of the main rotor. When the tip-path plane is tilted away from the horizontal, the lift/thrust force is divided into two components: horizontal thrust and vertical lift. The purpose of the cyclic pitch control (cyclic) is to tilt the tip-path plane in the direction that horizontal movement is desired. The thrust component then pulls the helicopter in the direction of rotor tilt. The cyclic control has no effect on the magnitude of the total lift/thrust force, but merely changes the direction of this force, thus controlling the attitude and airspeed of the ship.

It sounds simple, because it is simple. The rotor disc tilts in the direction that pressure is applied to the cyclic. The rotor

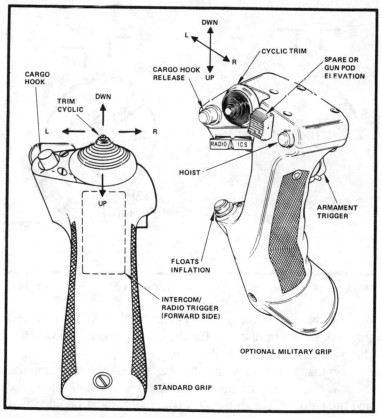

Cyclics range from a simple stick to this integrated cyclic grip.

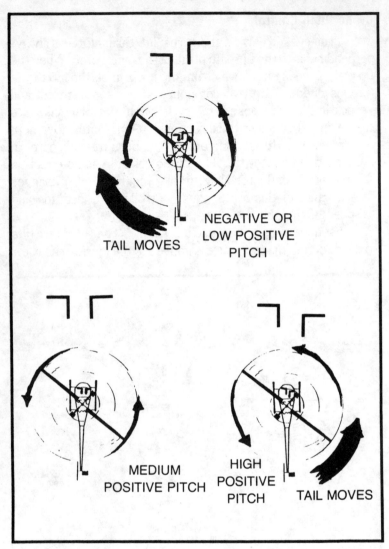

NEGATIVE OR LOW POSITIVE PITCH

TAIL MOVES

MEDIUM POSITIVE PITCH

HIGH POSITIVE PITCH

TAIL MOVES

Rudder pedal position in relation to tail rotor pitch and thrust, during cruise flight.

disc follows the input on the cyclic. If the cyclic is moved forward, the rotor disc tilts forward; if the cyclic is moved aft, the rotor disc tilts aft, and so on.

So that the rotor disc will always tilt in the direction the cyclic is displaced, the mechanical linkage between the cyclic and the rotor, through the "swash plate," must be such that the maximum downward deflection of the blades is reached in

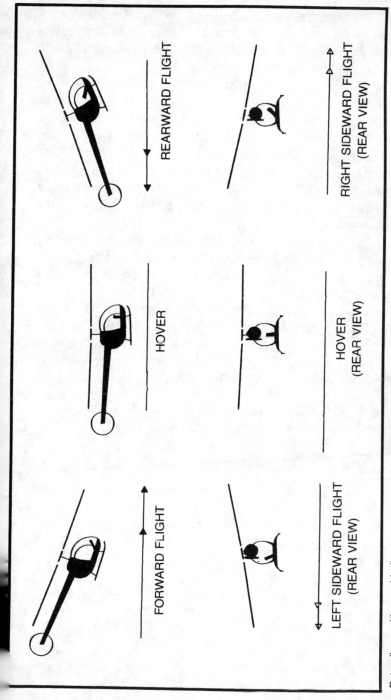

Rotor disc position and helicopter movement in relation to cyclic position.

65

the direction the stick is displaced; and maximum upward deflection is reached in the opposite direction. Otherwise, you would have a difficult job of relating the direction of cyclic displacement to the rotor disc tilt.

Remember, it was earlier stated about the 90 degrees between input and reaction. It also applies in this instance. Through mechanical linkage, which decreases the pitch angle of the rotor blades 90 degrees before they reach the direction of displacement of the cyclic; and increases the pitch angle of the rotor blades 90 degrees after they pass the direction of displacement of the cyclic stick. Any increase in pitch angle increases the angle of attack; any decrease in pitch angle decreases the angle of attack.

As an example, as the cyclic stick is displaced forward, the angle of attack is decreased as the rotor blades pass the 90 degree position to the pilot's right and increases as the blades pass the 90 degree position to the pilot's left. Because of gyroscopic precession, maximum downward deflection of the rotor blades is forward, and maximum upward deflection is aft, causing the rotor disc to tilt forward in the same direction as cyclic displacement. A similar analysis could be made for any direction of displacement of the cyclic.

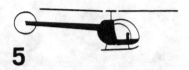

5

SYSTEMS AND COMPONENTS

In preceding chapters, we've discussed basic aerodynamics, aerodynamics of flight and flight controls. In this chapter, some of the other systems, components and their functions will be discussed to help familiarize you with the overall craft.

Transmission System

The transmission does just what its name implies: It transmits engine power to the main rotor, tail rotor, generator and other accessories. In a sense, it's what makes the machine go.

The engine must operate at a relatively high speed, while the main rotor turns at a much lower rpm. This speed reduction is accomplished through reduction gears in the transmission system.

A helicopter's reduction system is generally somewhere between 6:1-9:1. This simply means that, depending on which ratio is used, for every 6-9 engine rpm, the blades rotate one time. Using these ratios, then, it's easy to see that if the engine turns at 2700 rpm, for instance, the main rotor would turn up at 450 rpm at a 6:1 ratio and 300 rpm at a 9:1 reduction.

When the rotor tachometer needle and the engine tachometer needle are superimposed over each other in the same instrument unit, the ratio of the engine rpm to the rotor

Hughes 300 model power assembly.

rpm is the same as the gear reduction ratio. This single instrument unit, housing both engine and rotor rpm, makes for simple pilot readout and does away with superfluous instrument clutter.

Clutch

It's standard practice in the conventional, fixed-wing airplane to have the engine and the propeller permanently connected. Since the prop serves as a flywheel, there's no reason for the propeller to be at a standstill while the engine is running. With the helicopter, however, there's a different relationship between the engine and the rotor.

Since the helicopter's rotor weighs so much more than the prop of an airplane, it's necessary to have the rotor disconnect from the engine during start and warmup to relieve the load. It is, therefore, necessary to have a clutch between the engine and the rotor.

The clutch assembly allows the engine to be started and gradually assume the load of driving the heavy rotor system. The clutch doesn't necessarily provide disengagement of the engine from the rotor system for autorotation. This is accomplished through another device.

There are two basic clutch types: centrifugal and friction (belt). These two types of clutch operate differently but for the same purpose.

With the centrifugal clutch, contact between the inner and outer parts is made by spring-loaded clutch shoes. The inner portion of the clutch, the shoes, is rotated by the engine. The outer portion of the clutch, the drum, is connected to the main rotor through the transmission.

At low engine speeds, the clutch shoes are held out of contact with the clutch drum by the springs. As the engine speeds up, centrifugal force throws the clutch shoes outward until they contact the clutch drum. Motion is thus transmitted from the engine drive shaft to the input drive shaft of the transmission. The rotor starts to turn, slowly at first, but increases speed as friction develops sufficiently to drive the drum at engine rpm.

As the clutch becomes fully engaged, the rotor system is driven at the equivalent of engine rpm, and the rotor tachometer needle and engine tachometer needle join or "marry;" one needle superimposed over the other.

The rotor rpm equivalent to the engine rpm depends upon the gear reduction ratio between the engine and rotor system for that particular helicopter.

The friction or belt-driven system clutch is manually engaged by the pilot through a lever in the cockpit. Power from the engine drive shaft is transmitted to the transmission drive shaft by a series of friction discs or belts. With this type

Main rotor pitch links and pitch horn on R22. 1. Pitch link; 2. pitch horn; 3. teetering hinge, and 4. hub.

clutch, it's possible to start the engine and warm it up without engaging the rotors.

Freewheeling Unit

As previously discussed, the rotor system slowly engages and keeps up with engine rpm. When the engine slows below the equivalent of rotor rpm or stops altogether, the freewheeling unit-coupling automatically disconnects the rotor system from the engine. When the engine is disconnected from the rotor system through the automatic action of the freewheeling coupling, the transmission continues to rotate with the main rotor, thereby enabling the tail rotor to continue turning at its normal rate. This is important, because it allows the pilot to maintain directional control during autorotation.

Swash Plate Assembly

The swash plate consists of two primary elements through which the rotor mast passes: Stationary Star and Rotating Star.

The stationary star is a disc, linked to the cyclic pitch control. The disc is capable of tilting in any direction, but it doesn't rotate as the rotor turns. This non-rotating disc is attached by a bearing surface to a second disc, the rotating star, which turns with the rotor and is mechanically linked to the rotor blade pitch horns.

The rotor blade pitch horns are placed approximately 90 degrees ahead of, or behind the blade on which they control the pitch change. If this were not done, gyroscopic precession would cause the movement of the craft to be 90 degrees out of phase with the movement of the cyclic pitch stick. As an example, if the cyclic stick were moved to the right, the helicopter would move forward; if it were moved forward, the helicopter would move to the left, and so on, 90 degrees out of phase. Whether the pitch horns are ahead or behind, the blade will depend on the mechanical linkage arrangement between the cyclic stick, swash plate and pitch horns.

If pitch horns are 90 degrees ahead of the blade, pitch decrease of the blades take place as the horns pass the direc-

Top view rotorhead Hughes 500 series shows blade fairings.

tion the cyclic stick is displaced. Blade pitch increase takes place as the horns pass the direction opposite to the displacement of the stick. If the horns are 90 degrees behind the blades, pitch decrease will take place as the horns pass the direction opposite to the displacement of the cyclic. Blade pitch increase takes place as the horns pass the direction of displacement.

In either case, however, blade pitch decrease takes place 90 degrees ahead of cyclic stick position, and blade pitch increase takes place 90 degrees after passing the cyclic stick position. Thus, maximum downward deflection of the rotor blades occurs in the same direction as cyclic stick displacement, and maximum upward deflection occurs in the opposite direction.

In other words, when the cyclic stick is displaced forward, the swash plate's non-rotating disc tilts forward, and the swash plate's rotating disc follows this forward tilt. Since the mechanical linkage from the rotating disc to the rotor blades' pitch horns is 90 degrees ahead or behind the cyclic pitch change, the pitch angle is decreased as the rotor blades pass 90 degrees to the pilot's right and increased as the rotor blades pass 90 degrees to the pilot's left. Because of gyroscopic precession, maximum blade deflection occurs 90 degrees later in the cycle of motion. Thus, maximum downward deflection is forward; in the same direciton as cyclic stick placement, and maximum upward deflection is aft; causing the rotor disc to tilt forward in the same direction as cyclic stick placement.

Main Rotor System

Fully articulated rotor systems generally consist of three or more rotor blades. In a fully articulated rotor system, each rotor blade is attached to the rotor hub by a horizontal hinge, called the "flapping hinge," which permits the blades to flap up or down. Each blade can move up or down independently of the others. The flapping hinge can be located at varying distances from the rotor hub, and there can be more than one. The position is chosen by each manufacturer, primarily with regard to stability and control.

Scorpion Too antitorque rotor drive belt.

Each rotor blade is also attached to the hub by a vertical hinge, called a "drag" or lag hinge, which permits each blade, independently of the others, to move back and forth in the plane of the rotor disc. This forward and backward movement is called dragging, lead-drag or hunting. The location of this hinge is chosen with primary regard to controlling vibration. Dampers are normally associated with the fully articulated system to prevent excessive motion about the drag hinge.

Also, the blades can be "feathered" or rotated about their spanwise axis. Feathering means the automatic and periodic changing of the pitch angle of the rotor blades.

Semirigid rotor system's rotor blades are rigidly interconnected to the hub, but the hub is free to tilt and rock with respect to the rotor shaft. In this system, only two-bladed rotors are used. The rotor flaps as a unit, that is, as one blades flaps up, the other blade automatically flaps down an equal amount.

The hinge which permits the flapping or seesaw effect is called a "teetering" hinge. The rocking hinge that allows this teetering motion is perpendicular to the teetering hinge and parallel to the rotor blades. This hinge allows the head to rock in response to the tilting of the swash plate by the cyclic pitch control, thus changing the pitch angle an equal amount on each blade; decreasing it on one and increasing it on the other.

The rotor blades of a semirigid rotor system may or may not require drag hinges, depending on whether the system is "underslung." In an underslung system, the rotor blades lie in a plane below the plane containing the rotor hub pivot point. Because of coning, normal rotor operating rpm will place the center of mass of the rotor blades in approximately the same plane as the rotor hub pivot point. Consequently, the distance of the center of mass from the axis of rotation varies very little. Therefore, an underslung system is subject to coriolis effect, but to a lesser degree than a system that's not underslung. Drag hinges aren't needed, since the hunting action can be absorbed through blade bending.

Collective pitch control changes the pitch of each blade simultaneously and an equal amount, either increasing the pitch of both or decreasing the pitch of both.

In rigid rotor systems, the blades and mast are rigid with respect to each other. The blades can't flap or drag, but they can be feathered.

Because of their inflexibility, the rigid rotor system isn't one of the most popular. It's only been in the past few years that a great deal of progress has been made with their applications.

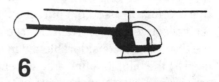

6

FLIGHT MANEUVERS: THE TAKEOFF

It should be obvious that the variable factors of wind, temperature, humidity, gross weight and structural differences of various helicopter models greatly affect their operation. Even when flying the same model, two flights are seldom exactly alike. Because of this variation, wind and density altitude, and flight characteristics must be adjusted accordingly.

It would be impossible, then, for a handbook to outline a specific nose attitude or power setting (these will be discussed in another chapter). The following maneuvers are accomplished at what can only be described as a normal day with the helicopter responding normally.

Although helicopter controls were discussed in an earlier chapter, a summary of their effects from the pilot's point of view will be helpful in understanding the various flying maneuvers presented in following chapters.

The "cyclic" or cyclic pitch control, tilts the rotor disc in the same direction as the cyclic is moved, and the helicopter moves in that direction. Thus, a backward displacement of the cyclic results in a nose-up tendency, followed by rearward flight; a sideward displacement results in a sideways tilt and sideways flight, etc. In normal, cruise flight, the cyclic is used much as is the control column or "joy stick" in a fixed-wing airplane. The main difference being, if a rearward displacement were held for long, the craft would, after climbing and losing airspeed, tend to fly backwards.

The "collective" or collective pitch control, in hovering flight is used to stabilize the helicopter's vertical movement. Raise the collective and the helicopter climbs; lower it and the craft descends. The primary effect of the collective is to control the engine's power; manifold pressure. If constant rotor rpm is maintained, the power will vary with the collective's position. Varying rpm is another collective function.

The twist-grip "throttle" control on the end of the collective is primarily used to control engine rpm. As stated above, the collective, to a certain degree, controls engine rpm, but the throttle is a considerable aid in maintaining rpm. It's often used by the pilot as a fine adjustment and can be used to obtain any desired rpm over the normal engine rpm range. Its second function is an alteration in power, and a small change can often result in a considerable change in boost.

The antitorque (rudder) pedals are used in powered flight to balance torque and to turn the craft in the yawing plane. As in an airplane, application of left rudder tends to yaw or turn the nose of the helicopter to the left and vice versa. In gliding flight (autorotation), rudder control is still available to maintain balanced flight or to turn.

The initial complexity of control coordination will be appreciated when it is stated that as one control is moved the other controls must generally be moved as well, especially in hovering maneuvers. As an example, consider the case of a helicopter about to move forward from a hover.

The stick is eased forward. The aircraft starts to move forward, but, because of the loss of the ground bubble, it also begins to sink. Up collective is applied to maintain the desired height, the throttle position must be altered to maintain rpm, which in turn changes torque. This means that the rudder pedal position must also be altered to maintain the desired heading. The change in rudder position affects the sideways drifting tendency, rpm and so on. When any forward speed builds up, the rotor disc will tend to flap backwards and more forward cyclic must be applied.

However, the control that consistently causes the most difficulty is the throttle. It's this twist-grip power control that

Bell Helicopter Textron's Model 222, the first U.S.-built commercial mid-size twin turbine helicopter.

has a direct or indirect action-reaction on all other controls. Increase or decrease power, and rudder, stick and collective adjustments must be made also.

Vertical Takeoff to a Hover

A vertical takeoff is a maneuver in which the helicopter is raised vertically from a spot on the ground to the normal hovering altitude, with a minimum of lateral and/or fore and aft movement.

To begin with, have the chopper headed into the wind. This is done to lessen complications when simplicity is the student's word. As your proficiency rises, this maneuver will be less of a problem. Place cyclic in a "neutral" position, and make sure the collective is in the full "down" position.

Make sure the craft is running in a warmed-up condition. You should now be sitting comfortably, with your feet on the pedals, right hand on the cyclic and left hand gripping the throttle control of the collective.

Open the throttle smoothly to acquire and maintain proper operating rpm. Raise the collective in a smooth, continuous movement, coordinating the throttle to maintain proper rpm. As the collective is increased and the craft becomes light on its skids (wheels or floats), torque will tend to cause the nose to swing to the right, unless you add a sufficient amount of left pedal pressure to maintain a constant heading.

As the helicopter becomes light on its skids, make the necessary control adjustments: cyclic corrections to ensure a level attitude on becoming airborne; pedal corrections to maintain heading; and collective corrections to ensure continuous vertical ascent to the desired hovering altitude.

When the desired hovering altitude has been reached, adjust throttle and collective as required to maintain rpm and altitude. Coordinate pedal changes with throttle and collective adjustments to maintain heading. Use the cyclic as necessary to maintain a constant position over the spot. Remember, the collective controls altitude, while the cyclic controls attitude and position.

Now, in a relatively stable position, check things out; engine and control operation, manifold pressure to hold hover,

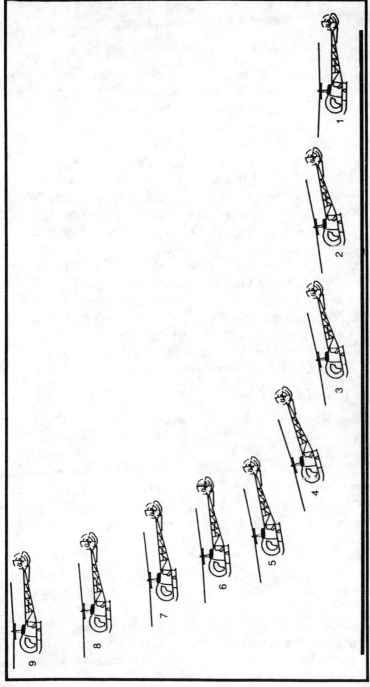

Normal takeoff from a hover. 1. Begin from normal hovering altitude. 2-4. Ease cyclic forward; increase collective to prevent settling. 5-7. Accelerate to normal climb speed, then raise nose to climbing attitude. 8-9. Make climb at normal climb airspeed.

and cyclic stick position. Cyclic position will vary with the amount and distribution of load and wind speed.

Errors

1. Failure to maintain level attitude upon becoming airborne. Any number of items can cause this, but to a greater degree it's caused by not anticipating the actions and reactions of elements present. Not to worry, as this will come with practice.
2. Pulling through on the collective after becoming airborne, causing the helicopter to gain too much altitude too quickly. This, in turn, will necessitate a comparatively large throttle and collective change, which will, in turn, produce even a greater degree of a problem, if not anticipated.
3. Overcontrolling the rudders, which not only changes the heading of the helicopter but also changes rpm, necessitating a constant throttle adjustment.
4. Reducing throttle too rapidly in situations where proper rpm has been exceeded, which usually means violent changes of heading to the left and loss of lift, resulting in loss of altitude.

Normal Takeoff From Hover

Takeoff from a hover is an orderly transition to forward flight and is executed to increase altitude safely and expediously.

After lifting the helicopter to a normal hover, check the engine and control operations. Note the cyclic stick position to determine if the copter is loaded properly. Check the manifold pressure required to hover to determine the amount of excess power available.

Make a 360 degree spot turn for clearing the area all around. Slowly, yet smoothly, ease the cyclic forward. Apply just enough forward cyclic to start the craft moving forward over the ground.

As the machine starts to move forward, increase collective as necessary to prevent settling when it departs ground effect. Adjust throttle to maintain rpm lost because of collective increase. The increase in power will, in turn, require an increase in left pedal to stay on heading. Keep a straight takeoff path throughout the maneuver, if necessary, picking two reference points.

As you accelerate to effective translational lift, and the helicopter begins to climb, the nose will begin to pitch up due to increased lift. Compensate for this nose-up tendency by adjusting collective to normal climb power, and apply enough forward cyclic to overcome nose pitching. Hold an altitude that will allow a smooth acceleration toward climbing airspeed and a commensurate gain in altitude so that the takeoff profile will not take you through any of the cross-hatched area or the height/velocity chart for that particular helicopter (see helicopter flight manual chapter). As airspeed increases, the streamlining of the fuselage will reduce engine torque effect, requiring a gradual reduction of left pedal pressure.

As the chopper continues to climb and airspeed approaches normal climb speed, apply rear cyclic pressure to raise the nose smoothly to the normal climb attitude. The normal climb attitude is approximately the attitude of the machine when it's sitting on level ground.

Errors

1. Failure to use sufficient collective to prevent settling between the time the helicopter leaves ground effect to when it picks up translational lift.
2. Adding power too rapidly at the beginning of the transition from hovering to forward flight without forward cyclic compensation, thus causing the craft to gain excessive altitude before acquiring airspeed.
3. Assuming an extreme nose-down attitude near the ground in the transition from hovering to forward flight.
4. Failure to maintain a straight flight track over the ground.
5. Failure to keep proper airspeed during the climb.
6. Failure to adjust the throttle to maintain proper rpm.

Note: If, for some reason, a takeoff can't be made into the wind, and a crosswind takeoff must be made, fly the helicopter in a slip during the early stages of the maneuver. To do this, the cyclic is held into the wind to maintain the selected ground track for takeoff, while the heading is kept straight along the takeoff path with rudder. Thus, the ground track and the fuselage are aligned with each other. In other words, the rotor is tilted into the wind to allow the aircraft to slip into the wind as much as the wind is pushing the copter sideways, effectively cancelling the wind's affect. To prevent the nose from turning in the direction of rotor tilt, you'll have to increase pedal pressure on the side opposite the rotor tilt. The stronger the crosswind, the greater the amount of rotor tilt and rudder pressure.

After gaining approximately 50 feet of altitude, establish a heading into the wind (crab), by coordinating a turn into the wind to maintain the desired ground track. The stronger the crosswind component, the more the chopper will have to be turned into the wind to maintain desired ground track. Once straight-and-level flight on the desired heading is reached, continue to use the rudders as necessary to compensate for torque to keep the craft in trim. Otherwise, there will be no other rudder correction for the wind in the crab attitude.

Running Takeoff

The running takeoff is used when conditions of load and/or density altitude prevent a sustained hover at normal hovering altitude. It's often referred to as a high-altitude takeoff. With insufficient power to hover, at least momentarily or at a very low altitude, a running takeoff is not advisable. No takeoff should be attempted if the helicopter can't be lifted off the ground momentarily at full power. There are two main reasons why this is always so:

1. If the helicopter can't hover, its performance is unpredictable.
2. If the helicopter can't be raised off the ground at all, sufficient power might not be available for a safe running takeoff.

A safe running takeoff can be accomplished only if ground area of sufficient length and smoothness is available and if no barriers exist in the flight path to interfere with a shallow climb.

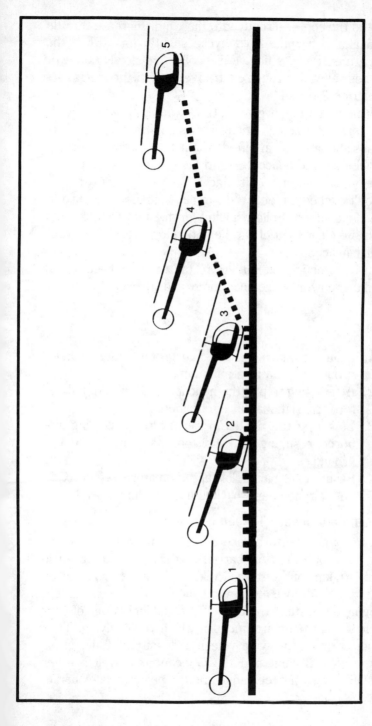

Running takeoff. 1-2 Adjust power for takeoff, usually one to two inches less than hovering power. Move the cyclic slightly forward of hovering position, for a gradual acceleration. 3. After translational lift is reached, ease cyclic rearward slightly to lift off. 4. Maintain 10-feet AGL or less until climb airspeed is reached, adjust to climb attitude. 5. Once climb airspeed is reached, adjust to climb attitude.

Head the copter directly into the wind. Increase throttle to obtain takeoff rpm. Hold cyclic slightly forward of the hovering "neutral" position. Raise collective slowly to one or two inches below that required to hover or until the craft starts to accelerate forward.

Maintain a straight ground track with both lateral cyclic and rudders for heading until a climb is established. As effective translational lift is attained, slight back pressure on the cyclic will take the helicopter into flight smoothly, in a level attitude, with little or no pitching.

Don't exceed 10-feet AGL, to allow airspeed to build to normal climb speed. Follow a climb profile that will take you through the clear area of the height/velocity curve for your particular helicopter.

During practice maneuvers, climb to 50-feet AGL, and then adjust power to normal climb and attitude to normal climb.

Errors

1. Failure to align heading and ground track to keep ground friction to a minimum.
2. Attempting to pull the helicopter off the ground before translational lift is obtained.
3. Lowering the nose too much after becoming airborne, resulting in the helicopter settling back to the ground.
4. Failure to remain below approximately 10-feet AGL, until airspeed approaches normal climb speed.

Maximum Performance Takeoff

A maximum performance takeoff is used to climb at a steep angle in order to clear barriers in the flight path. It can be used when taking off from small fields which are surrounded by high obstacles. Before attempting such a maneuver, though, thoroughly understand the capabilities and limitations of your equipment and the environment in which you're flying. Take into consideration the wind velocity, density altitude, gross weight of your machine and its CG location, as well as other factors affecting your technique and the performance characteristics of your craft.

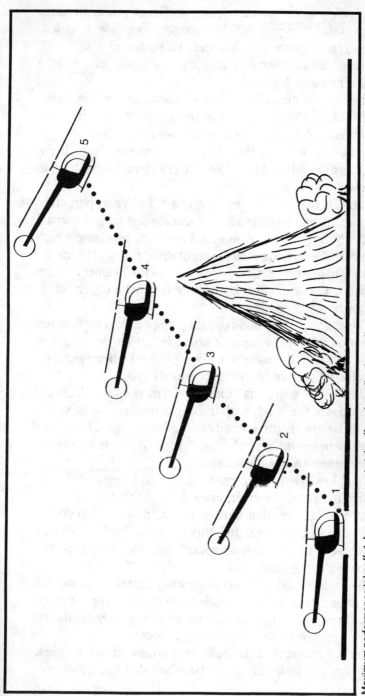

Maximum performance takeoff. 1. Increase: rpm to takeoff mode; collective until copter is light on skids. 2. Increase collective to maximum possible, without the loss of rpm. Add full throttle, as helicopter becomes airborne in the forward climbing attitude. 3-4. Maintain full power, without the loss of rpm. 5. Lower the nose to normal climb attitude to pick up climb speed, then adjust power to continue with normal climb.

To safely make such a takeoff, sufficient power to hover must be available to prevent the chopper from sinking back to the ground after becoming airborne. This maneuver will result in a steep climb, affording maximum altitude gain over a minimum distance forward.

The angle of climb for this type takeoff depends on existing conditions. The more critical these conditions—high density altitude, calm wind, etc.—the shallower the angle of climb. Use extreme caution in making a steep climb. If the airspeed is allowed to get too low, the craft could settle back to the ground.

Consult the height/velocity chart for your particular helicopter. An engine failure at low altitude and airspeed would place the helicopter in a dangerous position, requiring a high degree of skill in making a safe autorotative landing. It could be necessary to operate in the shaded area of the height/velocity chart during the beginning of this maneuver, when operating in a light or no-wind condition.

The angle of climb and resulting airspeed will be dictated by the proximity and height of obstacles to be cleared. You must be aware of the calculated risk involved when operating in the shaded area of the height/velocity chart.

The first step in a maximum performance takeoff should be to head into the wind, with the cyclic placed in what would normally be the neutral position for hovering. Check this position by hovering the helicopter momentarily prior to preparing to execute the maneuver.

Establish the proper rpm setting and apply sufficient collective to lighten the craft on its skids. Apply the maximum amount of collective that can be obtained without reducing rpm. Simultaneously add full throttle, and apply sufficient forward cyclic to establish a forward climbing attitude as the craft leaves the ground.

Use rudder pedals as necessary to maintain heading. Do not sacrifice rpm in order to obtain increased pitch on the rotor blades. If rpm starts to decrease under a full power condition, it can be regained only by reducing collective.

Use full power until the helicopter is clear of all obstacles, then a normal climb may be established and the power reduced.

Errors

1. Too much forward cyclic initially, allowed the nose to go down too far.
2. Failure to maintain maximum permissable rpm.
3. Movement of controls too abrupt.

7

FLIGHT MANEUVERS: THE HOVER

To a ground observer or even a passenger, hovering may look simple, because the pilot is apparently doing little and the helicopter is virtually motionless above the ground. However, since you've tried your hand at this maneuver or are about to, you should know that this isn't completely true: The pilot is maintaining position with the cyclic, keeping a fixed height with the collective, retaining the desired heading with rudder pedals and correcting any changes or rpm with the throttle.

The maneuver requires a high degree of concentration on your part as the pilot. Control corrections should be pressure rather than abrupt movements: A constant pressure on the desired rudder pedal will result in a smooth turn, while pronounced movements will tend to jerk the nose around causing other complications.

Smoothness on the controls can be accomplished by immediately making all corrections and not waiting out helicopter movement. Stopping and stabilizing the machine at a hover requires a number of small, pressure corrections to avoid overcontrolling. With practice, it becomes easier to anticipate the helicopter's movements.

The attitude of the copter determines its movements over the ground. While the attitude required to hover varies with the wind conditions and center of gravity (CG) locations, there's a particular attitude which can be found by experimentation that will keep the craft hovering over a selected point. After this attitude has been discovered, deviations can be easily noted and the necessary corrections made, often before the helicopter actually starts to move. This is really flying by the seat of your pants.

Coordination of all controls can't be overemphasized. Any change on one control will almost always require a correction on one or more of the other controls. Hovering can be accomplished in a precise manner by keeping in mind the small, smooth and coordinated control responses.

Errors

1. Tenseness which often causes late reactions to helicopter movements, or overreaction resulting in overcorrecting.
2. Failure to allow for lag in cyclic and collective which also leads to overcontrolling.
3. Confusing altitude changes for attitude changes, resulting in the use of improper cockpit controls.
4. Hovering too high; out of ground effect.
5. Hovering too low, resulting in occasional touchdown.

Hovering Turn

The hovering turn is a maneuver performed at hovering altitude. The nose of the helicopter is rotated either left or right, while maintaining position over a reference point on the ground. It requires the coordination of all flight controls and demands precision movement near the ground.

In calm air, a hovering turn is simple, but in a wind condition, the helicopter will be alternately moving forward, sideward, backward, sideward and then forward again, while turning on its axis. Also, the weathervaning stability of the copter is such that the initial turn out of the wind will be resisted, and on passing the downwind position the rate of turn will tend to speed up. Again, due to the wind, a fair amount of rudder will be necessary to make and control the turn, and this will have a considerable effect on the rpm.

Hovering in groun cushion during agricultural (aerial spraying/dusting) training.

Keeping the above factors in mind, the turn is accomplished with a feel for the helicopter's movements and by staying on top of the situation.

Start the maneuver from a normal hovering altitude, headed into the wind. Begin by applying rudder pressure smoothly in the direction you desire to turn.

When the nose begins to turn, and throughout the remainder of the turn, use cyclic to maintain position over the ground reference point. Use rudder pedals to maintain slow, constant rate of turn. Collective, along with the throttle, is used to maintain a constant altitude and rpm.

As the 180-degree position is approached in the turn, anticipate the use of a small amount of opposite rudder, as the tail of the helicopter swings from a position into the wind to one downwind. The machine will have a tendency to whip or increase its rate of turn as a result of the weathervaning tendency of the tail. Remember, the higher the wind, the greater will be this whipping action.

As you approach the desired heading for turn completion, apply opposite pedal pressure, as necessary to stop the turn on this heading.

During the hovering turn to the left, the rpm will decrease if power isn't reduced slightly. This is due to the amount of engine power that's being absorbed by the tail rotor, which is dependent upon the pitch angle at which the tail rotor blades are operating. Avoid making large corrections in rpm while turning, since the throttle adjustment will result in erratic nose movements due to torque changes.

Always make the first hovering turn to the left to determine the amount of left pedal available. If a 90-degree turn to the left can't be made, or if an unusual amount of pedal is required to complete a 45-degree hovering turn to the left, don't attempt a turn to the right, since sufficient left pedal might not be available to prevent an uncontrolled turn. Hover power requires a large amount of left pedal to maintain heading. Once the turn has started, sufficient left pedal in excess of this amount must be available to prevent an uncontrolled turn to the right.

Hovering turns should be avoided in winds strong enough to preclude sufficient back cyclic control to maintain the

Hughes 500 in hover.

helicopter on the selected ground reference point when headed downwind. Check the craft's flight manual for the manufacturer's recommendations on this limit.

Errors

1. Failure to maintain a slow, constant rate of turn.
2. Failure to maintain position over the reference point.
3. Failure to keep the rpm within normal operating ranges.
4. Failure to make the first turn to the left.
5. Failure to maintain a constant altitude.
6. Failure to apply rudder smoothly and cautiously.

Hovering Forward Flight

This maneuver is not so much a hover as it is keeping the helicopter from getting away from you, in what could be labelled as slow flight near the ground. Forward, hovering flight can generally be used to move the chopper to a specific area, unless strong winds prohibit crosswind or downwind hovering. A hovering turn is utilized to head the helicopter in the direction of the desired area, then forward flight at a slow speed is used to move to that area. During this maneuver, a constant, slow groundspeed, altitude and heading should be maintained. Care should be taken so as not to leave the ground-cushion effect.

Pick two reference points in front of and in line with the helicopter. These points can be any object that can be clearly seen. Keep them in line throughout the maneuver, since they guarantee a straight ground track while you're on the move.

Initiate the maneuver from a normal, hovering altitude by applying slight, forward pressure on the cyclic; only enough at first to start the helicopter moving.

As the craft begins to move, return the cyclic toward the neutral position to keep the groundspeed at a slow rate; no faster than normal walking pace. Ground effect will be retained at this speed, thus reducing the need for power and pedal corrections.

Keep a constant check on your reference points. Control groundspeed with the cyclic, a steady heading with the pedals,

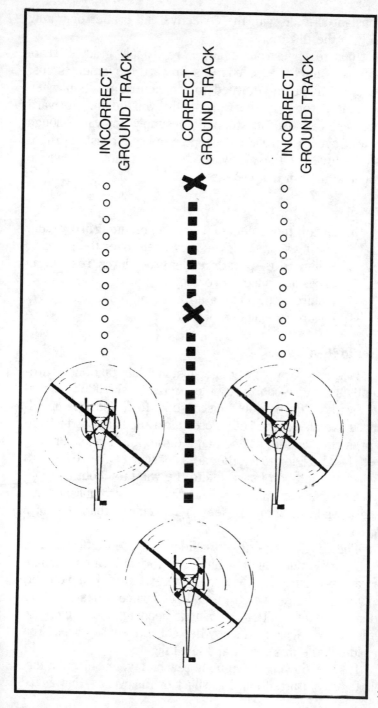

INCORRECT
GROUND TRACK

CORRECT
GROUND TRACK

INCORRECT
GROUND TRACK

Use reference points to hold a proper ground track while in forward or rearward hovering flight.

a constant altitude with the collective and proper operating rpm with the throttle.

Upon reaching your desired area, apply gradual, rearward cyclic until the helicopter's forward movement stops. The cyclic must be returned to the neutral position when movement stops or rearward flight will begin. Forward movement can also be stopped by simply applying enough rearwind cyclic to level the helicopter and let it coast or drift to a stop. However the rearward cyclic pressure will require more lead time in this instance.

Errors

1. Erratic movement of the cyclic, resulting in overcontrolling and an uneven movement over the ground.
2. Failure to use proper rudder procedures, resulting in excessive nose movement.
3. Failure to maintain a hovering altitude.
4. Failure to maintain proper rpm.

Hover to Hover

This is a form of a longer-distance air taxi and is frequently used as a coordination exercise. It shouldn't be confused with a "quick-stop" (discussed later), which is an advanced exercise carried out more quickly and one in which the rotor is autorotating at one stage during the maneuver.

The transition to another area consists of a hover, then a gradual acceleration forward into the wind to about 60 mph, then a gradual return to a hover again. It's accomplished at a fixed altitude of about 20-feet AGL; higher than that of a normal hover.

The first part of the transition isn't too difficult. The technique is much like beginning a forward climb. Initiate forward pressure on the cyclic to get forward movement; slight up collective when ground resonance is lost, to hold altitude; rudder position to maintain heading; and an increase in throttle to regain rpm lost when collective was raised. You should now be in straight and level flight.

It's the slowing down upon reaching your objective that calls for careful attention. Ease back on the cyclic—this should be a very small movement—accompanied, or even preceded, by a downward movement on the collective. A corresponding change of a rudder pedal position is needed to maintain heading and a change of throttle to retain correct rpm.

When slowing down, translational lift will be lost. Power must again be increased, with a corresponding balancing of torque and rpm.

Errors

1. Failure to maintain altitude when entering translational lift.
2. Losing or gaining rpm.
3. Uncoordination on controls.
4. Failure to maintain altitude when leaving translational lift.
5. Moving too fast or slow between the two areas.

Hovering Sideward Flight

It could become necessary to move a helicopter to a specific area or position, when conditions make it impossible to use forward flight. In such a case, sideward flight may be a possible solution. It's also an excellent coordination maneuver. The primary objective is to maintain a constant groundspeed, altitude and heading.

Begin the maneuver by picking two reference points in a line running in the direction sideward flight is to be made. These two points will help you maintain proper ground tracking. Keep these reference points in line throughout the maneuver.

Initiate hovering sideward flight from a normal hovering altitude by applying sideward pressure on the cyclic in the direction you want to move.

As movement begins, return the cyclic toward the neutral position, but not all the way to neutral. Adjust to keep a slow groundspeed. Remember, ground effect will be retained, thus reducing the need for power or rudder corrections, at the speed of a walking person.

During the complete maneuver, maintain a constant groundspeed and ground track with the cyclic; a constant heading perpendicular to the proposed ground track with the rudder, a constant altitude with the collective; and proper operating rpm with the throttle.

Apply cyclic pressure in the opposite direction to that of the helicopter's movement and hold until the craft comes almost to a stop. As the motion ceases, the cyclic must be returned to the neutral position to prevent movement in the other direction. Sideward movement also can be stopped by simply applying enough opposite cyclic pressure to only level the helicopter. It will then drift to a stop.

Errors

1. Movement of the cyclic is erratic, resulting in over-control and uneven movement over the ground.
2. Failure to use proper rudder control, resulting in excessive nose movement.
3. Failure to maintain a hovering altitude.
4. Failure to maintain proper rpm.
5. Failure to make clearing turns prior to starting the maneuver.

Hovering Rearward Flight

This maneuver may be necessary to move the helicopter to a specific area when forward or sideward flight can't be used, as in backing into a parking pad surrounded by other craft.

As with previous maneuvers, pick out two reference points in front of, and in line with, the helicopter. These will help you in keeping a proper ground track. Keep these reference points in line throughout the flight.

Start rearwind flight from a normal hovering altitude by applying rearward pressure on the stick. After movement has started, position the cyclic to maintain a slow enough groundspeed that ground effect is maintained.

Keep a constant groundspeed with the cyclic; a constant heading with the rudder; a constant altitude with the collective; and proper rpm with the throttle.

To stop rearward movement, apply forward cyclic and hold until the helicopter almost stops. As the motion does

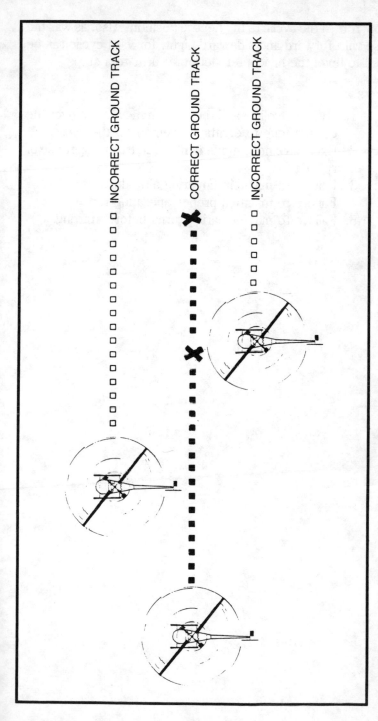

INCORRECT GROUND TRACK

CORRECT GROUND TRACK

INCORRECT GROUND TRACK

Use reference points in maintaining ground tracks. This includes sideward hovering flight, also.

stop, return the cyclic to the neutral position. Also, as was the case with forward and sideward flight, forward cyclic can be used to level the helicopter, letting it drift to a stop.

Errors

1. Overcontrolling and the uneven movement over the ground, due to erratic movement of the cyclic.
2. Excessive nose movements, due to improper use of rudder.
3. Failure to maintain hovering altitude.
4. Failure to maintain proper operating rpm.
5. Failure to make clearing turns before starting.

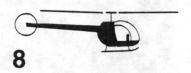

8

FLIGHT MANEUVERS: PRELIMINARIES

Flight in which a constant altitude and heading are mantained is considered "straight and level." The straight and level flight attitude is the attitude of the helicopter necessary to maintain straight and level flight. The level-flight attitude is the attitude of the helicopter necessary to maintain altitude.

Straight-And-Level

Airspeed is determined by the attitude of the helicopter. The attitude of the copter is controlled by the cyclic. Altitude is maintained by the use of the collective and throttle. In order to maintain forward flight, the rotor tip-path plane must be tilted forward to obtain the necessary horizontal thrust component from the main rotor. This will generally result in a nose-low attitude. The lower the nose, the greater the power required to maintain altitude and the higher the resulting airspeed. Conversely, the greater the power used, the lower the nose must be to maintain altitude.

When in straight and level flight, an increase in collective while holding airspeed constant with the cyclic causes the craft to climb; a decrease in collective while holding airspeed constant causes a descent. A correction on the collective requires a coordinated correction on the throttle in order to maintain a constant rpm; a correction on the rudder pedals to maintain

With wheels up for the first time Sikorsky's new advanced technology twin-turbine powered S-76 commercial helicopter maneuvers above the Florida countryside as part of its flight test and FAA certification program.

heading and longitudinal trim. Maintain coordinated flight without either slipping or skidding the helicopter.

To increase airspeed in straight and level flight, increase collective for more power, then gently apply forward pressure on the cyclic to maintain altitude. To decrease airspeed, decrease collective for reduced power, then add back pressure on the cyclic to maintain altitude.

As previously stated, expect a slight delay in control reaction from the time of correction input and the machine's response. The cyclic stick seems to be more prone to this delay than other controls. In making cyclic corrections to control the attitude or airspeed, take care not to overcontrol. Try to anticipate actual helicopter movement. If the nose of the craft rises above the level flight attitude, apply forward cyclic pressure to bring it down. If this correction is held too long, the nose will drop too low. Put in your correction, then wait for the resulting reaction. This is especially important, since the helicopter will continue to change attitude momentarily after you replace the controls to neutral, so anticipate such action

Hughes 500D over Southern California.

by bringing controls back to the neutral position just prior to reaching the desired attitude.

Most helicopters are inherently unstable. If gusts or turbulence cause the nose to drop, it will tend to continue dropping, instead of returning to a straight and level attitude. You must remain alert and fly the helicopter at all times.

Errors

1. Failure to trim properly.
2. Tending to hold pedal pressure and opposite cyclic (cross controlling).
3. Failure to hold best airspeed. Aft cyclic pressure dissipated airspeed without significant climb.
4. Failure to recognize proper control position for maintaining crab-type drift corrections.

Turns

This basic maneuver is used to change the heading of your craft. The aerodynamics of the turn have been discussed in previous chapters; lift components, vertical lift, resultant lift, load factors, etc. They should be thoroughly understood.

Before beginning, clear the area above, below and all around. It should be standard procedure with any maneuver. Enter the turn from straight and level flight. Apply sideward pressure on the cyclic in the direction of desired flight. This should be the only control movement necessary to start the turn.

(*Note:* Don't use the rudders to assist the turn. Use the pedals only to compensate for torque in keeping the helicopter in trim longitudinally.)

The more the cyclic is displaced, the steeper the resulting angle of bank. Therefore, adjust the cyclic to obtain, and maintain, the desired bank angle throughout the maneuver. Increase collective as necessary to maintain altitude, at the same time coordinating throttle to keep desired rpm. Increase left pedal pressure to counteract the added torque effect from the increased power. Depending on the angle of bank, swiftness of entry, power changes, etc., additional forward or rearward cyclic pressure may be necessary: forward pressure to maintain airspeed, or rearward pressure to keep the nose from falling out of the turn.

Recovery from the turn is the same as the entry, except the pressure on the cyclic is applied in reverse. Since the helicopter will continue to turn as long as it's in a bank, start the rollout before reaching the desired heading. Rollout lead-time is normally expressed in degrees, as you will usually be turning to headings. A rule-of-thumb is 5-10 degrees lead-time for angle of banks up to 30 degrees, and 10-15 degrees lead-time for more than 30.

Make climbing and descending turns the same as in straight and level, except that the helicopter will now be in a climbing or descending attitude. Establish entry by merely combining the techniques of both maneuvers; climb or descent entry and turn entry.

In a descending turn, however, an unusual feature occurs, especially noticeable to fixed-wing pilots. The craft can be turning to the left, but a considerable amount of right rudder is necessary to maintain balanced flight due to the low rotor torque.

A "skid" occurs when the helicopter slides sideways away from the center of the turn. It's caused by too much rudder pressure in the direction of the turn or too little in the direction opposite the turn in relation to the amount of collective (power) used. If the helicopter is forced to turn faster, with increased pedal pressure instead of increasing the degree of bank, it will skid sideways away from the center of the turn. Instead of flying in its normal, curved pattern, it will fly a straighter course. You could liken it to an automobile skid. If the steering wheel is the rudder, it's applying too much steering wheel for the speed or for the sharpness of the turn. Like the automobile, the helicopter will skid sideways in regards to the direction of wanted travel.

In a right, climbing turn, if insufficient left pedal is applied to compensate for increased torque effect, a skid will occur. In a left, climbing turn, if excessive left pedal is applied to compensate for increased torque effect, a skid will occur.

In a right, descending turn, if excessive right pedal is applied to compensate for decreased torque, a skid will occur.

In a left, descending turn, if insufficient right pedal is applied to compensate for the decreased torque effect, a skid will occur.

A skid can also occur when flying straight and level, if the nose of the helicopter is allowed to move sideways along the horizon. This condition occurs when improper pedal pressure is held to counteract torque, and the copter is held level with cyclic control.

A "slip" occurs when the helicopter slides sideways toward the center of the turn. It's caused by an insufficient amount of pedal in the direction of turn or too much in the direction opposite the turn, in relationship to the amount of collective or power used. In other words, if improper pedal pressure is held, keeping the nose from following the turn, the craft will slip sideways into (toward the center of) the turn.

In a right climbing turn, if excessive left pedal is applied to compensate for the increased torque effect, a slip occurs. In a left climbing turn, if insufficient left pedal is applied to compensate for the increased torque effect, a slip also occurs.

In a right descending turn, if insufficient right pedal is applied to compensate for the decreased torque effect, a slip will occur. In a left descending turn, if excessive right pedal is applied to compensate for the decreased torque effect, a slip also occurs.

A slip can also occur in straight and level flight if one side of the helicopter is low and the nose is held straight by rudder pressure. This technique is used to correct for a crosswind during an approach and during a takeoff when at a low altitude.

Errors

1. Failure to hold altitude when entering, during and exiting a turn.
2. Using unecessary pedal pressure for turns. Pedal pressure isn't necessary for small helicopters.

Normal Climb

Since entry into a climb from a hover has already been discussed, this section will be limited to climb entry from normal crusing flight.

Begin the maneuver by first applying rearward cyclic pressure to obtain an approximate climb attitude. Simultane-

Bell Helicopter's Model 206L Long Ranger is shown in IFR configuration with vertical fins extending from horizontal stabilizer. The seven-place, light turbine LongRanger features Bell's exclusive Noda-Matic TM suspension system for outstanding ride smoothness.

ously, increase collective until climb manifold pressure is established. Adjust the throttle to obtain, and maintain, climb rpm. An increase in left rudder pressure also is necessary to compensate for the increase in torque. As you approach the desired climb airspeed, further adjustment of the cyclic is necessary to establish and hold this airspeed.

Throughout the maneuver, keep climb attitude and airspeed with cyclic, climb mainfold pressure and rpm with collective and throttle. Longitudinal trim and heading are maintained with the rudder pedals.

To level off from a climb, start adjusting to level flight attitude a few feet prior to reaching the desired altitude. The amount of lead you choose will depend on the rate of climb at the time of leveling-off. The higher the rate of climb, the more the lead. Apply forward cyclic to adjust and keep a level flight attitude which will be slightly nose low. Maintain climb power until airspeed approaches cruise airspeed, then lower the collective to obtain cruising manifold pressure. Make a throttle adjustment to cruising rpm, and you're there. Throughout the level-off, maintain longitudinal trim and a constant heading with the rudders.

Errors

1. Failure to hold proper manifold pressure.
2. Failure to hold proper airspeed.
3. Holding too much or too little left rudder.
4. In level off, decreasing power before lowering the nose to cruising attitude.

Normal Descent

To establish a normal descent from straight and level flight at cruising airspeed, lower collective to obtain proper manifold pressure, adjust throttle to maintain rpm, and increase right rudder pressure to maintain desired heading. If cruising airspeed is the same as, or slightly above descending airspeed, simultaneously apply the necessary cyclic stick pressure to obtain the approximate descending attitude. If cruising airspeed is well above descending airspeed, the level flight attitude may be maintained until the airspeed approaches descending airspeed, at which time the nose should be lowered to the descending attitude.

Throughout the maneuver, maintain descending attitude and airspeed with the cyclic control, descending manifold pressure and rpm with collective and throttle. Control heading with the rudders.

To level-off from the descent, lead the desired altitude by an amount that will depend on the rate of descent at the time of level-off. Remember, the higher the rate of descent, the greater the lead. At this point, increase collective to obtain cruising manifold pressure, adjust throttle to maintain proper rpm, increase left rudder pressure to maintain heading, and adjust cyclic to obtain cruising airspeed and the level flight attitude as the desired altitude is reached.

Errors

1. Failure to hold constant angle of descent.
2. Failure to adjust rudder pressures for power changes.

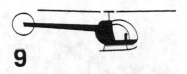

9
FLIGHT MANEUVERS: APPROACH AND LANDING

An approach is a transition maneuver which is flown from traffic pattern altitude, at cruising speed, to a normal hover. It is, basically, a power glide, made at an angle of descent matching the type of approach desired.

There are three basic approaches that you should be proficient in performing: normal, steep and shallow. You also should know how to analyze influential outside factors and how to plan an approach to fit any particular situation in which you find yourself.

Your choice of an approach is governed by the size of landing area, barriers in the approach path, type of ground surface, temperature, altitude, humidity (density altitude), wind direction, wind speed and the gross weight of your craft. Give a little tolerance for overshooting or undershooting a chosen landing spot, and in order to maintain a maximum safety margin in each type of approach, retain translational lift as long as practicable.

Evaluation of existing wind conditions must be made before initiating an approach. Although the approach is generally made into the wind, conditions can indicate the entry will have to be made from a downwind or crosswind position. The traffic pattern is generally flown at normal cruise airspeed. The velocity of the wind determines the airspeed that will be

The HueyCobra, designated AH-1G by the United States Army, is manufactured by Textron's Bell Helicopter Company in Fort Worth, Texas.

maintained after the approach is started. Increase airspeed in proportion to any increase in wind velocity. Keep the angle of descent constant, regardless of wind speed.

Crosswind approaches are made by crabbing or slipping or a combination of both. To make running landings in strong crosswinds, it may be necessary to touch down, initially, with the upwind skid (skid that's into the wind), to avoid drifting.

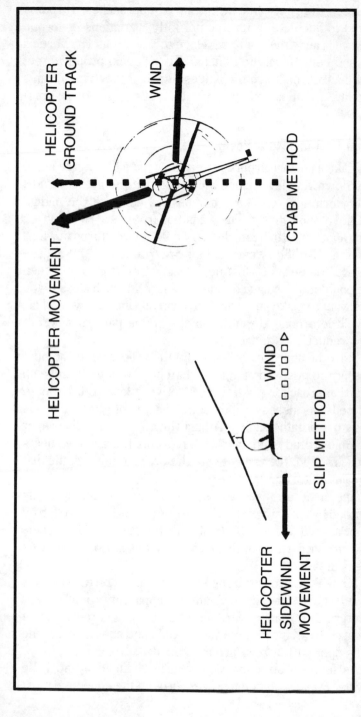

HELICOPTER GROUND TRACK

WIND

HELICOPTER MOVEMENT

CRAB METHOD

WIND

SLIP METHOD

HELICOPTER SIDEWIND MOVEMENT

Slip method as compared to the crab method of wind drift correction. Slip method is normally used for close to the ground work, such as in takeoff, air taxi and landings; crab method is used in normal flight configuration.

Keep the rpm constant during all approaches. If rpm is allowed to fluctuate or change abruptly, variations or torque forces will cause the craft's fuselage to yaw around its vertical axis, and control will be difficult. To maintain proper directional control, make rpm changes and/or collective settings smoothly, accompanied by appropriate changes in pedal pressure.

Normal Approach to a Hover

Make a normal airport pattern entry at a 45-degree angle to the downwind leg in such a manner that the actual turn to the downwind leg will be accomplished opposite the middle one-third of the runway. The transition from the downwind leg to final approach can be made by two 90-degree turns in which a definite base leg is established or by a single 180-degree turn. Remember, at all times during this transition, keep sufficient altitude in case of engine failure. In such a case, you would want to make an autorotative landing into the wind. This fact will determine the point in the traffic pattern where a power reduction is made.

Start the approach by lowering the collective the amount necessary to descend at approximately a 12-degree angle on the final approach leg. As the collective is lowered, increase right pedal as necessary to compensate for the change in torque to maintain heading. Adjust throttle to maintain proper rpm. Hold attitude with cyclic control until the airspeed nears approach speed, then adjust with the cyclic to the attitude that will maintain this approach speed.

The angle of descent and rate of descent are primarily controlled by collective; the airspeed is primarily controlled by the cyclic; and heading on final with the rudders. However, only with coordination of all controls can the approach be made successfully.

Maintain approach airspeed until the point on the circuit is reached where, through evaluation of apparent ground speed, it's determined that forward airspeed must be progressively decreased to arrive at hovering altitude and an attitude at the landing spot with a zero ground speed.

As forward airspeed is gradually reduced by applying rearward cyclic, additional power through the collective must

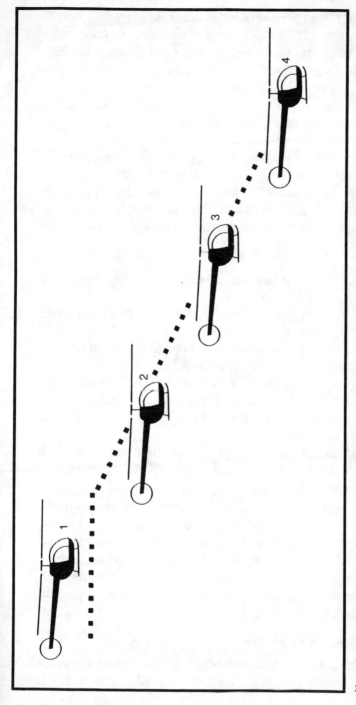

Normal approach to a hover: 1. Set to approach power and rpm. 2. Enter descent at proper airspeed, maintaining angle of descent with collective and airspeed with cyclic. 3. At approximately 50 ft AGL, progressively decrease ground speed to arrive at hover over selected spot. You'll have to increase collective as translational lift is lost to hold proper approach angle. 4. When approaching the hover, make sure your craft is level. Make final power adjustment and hover.

be applied to compensate for the decrease in translational lift and to maintain the proper angle of descent. As collective is increased, left rudder must be increased to keep heading; throttle adjusted to hold rpm; and cyclic coordinated to maintain the proper change in forward airspeed.

The approach is terminated at hovering altitude above your intended landing point with zero ground speed. Very little, if any, additional power is required to stop the forward movement and rate of descent if power has been properly applied during the final portion of the approach.

If the condition of the landing spot is unknown, the approach may be terminated just short of the spot so it can be checked out before moving forward for touchdown.

Errors

1. Failure to maintain proper rpm during the entire approach.
2. Improper use of the collective in controlling the rate of descent.
3. Failure to make rudder corrections to compensate for collective changes during the approach.
4. Failure to arrive at hovering altitude, hovering attitude and zero ground speed almost simultaneously.
5. Low rpm in transition to the hover at the end of the approach.
6. Using too much aft cyclic close to the ground, which could result in the tail rotor striking the ground.

(*Note*: During the early stages of a crosswind approach, a crab and/or slip may be used. During the final stages of the approach, beginning about 50-feet AGL, a slip should be used to align the fuselage with the ground track. The rotor is tilted into the wind with cyclic enough to cancel the wind drift. Heading is maintained along the ground track with the rudders. Use this technique on any type of crosswind approach; shallow, normal or steep.)

Steep Approach to a Hover

A steep approach is used primarily when obstacles in the approach path are too high to allow a normal approach. It will

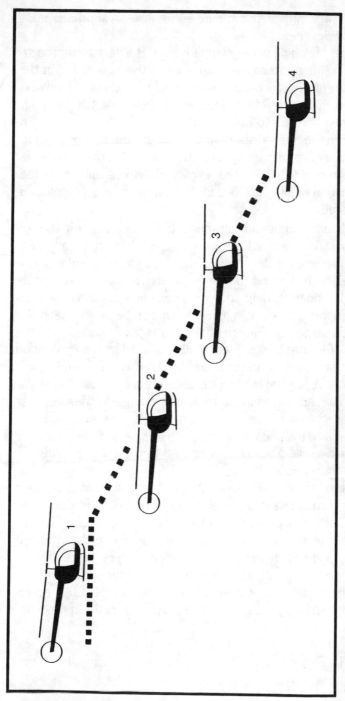

Steep approach to a hover: 1. Set to approach power and rpm. 2. Enter descent at proper airspeed, holding angle of descent with collective and airspeed with cyclic. 3. At approximately 50 ft AGL (unless manufacturer recommends otherwise), progressively decrease ground speed to arrive at hover over selected spot. 4. When approaching the hover, make sure the craft is level.

permit entry into most confined areas. Use an approach angle of 12-20 degrees.

Entry is made in the same manner as a normal approach, except that a greater reduction of collective is required at the beginning of the approach to start the descent. As collective is lowered, increase right rudder pressure to maintain heading, and adjust throttle to hold rpm.

As in the normal approach, the angle and rate of descent are primarily controlled by collective pitch, and the airspeed is primarily controlled by the cyclic. However only with the coordination of all controls can the approach be accomplished successfully.

Maintain approach airspeed until the point on the approach is reached where, through evaluation of apparent ground speed, it's determined that forward airspeed must be progressively decreased in order to arrive at hovering altitude at the intended landing spot with zero ground speed. This is very important, since a flare shouldn't be made near the ground due to the danger of the tail rotor striking.

As forward speed is gradually reduced by the application of rearward cyclic pressure, additional power from the collective must be applied to compensate for the decrease in translational lift and to maintain the proper angle of descent. As collective pitch is increased, left rudder pressure must be increased to maintain heading. Adjust throttle to keep proper rpm, and cyclic pitch is coordinated to control the change in forward airspeed.

Since the rate of descent on a steep approach is much higher than for normal approaches, the collective must be used much sooner at the bottom of the approach. The approach is terminated at hovering altitude above the intended landing point with zero ground speed. Very little, if any, additional power should be required to stop the forward movement and rate of descent of the helicopter if power has been properly applied during the final portion of the approach.

Errors

1. Failure to maintain proper rpm during the entire approach.

2. Improper use of collective in controlling the rate of descent.
3. Failure to make pedal corrections to compensate for collective pitch changes during the approach.
4. Slowing airspeed excessively in order to remain on the proper angle of descent.
5. Failure to arrive at hovering altitude, hovering attitude and zero ground speed almost simultaneously.
6. Low rpm in transition to the hover at the end of the approach.
7. Using too much rearward cyclic close to the ground, which could result in the tail rotor striking the ground.

Landing From a Hover

In Chapter Six, how to takeoff to a hover was discussed. Here's its sequel, how to land vertically from a hover.

From an already attained hover, begin your descent by applying a slow, but gradual, downward pressure on the collective. Maintain a constant rate of descent to the ground. As the skids come to within a few feet of the surface, ground cushion effect becomes very noticeable, and the helicopter tends to stop its descent altogether. At this point, it may be necessary to further decrease the collective in order to maintain the constant rate of descent.

When the skids touch the ground, lower the collective to the full down position, adjust the throttle to keep rpm in the proper range, and at the same time add right pedal pressure as needed to maintain heading.

Throughout the descent and until the time the skids are firmly on the ground and the collective is in the full down position, make necessary corrections with rudders to keep a constant heading. Make the necessary cyclic corrections to hold a level attitude and to prevent movements over the ground.

Errors

1. Cyclic overcontrolling during descent, resulting in movement over the ground on contact.

2. Failure to use collective smoothly.
3. Pulling back on the cyclic prior to or upon touchdown.
4. Failure to lower the collective smoothly and positively to the full down position upon ground contact.
5. Failure to maintain a constant rate of descent.
6. Failure to hold proper rpm.

Shallow Approach and Running Landing

A shallow approach and running landing are used when a high density altitude or a high gross weight condition or a combination thereof is such that a normal or steep approach can't be made because of insufficient power to hover. To compensate for this lack of power, a shallow approach and running landing makes maximum use of translational lift until ground contact is made. The glide angle is from 5-12 degrees, depending on wind conditions. Since a running landing follows the shallow approach, a ground area of sufficient length and smoothness must be available.

Start the shallow approach in the same manner as a normal approach except that a shallower angle of descent is maintained. The power reduction to begin the desired angle of descent will be less than that for a normal approach, since the angle of descent is less. As collective is lowered, maintain heading by increasing right rudder pressure, adjust throttle to maintain rpm, and use cyclic as necessary to hold the desired approach airspeed.

As in normal and steep approaches, the descent angle and rate of descent are primarily controlled by collective, and the ground speed is primarily controlled by the cyclic. The coordination of all controls is needed, however, if the approach is to be accomplished successfully.

Approach airspeed should be held until reaching an altitude of approximately 50-feet AGL. At this point, gradually apply aft cyclic to start losing airspeed. Coordinate a slight downward pressure on the collective to maintain the proper descent angle. Airspeed deceleration should be enough that the helicopter will settle to the ground, due to the decreased effect of translational lift just as the landing spot is reached.

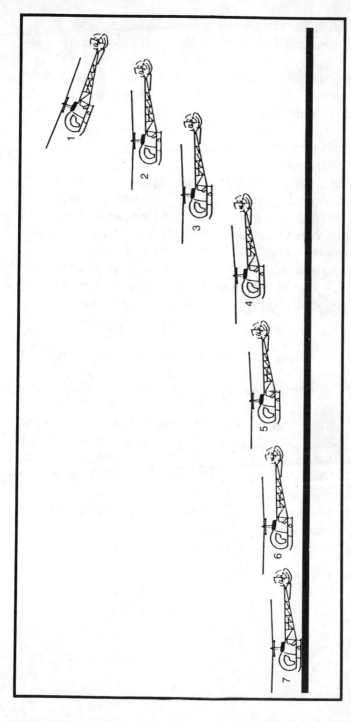

Running landing: 1. At approximately 50 ft AGL, raise nose slightly and slow airspeed for approach. 2-3. Bring the chopper to a level attitude and slow the rate of descent with the collective. 4-6. Use collective to continue slowing rate of descent and to cushion landing. 7. Continue skidding, braking with collective.

123

Deceleration must be smoothly coordinated, at the same time keeping enough lift to prevent the copter from settling abruptly.

On final approach, prior to making ground contact, place the helicopter in a level attitude with cyclic, use rudder to maintain heading, and cyclic necessary to keep heading and ground track identical. Allow the helicopter to settle gently to the ground in a straight and level attitude, cushioning the landing with the collective.

After ground contact, the cyclic is placed slightly forward of neutral to tilt the main rotor away from the tail boom; adjust throttle to hold rpm; maintain ground track with cyclic. Normally, the collective is held stationary after touchdown, until the helicopter comes to a complete stop. If braking action is desired or required, the collective may be lowered cautiously. To ensure directional control, normal rotor rpm must be maintained until the helicopter comes to a full stop.

Errors

1. Assuming excessive nose-high attitude at about 10 feet.
2. Insufficient collective and throttle to cushion the landing.
3. Failure to add left rudder as collective is added to cushion landing, resulting in a touchdown while in a left skid.
4. Touching down at an excessive ground speed.
5. Failure to touchdown in a level attitude.
6. Failure to maintain proper rotor rpm during and after touchdown.
7. Poor directional control upon touchdown.

10

AUTOROTATIONS

In helicopter flying, an autorotation is a maneuver that you can perform whenever the engine is no longer supplying power to the main rotor blades. A chopper transmission is designed to allow the main rotor hub and its blades to rotate freely in its original direction if the engine stops.

Keep in mind that at the instant of engine failure, the blades will be producing lift and thrust. By immediately lowering the collective, lift, as well as drag, will be reduced. This will cause the craft to begin an immediate descent, thus producing an upward flow of air through the rotor blades. The impact of this upward flow of air on the blades produces a ram effect which gives sufficient thrust to maintain rotor rpm throughout the descent. Since the tail rotor is driven by the main rotor during autorotation, heading control can still be maintained as if in normal flight.

Several factors affect the rate of descent in autorotation: density altitude, gross weight, rotor rpm and airspeed. Your primary control of the rate of descent is airspeed. Higher or lower airspeed is obtained with the cyclic, just as in normal flight.

You have a choice in angle of descent, varying from the vertical to maximum angle of descent or glide. Rate of descent is high at zero airspeed and decreases to a minimum somewhere in the neighborhood of 50-60 mph, depending on the particular copter and the factors just mentioned.

As the airspeed increases beyond that which gives you minimum rate of descent, the rate of your drop in altitude will again increase. When an autorotative landing is to be made, the energy stored in the rotating blades can be used to decrease the rate of descent even further and a safe landing made.

A greater amount of rotor energy is required to stop the helicopter with a high rate of descent than one that is descending more slowly. It follows, then, that autorotative descents at very low or very high airspeeds are more critical than those performed at the proper airspeed for the minimum rate of descent.

Each type of helicopter has a specific airspeed at which a power-off glide is most efficient. The best airspeed is the one which combines the greatest glide range with the slowest rate of descent. The specific airspeed is somewhat different for each type of copter, yet certain factors affect all configurations in the same manner. For specific autorotation airspeeds for a particular helicopter, refer to that particular helicopter's flight manual.

The exact airspeed for autorotation is established for each type of helicopter on the basis of average weather and wind conditions and normal loading. When operating a machine with excessive loads in high density altitudes or strong, gusty wind conditions, best performance is achieved from a slightly increased airspeed in the descent. On the other hand, for autorotations in light winds, low density altitudes and light loading, best performance is achieved from a slightly decreased normal airspeed. Following this general procedure of fitting airspeed to existing conditions, you can achieve approximately the same glide angle in any set of circumstances and estimate the probable touchdown point.

When making autorotative turns, generally use cyclic control only. Use of rudder pedals to assist or speed the turn only causes loss of airspeed and downward pitching of the craft's nose; especially when left pedal is used. When autorotation is initiated, sufficient right rudder should be used to

Nearly 800 Hughes TH-55A helicopter trainers were purchased by the U.S. Army during the late sixties.

127

maintain straight flight and to prevent yawing to the left. Don't change this rudder pressure to assist the turn.

If rotor rpm becomes too high during an autorotative approach, collective should be raised sufficiently to decrease rpm to the normal operating range, then lowered all the way again. This procedure may be repeated as necessary to keep rpm in the normal mode.

Due to the increased back cyclic pressure, which induces a greater airflow through the rotor system, rpm is most likely to increase above the maximum limit during the turn. The tighter the turn and the heavier the gross weight, the higher the rpm will be.

Hovering Autorotation

To practice hovering autorotations, establish the normal hovering altitude for your particular helicopter, considering its load and the atmospheric conditions, and keep it headed into the wind, holding maximum allowable rpm.

To enter autorotation, close the throttle quickly to ensure a clean split of the engine and rotor needles. This disengages the driving force of the engine from the rotor, thus eliminating torque effect. As throttle is closed, right rudder pressure must be applied to maintain heading. Usually, a slight amount of right cyclic will be necessary to keep the craft from drifting, but use cyclic control as required to ensure a vertical descent and a level attitude. Leave the collective pitch where it is on entry.

In helicopters with low inertia rotor systems, the aircraft will begin to settle immediately. Keep a level attitude, and ensure a vertical descent with the cyclic heading with the rudders, and apply up collective pitch as necessary to slow the descent and cushion the landing (generally, the full amount of collective is required). As upward collective is applied, the throttle will have to be held in the closed position to prevent the rotor from re-engaging.

Machines with high inertia rotor systems will maintain altitude momentarily after the throttle is closed. As rotor rpm decreases, the craft will start to settle. As it does so, apply upward collective, while holding the throttle in the closed position to slow the descent and cushion the landing. The

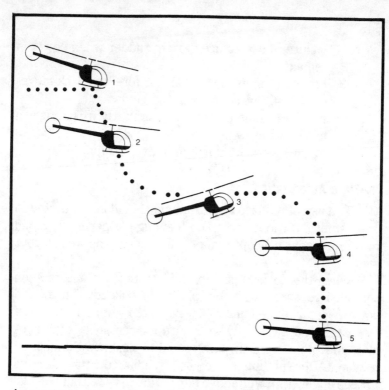

Autorotation: 1. Lower collective full-down, and close the throttle to "split the needles." 2. Maintain recommended autorotation speed. 3. Flare the craft to obtain the desired ground speed. 4-5. Move cyclic forward to level the helicopter, and increase collective to slow descent and cushion landing.

timing of this collective application, and the rate at which it is applied, depends on the particular helicopter being flown, its gross weight and the atmospheric conditions. Use cyclic to maintain a level attitude and to ensure a vertical descent. Keep heading with rudders.

When the weight of the helicopter is entirely on the skids, stop application of up collective. When the craft has come to a complete stop, lower the collective completely.

The timing of the collective is a most important consideration. If it's applied too soon, the remaining rpm will not be sufficient to effect a smooth landing. On the other hand, if collective is initiated too late, ground contact will be made before sufficient blade pitch is increased to cushion the landing.

129

Errors

1. Failure to use sufficient right rudder when power is reduced.
2. Failure to stop all sideward or fore and back movement with cyclic prior to touchdown.
3. Failure to time up collective properly, resulting in a hard touchdown.
4. Failure to touch down in a level attitude.

No-Flare Autorotation

The use of no-flare autorotations should be restricted to areas sufficiently long and smooth enough to permit a ground run. Know your helicopter and its limitations, as well as your own.

When the desired position for starting the autorotation has been reached, smoothly place the collective in the full down position, maintaining cruising rpm with the throttle. Decrease throttle quickly to ensure a clean split of the needles, and apply sufficient right pedal to maintain the desired heading. After splitting the needles, readjust the throttle so as to keep engine rpm well above normal idling speed but not high enough to cause the rejoining of the two needles. (Manufacturers will often recommend proper rpm for this use.)

Adjust attitude with cyclic to obtain the best gliding speed that will result in the slowest rate of descent. Be sure to hold collective in the full down position. If it's permitted to rise, rotor rpm will decrease due to the increased drag from the increased pitch angle of the blades. At about 50-feet AGL (check manufacturer's recommendation), raise the nose slightly to obtain the desired landing speed and to slow the rate of descent.

If a landing is to be made from the autorotative approach, rotate throttle to the closed or override position, and hold in this position as collective is raised, so the rotor will not re-engage. As the helicopter approaches normal hovering altitude, maintain a level attitude with the cyclic; heading with right rudder; apply sufficient collective (while holding the throttle in the closed position) to cushion touchdown; and be sure the craft is landing parallel to its direction of motion upon ground contact. Avoid landing on the heels of the skid gear. The timing of the collective application, and the amount applied, will be dependent on the rate of descent.

After ground contact is made, collective may be increased smoothly (still holding the throttle in the closed position), to keep the helicopter light on the skids and allow it to slow down gradually; or it may be held stationary, resulting in a shorter ground run; or it may be lowered cautiously for additional braking, if required, due to a fast touchdown and limited landing area. Hold cyclic slightly forward of neutral and use to keep directional control if landing is made in a crosswind. Maintain heading with rudders. In the event of insufficient rudder travel to maintain heading control when the rotor rpm decreases after touchdown, apply cyclic in the direction of the turn.

After the helicopter has stopped, decrease collective to the full down position. If a power recovery is to be made from the practice approach, replace certain of the above procedures with those found in "Power Recovery From Practice Autorotations," found in this chapter.

Errors

1. Failure to use sufficient right rudder when power is reduced.
2. Lowering the nose too abruptly when power is reduced, thus placing the craft in a dive.
3. Failure to maintain full down collective during the descent.
4. Application of up collective at an excessive altitude, resulting in a hard landing, loss of heading control and, possibly, damage to the tail rotor and main rotor blade stops.
5. Pulling the nose up just prior to touchdown.

Flare Autorotation

This maneuver enables you to land at any speed between a no landing run to that of a running one; that is to say, anywhere between a zero ground speed and the speed of touchdown from a no-flare autorotation. The speed at touchdown and the resulting ground run will depend on the rate and amount of the flare: The greater the degree of flare and the longer it is held, the slower the touchdown speed and the shorter the ground run. The slower the speed desired at touchdown from an autorotation, the more accurate must be the timing and speed of the flare, especially in craft with low inertia rotor systems.

Enter the flare autorotation in the same manner as the no-flare autorotation. The technique is the same down to the point where the flare is to begin. This point is slightly lower than the point at which the nose is raised in the no-flare autorotation.

At approximately 35-60-feet AGL, depending on the particular helicopter (check the manufacturer's recommendation), initiate the flare by moving the cyclic smoothly to the rear. Heading is maintained by the rudders. Care must be exercised in the execution of the flare so the cyclic isn't moved rearward so abruptly as to cause the helicopter to climb or so slowly as to allow it to settle so rapidly that the tail rotor strikes the ground.

As forward motion decreases to the desired ground speed, move the cyclic forward to a level attitude in preparation for landing. If a landing is to be made, rotate the throttle to the closed or override position. If power recovery is to be made, do so as the copter reaches the level position.

The altitude at this time should be about 3-10 feet, depending on the helicopter. If a landing is to be made, allow the craft to settle vertically. Apply collective smoothly as necessary to check the descent and cushion the landing. As collective pitch is increased, hold the throttle in the closed position so that the rotor will not re-engage. Additional right rudder is required to maintain heading, as collective is raised, due to the reduction in rotor rpm and the resulting reduced effect of the tail rotor.

After touchdown, when the chopper has come to a complete stop, lower the collective to the full down position.

Errors

1. Failure to use sufficient right rudder when power is reduced.

132

2. Lowering the nose too abruptly when power is reduced, thus placing the craft in a dive.
3. Failure to maintain full down collective during the descent.
4. Application of up collective at an excessive altitude, resulting in a hard landing, loss of heading control and possible damage to the tail rotor and the main rotor blade stops.
5. Applying up collective before a level attitude is attained: If timing is late, it may be necessary to apply up collective before a level attitude is attained.
6. Pulling the nose up just prior to touchdown on full autorotation.

Power Recovery From Practice Autorotations

A power recovery is used to terminate practice autorotations at a point prior to actual touchdown. If so desired, a landing can be made or a go-around initiated after the power recovery is made.

To effect a power recovery after the flare or level-off, coordinate upward collective and increase throttle to join the needles at operating rpm. The throttle and collective must be coordinated properly. If the throttle is increased too fast or too much, an engine overspeed will occur. If the throttle is increased too slow or too little in proportion to the increase in collective, a loss of rotor rpm will result. Use sufficient collective to check the descent, and coordinate left rudder with the increase in collective to maintain heading.

If a go-around is to be made, move the cyclic control smoothly forward to re-enter forward flight. If a landing is to be made following the power recovery, the helicopter can be brought to a hover at normal hovering altitude.

In transitioning from a practice autorotation to a go-around, care must be exercised to avoid an altitude-airspeed combination which could place the craft in an unsafe area of the height-velocity chart for that particular helicopter.

Errors

1. Initiating recovery too late, requiring a rapid application of controls, resulting in overcontrolling.

2. Failure to obtain and maintain a level attitude near the ground.
3. Adding throttle before the collective.
4. Failure to coordinate throttle and collective properly, resulting in an engine overspeed or loss of rpm.
5. Failure to coordinate left rudder with the increase in power.

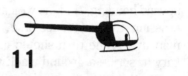

11
PRACTICE MANEUVERS

The purpose of practice maneuvers is to build coordination and to keep you familiar with your aircraft and your own skill level. They give you the opportunity to practice many single maneuvers in one, by grouping them as a single unit. They also instill an automatic reflex to certain configurations.

Two major practice maneuvers are the S-turns and rapid deceleration or "quick-stop."

S-Turns

This single maneuver presents one of the most elementary problems in the practical application of a turn, and also for wind correction or drift while in a turn. To set up for S-turns, a reference line is used. This line can be a road, railroad, fence or section line, however, it should be straight for a considerable distance. It should extend as nearly perpendicular to the wind as possible.

The objective of the S-turn is to fly a pattern of two half-circle of equal size on opposite sides of a reference line. The maneuver should be started at an altitude of about 500-feet AGL and flown at a constant altitude above the terrain throughout. S-turns may be started at any point, however, during early training, it may be beneficial to start on a downwind heading.

As your helicopter crosses the reference line, a bank is immediately established. This initial bank will be the steepest used throughout the maneuver since the craft is headed directly downwind. The bank is gradually reduced as necessary to scribe a ground track in a half-circle. The turn should be timed so that as the rollout is completed, the helicopter is crossing the reference line, perpendicular to it and headed directly upwind.

A bank is immediately entered in the opposite direction to begin the second half of the S-turn. Since the copter is on an upwind heading, this, as well as the one just completed before crossing the reference line, will be the shallowest in the maneuver. The turn should gradually be increased as necessary to scribe a ground track which is a half-circle identical in size to the one previously completed on the other side of the reference line. The steepest bank in this turn should be attained just prior to rollout when the craft is approaching the reference line nearest to a downwind heading. This bank, along with the initial bank entered at the beginning of the maneuver, will be the steepest bank used in S-turns. The turn should be timed so that, as the rollout is completed, the helicopter is crossing the reference line perpendicular to it and headed directly downwind.

From here, the maneuver can be started over again without breaking the pattern. It can be continued as long as the reference line runs true without a break. You can do a number in one direction, then do a 180-degree turn and head back along the same track in the direction from which you just came.

As a summary, the angle of bank required at any given point in the maneuver is dependent on the groundspeed—the faster the groundspeed, the steeper the bank of the turn. Or, to express it another way, the more nearly the helicopter is to a downwind heading, the steeper the bank; the more nearly it is to an upwind heading, the shallower the bank.

In addition to varying the angle of bank to correct for wind drift in order to maintain the proper radius of turn, the chopper must also be flown with a drift correction angle (crab) in relation to its ground track, except, of course, when it's on direct upwind or downwind headings, or there's no wind. You

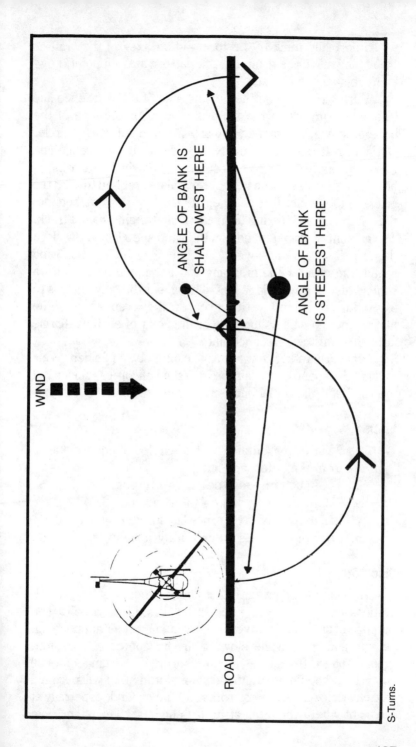

WIND

ANGLE OF BANK IS SHALLOWEST HERE

ANGLE OF BANK IS STEEPEST HERE

ROAD

S-Turns.

would normally think of the fore and aft axes of the craft as being tangent to the ground track pattern at each point, however, this isn't the case.

During the turn on the upwind side of the reference line (the side from which the wind is blowing), the nose of the helicopter will be crabbed toward the outside of the circle. During the turn on the downwind side of the reference line (the side opposite to the direction from which the wind is blowing), the nose of the helicopter will be crabbed toward the inside of the circle. In any case, the craft will be crabbed into the wind, just as if trying to maintain a straight ground track. The amount of crab depends on the wind speed and how close the ship is to its crosswind position. The higher the wind speed, the greater the crab angle at any given position for a scribed turn of a specific radius. The closer the helicopter is to a crosswind position, the greater the crab angle. The maximum crab angle should be at the point of each half-circle farthest from the reference line.

Standard radius for S-turns cannot be specified. This radius will depend on the airspeed of the helicopter, velocity of the wind and the initial bank angle required for the entry.

Errors

1. Failure to maintain two half-circles of equal distance from the reference line.
2. Too much or too little crab for crosswind.
3. Sloppy coordination on the controls.
4. Failure to cross reference line in level flight attitude.
5. Loss or gain in altitude during maneuver.

Quick Stops

Although used primarily for coordination practice, decelerations can be used to effect a quick stop in the air. The purpose of such a maneuver is to maintain a constant heading, altitude and rpm, while slowing the helicopter to a desired ground speed. It requires a high degree of coordination of all controls. It should be practiced at an altitude that will permit a safe clearance between tail rotor and the ground, especially at the point where the pitch attitude is highest. Telephone pole

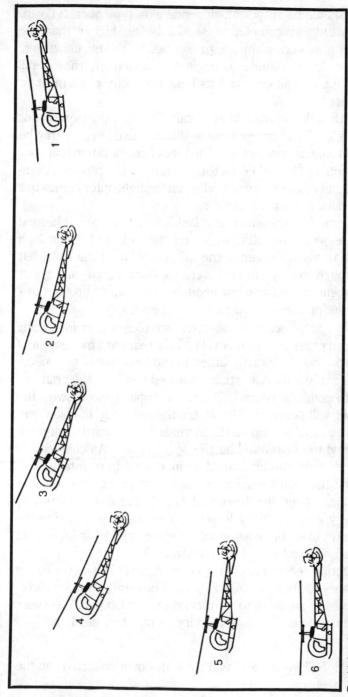

Rapid deceleration (quick-stop). 1. Begin at cruise airspeed, at a safe altitude. 2. Synchronize a decrease in collective, with a slightly rearward cyclic. 3-4. Continue with down collective and back cyclic to decrease groundspeed. 5. Bring cyclic forward and increase collective. 6. Follow through with a normal hover landing.

height should be sufficient, depending on type of craft flown. The altitude at completion should be no higher than the maximum, hovering altitude prescribed by the manufacturer. In selecting an altitude to begin the maneuver, the overall length of the helicopter and its height-velocity chart must be considered.

Although the maneuver is called a rapid deceleration or "quick stop," this doesn't mean that it should necessarily be used through to completion. The rate of deceleration is at your discretion, but blade "G" factors must be taken into consideration. A quick stop is completed when the helicopter comes to a hover during the recovery.

Begin the maneuver at a fast hover taxi speed, headed into the wind. An altitude should be selected that's high enough to avoid danger to the tail rotor during the flare, but low enough to stay out of the craft's shaded area throughout the maneuver, and also low enough that it can be brought to a hover during the recovery.

To start, decrease collective, simultaneously increasing rearward pressure on the cyclic. This rearward movement of the stick must be exactly timed to the lowering of the collective. If rearward cyclic stick is applied too fast, the craft will start to climb; if rearward cyclic is applied too slowly, the chopper will descend. The faster the decrease in collective, the more rapid should be the increase in rearward stick pressure, and the faster will be the deceleration. As collective is lowered, right rudder should be increased to maintain heading, and the throttle should be adjusted to maintain rpm.

Once speed has been reduced to the desired amount, recovery is initiated by lowering the nose and allowing the helicopter to settle to a normal hovering altitude, in level flight and zero ground speed or that desired.

During recovery, collective pitch should be increased as necessary to stop the craft at normal hovering altitude; throttle should be adjusted to maintain rpm; and left pedal pressure should be increased as necessary to maintain heading.

Errors

1. Failure to lead slightly with down collective on the entry.

2. Failure to raise the nose high enough, resulting in slow deceleration.

3. Applying back cyclic too rapidly initially, causing the helicopter to "balloon," gaining altitude suddenly.

4. Failure to lead with, and maintain, forward cyclic during recovery. If a quick stop isn't performed properly, it may be necessary to lead with collective, to prevent touching down too hard or on the heels of the skids.

5. Allowing the helicopter to stop forward motion in a tail low attitude.

6. Failure to maintain proper rpm.

Tree Topper

This maneuver is another coordination stratagem, one to practice using all controls in making minute corrections, while enjoing yourself. It's much like the S-turn, in that wind correction is involved.

Pick a wide-open area with a tree, pole or some object in the middle. Make sure there's good all around clearance. The objective is to look the chosen object over by moving your craft around it, as well as up and down.

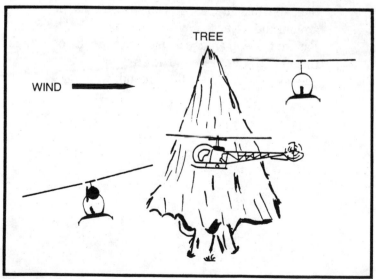

Tree Topper.

To start the maneuver, approach the object slowly from upwind at about hovering altitude. An upwind entry is desired to get the feel of wind speed and what it takes to stop short of the object.

Move to the object, being extremely careful not to touch it with blade tips. Notice your blade clearance. Move the helicopter lower and lower, gradually, making corrections with collective, cyclic, rudder and throttle. You should be moving forward, around the object, at the same time.

Once this has been done, move higher and higher, looking the object over. Again, extreme care should be used in keeping the blades away from the object. Make necessary corrections on the controls to keep the craft moving at a steady pace, keeping your distance from the object.

Once you've made a trip or two around it, and you have the feel of both the machine and wind, coordinating the controls, find another object and try the whole sequence over. Remember, caution is the word.

Errors

1. Failure to take into account the effect of wind as you move around the object.
2. Failure to coordinate controls with changes in collective, rpm and rudder, as you move up and down and around the object.
3. Failure to keep an equal distance from the object, as the craft moves around it. An equal-radius circle should be scribed on the ground.

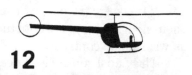

12

EMERGENCY PROCEDURES

Since emergency procedures differ with particular aircraft, before simulating any emergency, check the manufacturer's recommendations. There are, however, general emergency steps that every helicopter pilot should be familiar with, no matter what type of copter is being flown. It's the purpose of this chapter to acquaint you with this information.

Recovery From Low Rotor RPM

Recovery from low rotor rpm procedure is one used to return the rotor to normal operating rpm. This recovery is often referred to as "milking." If performed properly, it will normally regain lost rotor rpm while still maintaining flight. This condition is the result of having a high angle of attack on the main rotor blades, induced by too much collective. It creates a drag so great that engine power available, or being used, isn't sufficient to maintain normal rotor operating rpm.

When you realize what's happening, immediately add full throttle, and briskly decrease the collective to relieve, momentarily at least, the excess engine load. As the helicopter begins to settle, smoothly increase the collective, but only enough to stop the settling motion. Remember, down briskly, up smoothly and slower. This procedure, under critical conditions, might have to be repeated several times in order to regain normal rotor operating rpm. The amount that the collective can be decreased will depend on the altitude available at the time of the emergency condition. In practice, give yourself plenty of room to spare.

When operating at sufficient altitudes above the terrain, it will be necessary to decrease the collective only once to regain sufficient rotor rpm. When the rotor rpm begins to rise and attains about normal rotor operating rpm, anticipate decreasing the throttle slowly to prevent the engine from overspeeding.

If recovery from a low rotor rpm condition isn't effected soon enough, lifting power of the main rotor blades will be lost, as will rudder control.

This pedal control loss occurs as a result of the decrease in tail rotor rpm. Remember, the tail rotor is driven by the main rotor, and its rpm is directly proportional to that of the main rotor. If rudder control is lost and the altitude is such that a landing can be effected before the turning rate increases dangerously, decrease collective pitch slowly, maintain a level attitude with the cyclic and land.

Recovery From Blade Stall

Blade stall occurs when, at a high forward speed, the angle of attack of the retreating blade is made so acute that the streamline flow of air over its upper surface, especially toward blade tip, reaches the burbling point and begins breaking down. Each blade will stall when it becomes the retreating blade. The high angle of attack can also be increased beyond the "critical angle" and cause complete blade stall, as in such maneuvers as a steep turn or sudden up-gusts of air. Again, the airspeed at which blade stall commences will be reduced when the craft has a high, all-up weight or when it's at high altitudes, as a greater degree of collective must be used in these conditions.

You will first feel blade stall as a vibration equivalent to the number of blades in the main rotor, per revolution. That is to say, a three bladed rotor will have three vibrations per revolution, two bladers will have two, and so forth. The vibration can be fairly severe and a kicking at the controls can be present.

Aerospatiale 350C A Star.

145

When blade stall occurs, you can correct the situation by reducing the severity of the maneuver, reduce collective pitch, reduce airspeed/and increase rotor rpm, or combination thereof. It depends on your situation at the time.

A blade stall which is encountered because of the severity of a maneuver will normally correct itself, as soon as you reduce the harshness of, or cease entirely, the maneuver. This is applicable if the blade stall occurs in a steep turn, a sharp pull out at a high speed, etc.

In the majority of blade stall cases, reducing collective pitch is the right action, especially when flying fast in turbulent weather. In copters that are prone to high speed stalling of advancing blades (usually due to their reaching a high, critical, mach number), it's possible not to know which of the two possible causes is producing the vibrations felt. A slight reduction in rpm would, therefore, be advisable at the same time as the collective is lowered.

There's some debate against an immediate reduction of airspeed in the case of a blade stall at high cruising speed. Some feel the result of easing back on the cyclic would be to increase the G load and further aggravate stall symptoms. It's recommended that a reduction of airspeed should be accomplished slowly, and the collective should be lowered at the same time.

If higher rotor rpm can be used with a lower collective setting, then blade stall will occur at a higher cruising speed. In some helicopters, the possibility of reaching critical mach numbers with the advancing blades must be kept in mind when rpm is increased.

Much depends upon the type of helicopter being used as to the manner in which blade stall is induced. With some craft, blade-stall onset could be experienced frequently during routine exercises, however, in others extreme steep turns, with high G effects at altitude, may have to be carried out before blade stall is encountered.

Vortex Ring Condition

This situation can occur during a vertical descent through the air with power on, with a rate of descent in excess of 300 fpm usually being necessary. Although less common, it can also occur in conditions where considerable power is applied, with the helicopter mushing through the disturbed air. The latter case is generally only momentary but can cause considerable buffeting and a loss of lift.

In the case of the vertical descent, the effect can be prolonged, resulting in a high rate of descent, vibration and partial loss of control. The symptoms may vary among different helicopter types.

The vortex ring isn't dangerous, unless carried out at a low altitude. The rate of descent is high, both during the condition and recovery. Altitude should, therefore, not be held deliberately below 600-feet AGL. Steep or vertical approaches to small sites in calm air should be carried out at a low rate of descent in order to avoid the vortex ring condition.

This problem is so named because of the airflow pattern around the rotor. From the pilot's point of view, it may be thought of more simply as the fact that the rotor is forcing air downward, and the aircraft is then sinking into this downward-moving, disturbed air. It's not always easy to initiate the condition for demonstration purposes, as sideways, forward or backward movement through the air could prevent its occurring.

When the condition is encountered in a vertical descent, there are two main ways of recovery:

1. Easing the stick forward and diving out.
2. Entering autorotation; placing the collective full down and diving out.

Engine Failure

This emergency can happen any time, any place. It should be kept foremost in mind and a precautionary landing made any time there's indication of engine trouble. It's better to land with some power than none at all. Obviously, the most critical time for an engine out would be when working close to the ground in such attitudes as takeoff, landing or a low hover.

If time and altitude permit when engine failure occurs, rapidly reduce the main rotor's pitch with the collective a proportional amount to your altitude AGL. At an altitude of

300 feet and up, say, reduce collective to the maximum, which will reduce the rotor blade's pitch to a minimum. At altitudes of 10 feet or less, reduce the collective only a slight amount, if at all.

If altitude permits, obtain some forward airspeed. Transition to a forward glide advantageously reduces the rate of descent. From here, a normal landing without power can be made.

At an altitude of five to 10-feet AGL, rapidly increase the main rotor's pitch angle with the collective, depending on your rate of descent. You should make every effort to utilize all available rotor energy to cushion the landing. However, you should save some collective for the last few feet before touchdown.

If you're above 50-feet AGL, instantly execute an autorotative glide by applying appropriate forward cyclic and maximum down collective. This will permit the copter to descend along a forward path at complementary forward speed.

When approaching normal hovering altitude, apply backward cyclic to flare. This will reduce forward speed and further decrease the rate of descent. At about head high, five to eight-feet AGL, level the flare enough to bring the helicopter to an almost level attitude. A final cushioning effect with increased rotor blade pitch by up collective at approximately two to four feet AGL. This should set the craft nicely on the chosen spot.

After touchdown, turn battery switch, selector valve and ignition switch to the "off" position. Also place the mixture control in the "cut-off" position. Climb out of the craft, and you're home free.

Tail Rotor Control System Failure

Failure of the tail rotor is one of the more dangerous of helicopter emergencies, but if you're ready for it, for immediate action, it's just another emergency maneuver. Since it controls the directional stability of the craft, without the tail rotor, there's a tendency of the helicopter to begin turning in the opposite direction of the rotor blades, causing a landing or inflight problem, if forward speed gets too low.

Immediately go into an autorotative attitude and, maintain an airspeed sufficient to keep the craft aligned parallel with its forward ground track. Make an autorotational landing, while heading in a direction that's parallel to the flight or glide path. A "running landing" here would be most appropriate; enough so to keep the tail from swinging around.

Antitorque system failure could be the result of a failure in the tail rotor blades, the mechanical linkage between the rudders and the pitch-change mechanism of the tail rotor or the tail rotor drive-shaft between the transmission and the tail rotor.

If the system fails in cruising flight, the nose of the helicopter will usually pitch slightly and yaw to the right. The direction in which the nose pitches will depend on your particular craft and how it's loaded. Violence in pitching and yawing is generally greater when the failure occurs in the tail rotor blades and also is usually accompanied by severe vibration.

Pitching and yawing can be overcome by holding the cyclic stick near neutral and immediately entering autorotation. Keep cyclic movements to a minimum until the pitching subsides. Abrupt rearward movements of the cyclic should be avoided. If the stick is moved rearward too fast the main rotor blades could flex downward with sufficient force to strike the tail boom.

The fuselage will remain fairly well streamlined if sufficient forward speed is maintained. However, if you attempt a descent at slow speeds, a continuous turning movement to the left can be expected. Know the manufacturer's recommended speeds and procedures for each particular helicopter you fly. This will generally be found under "Emergency Procedures" in the aircraft flight manual. Directional control should be maintained primarily with cyclic and secondarily by gently applying throttle momentarily, with needles joined, to swing the nose to the right.

A running landing may be made or a flare-type. The best, and safest, landing technique, terrain permitting, is to land directly into the wind with about 20 mph airspeed. In a flare landing, the helicopter will turn to the left during the actual flare and subsequent vertical descent. An important factor to remember is that the craft should be level, or approximately level, at ground contact, in any case.

Immediate and quick action must be taken. The turning motion to the right builds up rapidly, because of the torque reaction produced by the relatively high power setting. To eliminate this turning effect, you should close the throttle immediately without varying collective pitch. Simultaneously, adjust the cyclic to stop all sideward or rearward movements and to level the chopper for touchdown. From this point, the procedure for a hovering autorotation is followed.

Low-Frequency Vibrations

Abnormal, low-frequency vibrations are always associated with the main rotor. These vibrations will be at some frequency related to the rotor rpm and the number of blades of the rotor, such as one vibration per rotor revolution, two per rev., three per rev., etc. Low frequency vibrations are slow enough that they can be counted.

The frequency and strength of the vibrations will cause you and/or your passengers to be noticeably bounced or shaken. If the vibration is felt through the cyclic, it'll have some definite kick at the same point in the rotor-blade cycle. These low-frequency vibrations can be felt in the fuselage, in the stick, or they can be evident in all simultaneously. Whether the tremor is in the fuselage or the stick will, to some extent, determine the cause.

Vibrations felt through the fuselage can be classified in four ways: lateral, longitudinal, vertical or a combination of the others. A lateral vibration is one which throws the pilot from side-to-side. A longitudinal vibration is one which rocks the pilot forward-and-backward, or in which the pilot receives a periodic kick in the back. A vertical vibration is one in which the pilot is bounced up-and-down, or it may be thought of as one in which the pilot receives a periodic "kick in the seat of the pants." Describing the vibrations to a mechanic in the above forms will also help him in determining the exact cause.

Vibrations felt through both the stick and fuselage are generally indicative of problems in the rotor or rotor support. A failure of the pylon support at the fuselage connection is also a possible cause.

If the low-frequency vibration in the fuselage occurs during translational flight or during a climb at certain airspeeds, the vibration could be a result of the blades striking their rest stops. This problem can be eliminated until mechanical correction by avoiding the flight conditions that cause it.

For low-frequency vibrations felt predominantly through the stick, the trouble is most likely in the control system linkage, from the stick to the rotor head.

Medium-Frequency Vibrations

In most helicopters, medium-frequency vibrations are a result of trouble with the tail rotor. Improper rigging, unbalance, defective blades or bad bearings in the tail rotor are all sources of this type vibrations. If it occurs only during turns, the trouble could be caused by insufficient tail-rotor flapping action. Medium-frequency vibrations are very difficult, if not impossible, to count, due to their fast rate. See a mechanic for a thorough check out.

High-Frequency Vibrations

These vibrations are associated with the engine in most helicopters and will be impossible to count, due to their high rate. However, they could be associated with the tail rotor in helicopters with tail rotor rpm about equal to, or greater than engine rpm. A defective clutch or missing or bent fan blade will cause vibrations. Any bad bearing in the engine, transmission or tail rotor drive shaft will result in vibrations with frequencies directly related to the speed of the engine.

Experience in detecting and isolating the three main different classes of vibrations when they first develop makes it possible to correct the situation long before it becomes serious. Take a good look, feel and listen. If you don't like what you find, see a mechanic.

13

SPECIAL OPERATIONS

A special operation is one that is out of the ordinary. Such an operation would include flight in confined areas, high, low and ground reconnaissance maneuvers.

Slope Operations

Approaching a slope, mountain, hill or knoll for landing isn't much different from an approach to any other helicopter landing area. However, during this type of operation, an allowance must be made for wind, obstacles, and a possible forced landing. Since the terrain incline could constitute a barrier to the wind, turbulence and down-drafts must be anticipated because of air spilling over and down.

It's usually best to land the helicopter cross-slope rather than upslope. And, landing downslope or downhill is definitely *not* recommended because of the possibility of striking the tail rotor on the ground during normal flare out.

Manuever slowly toward the incline, being especially careful not to turn the tail upslope. The helicopter should be hovered in a position cross-slope, directly over the spot of intended landing.

A slight downward pressure on the collective will put the copter in a slow descent. As the upslope skid touches the ground, apply cyclic pressure in the direction of the slope.

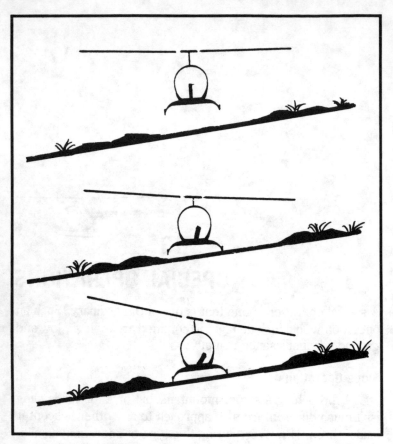

Slope landing and takeoff.

This will hold the skid against the incline, while you continue a gradual letdown with the collective.

As collective is reduced, continue to move the cyclic toward the slope as needed to maintain a fixed position. The slope must be shallow enough to allow you to hold the craft against it with the cyclic during the entire landing.

A five-degree slope is considered maximum for normal operation of most helicopters. Each make of machine will generally let you know in its own particular way when you're about to run out of lateral cyclic, such as the rotor hub hitting the rotor mast, vibrations felt through the cyclic, etc. If you encounter such warnings, don't land. They indicate the slope is too steep for safe operations.

Aerospatiale SA 365.

Once the downslope skid has touched the ground, continue to lower the collective until reaching the stop. Maintain normal rotor operating rpm until the full weight of the chopper rests on the skids. This will assure adequate rotor rpm for immediate takeoff if the craft should start to slide downhill. Use the rudders as necessary throughout the landing to maintain heading.

The procedure for a slope takeoff is almost the exact reverse of that for a slope landing. Adjust the throttle to obtain takeoff rotor rpm and slowly move the cyclic in the direction of the slope so that the rotor rotation plane is parallel to the true horizontal rather than the slope. Apply up-collective smoothly. As the helicopter becomes light on the skids, apply rudders as needed to maintain heading.

Upon raising the downslope skid and the helicopter approaches a level attitude, return the cyclic to the neutral position. Continue to apply up collective, taking the craft straight up to a hover, before moving away from the slope. As you depart, care should be taken that the tail doesn't turn upslope. Remember the danger of the tail rotor striking the ground.

Errors

1. Failure to maintain proper rotor rpm throughout the entire maneuver.
2. Letting the craft down too rapidly.
3. Failure to adjust cyclic to keep the craft from sliding downhill.

Confined Area Operations

A confined area is a local where the flight of your helicopter is limited in some direction by terrain or the presence of obstructions, natural or man made: a clearing in the woods, a city street, a road, a building roof, etc.

Barriers on the ground, or the ground itself, can interfere with the smooth flow of air, resulting in turbulence. This interference is transmitted to upper air levels as larger, but less, intense disturbances. Therefore the greatest turbulence is usually found at low altitudes. Gusts are unpredictable variations in wind velocity. Ordinary gusts are dangerous only in slow flight at very low altitudes. You might be unaware of such a gust. Its cessation could reduce airspeed below that required to sustain flight, due to the loss of effective translational lift. Gusts cannot be planned for or anticipated. Turbulence, however, can generally be predicted. You'll find turbulence in the following areas, when wind velocity exceeds 10 mph:

1. Near the ground on the downwind side of trees, buildings, hills or other obstructions. The turbulence area is always relative in size to that of the obstacle, and relative in intensity to the speed of the wind.
2. Near the ground on the immediate upwind side of any solid obstacle, such as trees in leaf and buildings. This condition isn't generally dangerous, unless the wind velocity is 15 knots or higher.
3. In the air, above and slightly downwind of any sizable obstruction, such as a hill or mountain range. The size of the obstruction and the wind speed govern the height to which the turbulence extends and also its severity.

You should know the direction and approximate speed of the wind at all times. Plan landings and takeoffs with the wind conditions in mind. This doesn't necessarily mean that takeoffs and landings should always be made into the wind, but wind must be considered, and its velocity will, many times, determine proper avenues on approach and takeoff.

In case of engine failure, plan flights over areas suitable for forced landing, if possible. You might find it necessay to choose between a crosswind approach over an open area and one directly into the wind but over heavily wooded or extremely rough terrain where a safe forced landing would be impossible. Perhaps the initial approach phase can be made crosswind over the open area, and then it may be possible to execute a turn into the wind for the final approach portion.

Always operate the copter as closely to its normal capabilities as possible while considering the situation at hand. In all confined area operations, with the exception of the pinnacle operation, of course, the angle of descent should be no steeper than is necessary to clear any barrier in the avenue of approach and still land on the pre-selected spot. The angle of climb on takeoff shouldn't be any steeper than is necessary to clear any barrier. It's far better to clear the barrier by just a few feet and maintain normal rotor operating rpm with, perhaps, a reserve of power, than it is to clear the obstruction by a wide margin but with dangerously low rotor rpm and no power reserve.

Always make the landing to a specific point and not to just some general area. The more confined the area the more essential it is that you land the helicopter precisely on a definite point. Keep this spot in sight during the entire final approach phase.

Any increase in elevation between the point of takeoff and the point of intended landing must be given due consideration, because sufficient power must be available to bring the chopper to a hover at the point of the intended landing. A decrease in wind speed should also be allowed for with the presence of obstructions.

If you're flying a helicopter near obstructions, it's critical that you consider the tail rotor. Therefore, a safe angle of descent over barriers must be established to ensure tail rotor clearance. After coming to a hover, avoid swinging the tail into obstructions.

Make a high reconnaissance to determine the suitability of the area for a landing. In a high reconnaissance, the following items should be accomplished:

1. Determine wind direction and speed.
2. Select the most suitable flight paths in and out of the area, with particular consideration being given a forced landing.
3. Plan the approach and select a touchdown point.
4. Locate and determine the size of obstacles immediately around the chosen area.

A high reconnaissance is flown at about 500-feet AGL, however, a higher altitude may be required in some craft.

Always ensure sufficient altitude to land into the wind in case of engine failure. This means the greatest altitude will be

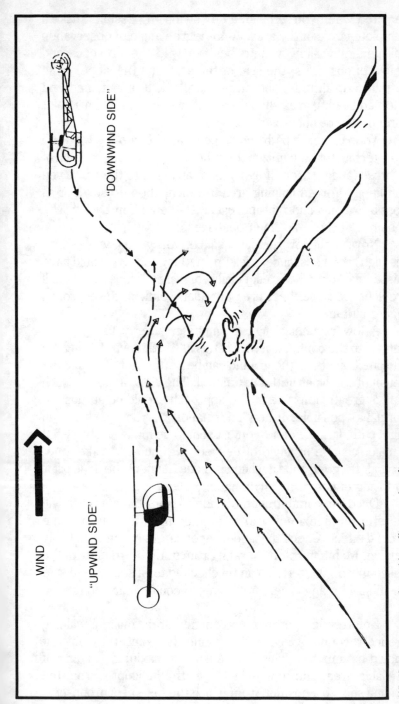

WIND

"UPWIND SIDE"

"DOWNWIND SIDE"

Windflow over mountain and its effect on aircraft.

required when you're headed downwind. If possible, make a complete circle of the area. A 45-degree angle of observation will generally allow you to best analyze the presence and height of obstacles, the size of the area and the slope of the terrain. Safe altitudes and airspeeds should be maintained, and a forced landing area should be kept within reach. This point can't be overemphasized.

Your approach path should generally be into the wind and over terrain that minimizes the time that you're out of reach of a forced-landing area. If by flying at an angle to the wind, you can keep a forced landing area in reach, then do so. If at all possible, make a normal approach. A steeper approach will be required, if there are high obstacles.

Now, in the low reconnaissance, verify what was seen in the high reconnaissance. Pick up anything that you could have missed earlier. Check especially for wires, slopes and small crevices, because these are particularly difficult to see from a higher altitude.

A low reconnaissance begins just after your approach entry into the confined area. It ends at touchdown. During the interim, objects on the ground can be better identified and the height of obstacles better estimated. The view of the approach path is greatly improved. The approach should be as close to normal as possible. If new information warrants a change in flight path or angle of descent, it should be made. However, if a major change in angle of descent is required, make a go-around. If a go-around decision is made, it should be done prior to losing effective translational lift.

Once the commitment is made to land, the approach will be terminated in a hover at an altitude that will conserve the ground effect. Check the landing spot carefully before actually landing. Maintain rotor operating rpm until the stability of the helicopter on the terrain can be checked for a secure and safe position. In many cases, not doing so could mean a long walk out.

Before taking off from a confined area, make a walking ground reconnaissance to determine the point from which it should be initiated. This is to ensure a maximum amount of available area, and how best to get the helicopter from the landing spot to a position from which the takeoff is proposed.

First thing, check the wind. If the rotor was left turning after landing, walk a sufficient distance from the craft to ensure that the downwash of the blades doesn't interfere. Light dust or grass may be dropped and the direction they are blown observed.

Next, go to the downwind end of the area, and mark a position for takeoff, so that the tail and main rotors will have sufficient clearance from obstructions. A sturdy marker, such as a heavy stone or log, should be used as this marker.

If rearward flight is required to reach the takeoff position, reference markers should be placed in front of the helicopter in such a way that a ground track can be safely followed to the takeoff position. If wind conditions and available area permit, hover-taxi downwind from the landing position to the takeoff spot.

In preparing for the actual takeoff from a confined area, first visualize the angle over obstacles from the takeoff position. The flight path should be over the lowest barrier that allows for taking best advantage of wind and terrain. Make the takeoff and climb as near normal as possible. Again, it's better to clear the obstructions by a few feet at normal rotor rpm than to sacrifice rotor rpm by attempting to clear by a large margin. Wind conditions should seriously be considered during the takeoff.

In general, flying over good terrain is preferable to heading directly into the wind, depending, of course, on the speed of the wind and the relative height of obstacles.

Because of its unique flight characteristics, a helicopter is capable of many missions no other aircraft can perform. You must, however, realize the hazards involved and know also what precautions to take in preserving the craft, as well as your life.

Here are a few basic and general precautionary rules that you should consider and keep in mind:

1. Don't perform acrobatic maneuvers.
2. Don't check magnetos in flight in lieu of ground checks during runup.
3. Use caution when adjusting mixture in flight.
4. Always taxi (air) slowly (about as fast as you can walk).

5. Always check balance prior to flying.
6. Use caution when hovering on the leeward side of buildings or obstruction.
7. Don't hover at an altitude that will place you in the shaded area of the height-velocity chart.
8. Always hover for a moment before beginning a new flight.
9. When practicing hovering turns, sideward flight and similar low airspeed maneuvers, be especially careful to maintain proper rpm.
10. When flying in rough, gusty air, use special care to maintain proper rpm.
11. Always clear the area overhead, ahead, to each side and below before entering practice autorotations.
12. Make sure any object placed in the cockpit of your helicopter is secured to prevent fouling of controls or mechanisms.
13. Except in sideward or rearward flight, always fly the aircraft from references ahead.

Rotor RPM Operating Limits

Limits of rotor rpm vary with each type of craft. In general, the lower limit is determined primarily by the control characteristics of a particular helicopter during autorotation. Since the tail rotor is driven by the main rotor, a minimum main rotor rpm exists at which tail rotor thrust is sufficient for proper heading control. Below this minimum main-rotor rpm, full rudder travel will not maintain heading under certain conditions of flight.

The upper limit for rotor rpm is based on both autorotative characteristics and structural strength of the rotor system. Structural tests, plus an adequate margin for safety, are required by FAA safety standards for the certification of the aircraft.

Extreme Attitudes and Overcontrolling

Avoid all maneuvers which would place the craft in danger of extreme and unusual attitudes. Design characteristics of a helicopter preclude the possibility of safe inverted flight.

Avoid helicopter loading that will cause an extreme tail-low attitude when taking off to a hover. Aft center CG is dangerous while hovering, and even more so in flight because of limited forward cyclic travel.

Avoid heavy loading forward of the CG. The result is limited aft cyclic travel, endangering controllability.

Avoid an extreme nose-low attitude when executing a normal takeoff. Such an attitude may require more power than the engine can deliver, and it will also allow the helicopter to settle to the ground in an unsafe landing attitude. In the event of a forced landing, only a comparatively level attitude can assure a safe touchdown.

Avoid abrupt applications of rearward cyclic. The violent backward-pitching action of the rotor disc may cause the main rotor to flex downward into the tailboom.

Avoid large or unecessary movements of the cyclic, while in a hover. Such movements of the cyclic can, under certain conditions, cause sufficient loss of lift to make the craft settle to the ground.

Flight Technique in Hot Weather

As discussed in an earlier chapter, hot temperatures drive density altitude up. When you encounter hot weather, piloting skill calls for special techniques. Follow these rules religiously:

1. Make full use of wind and translational lift.
2. Hover as low as possible and no longer than absolutely necessary.
3. Maintain maximum allowable engine rpm.
4. Accelerate very slowly into forward flight.
5. Employ running takeoffs and landings, whenever possible.
6. Use caution in maximum performance takeoffs and landings from steep approaches.
7. Avoid high rates of descent in all approaches.

High Altitude Pilot Technique

Of the three major factors limiting helicopter performance at high altitudes (gross weight, density altitude and wind), only gross weight may be controlled by the pilot of an unsupercharged helicopter. At the expense of range, you may carry smaller amounts of fuel to improve performance, increase the number of passengers or the amount of baggage. Where practical, use running landings and takeoffs. Make maximum use of favorable winds, with landings and takeoffs directly into them when possible. Other factors sometimes dictate otherwise.

When the wind blows over large obstructions, such as mountain ridges, turbulent conditions are set up. The wind blowing up the slope on the windward side is usually relatively smooth. However, on the leeward side, the wind spills rapidly down the slope, similar to the way water flows down a rough streambed. This tumbling action sets up strong downdrafts and causes very turbulent air. These violent downdrafts can cause aircraft to strike the sides of mountains. Therefore, when approaching mountain ridges against the wind, make an extra altitude allowance to assure safe terrain clearance. Where pronounced mountain ridges and strong winds are present, a clearance of 2000- 3000-feet AGL is considered a desirable minimum. Also, it's advisable to climb to the crossing altitude well before reaching the mountain barrier to avoid having to make the climb in a persistent downdraft.

When operating over mountainous terrain, fly on the upwind side of ridges. The safest approach is usually made lengthwise of the ridge at about a 45-degree angle. Fly near the upwind edge to avoid possible downdrafts and to be in position to autorotate down the upwind side of the slope in case of forced landing. Riding the updraft in this manner results in a lower rate of descent, improved glide ratio, and a greater choice of a landing areas.

Tall Grass and Water Operations

Tall grass will tend to disperse or absorb the ground cushion that you're used to over firm ground. More power will be required to hover, and takeoff could be tricky. Before attempting to hover over tall grass, make sure that at least two to three inches more manifold pressure are available than is required to hover over normal terrain.

Operations over water with a smooth or glassy surface makes altitude determination difficult. Exercise caution to prevent the helicopter from inadvertently striking the water. This problem doesn't exist over rough water, but a very rough water surface could disperse the ground effect and thereby require more power to hover. Movements of the water surface, wind ripples, waves, current flow or even agitation by the chopper's own rotor wash, will tend to give you a false sense of aircraft movement.

Carburetor Icing

Carburetor icing is a frequent cause of engine failure. The vaporization of fuel, combined with the expansion of air as it passes through the carburetor, causes a sudden cooling of the mixture. The temperature of the air passing through the carburetor can drop as much as 60-degrees F within a fraction of a second. Water vapor in the air is squeezed out by this cooling, and if the temperature in the carburetor reaches 32-degrees F or below, the moisture will be deposited as frost or ice inside the carburetor passages. Even a slight accumulation of such deposits reduces power and can lead to a complete engine failure, particularly when the throttle is partially or fully closed.

On dry days or when the temp is well below freezing, moisture in the air isn't generally enough to cause much trouble. But, if the temperature is 20-70-degrees F, with visible moisture or high humidity, the pilot should be constantly on the alert for carb ice. During low or closed throttle settings, an engine is particularly susceptible to carburetor icing.

Indications of carb ice include unexplained loss of rpm or manifold pressure; the carburetor air temp indicating in the "red" (danger) arc or "yellow" (caution) arc; and engine roughness. A loss of manifold pressure will generally give the first indication. However, due to the many small control changes (settings) made in the throttle and collective, this might be less noticeable. So, a close check of the carb air temperature gauge is necessary so that carburetor heat may be adjusted to keep the carb air temp gauge out of the red and yellow arcs.

Carburetor air temperature gauges are marked with a green arc, representing the range of desired operating temps; a yellow arc represents the range of temperatures in which caution should be exercised, since icing is possible; and a red arc represents the maximum operating temperature limit, or is used to represent the most dangerous range in which carb ice can be anticipated. The carb heat control should be adjusted so that the carburetor air temperature remains in the green arc.

The carburetor heater is an anti-icing device that preheats air before it reaches the carburetor. This preheating can be used to melt ice or snow entering the intake duct; melt ice that forms in the carburetor passages (provided the accumulation isn't too great); and to keep the fuel mixture above the freezing point, preventing formation of carb ice.

When conditions are favorable for carb ice, you should make the proper check for its presence often. Check the manifold pressure gauge reading, then apply full carburetor heat and leave it on until you're certain that if ice was present, it has been removed. (During this check, a constant throttle and collective setting should be maintained.) Carb heat should then be returned to the "off" position (cold). If the manifold pressure gauge indicates higher than when the check was started, and carb air temp gauges indicates a safe operation range, carb ice has been removed.

Fuel injection systems have replaced carburetors in some craft. In the fuel injection system, the fuel is normally injected into the system either directly ahead of the intake valves or into the cylinders themselves. In the carburetor system, the fuel enters the airstream at the throttle valve. The fuel injection system is generally considered to be less susceptible to icing than the carb system.

Effect of Altitude on Instrument Readings

The thinner air of higher altitudes causes the airspeed indicator to read slow in relation to True Airspeed. True airspeed may be roughly computed by adding to the Indicated Airspeed two per cent of the indicated airspeed for each 1000 feet of altitude MSL. For example, an indicated speed of 80 mph at 5000-feet MSL will be a True airspeed of about 88 mph. This computation may be made more accurately with the use of a computer.

Manifold pressure is reduced approximately one inch per 1000 feet above sea level. If you have 28-inches manifold pressure at 1000 feet, only 22-inches manifold pressure will be available at 7000. This loss of manifold pressure must be considered when planning flights to higher altitudes.

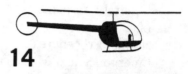

14

INTRODUCTION TO THE HELICOPTER FLIGHT MANUAL

It's your responsibility as pilot in command (PIC) to know all pertinent information for each helicopter you fly. The helicopter flight manual is designed to provide you with a general knowledge of the particular helicopter and the information necessary for its safe and efficient operation. Its function isn't to teach you to fly but, rather, to provide you with the best possible operating instructions, under most circumstances. The manual isn't intended as a substitute for sound judgement, however, as emergencies and other unforeseen situations may require modification of these procedures.

A helicopter flight manual accompanies each certificated helicopter. Although the manual for a particular craft may contain information identical to that contained in the flight manual for other helicopters of the same make and model, it may also contain data which is peculiar only to that one helicopter, especially the information on weight and balance. Helicopter flight manuals are prepared and furnished by the aircraft's manufacturers. Much of the information contained in them is required by FARs, Part 27, "Airworthiness Standards: Normal Category Rotorcraft." However, manufacturers often include additional information that is helpful to the pilot but which isn't specifically required.

When the helicopter manual contains information required by regulations that doesn't appear as placards in the craft, the manual must be carried in the machine at all times. The statement, "This document must be carried in the aircraft at all times," will appear somewhere on the manual if such conditions exist.

Most flight manuals would include the following, under chapters, sections, headings or a similar breakdown in information:

General Information
Limitations
Normal Procedures
Emergency and Malfunction Procedures
Performance Data
Weight & Balance
Aircraft Handling, Servicing & Maintenance

General Information

Data presented here would include an introduction, if there is one, method of presentation, helicopter description, certification, design and construction, and general dimensional data.

The Introduction might read someting to the effect: "The pilot's flight manual has been prepared with but one very fundamental goal in mind; that is, to provide the pilot with all information necessary to accomplish the intended mission with the maximum amount of safety and economy possible..."

The method of presentation means just that: Information in various sections is presented in different formats. It can be presented as a narrative, charts, tabular form, etc., or a combination. In any case, it will be described here. Notes, step-by-step procedures are also explained, such as the following examples:

The "Caution" symbol is used to alert you that damage to equipment could result, if the procedure step isn't followed exactly.

The "Warning" symbol is used to bring to your attention that not only damage to equipment but personal injury could occur, if the instruction is disregarded.

WARNING

The Helicopter Description gives an overall description of the craft. It may describe it as fast, lightweight, turbine-powered, all-purpose, etc. It would also give other key tidbits, such as its different uses and configurations: ambulance, internal/external cargo capability, aerial survey, patrol, photographic, air/sea rescue, agricultural, forestry and police applications, to name a few.

"Design and Construction" gives details as to material make-up, crew and passenger seating, power-plant and some of the craft's outstanding features, among others.

As an example, one entry in the Hughes 500D (Model 369D) explains: "...is a turbine powered, rotary-wing aircraft constructed primarily of aluminum alloy. The main rotor is

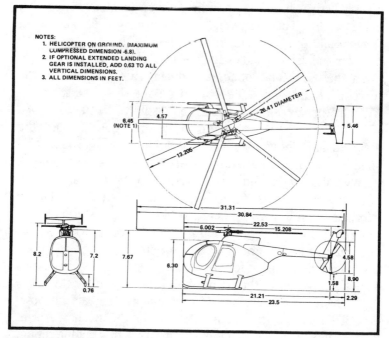

369D Helicopter principal dimensions.

five-bladed and fully articulated, the tail rotor is a two-bladed, antitorque semi-rigid type. Power from the turboshaft engine is coupled to the main and tail rotors by drive shafts and two transmissions. An overrunning (one-way) clutch in the drive between the engine and main transmission permits free-wheeling of the rotors for autorotational descent."

"General Dimensional Data" would include rotor characteristics, rotor speeds, control rigging of the main and tail rotor. Often general information graphs and charts are included for such conversions dealing with velocity, temperature, liquid, linear, weight and pressure. Also, a three-view drawing of the particular craft, showing its principal dimensions may be included.

Limitations

All aircraft have certain parameters within which they must fly. With the helicopter, these limitations would include airspeed limits, rotor-speed, weight and balance, powerplant and others. In some instances, limitations are as easy to comply with as keeping a needle within a green or yellow arc, while others, such as weight and balance, will take more thought and preplanning.

This section would include all important operating limitations that must be observed during normal operations. Airspeed Limits must be shown on the airspeed indicator (ASI) by a color coding or must be displayed in the form of a placard. A red radial line must be placed on the ASI to show the airspeed limit beyond which operation is dangerous. This speed is also known as the "never-exceed" speed or Vne. A yellow arc is used to indicate cautionary operating ranges, and of course, a green arc for safe or normal operation. Required information on Rotor Limits are marked on the tachometer by red radial lines and yellow arcs respectively, with normal operating ranges marked with a green arc, much as speed markings. Information for rotor limits, as well as airspeed, is sometimes given in the form of a chart or graph.

Powerplant limitation information will explain all powerplant limits and the required markings on the powerplant instruments. This will include such items as fuel octane rating, idling rpm, manifold pressure, oil pressure, oil temperature, cylinder-head temp, fuel pressure, mixture and others.

Normal Procedures

This section of the manual contains information concerning normal procedures for takeoff and landing, appropriate airspeeds peculiar to the rotorcraft's operating characteristics and other pertinent information necessary for safe operations. This portion may include the following procedures: checklists for preflight, before starting engine, starting engine, warmup, takeoff, inflight procedures and landing.

Normal procedures would also include such operations as low-speed maneuvering, practice autorotations, doors-off flight and post flight. Depending on the machine, of course, it could give you an instrument panel rundown, explain pilot controls and even give you a rundown on the fuel system.

Engine Start Procedures:

1. Mixture, IDLE CUT-OFF.
2. Fuel valve, ON.
3. Throttle friction released, Throttle closed.
4. Fuel boost, ON; check pressure.
5. Mixture FULL-RICH, 2.5-3.0 seconds; return to IDLE CUT-OFF.
6. Fuel boost, OFF.
7. Ignition switch, BOTH.
8. Engage starter.
9. When engine starts, mixture FULL-RICH.
10. Heater fan (exhaust muff heater), ON.
11. Set engine rpm at approximately 1400.
12. Fuel boost, ON.
13. Check engine oil pressure 25 psi minimum.
14. Alternator switch, ON.

Emergency & Malfunction Procedures

These procedures may warrent a section of their own, or they could be combined with "Normal Operating Procedures." However, in either case, they should be studied, until they

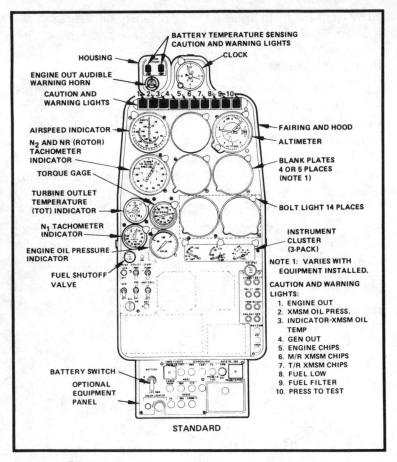

Instrument Panel

become second nature to you, and marked off for quick reference.

This section should cover such items as engine failure, ditching, tail rotor failure, and how to recognize and correct such emergencies. It would also contain failure of specialized, optional equipment, such as cyclic trim or the power turbine governor.

Recommendations for correcting such situations may read like this example on engine failure:

1. Establish a 60 mph autorotation.
2. If less than 2000-feet AGL, pick a landing spot, and proceed with autorotation landing.

3. Pull mixture control to IDLE CUT-OFF, when time permits, to stop flow of fuel from nozzles.

4. If altitude permits (cyclic can be gripped between knees to achieve the following):
   a. With mixture in IDLE CUT-OFF.
   b. Throttle—crack about ½ inch.
   c. Starter—press to engage.
   d. Mixture—push to FULL RICH position when engine fires.

(Note: If fuel boost pump was on at time of engine stoppage, a flooded condition could have resulted, necessitating additonal use of the starter.)

Performance Data

It's primarily from the information taken from graphs and charts found in this section that you're able to plot and figure how the craft will operate. This section should include such information as: rates of climb and hovering ceilings, together with the corresponding airspeeds and other pertinent information, including the calculated effect of altitude and temperature, maximum allowable wind for safe operation near the ground, and sufficient other data to outline the limiting heights and corresponding speeds for safe landing after power failure.

Using the Density Altitude and Best Rate of Climb Speed charts, find the best rate of climb speed you should use when at a pressure altitude of 7000 feet with a temperature of 20 degrees C.

1. Locate 20 degrees C along the bottom of the DA chart. Follow its line vertically, until it intersects 7000-feet pressure altitude. Move horizontally left to read a density altitude of approximately 9000 feet.

2. Using the Best Rate Of Climb chart, locate 9000-feet DA on the left side. Move horizontally from this point until intersecting the dark vertical line. From this point drop vertically straight down the graph to the craft's best rate of climb speed of 59-60 knots.

"Maximum allowable wind" for safe operations near the ground will be noted by a statement in most flight manuals, similiar to the following: "When hovering with wind from the

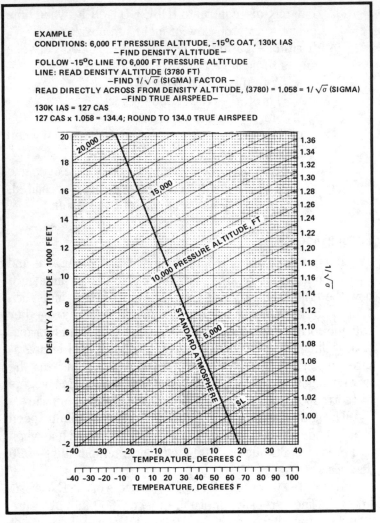

EXAMPLE
CONDITIONS: 6,000 FT PRESSURE ALTITUDE, -15°C OAT, 130K IAS
—FIND DENSITY ALTITUDE—
FOLLOW -15°C LINE TO 6,000 FT PRESSURE ALTITUDE
LINE: READ DENSITY ALTITUDE (3780 FT)
—FIND $1/\sqrt{\sigma}$ (SIGMA) FACTOR —
READ DIRECTLY ACROSS FROM DENSITY ALTITUDE, (3780) = 1.058 = $1/\sqrt{\sigma}$ (SIGMA)
—FIND TRUE AIRSPEED—

130K IAS = 127 CAS
127 CAS x 1.058 = 134.4; ROUND TO 134.0 TRUE AIRSPEED

Density Altitude Chart

left, expect random yaw oscillations; with wind from right, expect random pitch and roll oscillations in winds 10 knots and above."

Limiting heights and corresponding speeds for safe landing after power failure are generally incorporated in a chart called the "Airspeed vs. Altitude Limitations Chart" or "Height-Velocity Curve, Diagram or Chart." This chart generally appears in the performance section of the manual, but occasionally can be found in the "Operating Limitations Section."

You'll notice in the Height-Velocity Chart presented here the recommended takeoff profile. A normal takeoff would be to lift off to about eight feet AGL and accelerate to around 36 knots, before initiating a climb. Once the climb is started, it recommends a gradual increase in airspeed to 60 knots as a height of 75-feet AGL is attained.

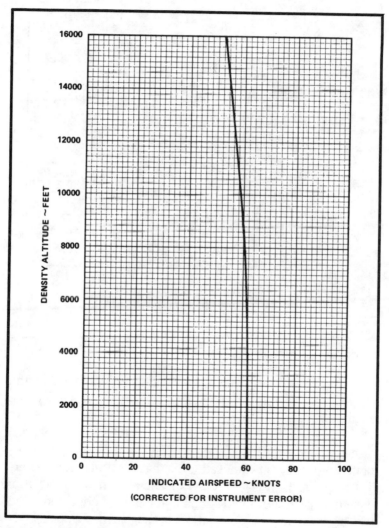

Speed for Best Rate of Climb.

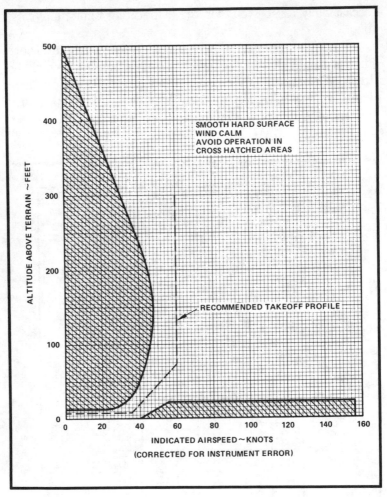

Height Velocity Diagram.

Care should be taken to avoid operations within the shaded area of the Height-Velocity Chart, as it signifies an unsafe operation.

All helicopters will normally have at least one placard displayed in a conspicuous position that has a direct and important bearing on safe operation of that particular helicopter. These placards will generally appear also in the machine's flight manual in the "Operating Limitations" section under the heading of "Placards, Caution or Warning." An example of this might be, "Strobe anticollision lights should be turned OFF during prolonged hover or ground operation over concrete, to avoid possible pilot distraction." Another example might be, "Solo pilot operation from the LEFT seat only."

Weight & Balance

The Weight & Balance portion must include rotorcraft weights and center-of-gravity (CG) limits, together with the items of equipment on which the empty weight is based. This will generally require the use of a chart or graph from which you can compute the CG position for any given loading situation.

If the unusable fuel supply in any tank exceeds one gallon or five percent of the tank capacity, whichever is greater, a warning shall be provided to indicate to flight personnel that when the quantity indicator reads "zero" the remaining fuel in the tank can't be used for flight. A complete explanation and sample problem on weight and balance follows in the next chapter.

Aircraft Handling, Servicing and Maintenance

Covered in this portion will be procedures for accomplishing the everyday operations. Such items as ground handling, the use of external power, moving and towing the copter, as well as parking, mooring and servicing. It also deals with the normal servicing operations, such as filling the fuel and oil system. Here's an example:

Replacing Transmission Lubrication Pump Oil Filter

1. Remove interior trim and blower access door.
2. Position container of cloth to catch residual oil. Loosen and remove filter housing by turning counterclockwise.
3. Remove filter element.
4. Inspect filter element for metal particles. If metal particles are present, remove main transmission chip detectors and inspect for other evidence of internal failure in the gearbox.
5. Install new filter element and new O-rings.
6. Install and tighten housing.

7. If necessary, replenish transmission oil supply, then perform ground runup of helicopter, and check split-line for oil leakage.
8. Reinstall, in order, blower access door and interior trim.

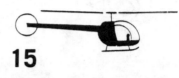

15

WEIGHT & BALANCE

All helicopters, like all aircraft, are designed for certain weight and balance conditions. But it's you, the PIC, who is responsible for making sure that the specified weight and balance limitations are met before takeoff. Any pilot who does takeoff in a helicopter that isn't within the designed weight and balance condition isn't only violating FAA regulations but is inviting disaster.

Four kinds of weight must be considered in the loading of every machine. They are empty weight, useful load, gross weight and maximum (allowable) gross weight.

Empty Weight can be described as the weight of the helicopter, including the structure, the powerplant, all fixed equipment, all fixed ballast, unusable fuel, undrainable oil and the total quantity of both engine coolant and hydraulic fluid.

Useful Load is the weight of the pilot, passengers, baggage (including removeable ballast) usable fuel and drainable oil.

Gross Weight is simply the empty weight plus the useful load. The sum of these two weights must now be compared with the fourth weight to be considered—maximum gross weight.

Maximum Gross Weight is the heaviest weight for which the craft is certificated to fly or operate under varying condi-

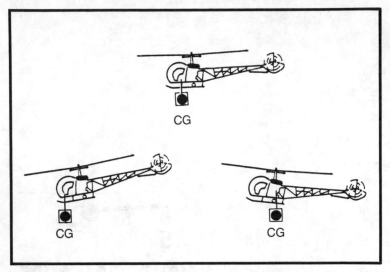

Notice the CG effect on cyclic position and helicopter attitude during hovering flight.

tions. Some helicopter manufacturers use the term "basic weight" in determining the weight and balance of their helicopters. Basic weight includes the empty weight, as previously defined, plus the weight of the drainable oil. Whenever the term "basic weight" is used, it should be understood that this is its meaning.

Although a helicopter is certificated for a specified maximum gross weight, it will not be safe to take off with this load under all situations. Conditions that affect takeoff, climb, hovering and landing performance may require the off-loading of fuel, passengers or baggage to a weight less than the maximum allowable. Such conditions would include high altitudes, high temperatures and high humidity, the combination of which makes for a high density altitude. Additional factors to consider are takeoff and landing surfaces, takeoff and landing distances and the presence of obstacles.

Because of the various adverse conditions that may exist, many times you'll have to decide the needs of the type of mission to be flown, and load your craft accordingly. For example, if all seats are occupied and maximum baggage is carried, gross weight limitations could dictate that less than max fuel be carried. On the other hand, if you're interested in

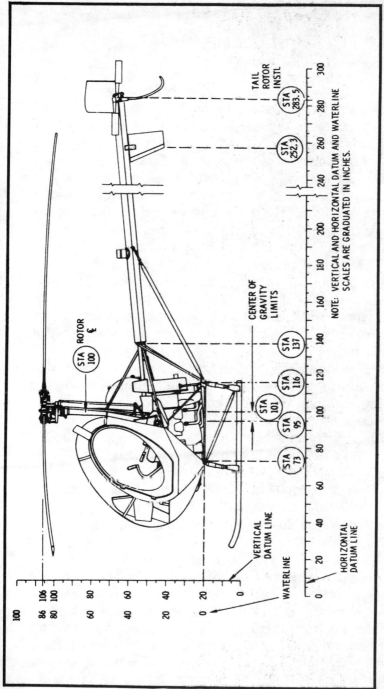

Balance Diagram.

183

range, you may elect to carry a full load but fewer passengers and less baggage.

Balance

Not only must you consider the gross weight of the helicopter, but you must also determine that the load is arranged to fall within the allowable center-of-gravity (CG) range, which is specified in the helicopter flight manual. The CG is the point where the copter is in balance—the point at which all the weight of the system is considered to be concentrated. If the helicopter were suspended by a string attached to the "CG Point," the craft's fuselage would remain parallel to the ground, much as a perfectly balanced teeter-totter. The allowable range in which the CG must fall is referred to as the "CG Range." The exact location and length of this range is specified for each machine, but it usually extends a short distance fore and aft of the main rotor mast. For most helicopter types, the location of the CG must be kept within much narrower limits than for airplanes—in some cases less than three inches.

The ideal condition is to have a machine in such perfect balance that the fuselage will remain horizontal in hovering flight, with no cyclic pitch control necessary, except that necessary for windage. The fuselage acts as a pendulum suspended from the rotor.

Any change in the CG changes the angle at which it hangs from this point of support. If the weight is concentrated directly under the rotor mast, the helicopter hangs horizontal; if the center-of-gravity is too far aft of the mast, the machine hangs with nose tilted up; and if the CG is too far forward of the mast, the nose tilts down. Hence, out of balance loading of the chopper makes control more difficult and decreases maneuverability, since cyclic travel is restricted in the direction opposite of the CG location. Because helicopters are relatively narrow and high sideward speeds will not be attained, lateral balance presents no problems in normal flight instruction and passenger flights, but some light helicopters specify the seat from which solo flight must be made. However, if external loads are carried in such a position that a large, lateral displacement of the cyclic is required to maintain level flight, fore and aft cyclic movements might be limited.

CG Forward Of Allowable Limits

This condition arises more often in two-place helicopters; a heavy pilot and passenger take off without baggage or proper ballast located aft of the rotor mast. The condition will become worse as the flight progresses, due to fuel consumption, if the main fuel tank is located behind the rotor mast.

You'll recognize this condition after coming to a hover, following a vertical takeoff. The copter will have a nose-low attitude, and an excessive rearward cyclic will be required to hold a hover in a no-wind condition, if hovering flight can be maintained at all. Flight under this condition shouldn't be

If new equipment is added or taken away from the helicopter after leaving manufacturer, it must be corrected on the craft's weight & balance. These two items could be enough to warrant a change.

continued, since the possibility of running out of rearward cyclic control will increase rapidly as fuel is consumed. You might even find it impossible to increase the pitch attitude sufficiently to bring the chopper to a stop. Also, in case of engine failure and the resulting autorotation, sufficient cyclic might not be available to flare properly for the landing.

Hovering in a strong wind will make a forward CG less easy to recognize, since less rearward displacement of the cyclic will be required than when hovering in a no-wind condition. You should, therefore, consider the wind speed in which you're hovering and its relation to the rearward displacement of the cyclic in determining if a critical balance condition exists.

CG Aft of Maximum Limits

Without proper ballast in the cockpit, this condition could arise when: a lightweight pilot takes off solo with a full load of fuel located aft of the rotor mast; a lightweight pilot takes off with maximum baggage allowed in a compartment located behind the rotor mast; or a lightweight pilot takes off with a combination of baggage and substantial fuel where both are aft of the rotor mast. You'll recognize this condition after bringing the craft to a hover, following a vertical takeoff. The chopper will have a tail-low attitude, and an excessive forward cyclic will be required to hold a hover in a no-wind condition, if a hover can be maintained at all. If there's a wind, an even greater forward displacement will be required.

If you continue flight in this condition, you could find it impossible to fly at high airspeeds due to insufficient forward cyclic displacement to hold a nose-low attitude. This particular condition could become quite dangerous if gusty or rough air accelerates the machine to a higher airspeed than forward cyclic will allow. The nose will start to rise and full forward cyclic might be insufficient to hold it down or lower it once it does rise.

Weight & Balance Information

When a helicopter is delivered from the factory, the empty weight, empty weight CG and useful load for each particular craft are noted on a weight & balance data sheet included in the helicopter flight manual. These quantities will vary for different helicopters of a given series, depending on variations in fixed equipment included in each helicopter when delivered.

If, after delivery, additional fixed equipment is added, or if some is removed, or a major repair or alteration is made which may affect the empty weight, empty weight CG or useful load, the weight and balance data must be revised to reflect this new information and its effect on that particular craft. All weight and balance changes will be entered in the appropriate aircraft records. This generally will be the aircraft logbook. Make sure you use the latest weight and balance data in computing all loading problems.

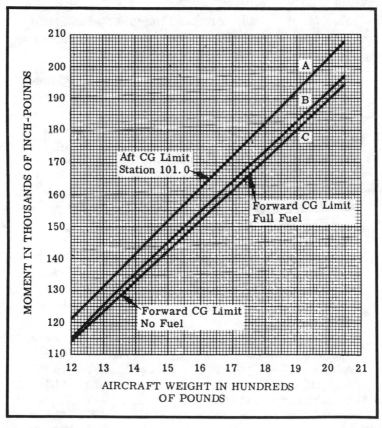

Loading Chart.

Sample Weight & Balance Problem

In loading a helicopter for flight you have to answer two very basic questions: Is its gross weight within the "maximum allowable gross weight," and does that weight's CG fall within the allowable "CG range?"

To answer the first question, merely add the weight of the items comprising the useful load (pilot, passengers, useable fuel, drainable oil and baggage) to the empty weight of the machine. Then check the total weight obtained to see that it doesn't exceed maximum allowable gross weight. If basic weight is used in computing weight and balance, then the weight of the oil is included with this weight.

To answer the second question, use the loading chart or loading table in the aircraft's flight manual for the particular helicopter being flown.

Sample Problem: Determine if the gross weight and CG are within allowable limits under the following conditions based on the sample loading charts.

	Pounds
Basic Weight	1070
Fuel (full tank—30 gallons).................................	180
Pilot (Station 83.2)...	170
Passenger (right hand—Station 83.2).....................	170
Passenger (center—Station 80.0)...........................	170

By adding the individual weights together, you should come out with a gross weight sum of 1760 pounds. Now, does the gross weight fall at or below the maximum allowable gross weight specified for this helicopter? With a maximum gross of 2050 pounds, 1760 gross is well below max.

How about CG range, does the "CG point" fall within the CG range? With the use of the "Load Weight—Pounds" chart, find the moment in thousands of inch-pounds for each position or station. With the sample, as stated above, it should look something like this:

	Pounds	**Moment**
Basic Weight	1070	108,915
Fuel (full tank—30 gallons)......................	180	19,260
Pilot (Station 83.2)...............................	170	14,144
Passenger (right hand—Station 83.2).........	170	14,144
Passenger (center—Station 80.0)..............	170	13,600
	1760	170,063

Where will the total moment and weight fall within the CG Range? To find out, simply go to the loading chart and plot the CG. First, plot the aircraft's gross weight in hundreds of pounds across the bottom of the chart, and the total moment in thousands of inch-pounds vertically on the left side. Once these two points have been found, it's simply a matter of drawing a line vertically up the chart from pounds and a line horizontally across the chart from the moment. Where these two intersect on the chart will be your craft's CG point. Does this CG point fall within the CG range (the bold, black lines)? Sure it does. It's between lines "A" and "B" and, therefore, your loading meets all balance requirements.

Sample problems such as this should be worked until you feel comfortable using the craft's charts and graphs. It also makes you more familiar with the operation of your particular helicopter, and this means a safer operation.

GLOSSARY

GLOSSARY

advancing blade: As the rotor spins around its shaft, the blade turning into the wind is the advancing blade. If the helicopter is moving forward, the advancing blade will be in the right half of the rotor disc; if moving backward, it will be in the left; if moving sideward to the left, it will be in the forward half; and if moving sideward to the right, it will be in the rear half.

airfoil: Any surface designed to obtain a useful reaction from the air through which it moves in the form of lift. A streamline shape of aerodynamic surfaces which are designed to produce a minimum of drag and a maximum of lift.

angle of attack: The acute angle measured between the chord of an airfoil and the relative wind.

articulated rotor: A rotor system in which the blades are free to flap, drag and feather. A mode of attaching the rotor blade to the mast. A blade is said to be "fully articulated" when it's similar to the shoulder joint in its root attachment. This joint allows the rotor blade to flap up and down, move fore and aft to lead and lag and twist around its own axis in a feathering motion.

autorotation: Self-energized turning of the rotor. Unlike "windmilling," where blade pitch is negative and energy is extracted from the rotor, autorotation is obtained with slightly positive pitch settings and no energy is extracted from the rotor. This creates maximum amount of lift.

bank: Sideward tilt of. It may be necessary to keep the craft from skidding, or side-slipping, during a turn. In a correctly executed turn, the bank compensates for the centrifugal force, and the pilot is pressed straight down into the seat, without any side force.

blade: One of the blades of the rotor. Usually more than just one is used. If the rotor has two or three or more blades, it's described as a two-bladed or three-bladed rotor, respectively.

blade damper: A device; spring, friction or hydraulic, installed on the vertical (drag) hinge to diminish or dampen blade oscillation (hunting) around this hinge.

blade loading: The load placed on the rotor blades of a helicopter, determined by dividing the gross weight of the copter by the combined area of all rotor blades.

camber: Is the curvature of the centerline of an airfoil. A symmetrical airfoil is said to have zero camber, because its mean contour is flat and the upper surface of the airfoil is a mirror image of the bottom surface.

ceiling: Maximum height to which a given helicopter can climb. Air is thinner at higher altitudes and the ceiling is reached when either the engine loses too much power or the blade airfoil begins to stall, or both. This happens at "absolute ceiling." An altitude at which the craft still has the ability to climb 100 fpm is "service ceiling."

center of gravity (CG): An imaginary point where the resultant of all weight forces in the body may be considered to be concentrated for any position of the body.

center of pressure: The imaginary point on the chord line of an airfoil where the resultant of all aerodynamic forces of the airfoil section may be considered to be concentrated.

centrifugal force: The force created by the tendency of a body to follow a straight-line path against the force which causes it to move in a curve, resulting in a force which tends to pull away from the axis of rotation. Applied to the helicopter, the force that would make the rotor blade fly out if it were not attached at the hub.

chord: The length of an airfoil as depicted by an imaginary straight line between the leading and trailing edges of that airfoil.

chordwise balance: An engineering term that refers to the mass balance of the airfoil. It's usually made to coincide with its center of lift. If this is not done, blade flutter could develop in flight, which might destroy the entire blade.

collective pitch control (collective): Affecting all rotor blades in the same way. Collective pitch control changes the pitch of all rotor blades in unison, thus varying the total lift of the rotor. The method of control by which the pitch of all rotor blades is varied equally and simultaneously.

cone angle (coning angle): The angle a rotor blade makes with the plane of rotation, similar to the dihedral angle of a fixed wing. Since the rotor blade is hinged at the hub, it's held out by centrifugal force, but since it also produces lift, it's deflected upward.

coriolis effect: The tendency of a mass to increase or decrease its angular velocity, when its radius of rotation is shortened or lengthened, respectively.

cyclic pitch control: Repetitive once-around-the-circle change in the pitch angle of each rotor blade as it turns around the axis. Cyclic control is also known as "azimuth" control, and its purpose is to tilt the direction of lift force of the rotor, rather than to change its magnitude. The control which changes the pitch of the rotor blades individually during a cycle of revolution to control the tilt of the rotor disc and, therefore, the direction and velocity of horizontal flight.

delta hinge (flapping hinge): The hinge with its axis parallel to the rotor plane of rotation, which permits the rotor blades to flap to equalize lift between the rotor disc.

damper: A mechanical device, similar to a shock absorber, installed on helicopters for the purpose of preventing the buildup of destructive oscillations. Dampers are found in rotorcraft in two critical areas: on the landing gear and on lag hinges of rotor blades. Without dampers, dangerous "ground resonance" would occur on many modern copters.

density altitude: Pressure altitude corrected for temperature and humidity. An altitude that's computed from the three H's (high altitude, high temperature and high humidity). Your craft performs like it's at that altitude, even though it's actually at a different altitude MSL.

disc: An area swept by the rotor blades. Although the rotor in flight actually sweeps a cone surface, for purposes of calculations, it's customary to speak of it as a disc. This is a circle, with its center at the hub axis and a radius of one blade length.

disc loading: Is similar to "wing loading" of a fixed winger. It's the ratio of helicopter gross weight to rotor disc area (total chopper weight divided by the rotor disc area). The greater the disc loading the greater is the craft's sinking speed with power off and the steeper its angle of glide. Most helicopters are disc-loaded three to five, but some heavy cargo copters' disc loading goes up to 10.

dissymmetry of lift: The unequal lift across the rotor disc resulting from the difference in the velocity of air over the advancing blade half and retreating blade half of the rotor disc area.

fatigue: A property of structural materials, similar to that of human beings, which makes them break down under repeated stresses, while they wouldn't break down under stresses twice as high if applied only a few times. Vibration is the major cause of fatigue failures in helicopters. Because vibration cannot be completely eliminated from rotorcraft, fatigue is still the number one enemy of its designers and also the user.

feathering axis: The axis about which the pitch angle of a rotor blade is varied. Sometimes referred to as spanwise axis. Rotating around the long axis of the rotor blade, changing its pitch angle. In helicopters, feathering axis usually is designed to go through the quarter-chord of the airfoil to minimize control stick forces.

feathering action: That action which changes the pitch angle of the rotor blades periodically, by rotating them around their feathering (spanwise) axis.

flapping: The vertical movement of a blade about a delta (flapping) hinge. Rotor blades flap as much as eight degrees in forward flight. Without flapping, a craft would roll over on its side, because the advancing blade would produce more lift than the retreating blade.

flare (flareout): A landing maneuver in which the angle of attack is increased near the ground, executed in helicopters as well as fixed wing craft and birds, which consumes the kinetic energy of forward velocity to arrest the descent. In a correctly executed flareout, horizontal velocity and vertical velocity come to zero at the same time, making a perfect zero-speed touchdown.

flutter: A self-induced oscillating motion of an aerodynamic surface, such as the main or tail rotors. It resembles, somewhat, the flapping motion of a bird's wings, except that energy is extracted from the airstream rather than pumped into it. Noseweights on rotor blades are installed to prevent flutter. Occurences of flutter in copters can be catastrophic and must be avoided at all costs.

freewheeling unit: A component part of the transmission or power train which automatically disconnects the main rotor from the engine when the engine stops or slows below the equivalent of rpm.

gimbal: A mechanism which permits the tilt of the rotor head in any direction, but restrains its rotation. If axes of tilt don't intersect the axis of rotation of a rotor, the gimbal is said to be "offset." A correctly designed Offset Gimball Head allows the craft to fly hands-off for an unlimited length of time.

ground effect: The "cushion" of denser air confined beneath the rotor system of a hovering helicopter, which gives additional lift and, thus, decreases the power required to hover. It's the extra buoyancy near the ground, which makes the craft float a few feet off the ground on a pillow of air. Ground proximity does, in fact, increase the lift of a rotor up to the height of one diameter above the surface.

ground resonance: A violent "dance jig" that a helicopter sometimes develops when its rotor is turning while it stands on the ground. It happens only to choppers equipped with lag hinges and inadequate dampers. Lag motions of the blades become amplified by the flexibility of the landing gear, and the craft can destroy itself in a few seconds, if power is not shut off at once.

gyroscopic precession: A characteristic of all rotating bodies. When a force is applied to the periphery of a rotating body parallel to its axis of rotation, the rotating body will tilt in the direction of the applied force 90 degrees later in the plane of rotation.

hovering in ground effect (HIGE): Maintaining a fixed position over a spot on the ground or water which compresses a cushion of high-density air between the main rotor and the ground or water surface and, thus, increases the lift produced by the main rotor. Normally, the main rotor must be within one-half rotor diameter to the ground or water surface in order to produce an efficient ground effect.

hovering out of ground effect (HOGE): Maintaining a fixed position over a spot on the ground or water at some altitude above the ground at which no additional lift is obtained from ground effect.

hunting: The tendency of a blade, due to coriolis effect, to seek a position ahead of, or behind, that which would be determined by centrifugal force alone.

lag-lead: Motions of blades in the plane of the rotor around "lag hinges." They were introduced on rotors with three or more blades to minimize severe, in-plane stresses caused by the difference in drag on the blade as it went from advancing to retreating positions. Not all rotors have lag hinges, some two-bladed rotors don't have them. They obtain the same lag-lead stress relief by using a flexible mast.

life: Maximum safe duration of operation of any part of a helicopter. It is limited by the probability of either fatigue failure or excessive wear. Life of ball bearings could be 10,000 hours; V-belts 500, rotor blades 2000 hours, etc. Everything on a helicopter must be regarded as having limited life of uncertain duration, unless designed by qualified, professional engineers for unlimited life.

milking: A term applied to a procedure for regaining main rotor rpm.

mast: Main structural member of the rotor craft which connects the airframe to the rotor. In spite of its simple function, the mast must be very carefully designed to minimize the feedback of damaging vibrations between the rotor and the airframe.

noseweight: A lead weight attached to the leading edge of an airfoil. Its function is to prevent flutter.

pattern: In-plane lineup of rotor blades so they perfectly balance each other. For example, in a two-bladed rotor, if the line connecting the center of gravity of each blade doesn't pass through the center of rotation, the blades are said to be "out of pattern." Such a rotor would develop a one-per-rev vibration similar to out-of-balance.

pitch angle: The angle between the chord line of a rotor blade and the reference plane of the main rotor hub or the rotor plane of rotation.

radius of action: Maximum distance a helicopter can fly from its home base and return, without refueling.

range: Maximum distance a helicopter can fly without landing or refueling.

redundancy: A fail-safe design which provides a second standby structural member should the main one fail, or providing two members to do the same function. Dual ignition in aircraft engines is a typical redundancy. Because doubling up of everything would be expensive in both the weight and money, engineers use redundancy only in those areas where the probability of failure of a single member is high, or where it would result in catastrophic damage.

retreating: Retreating blade is on the opposite side of the advancing blade. It travels with the wind created by the forward motion. If forward velocity of the craft is zero, and there is no wind, simply opposite the advancing blade.

rigid rotor: A rotor system with blades fixed to the hub in such a way that they can feather but cannot flap or drag.

roll: Tilt of the rotorcraft around its longitudinal axis. Controlled by lateral movements of the cyclic.

rotor: The lift-producing, rotarywing part of the rotorcraft. It consists of one or more blades and is correctly described as a two-bladed rotor, three-bladed rotor, etc. "Rotor blade" refers to a single blade only.

semirigid rotor: A rotor system in which the blades are fixed to the hub but are free to flap and to feather.

slip: The controlled flight of a helicopter in a direction not in line with its fore and aft axis.

solidity ratio: Portion of the rotor disc which is filled by rotor blades; a ratio of total blade area to the disc area. The ratio of total rotor blade area to total rotor disc area.

spar: The main, load-carrying, structural member of the rotor blade. It carries the centrifugal force as well as lift loads from the blade tip to the root attachment. A second spar sometimes is added for redundancy.

standard atmosphere: Atmospheric conditions in which the air is a dry, perfect gas; the temperature at sea level is 59 degrees F (15 degrees C); the pressure at sea level (or reduced to sea level) is 29.92 inches Hg; and the temperature gradient is about 3.5 degrees F per 1000-feet change in altitude.

swashplate: A tilting plate, mounted concentrically with the rotor shaft. It consists of rotating and non-rotating halves, the rotating part being connected to the pitch horns of each rotor blade, and the non-rotating part to the cyclic. Thus the pilot can control the pitch of each blade while the rotor is turning.

teetering: Hinge and motion around it, in see-saw fashion, in two-bladed rotors. It allows one blade to flap up and forces the other blade to flap down. Use of teetering hinge allows direct transfer of centrifugal forces from one blade to the other, without going through the mast and separate flapping hinges.

tip path: The plane in which rotor blade tips travel when rotating.

tip speed: Airspeed at the tip of the rotor blade. Too high a tip speed is wasteful in power, too low a tip speed gives problems of controlling the retreating blade. Tip speed of small rotorcraft varies from 300 fps (200 mph) to 750 fps (500 mph). Lower tip speed yields greater lifting efficiency.

tip stall: The stall condition on the retreating blade which occurs at high forward speeds.

torque: A force, or combination of forces, that tends to produce a countering rotating motion. In a single rotor helicopter, where the rotor turns counterclockwise, the fuselage tends to rotate clockwise (looking down on the helicopter). Anything that rotates and consumes power, produces a reaction torque in the direction opposite to its rotation. Tail (antitorque) rotors are added to helicopters to overcome torque produced by main rotor rotation.

tracking: Tracking of the rotor is an operation necessary to assure that every blade rotates in the same orbit. This means that each blade tip must follow the path of the preceeding one. If not, a vibration will develop, which is similar to the dynamic unbalance of a wheel. To put a rotor "in track," the trim tab of the low blade should be bent up and vice-versa.

transition: A narrow region of flight speed in helicopters, usually between 10-20 mph, when they slide off the ground cushion, and before they pick up the added lift of forward translation. The airflow pattern through the rotor changes erratically during transition and is often accompanied by roughness and partial loss of lift.

translational lift: The additional lift obtained through airspeed because of increased efficiency of the rotor system, whether when transitioning from a hover into horizontal flight or when hovering in a high wind.

trim tab: A small metal plate projecting behind the trailing edge, near the tip, of a rotor blade. Its purpose is to aid in "tracking" the rotor. Without trim tabs, the pitch of the entire rotor blade would have to be changed to adjust its track.

weave: A form of rotor-blade instability, which may be caused by excessive, elastic softness of the rotor blade or of the control system. When weave occurs in improperly designed craft, the rotor suddenly stops following the pilot's commands and darts, seemingly, out of control. Like flutter, it must not be permitted to occur in flight.

yaw: Turning of the helicopter right or left around its vertical axis. In helicopters, its done by changing the pitch of the tail rotor.

INDEX

MAN-POWERED AIRCRAFT

Other TAB books by the author:

No. 2205 *Aircraft Metalwork*
No. 2230 *Restoration of Antique & Classic Planes*

MAN-POWERED AIRCRAFT
BY DON DWIGGINS

Copyright © 1979 by TAB BOOKS

Library of Congress Cataloging in Publication Data

Dwiggins, Don.
    Man-powered aircraft.

    Includes index.
    1. Human powered aircraft. I. Title.
TL769.D94   629.133'34   78-11137
ISBN 0-8306-9851-5
ISBN 0-8306-2254-3

Foreword

The story of man-powered flight has held the interest of the author since the 1930s, when he set out to chronicle the history of flight in the United States prior to the Wright Brothers' success at Kitty Hawk in 1903. Considerable correspondence was held with many inventors long since gone, and much of this material, never before in print, appears here for the first time.

The 1977 success of the *Gossamer Condor* in capturing the £50,000 Kremer Prize for the first MPA flight around a figure-8 course does not, in the author's view, mark the end of the ages-old quest for controlled human powered flight.

Rather it stands as a challenge for the future, where many more astounding flights under muscular power are surely in store for adventurous souls who still long to fly with the freedom of the birds.

Don Dwiggins

Acknowledgements

The author is deeply indebted to many persons who over the years have contributed unpublished stories and anecdotes of their experimental efforts to achieve man-powered flight.

Special recognition must also be given to the curators of several museums, and librarians, who assisted in researching this history of human flying.

Among these are: The Smithsonian Institution's National Air and Space Museum, the Library of Congress, the Royal Aeronautical Society, and the Aviation History Library Committee of Northrop Institute of Technology.

Among the published works consulted were: Astra Castra, by Hatton Turnor, Chapman & Hall, London, 1865; The History of Aeronautics in Great Britain, by J. E. Hodgson, Oxford University Press, London, 1924; Histoire de L'Aeronautique, Charles Dollfus & Henri Bouche, L'Illustration, Paris, 1932; Artificial and Natural Flight, Sir Hiram Maxim, Whittaker & Co., New York, 1908; Through the Air, by John Wise, To-Day Printing & Publishing Co., Philadelphia, 1873; Progress in Flying Machines, by Octave Chanute, The American Engineer & Railroad Journal, New York, 1894; Travels in Space, by E. Seton Valentine & F. L. Tomlinson, Hurst & Blackett, Ltd., London, 1902; Man Powered Flight, by Dr. Keith Sherwin, Model & Allied Publications, Ltd., Herts., UK, 1971; and The History of Man-Powered Flight, by D. E. Reay, Pergamon Press, Elmsford, N. Y., 1977.

Several fine biographies of Leonardo da Vinci are available, including: The World of Leonardo da Vinci, by Ivor B. Hart, Viking Press, N. Y., 1961; The Mind of Leonardo da Vinci, by Edward MacCurdy, Jonathan Cape, London, 1928; and da Vinci's own Codice Atlantico, in the Biblioteca Ambrosiana at Milan, Italy, and a dozen da Vinci notebooks identified as A to M, in the Institut de France.

Contents

Chapter 1
The Gossamer Condor

The huge hangar at the edge of Shafter-Kern County Airport is silhouetted against the skylight of a false dawn. Toward the east, the start of a new day outlines the black contours of the Sierra Nevada, California's major mountain range, behind the lights of Bakersfield. Inside the hangar a monster sleeps.

This is the lair of the *Gossamer Condor*, an unbelievably grotesque giant flying machine held together with a maze of piano wire and aluminum tubing, a chimera, unlike any other aircraft in the whole world. It has absolutely no practical value, except for one thing—its entire raison d'etre is to win a $50,000 prize, the coveted Kremer International Competition Award, posted by the Royal Aeronautical Society of Great Britain.

Since ancient times, man has dreamed of flying under his own power, the ultimate freedom. In recent years human flight actually has been achieved a number of times, in different parts of the world. But such flights were merely extended straight-line ventures into the air.

To *really* fly, to be one with the birds, a man must be able to bank and turn, climb and glide, maneuver at will through the three dimensions of the sky. A few machines have in fact made right-angled turns, but none so far had the inherent ability to fly through a figure-8 course.

Dr. Paul MacCready (r) with son Tyler.

This was the whole idea behind the challenge of Henry Kremer, a British research engineer, whose hobby was developing the muscles of his body to lift weights. Could man's muscles really lift himself into the sky, and propel him around a figure-8 course, between two loci set half a mile apart?

Could he design a machine that could cross a ten-foot hurdle at the start and finish of the course? If he could, Kremer mused, then ancient dreamers like Leonardo da Vinci could be proven right. Man *could* fly like the birds!

Bryan Allen arrived at the big hangar from his home in nearby Bakersfield feeling optimistic. This would be the day! The day he would make history by being the first man in the world to complete the Kremer course. He hoped. He was uniquely qualified for the challenge before him.

At 25, Bryan had that unusual blend of genetic, athletic, and aeronautical characteristics required for the task. At 6 feet and 137 pounds, he also possessed the strength/weight ratio necessary for human-powered flight. For the past four months he had been training for this day.

Besides making numerous practice flights in *Gossamer Condor*, he had shaped up physically by bike riding and exercising on a device

Tyler MacCready checks controls of Gossamer Condor.

called an Ergometer. On this device, loads are applied to typical bicycle pedals and crank, and dials tell what speed and horsepower output the rider is achieving. Bryan learned he could sustain .35 hp for 30 minutes, .45 hp for seven minutes, and 1.2 hp for short bursts.

Gossamer Condor was designed with such a specific horsepower output-per-unit-time in mind, to make the man-machine relationship successful in meeting the demands of the Kremer course.

A special physical fitness program had already been set up for the project by Dr. Joseph Mastropaolo of Long Beach State University, at the request of Dr. Paul MacCready, designer of the *Gossamer Condor*. Months before, Dr. MacCready and his son Tyler, 14, had embarked on a rigorous exercise program, to shape them up for test flying the *Gossamer Condor*. In only six weeks, Dr. MacCready, at 51, developed the stamina of an average good college athlete.

Bryan Allen had another qualification for the task—besides winning his high school's annual Bicycle Day track race three years in succession, he also was an experienced hang glider pilot. While no special piloting skills were found necessary to fly the *Gossamer Condor*, Bryan already was familiar with the sensations of ultralight flight.

Dr. MacCready, too, had a background in flying, that was essential to his grasp of the requirements of man-powered flight. As a youth he built model airplanes and won his private pilot license at 16. As a glider pilot he became International Champion at a soaring meet in France in 1956, the first American to achieve that goal.

In addition, he earned his Master's Degree in Physics at Cal-Tech in 1948 and his Ph. D. in Aeronautics at the same institution in 1952. Professionally, Dr. MacCready is president of a company he formed in 1970—AeroVironment, Inc.—involved in such areas as aircraft wake vortex investigations for flight safety, and wind power systems development.

The idea for building a machine to compete for the Kremer prize came to Dr. MacCready in July 1976, as he was working on an article comparing the flight of hawks to the flight of hang gliders. He saw that adapting hang glider construction techniques would permit construction of a very light, large, slow-moving vehicle. It would be easy to build, modify, and repair, and would require very little power to stay aloft.

First flight model of Gossamer Condor at Mojave.

Single-surface wing of first Gossamer Condor.

Within a few weeks he had built crude models of his proposed MPA, and then called in his close friend and vice-president of AeroVironment, Dr. Peter B. S. Lissaman, a South African by birth, who headed the firm's research work on wind energy programs for the government.

Dr. Lissaman had at his disposal a Hewlett-Packard 9821A computer, with which he was able to compress years of aerodynamic research and months of tedious computations into almost instant readouts. His goal was to develop critical airfoils for the main wing, the canard, and the propeller. The first two would be operating at very low airspeeds and at Reynolds Numbers between 500,000 and 1,000,000. Even the NASA wind tunnel people had left that region virtually virgin territory.

By October 1976, the *Gossamer Condor* was ready for rollout from its birthplace—the giant pavilion in Pasadena where the Tournament of Roses floats were constructed. Jack Lambie, a veteran soaring pilot and hang glider designer, helped to build the big machine, which spanned 88 feet and weighed a mere 50 pounds.

The building had to be vacated the next day, so the *Gossamer Condor* was rolled out at midnight of October 9, after only ten days' construction time. Curious visitors wondered what they were up to, but Dr. MacCready wanted the project kept absolutely secret, for good reason. The utter simplicity of the design might easily be copied and a rival machine might win the £50,000 Kremer prize ahead of the *Gossamer Condor*. In U. S. Dollars that was a tidy sum—about $87,500!

When one visitor asked Lambie what the darned thing was, he shrugged and replied: "Why, it's a new parade float, depicting the theme of government meddling in private affairs!"

There was a good reason for making the *Gossamer Condor* a crude machine—it could be rebuilt easily and quickly after the inevitable crashes it would endure, rather than taking months or a year to reassemble as the more sophisticated MPA's required.

The first version built in Pasadena, to check structure and pitch stability, had a wingspan of 88 feet, built around a single spar of 2-inch aluminum tubing. A maze of piano wires supported the wing from the top of an aluminum kingpost. Drag penalty of the wires, roughly 10% of the total parasitic drag, was negligible at the slow speeds the huge wing would be flying.

The wingspan and chord were determined by standard aerodynamic theory, while subsequent structural and aerodynamic design was aimed at permitting this wing plus a pilot to fly with a minimum of additional material. The initial criteria was limited to reliability and low power; the ability to maneuver in turns would come through trial and error.

Systems engineering and project management, often rather informal, were keys to the program's ultimate success. The overall approach was to try a simple solution for each problem encountered, thus more attention could be devoted to concepts that didn't work.

Eventually a new home was found for the project at Mojave Airport north of Los Angeles, where a pilot friend, Sean Roberts, had a huge hangar available. There the first operational prototype was built, with a bigger span of 95 feet, a chord of 11-¾ feet, and no streamlining of the pilot area.

The basic design concept was (a) support the wing spar with piano wire from the ends of a bottom post, king post, keel tube, and bowsprit, (b) have the pilot near the bottom of the bottom post to

Paul MacCready (on ladder) checks propeller blade of Gossamer Condor.

assist stability and pilot entry, (c) use the supine position to provide good forward visibility, to free the pilot's hands for controls, and to allow the main sprockets to be set right alongside the bottom post to take the chain tension, (d) put the propeller behind the wing for clearance and to keep its slipstream off the flight surface, (e) use a single surface airfoil for simplicity, (f) leave the pilot exposed for the time, but allow for future streamlining, and (g) ignore lateral control until satisfactory low-power straight flight was achieved.

After several design changes, the single-spar wing got a second spar to relieve compression and distortion of the ribs. Spreaders and wire bracing atop the airfoil helped relieve this problem.

Lissaman designed a 12-½ foot propeller with his computer magic, and developed a second, wider-blade version to permit the thrust to be increased 3 or 4-fold briefly for climbing or other

Plastic drive chain and idler wheel turns prop shaft of Gossamer Condor.

Pilot seat of Gossamer Condor #1.

"emergency" maneuvers. The latter propeller was used throughout the rest of the program.

Dr. MacCready's son Tyler made the first filght with the single-surface machine the day after Christmas, 1976, and stayed aloft 45 seconds after an assisted start. Through the next three months it was flown numerous times, and found to be too crude to fly for more than 2-½ minutes, far short of the time required to complete the Kremer course. It also flew badly in the slightest turbulence.

It was found that at the slow flying speed, even the lightest vertical turbulence altered the angle of attack along the wing locally, so that at any moment only a small portion of the wing would be operating within its narrow drag bucket. Lift distribution also would be altered far from the elliptical pattern desired.

Turns were next to impossible, due to high yaw forces that required extra power to overcome simply to stay aloft. A new "pilot" was found—Gregg Miller, a champion-caliber bike racer, with no flying experience but a fine set of well-coordinated muscles. Gregg

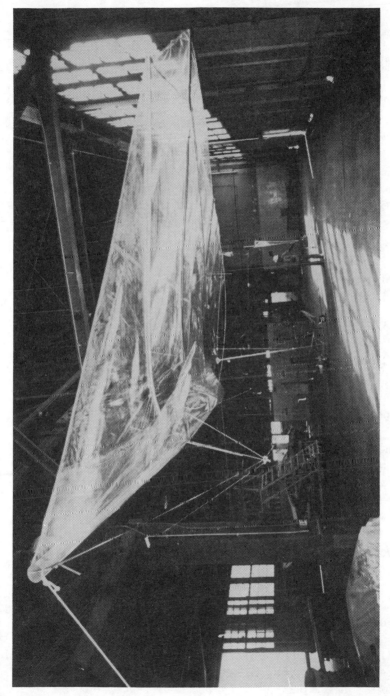

Gossamer Condor #1 at Mojave fills hangar.

could take off under his own power, and on his longest flight of 2-½ minutes covered more than 1,000 feet.

The author witnessed that amazing flight, which established a United States record for MPA's as it sailed serenely down the 10,000-foot runway of the ex-WWII Marine base at Mojave. Field elevation is 2,787 feet, but on that hot afternoon in January, the density altitude was maybe 4,000 feet.

Gregg Miller, a stocky 135-pounder, cranked slowly into the setting sun, some 10 feet off the deck, the red and yellow plastic propeller turning lazily at 110 rpm. He gripped the small steering wheel, turning it left and right to activate wingtip spoilers, and pushing and pulling to activate the canard out front for pitch control There was no rudder—do birds have rudders?

Paul MacCready sprinted alongside the machine, with his two sons, Tyler and Parker, both qualified MPA test pilots, and Jack Lambie. I could sense their overconfidence, and approved of it. Enthusiasm is needed on such a project.

There were even official observers on hand, in case Gregg did make it around the figure-8 course—M. W. (Woodie) Phillips, Technical Committee Chairman of the National Aeronautic Association, with two assistants, Alden DeWitt and Jess Bradshaw, stationed at the half-mile pylons. It was a bit ironic for these officials—only the summer before, they'd officially timed the world's fastest closed course flight of a USAF SR-71 bomber, at 2096 mph!

Gregg's legs finally tired, the *Gossamer Condor* settled down onto the runway, and Dr. MacCready knew the Kremer Prize was still unattainable. For a while, at least. A redesign was in order, and a new site had to be found, one with a much lower density altitude, and free from the unpredictable desert winds that lashed across the Mojave.

In March, 1977, operations were shifted to Shafter-Kern County Airport, in California's San Joaquin Valley. Work was immediately begun on a second flying *Gossamer Condor*, this one with a span of 96 feet, height 19-½ feet, length 30 feet, weight 30 pounds. The wing was double-surfaced, covered with ½ mil Mylar on top and ¼ mil Mylar underneath.

Design work now concentrated on stability and controllability, and a computer study revealed something interesting. Direct alteration of lift would have only a weak effect on roll, and a decrease in apparent mass at the wingtips was necessary, along with a decrease

Bike racer Gregg Miller flies Gossamer Condor #1.

21

in roll damping and considerable reliance on some yaw-roll (and roll rate) coupling.

A crude 36-inch balsa model was built, and pushed by hand through a swimming pool to study fluid accelerations, particularly those associated with the concept of apparent mass. The water tests confirmed results of the computer analysis, and so the wingtip chord was reduced to 5 feet, leaving the root chord at 10 feet.

This reduction in total wing area dictated that the pilot area be streamlined, and an 8-foot sweepback was added to meet balance and structural needs and help with the dihedral effect. The wing spar was moved back from the leading edge to the 28-½% chord position, and the ribs were made to cantilever on the spar and to hold their shape under load.

The double-surface airfoil was developed by Dr. Lissaman, using an interactive computer-human technique he developed for tailoring airfoils to special tasks. What he wanted was an airfoil of 11% thickness, nearly flat on the bottom, with a small pitching moment coefficient, high maximum C_l, low C_d over a wide C_l range, and sufficiently non-critical to cover mistakes in construction. Reynolds Numbers were between 500,000 and 1,000,000 in the concept.

In its final configuration, the *Gossamer Condor* wing used what was called the Lissaman 7769 airfoil, and its efficiency proved to be better than expected. The wing flew well and in combination with a rocking stabilizer, to provide a yawing force, it began showing good turning capability.

The final propeller, built by Lambie from Dr. Lissaman's computer figures, was made with balsa ribs and leading and trailing edges, set on a 1" OD, 0.020" wall tube, and covered with Monocote. It turned at 120 rpm, geared up from 90 rpm at the pedals.

By now Gregg Miller had left the project to go bike racing in Europe, and Bryan Allen took his place. On an early test hop, inadequate controllability resulted in an accident, and after rebuilding the wing it was found that false ribs were necessary to hold the proper shape. A fatter wing of 13.7% thickness was tried and rejected; it developed too much drag.

At this point Dr. MacCready knew he faced the most serious problem of all—how to make the *Gossamer Condor* turn properly. It was a problem that had stumped all other competitors in the Kremer

Gregg Miller flying Gossamer Condor #1.

The *Gossamer Condor* wing was more efficient than expected and showed turning capability.

competition. Initially, small ailerons were added to the trailing edge of the canard stabilizer in front, so that they could bank that surface, to lead the wing into a turn.

But what happened was, once the craft banked, instead of following through in an equilibrium turn, it just flew straight ahead, one wing low. "If you turned to the left," Dr. MacCready explained, "the left wing stayed low, but the nose pointed a bit to the right and you sort of sideslipped ahead."

He'd hoped that with the stabilizer putting in some side force, there would be sufficient dihedral effect to keep both wings balanced, with one wing traveling slower than the other, but it didn't work that way.

"Then, one Saturday I spent practically a whole day with my pocket computer, calculating what wing angles there should be in an equilibrium turn," he said. "It was an exercise where you note the airspeed differences between the inner and outer wings and figure how much the lift coefficient should be increased on the inner wing versus the outer wing. So, we put in the proper amount of twist, and it seemed to work okay!"

It was an historic breakthrough—never before had the problem of turning a low-speed aircraft of the MPA variety been licked. "The wing twist also maintained wing drag fairly constant," Dr. MacCready explained further, "and yielded a well-coordinated turn which could be trimmed with the canard roll. It turned out that the wing twist control, suitable for an equilibrium left turn, also served to initiate the left turn."

It was just the opposite of what you'd expect from adverse yaw on a lowered aileron, which in a conventional aircraft is neutralized with opposite rudder. In the *Gossamer Condor*, adverse yaw worked in the direction desired (left aileron or wingtip, down for a left turn). Instead of causing the left wing to rise in a bank to the right, the adverse yaw in reality swung the vehicle to the left, and yaw-roll coupling rolled the wing left, in a turn radius of about 250 feet, with a 3-degree bank angle.

Dr. MacCready now felt sure the Kremer prize was within grasp, but competition was becoming critical—in this country, two entries were making fast progress; Joe Zinno, in Rhode Island, was pedaling toward victory in his *Olympian* ZB-1, and Taras Kiceniuk, a CalTech student, was successfully testing his *Icarus* ground-effect

Ailerons on the stabilizer banked the craft, but the craft wouldn't turn.

MPA. Meanwhile in Japan, Professor Hidemasa Kimura's balsa-wood *Stork* MPA has covered more than 6,000 feet!

The *Gossamer Condor* had made more than 400 flights, and frequently had been wrecked, six times at Mojave and three times at Shafter. Sometimes the wing snapped, other times the fuselage

Gregg Miller warms up on bike prior to flight.

Dr. Peter Lissaman designed wing of Gossamer Condor on computer.

collapsed. But Dr. MacCready had expected that, and each time she was rebuilt, better than before.

Finally, comes the day when both man and machine are ready for the big one. Bryan Allen takes his place inside the Mylar cocoon, and warms up on the pedals in the light of the predawn glow. The official observers are in position. The whole crew is tense, waiting.

Standing beside the *Gossamer Condor*, watching, are Dr. Mac-Cready, his two sons, Jim Burke, Vern Oldershaw, the main constructor, and others. The propeller turns slowly, driven by a plastic cable-chain linking two aluminum wheels, one of 62 teeth, the other of 52 teeth. Its translucent red and yellow blades become a blur. The machine moves forward, slowly, on its two tiny plastic wheels.

Suddenly the *Gossamer Condor* is flying, climbing slowly toward the starting point, midway between the two pylons, half a mile

Tyler MacCready flies Gossamer Condor #1.

apart. Lambie is waiting there now, holding the ten-foot hurdle Bryan must pass over. Lambie watches intently, counting Bryan's pedal strokes…16 strokes every ten seconds, roughly 98 rpm.

"Come on, Bryan!" someone yells. "You'll make it!"

Rhythmically and gracefully, Bryan Allen pedals on toward the first pylon. He easily banks his wing, sweeps around it, smoothly. Back on the straightaway, he heads for the second pylon, as the noise of an approaching Ag plane disturbs the early morning stillness in the distance.

"You're doing great!" a voice cries. "Don't stop now!"

The *Gossamer Condor* approaches the second pylon, banking in the opposite direction to circle it, and fly back across the finish line at the midway point. A wing goes down, then suddenly it shudders. The stabilizer pitches up, the wing snaps, and folds back.

"Oh, no!" someone cries. Everybody rushes forward to catch the slowly collapsing machine. It sinks to the ground, a broken bird. Dr. MacCready's heart sinks too. With triumph so close, what happened?

Ironically, a trailing vortex from the Ag plane, landing half a mile away, has snapped the wing like a match-stick! The very thing his firm, AeroVironment, has spent so much effort studying!

Glumly, they carry the *Gossamer Condor* back to the huge hangar, for one more reconstruction. But is there time left? Dr. MacCready's mind turns back, across the centuries, to the long distant past, when man first dreamed of accomplishing what he was trying to accomplish—controlled flight on the power of the human muscle alone. To the time of Leonardo da Vinci, nearly five centuries ago…

Chapter 2
Da Vinci's Great Bird

Leonardo da Vinci stood gazing at a V-formation of soaring birds floating effortlessly in the sky above Monte Ceceri, near his villa at Fiesole, in the environs of Florence in northern Italy. The lovely, green hill, 1358 feet high, was shaped like the body of a swan (Monte Ceceri means "Swan Mountain"). His keen eyes studied how skillfully the birds maneuvered their wings and tail feathers to catch the slope winds, instead of beating furiously against the air.

Soaring birds simply let the winds do their work for them, "like the bird of prey, the vulture, which I saw on my way to Fiesole, on March 14, 1505," he wrote later. Here, he was certain, lay the secret of man flight. He had been all wrong in the past. For sixteen years da Vinci had dreamed of flying, and in those years, from 1483 to 1499, he had secretly invented and sketched no less than 14 manpowered aircraft to be propelled by flapping wings.

The study of birds had, in fact, been a lifelong obsession for da Vinci. During his turbulent years as a famous painter, he found relaxation sketching lovely mechanical drawings of ornithopers, helicopters, and parachutes. Any device he could think of to escape to the freedom of the sky.

It was an urge that had gripped men before him, but da Vinci was first to get it all down on paper, in detailed sketches. He described these flying machines carefully in his secret code—da Vinci was left-handed, and wrote from right to left, in a tight scrawl.

People today call it mirror writing, because it appears normal when viewed in a mirror.

Many of his drawings have been lost, but today two prime sources are filled with his fascinating concepts of mechanical birds. One is a collection of his work known as *Manuscript B*, in the Institut de France, which he started in 1488 at the age of 36. The other is his famous *Codex Atlanticus*, in the Ambrosiana Library in Milan.

In 1505, the year he turned from mechanical wing-flappers to the study of soaring birds and the unknown science of meteorology, da Vinci compiled a small notebook of some thirty pages, now in the Royal Library in Turin. In this notebook, called the *Codice Sul Volo degli Uccelli* (Manuscript on the Flight of Birds), da Vinci reveals how close he came to grasping the true secret of flight.

In his *Codex Atlanticus* he had written: "A bird is an instrument working according to mathematical law, an instrument which is within the capacity of man to reproduce with all its movements, though not with a corresponding degree of strength, for it is deficient in the power of maintaining equilibrium. We may therefore say that such an instrument constructed by man is lacking in nothing except the life of the bird, and this life must needs be supplied from that of man."

Later on da Vinci would write: "To attain to the true science of the movement of birds in the air, it is necessary to give first the science of the winds, which we will establish by means of the movements of water."

Da Vinci had long been fascinated by hydrodynamics, and marveled at the similarity of the flow of water down-stream around rocks and that of air over hills and valleys. He studied the action of wind on sails, and how a breeze could draw a sailboat forward, into the wind.

Some 400 years later, Professor Samuel P. Langley of the Smithsonian Institution would write a book on *The Internal Work of the Wind*, one of the earliest studies of the kinetic energy of the wind.

But in the 15th Century, da Vinci had no predecessor to study, only his own keen powers of observation, with his artist's eyes. This dependency on originality in his investigations has been cited as the main reason da Vinci "never got off the ground." Waldemar Kaempffert, science editor of the *New York Times*, wrote in the 1961 edition of the prestigious *Encyclopedia Britannica:* "It was

Self portrait by Leonardo da Vinci.

largely lack of a technical heritage that made it impossible for Leonardo da Vinci to invent a practical flying machine."

Da Vinci, of course didn't know he was up against the impossible. He clung to his great dream of flying, and wrote in his notebook: "The great bird will make its first flight—upon the back of its great swan—filling the whole world with amazement, filling all records with its fame, and bringing eternal glory to its birthplace."

Sketch shows how da Vinci MPA pilot would fly prone with feet in stirrups to flap wings.

No record exists that da Vinci ever succeeded in flying from the top of Swan Mountain, or elsewhere, but there is good evidence that he tried. In his *Codex Atlanticus* he wrote:

"Tomorrow morning, on the second of January 1496, I will make the leather for the straps and the trial." (At that time da Vinci had proposed making experimental flights from the roof of a house in the Corte Vecchia at Milan, where he could practice unobserved by workmen then engaged elsewhere, on the dome of the Cathedral.)

But it was the crest of Swan Mountain where da Vinci hoped to find glory. To him, painting and sculpture were simply expressions of his own talent. He believed he would be remembered rather as the first man to escape the bondage of gravity and soar off into the sky. That would be real immortality!

Da Vinci had reasons to become so introverted where his mechanical inventions were concerned. These machines were pure creations of his brilliant mind, the end result of powerful forces at work—keen observation, intellectual understanding, and a practical approach to solving seemingly insurmountable problems.

Other things had gone badly for him. A vast effort to divert the Arno River and isolate the rival town of Pisa from the sea ended in disaster, when spring flooding and a violent storm wrecked the project. Gascon invaders had vandalized his great equine colossus in Florence, by using it for archery target practice. His great mural of a

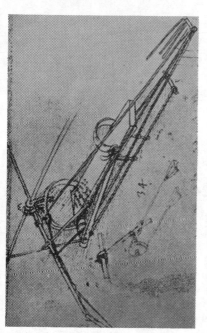

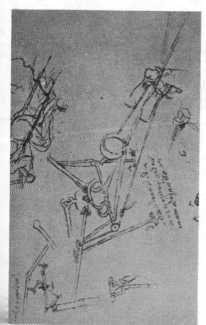
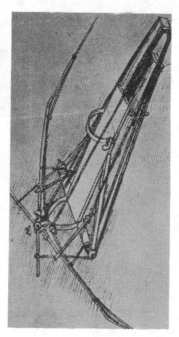

Various ornithopter MPA designs by da Vinci.

battle scene at the Sala de Consiglio was ruined, when the paint ran when he tried to speed its drying with a bonfire.

Younger artists in Florence were challenging his position and reputation. Michaelangelo publicly attacked him. Raphael unconscionably copied some of his greatest works. Of these, one—his beloved Madonna (Mona) Lisa—was the one painting that would establish his reputation through the ages as the greatest of the Florentines.

All this was nothing to da Vinci compared to his desire to fly. It was a desire misunderstood through the years, by "experts" seeking to understand his genius. A childhood fantasy, of a great vulture landing in his crib, was interpreted by Dr. Sigmund Freud as evidence of homosexuality. Charles H. Gibbs-Smith, the noted British aviation historian, wrote that in his opinion da Vinci's flying machine designs were simply too heavy to fly, and that he could not have invented the helicopter because spinning propeller toys already were common.

Da Vinci's personal life has no bearing on his achievements of the mind in inventing mechanical devices. His sketches were just that—an artist's renderings of ideas, not blueprints. And surely he was the first of record to consider the vertical screw as a possible means of lift for man-powered aircraft.

Many of his basic observations were far ahead of their time in the science of aerodynamics, which would not come to full flower until the beginnings of the 20th Century, with the 1905 statement of the Circulation Theory of Lift by Kutta and Zhukovski.

Until that time, and in fact since then, many observers pinpointed only a part of a wing's total circulation as responsible for lift. In both ornithopter and rigid wing aircraft designs, lift was assigned to a negative pressure area on top and a positive pressure area below the wing. The effect of vortex flow *behind* the wing was entirely overlooked.

Thus, da Vinci may be excused for not grasping the full picture of how lift is created by a wing moving through the air, although he was first to postulate the partial theory of positive and negative regions of air pressure below and above a bird's wing.

Perhaps he had in mind the analogy of a swimmer's hand in water, or that of a boat's oar, when he considered the behavior of air as a fluid. He actually preceded Sir Isaac Newton's law of action and reaction by a good 200 years—in his early studies of bird flight, da

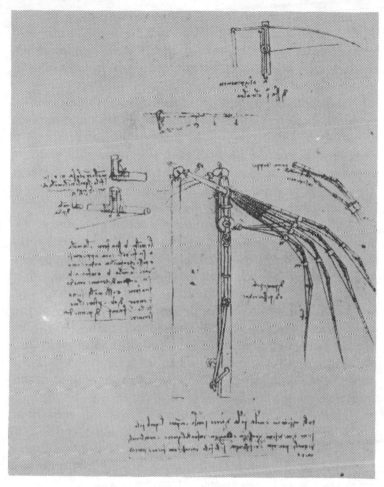

Da Vinci sketch shows mechanical linkage of MPA wing.

Vinci wrote in his Codex Atlanticus: "An object exerts the same force against the air as the air against the object. A man with sufficiently broad and properly constructed wings could learn to overcome the resistance of the air, and, by conquering it, subjugate it and rise above it."

To da Vinci, nature was the best teacher; to fly like a bird, one must have wings that flap, he considered early in his studies. Frequently he would go to the market place and purchase small birds from hawkers, then set them free. Birds did not belong in cages, and besides, he could study their flapping mechanism closely that way.

In his earliest aircraft design, da Vinci had the pilot lying flat on a board, secured by iron hoops. He operated the wings by pulling with his arms and treading with his more powerful legs. From his anatomical studies, he was well aware that a man's chest muscles were far inferior to those of birds in strength.

In another model, the weight of the apparatus rested mainly on the pilot's shoulders, rather than the board he lay on. It carried a double set of wings, operated by foot stirrups and levers. It is interesting to note how da Vinci used his extensive knowledge of leverage and systems of pulleys to increase the "thrust" of the wings when used as propellers, in a manner analagous to employment of reduction units today between engine and propeller.

Da Vinci came to feel that the flyer could operate more comfortably and efficiently in a standing position than when lying down. His third flying machine model thus had the pilot sitting upright in a gondola, driving the wings with foot pedals linked by a system of pulleys.

An unusual feature of this design was a retractable tricycle landing gear, which also served as steps to enter the machine. With a stretch of the imagination, one can also see a rudimentary "autopilot" in a sketch of a pendulum suspended in a glass ball. "This ball within the ring," he noted, "will enable you to guide the apparatus straight ahead or aslant, as you wish."

There quickly followed a design for a vertical screw lifting mechanism, frequently referred to by historians as the "first helicopter" design. A steel spring would actuate the 16-foot blades, with stored energy. Spinning blade toys were then common in Europe, based on imported Chinese spinning tops, but da Vinci seems to have been the first to suggest using a lifting screw for a man-carrying aircraft.

In 1496 da Vinci designed still another flying machine powered with coiled springs, which transmitted power to flap the wings through a system of reciprocating cranks and levers. With this device, da Vinci temporarily abandoned his researches into flying mechanisms, turning to other projects.

The last decade of the 15th Century was one of turmoil. The New World discoveries begun by Christopher Columbus were well under way, and in Florence French invaders of Charles VII held sway.

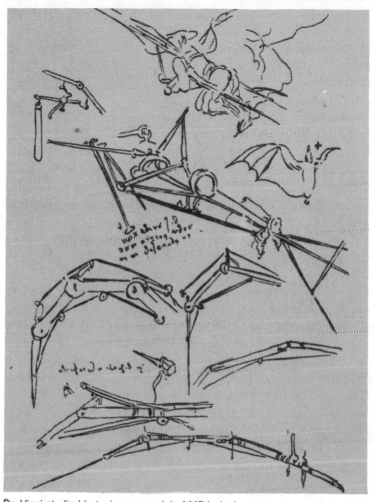

Da Vinci studied bat wing as model of MPA design.

Offering his services to Ludovico Sforza, the tyrant of Milan, da Vinci designed an amazing collection of military machines, including chariots with revolving knives on the axles. In a playful mood, he left instructions for the launching of stinkbombs to repel enemy invaders.

When Sforza's rule was overthrown, da Vinci returned to Florence, only to learn that another inventor, the mathematician Giovanni Battista Danti, had attempted to fly in a man powered aircraft, in January, 1503. Danti had jumped from the tower of the Church of Santa Maria della Vergine, but his wings hung up on a cornice and he fell to earth, breaking a leg. Da Vinci felt it was time to settle down to serious study of aeronautics.

Abandoning his earlier work on mechanical flapping contraptions, he turned to a study of air currents blowing up and over Swan Mountain, and how the great birds flew for hours on silent wings, drawing energy from the winds.

Da Vinci's writings contain numerous statements of broad concepts he called the "four potentials of nature"—*weight*, *force*, *motion*, and *impact*. Here was a starting point, from which to solve the riddle of heavier-than-air flight—an understanding of the same forces responsible for flight we now call lift, gravity thrust, and drag.

At this time, da Vinci reexamined his designs of man-powered aircraft patterned after birds. There was one thing wrong, he felt— the feathers. There was no practical way to duplicate their amazing lightness and interlocking construction. Air leaked through them, when he built artificial wings covered with feathers.

Da Vinci drew sketches of wings constructed with slats that opened on the upstroke and closed on the downstroke, something like Venetian blinds. In later years, similar patented devices were tried, but failed to work, when others sought to imitate da Vinci.

Then he thought of the bat. In his notebook *Sul Volo degli Uccelli* he reminded himself: "You are to remember that your bird (flying machine) ought not to imitate anything but the bat, because the membranes form an armour, a strength to the wings. The bat is aided by the membrane, which binds the whole and is not pervious."

His batwings were to be built of cotton fustian cloth, starched silk, and a fiber mesh for the outer trailing edge surfaces. Ribbing was to be of cane. In appearance, the Great Bird of da Vinci was not unlike one of Otto Lilienthal's successful early monoplane gliders, of the 1890's.

Plunging further into basics, he formulated the law of inertia more than a century before Galileo, in 1638, claimed credit for it. Da Vinci wrote: "Every movement tends to maintain itself, or rather, every body in motion continues to move so long as the influence of the force of its motor is maintained in it."

Once launched from Swan Mountain, a glider should thus continue on its way, the same way a bird soars. But what of equilibrium and balance? He invented a device to determine a bird's center of gravity, and wrote: "When a bird sinks, the center of gravity is moved beyond the center of resistance, and when the bird wishes to

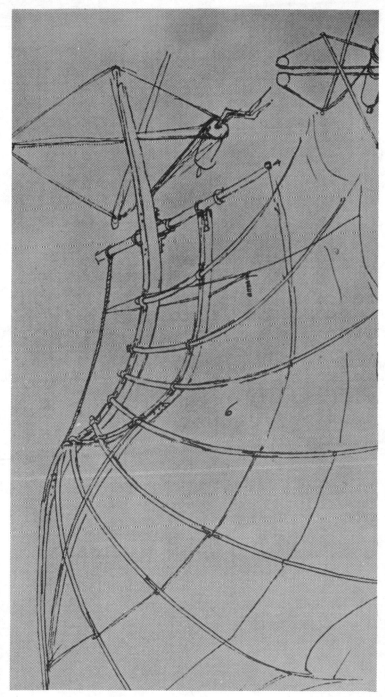

Da Vinci switched from birds to bats for MPA wing design.

rise, the center of gravity remains behind the center of its resistance."

In one of his later sketches, da Vinci included a cruxiform design for a tail with both horizontal and vertical surfaces, to be controlled by head movements. It was a forerunner of today's aircraft empennages.

In the spring of 1506, da Vinci's problems had reached a high point. He had quarreled with Pope Julius II, Michaelangelo, and others. His painting was going badly, particularly his great battle scene in the Sala del Consiglio, whose colors had run all together when the room was overheated.

From the villa of his adoptive uncle, Alessandro Amadori, at Fiesole, he gazed longingly at the summit of Swan Mountain. What an achievement it would be, to fly from there and soar with the birds!

What happened may never be known.

A legend has been reported by da Vinci's biographer, Antonnia Vallentin, that "one day there rose up from Monte Cecero a huge bird, as though Swan Mountain handlifted itself into the air. Suddenly the bird disappeared, as though swallowed up by the skies."

After da Vinci's death, Girolamo Cardano, son of Leonardo's close friend Fazio Cardona, would write: "Both those who have recently attempted to fly came to grief. Leonardo da Vinci also tried to fly, but he, to, failed. He was a magnificent painter."

Not until the 18th Century were da Vinci's amazing diaries made public, with their intricate notes and drawings of flying machines. According to Cecil Hilton Monk Gould, Assistant Keeper of the National Gallery in London, "It is on his drawings that Leonardo's claim to be considered one of the greatest of artists must chiefly rest..."

Certainly his brilliant mind and quick eye looked into the future, and saw the sky filled with flying machines. Whether or not he actually flew one remains unimportant. His contribution to aeronautics was originality of perception and design. By the same token, when the Wright Brothers first flew, four hundred years later, their contribution was not the invention of the airplane—da Vinci, Lilienthal, Moulliard, Chanute, Langley, and others already had invented it. The Wrights were the first to *learn how to fly*.

Chapter 3
The Birdmen

The origins of man-powered aircraft are lost in antiquity. In mythology, the best known legend of manned flight is the story of Daedalus and Icarus, with its counterpart in the Scandinavian legend of Wayland, the smith who forged his wings. Skipping over Bladud, the legendary Flying King of Britain, in the ninth century, and the apocryphal flight of the sorcerer Simon Magus, we come to Roger Bacon (1214-94), who dreamed of flying 200 years before Leonardo da Vinci.

Imprisoned for his radical teachings against beliefs of theologians and scholars of his day, Bacon's ideas on flying have frequently been misunderstood by aviation historians. In Bacon's time it was thought that the atmosphere, like the oceans, had an upper surface that could be sailed upon. Bacon envisioned an aerial machine as a "hollow globe of copper, or other suitable material, wrought extremely thin and filled with 'etherial air or liquid fire' and launched from a mountaintop."

"There may be some flying instrument," he wrote, "so that a man sitting in the middle of the instrument, and turning some mechanism, may put in motion some artificial wings which may beat upon the air like a bird flying."

According to the American balloonist and aeronautical historian, Professor John Wise, "Soon after Bacon's time projects were instituted to train up children from their infancy in the exercise of

Legendary flight of Icarus took him too near the sun, which melted wax in wings and caused crash.

flying with artificial wings, which seemed to have been the favorite plan of the flying philosophers and artists of that day."

We have seen how completely absorbed da Vinci was with the subject of imitating bird flight, but over the ensuing centuries the goal of constructing a practical ornithopter, or wing-flapper, has remained elusive.

Curiously, an attempt to cross the English Channel in a Man Powered Aircraft (MPA) seems to have occurred more than four centuries ago, in the fall of 1507, the year after da Vinci was contemplating a flight from the summit of Monte Ceceri.

John Lesley, in his *History of Scotland*, published in 1578, relates that an Italian-born adventurer, John Damian, leaped from the top of Stirling Castle with homemade wings of chicken feathers, hoping to overtake a boatload of ambassadors headed for France. "But he fell to the ground and brake his thee bane," Lesley related, ascribing the failure to "a natural affinity of the hens' feathers to return to the dunghill."

Two accounts of MPAs appear in the 17th Century. A French tightrope dancer named Allard reportedly tried to fly from the terrace at St. Germain before Louis XIV in 1660, but crash-landed. In 1678 another Frenchman, the locksmith Besnier, designed a pair of oscillating wings of muslin, with shutters that opened on the upstroke and closed on the downstroke, in the manner of da Vinci's device.

In his 1894 book, *Progress in Flying Machines*, the brilliant American civil engineer and aviation enthusiast Octave Chanute reported that Besnier actually sailed over the roof of an adjoining cottage, then later sold his wings to a traveling mountebank, who performed with them at fairs.

Eighteenth Century would-be birdmen continued the quest of man-powered flight in crude ornithopters, before invention of the hot-air balloon by the Montgolfier brothers in 1783 changed the whole picture.

The Marquis de Bacqueville in 1742 made a valiant try, hoping to flap his way across the Seine River in Paris, from a window of his mansion to the Tuilleries Gardens, some two hundred yards away. At mid-river he faltered and fell onto the desk of a washerwoman's barge, breaking a leg.

More fortunate was the Abbe Desforges, a canon of the church of Saint-Croix at Etampes, who tried to get airborne in a winged

Octave Chanute published history of MPA's in 1894.

chariot in 1772. The machine featured a pair of wings and a horizontal plane, with a total area of some 145 square feet. Four men assisted in the launch, but the harder he flapped the worse things became—the action of the wings, Chanute relates, pulled him down instead of up.

With the introduction of ballooning, inventors of wing-flapping devices could devote their full energies toward achieving forward propulsion rather than lift. Among the first was Jean-Pierre Blanchard, a 28-year-old Frenchman who in 1781 had attempted to fly a MPA fitted with four wings. He later admitted the wings merely "served to agitate an indocile element, with no more effect than those of a heavy ostrich."

In March, 1784, Blanchard adapted his "vaisseau volant" wings and rudder to a hot air balloon, history's first attempt to navigate the air in a lighter-than-aircraft. He discarded the devices as too heavy, but later successfully used a pair of silken oars and a revolving fan to tack upwind. Blanchard, incidentally, became the first airman to cross the English Channel, in 1785, and later introduced ballooning to America.

On August 23, 1783, some 50,000 Frenchmen gathered in the Champ-de-Mars in Paris to witness the first public balloon ascension in that city—a hydrogen sphere built by Anne-Jean and M. N. Roberts for the noted physicist Jacques Alexandre Cesar Charles. Among the witnesses was the United States Ambassador to France, Benjamin Franklin.

After the ascension, someone remarked to Franklin: "What good can a balloon be?"

Franklin's retort was the bon mot of the day: "Eh, a quoi bien l'enfant qui vient de naiture?" (What good is a new-born babe?)

If Franklin was skeptical of ballooning, his ingenious mind was fired with the concept of man powered flight. He sat down in his study and sketched an MPA design that historians have largely overlooked. It consisted of a flying machine with a huge umbrella of quill feathers to be flapped up and down by a rider suspended below, his feet in stirrups.

Like da Vinci before him and Dr. Paul MacCready nearly 200 years later, Franklin recognized that legpower would be the prime mover of the human engine in any sucessful MPA.

As to ballooning, he would write: "These machines must always be subject to be driven by the winds. Perhaps mechanic art may find easy means to give them progressive motion in a calm, and to slant them a little in the wind."

Dirigibles are another story, of course, but over the years aeronauts have sought to navigate the air with muscle power. In the 1880s, Carlotta Meyers, a lady balloonist of Mohawk, New York, used a folded newspaper to waft her way across the sky in a sport balloon, and at the beginning of this century, Roy Knabenshue used

American dirigible pilot Roy Knabenshue rowed his craft across the sky with silken oars in early 1900s, copying feat of 18th Century Italian balloonist Vincent Lunardi.

silken oars like those of Blanchard and Vincent Lunardi to "row" his dirigible across the skies of Pasadena, California.

Another aeronautical pioneer inspired by the invention of the balloon in 1783 was Sir George Cayley, remembered today as "the Father of Aeronautics" in Great Britain. Like da Vinci, he studied bird flight and came to the conclusion that wing flapping "was for the birds" and not for man. He summarily dismissed ornithopter flight as "ridiculous."

Cayley would win fame with a series of successful glider flights in a machine of some 300 square feet of surface, beginning in 1808. A story is told that his coachman flew the machine 300 yards across a valley and crashed.

Afterward, the coachman, in his broadest Yorkshire dialect, said, "Please, Sir George! I wish to give notice! I was hired to drive, not to fly!"

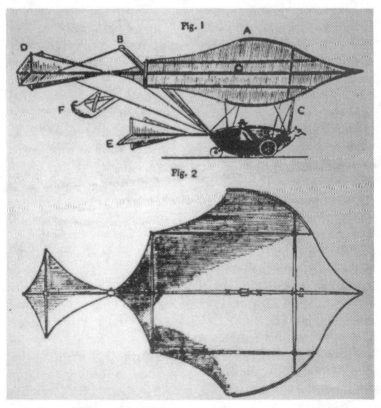

Early aircraft design of Sir George Cayley.

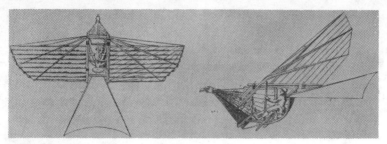
1810 MPA design of Thomas Walker.

A contemporary of Cayley, Thomas Walker, in 1810 published a work entitled *Treatise upon the Art of Flying by Mechanical Means*, with a subtitle: *Instructions and Plans for making a flying car with wings, in which a man may sit, and by working a small lever, cause himself to ascend and soar through the air with the facility of a bird."*

Like da Vinci, Cayley and others, Walker studied bird flight and dissected many birds, studying "very minutely the mechanism of their wings, tails, and all parts which they employ in flying." The secret of bird flight apparently eluded Walker, however, as no record exists that he built such an MPA as he envisioned and wrote about.

The work of Cayley and Walker, nevertheless, had their impact on the history of flight. William Samuel Henson and John Stringfellow, two contemporary Britishers, were inspired by their ideas to build steam-powered model aircraft, one of which actually flew in 1848, 55 years before the first powered flights of the Wright Brothers at Kitty Hawk, North Carolina. Work on ornithopters continued with little or no success in Euope through the 19th Century, with the possible exception of Charles Spencer, who exhibited his machine at the first Exhibition of the Aeronautical Society of Great Britain in 1868. A 140-pound athlete, Spencer tucked under his arms a machine weighing only 24 pounds. Two articulated wings of 15 square feet each were attached to a rigid plane of 100 square feet, with a small tail behind. By sprinting down a small hill, he was able to flap along above the ground for distances up to 130 feet, probably despite the movable wingtips.

Something new was suggested in 1873 with publication of J. Bell Pettigrew's *Animal Locomotion, or Walking, Swimming, and Flying*, in which the author pointed out that birds in flapping flight flex their wings so that the tip feathers describe a figure-8 motion. In

1879 an experimeter named Dandrieux built an ornithopter in which the wings were attached to an oblique axle to attain the figure-8 motion, but nothing came of it.

For a time, the ornithopter idea was put aside in favor of other MPA devices, none of which worked. As early as 1808 Cayley had tried a set of umbrella-shaped wings unsuccessfully, and from 1809-12 Jakob Degen, an Austrian clockmaker, failed to fly in a similar device of taffeta wings that operated with a valvular action. He did rise to a height of 54 feet beneath a small balloon, but went nowhere.

In July, 1854, the French aeronaut Letur ascended beneath a balloon from London's Cremorne Gardens in a flying machine that combined a parachute and wings operated by a treadle. Adverse winds blew him into a forest near Tottingham, tumbling him to earth. He died ten days later.

Vincent de Groof, a Belgian shoemaker, was killed in a similar accident 20 years later at Cremorne Gardens, attempting to fly from a balloon launch in a contraption that was basically an ornithopter with wings of 20 square meters area. He flapped the wings with his arms and wiggled a tail with his feet, but during the fall the wings folded upward and collapsed. He was killed on the spot.

Further experimentation in MPAs during this early period involved the design of ornithopters with much larger wings. While more likely to sustain the pilot, they were simply too big to flap fast enough. An example was the MPA of C. F. Meerwein, architect to the Prince of Wales, whose calico wings measured 111 square feet of area, for a wing loading of roughly .55 lb/sq. ft., about that of a wild duck. It wouldn't budge.

Chanute reports that an inventor named Breant in 1854 attempted to find a solution to flapping big wings by using elastic cords to assist the upstroke, along with three valves. His wing area totaled 108 square feet. Nothing happened.

Jean-Marie Le Bris, a sea captain of Brittany, in 1857 got airborne in an unusual MPA patterned after the albatross, a graceful soaring seabird he had studied during voyages around Cape Horn. He had placed his machine on a horse-drawn cart at the top of a rise facing into the wind, on the coast of France near Brest. The wings spanned 23 feet and had a surface of 220 square feet, and their angle of incidence was controlled by pulleys and cords actuated by levers. The horse galloped downhill, the machine rose to 300 feet, at the end

Belgian shoemaker Vincent de Groof's MPA collapsed in launch from balloon. He was killed.

of a tether. Encouraged, Le Bris tried again in 1868, took off, crashed and broke a leg.

To Chanute, this failure was evidence that man would never fly under his own muscle power. He wrote in 1894: "There seems to be no hope that any amount of ingenuity or skill can enable man to accomplish this feat."

He concluded that the fixed-wing aeroplane held greatest promise for conquest of the air, and in fact could support nearly twice the

French sea captain Jean-Marie Le Bris patterned his MPA after the graceful albatross, once rose 300 feet.

weight per horsepower as the ornithopter. The big problem remaining, he believed, was the matter of equilibrium. If one intended to pattern an MPA after birds, he would do well to forget the flappers and study the soaring species. "All birds are acrobats," he wrote, "but the soaring kind, if closely observed in a gusty wind, will be seen to perform feats of balancing more delicate and wonderful than those of any human equilibrist."

Chanute traces the antiquity of rigid-wing aircraft back to the legendary Saracen of Constantinople, who in 1178 attempted to fly from the Hippodrome tower before Emperor Manuel Comnenus. "He stood upright, clothed in a white robe, very long and very wide, stiffened by willow wands," wrote a contemporary. "The Saracen kept extending his arms to catch the wind. At last he rose into the air like a bird."

That he fell and was seriously injured didn't matter to Chanute—he saw in the Saracen's white robes the first design of a rigid-wing MPA.

Such concepts, of course, were forerunners of today's sailplanes, whose motive power comes from gravity and rising air currents. But before soaring craft could become practical, much study and experimentation would have to be done in the areas of wing design to achieve efficient lift/drag ratios, stability about the longitudinal, vertical, and lateral axes, and other aerodynamic refinements.

In the next chapter you will meet some of the pioneers who stripped away earlier concepts of "secret" forces of bird flight. To one delegate to the International Conference on Aerial Navigation held at Chicago in 1893, however, the secret of flight lay in goose feathers.

"How can a 20 pound wild goose carry itself so easily?" he demanded. "Weigh every feather you can pick off from a wild goose, and they will not weigh one pound. Now if the feathers be picked off from a wild goose, he can come no nearer to flying than we can."

It was very simple to him—"a magnetic negative earth-force does the lifting, and that is all produced by the feathers!"

Chapter 4
Why Airplanes Fly

Before man could design and fly a successful man-powered aircraft, a clear understanding of the basic principles of aerodynamics had to be formulated, and some old ideas abandoned. The ancients believed that the atmosphere itself provided a sustaining or impelling force, one that assisted rather than resisted the flight of an object through it.

Leonardo da Vinci did, in fact, recognize that air offered resistance to the movement of a solid object, which he attributed to compressibility effects.

The rapid flapping of a bird's wing, he believed, created a region of compressed air beneath it and so provided lift. He was only partly right.

Similarly, he believed that air flow closing behind a projectile helped to impel it, rather than producing resistance to its flight. (Curiously, Don Luscombe designed the fast little Monocoupe sport plane with a sharply downswept fuselage top surface with this idea in mind—he meant it to act like a wet grape when you squeezed it between your fingers, to make it squirt ahead. Amazingly, it seemed to work.)

Thus misconceptions about aerodynamics have persisted over the centuries. Early investigators, with no wind tunnels at hand, quite naturally had difficulty envisioning what was happening to invisible air at work.

Early French observers were puzzled by the fact that windmills wore out their front axle bearings faster than their rear bearings. There seemed to be some mysterious force in the wind that, under certain circumstances, made an object move toward it rather than away from it. They called this mysterious force "Aspiration."

Captain Le Bris, the French mariner who studied the albatross as a flying model, once wrote: "I took the wing of an albatross and exposed it to the breeze; and lo! in spite of me it drew forward into the wind; notwithstanding my resistance it tended to rise. Thus I had discovered the secret of the bird! I comprehended the whole mystery of flight!"

Professor John Wise, the aeronaut-historian, wrote in 1873 in *Through The Air*: "The philosophers, from Bacon's time down to the discovery of the true nature of atmospheric pressure, as illustrated by the Torricellian tube and air pump, in their speculations upon aerial navigation, all had an opinion that the atmosphere had a defined limit or border, not very high above he earth, upon which the aerial vessel must necessarily be placed in order to have it bouyed up by the air underneath, like the water under a ship. Reasoning from their knowledge of hydrostatics, they took it for granted that the atmosphere was a vast ocean of air surrounding our globe, upon the outer border of which rested another ethereal ocean of a much rarer kind, separate and distinct, as the air rests upon the water."

Of all the early experimenters who were inspired by the example of bird flight to imitate them with mechanical devices, Samuel Pierpont Langley, director of the Smithsonian Institution in Washington, D. C., was first to grasp the notion that MPA designers and builders were going at the problem all wrong.

"Nature had solved the problem of heavier-than-air flight, and why not man?" he asked himself. "Perhaps it was because he had begun at the wrong end, and attempted to construct machines to fly before knowing the principles on which flight rested. I turned to my books and got no help. Sir Isaac Newton had indicated a rule for finding the resistance to advance through the air, which seemed, if correct, to call for enormous mechanical power."

Langley forthwith discarded all the old rules "to commence new experiments, not to build a flying machine at once, but to find the principles upon which one should be built—to find with certainty by direct trial how much horsepower was needed to sustain a surface of given weight by means of its motion through the air."

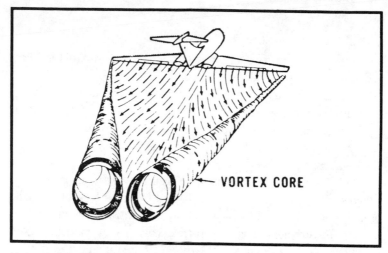

VORTEX CORE

Vortex theory of lift revolutionized aerodynamics.

Long before Langley, other scientists had worried over the problem of air resistance, as opposed to the concept of air "assistance" or "aspiration." Galileo experimentally laid to rest the idea of aspiration and concluded that air resistance was proportional to its relative velocity. Near the end of the 17th Century, the Dutch physicist Christian Huygens went a step further—he showed that resistance of air to the motion of a body was proportional to the square of the velocity.

Sir Isaac Newton's laws of mechanics later formed the basis for classical theories of aerodynamics, based on studies of pressures acting on a flat plate inclined toward an air stream. The pressure, he concluded, was proportional to the product of air density, plate area, the square of the velocity, and the square of the sine of the angle of inclination. Leonhard Euler refined the formula, stating that the effect of the plate's inclination was proportional to the sine, not to its square. But, none of these early experiments revealed the effects of flow over the upper surface of the plate, where low pressures helped to produce the major portion of a wing's lift.

Not until much later would the bigger picture emerge, of total circulation flow, and of air as a continuum, with a pressure field extending for considerable distances from the plate.

By bits and pieces, the jigsaw puzzle picture of how air works, and how an airplane flies, became clearer. In the mid-18th Century, Daniel Bernoulli, a Swiss physicist, arrived at his well-known theorem:

$$q + \frac{1}{2} PV^2 = \text{constant}$$

where q is the pressure in an airstream, P is the density of the fluid, and V its velocity.

Jean Le Rond d'Alembert in the same century became dissatisfied with the theories for resistance, and after some mathematical juggling concluded that resistance, being related to loss of momentum on impacting a moving body, was zero. This was known as "D'Alembert's paradox."

Others tackled the relationship of resistance to the viscosity of a fluid such as air or water. In the 1880s, Osborne Reynolds discovered laminar flow and the abrupt transition, away from the wing's surface, to turbulent flow. From this work a new yardstick, the "Reynolds Number,"evolved. It expressed the ratio of mass forces to viscous forces in a fluid, and enabled designers to compare aircraft models to full scale machines in airflows of equal Reynolds Numbers.

Researchers now had a better understanding of air at work, and mathematical formulae with which to grasp the meaning of measurements inside wind tunnels. But not until the beginning of the 20th Century did a fuller understanding of total circulation appear.

In England, Frederick W. Lanchester set forth the circulation theory of lift of an airfoil of infinite span, and the concept of a vortex theory of the lift of a wing of finite span. Coincidentally, two other researchers came to the same understanding and provided a mathematical theory to explain it. They were M. Wilhelm Kutta in Germany, and Nikolai E. Zhukovski in Russia.

Another brilliant researcher, Ludwig Prandtl, at Gottingen, Germany, independently arrived at the same concept, forming the basis of modern aerodynamic theory. Prandtl, incidentally, was first to recognize that total resistance of an aircraft consists of three parts—skin friction (viscosity), form or pressure drag, and induced drag.

Understanding the latter form of drag, resulting from production of lift by airflow over a wing, revolutionized aerodynamic theory. It was apparent that induced drag is smaller as the wingspan increases, primarily because it is associated with the vortices trailing from each wingtip.

Here was a fresh starting point for designers of manpowered aircraft—because the human machine is low powered, drag had to be

Octave Chanute's tri-decker hang glider of 1896.

Chanute experimented with as many as four and five multiplane gliders.

minimized. And as induced drag is the bigger part of total drag, a longer wingspan is essential.

A lack of theoretical understanding of aerodynamics in the 19th Century did not deter MPA experimenters from pushing ahead with aircraft patterned after wings of birds. More serious researchers like Professor Langley tested their designs in model form, whirled through the air at the end of rotating beams.

Both in the United States and abroad, efforts were made to get together all the existing knowledge of mechanical flight for serious study. Thus in January, 1866, was born the Aeronautical Society of Great Britain, and two years later it sponsored the first Aeronautical Exhibition, at the Crystal Palace at Sydenham. A total of 77 exhibits were on display for eight days, and MPAs were predominant.

In America, Dr. Albert F. Zahm, a Notre Dame University physics professor, invited the world's leading aeronautical experimenters to gather at the Chicago World's Fair grounds in 1893 to share ideas. Octave Chanute at first refused to chair the Conference

Chanute multiplane glider in flight.

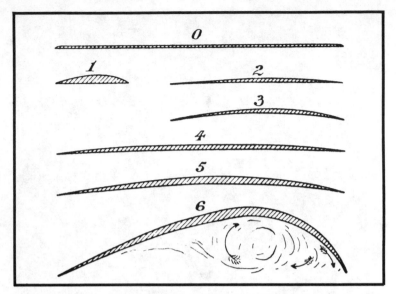

Horatio Phillips patented a series of airfoils in 1891. Number 5 seemed to work best.

on Aerial Navigation, fearing an invasion of "cranks." He finally accepted the honor—his publication of *Progress in Flying Machines* in 1891 made him the logical choice.

Inspired by the Crystal Palace exhibition, Horatio Frederick Phillips launched a study of wing curves in a crude wind tunnel, demonstrating that flat plates were useless for supporting weight in air. In 1884 Phillips patented a series of airfoils of concave-convex shape. In his patent description, Phillips noted that "particles of air

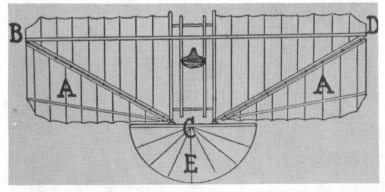

Early Montgomery glider featured modern ailerons in 1880's, long before the Wright Brothers and Aerial Experiment Association battled in court over design.

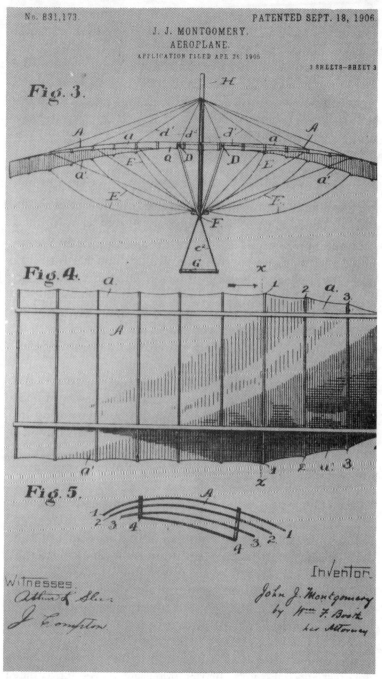

John J. Montgomery won patent on curved wing aeroplane in 1906.

struck by the convex upper surface are deflected upward, thereby causing a partial vacuum over the greater portion of the upper surface."

Professor Langley drew criticism at the Chicago meeting by suggesting, in his paper, *The Internal Work of the Wind*, that a mysterious force within the wind in some way pulsated, allowing birds to soar. Chanute, however, agreed with Langley—to him it was simply "aspiration."

There were startling developments at Chicago—at least two papers proved that successful heavier than air flight already had been achieved, by John J. Montgomery and Louis P. Mouillard.

Back in 1884, Montgomery revealed, he had been making 600-foot glides down a sandy slope at Otay Mesa in Southern California. In 1883 he had failed to get a wing-flapper off the ground, then designed a rigid-wing craft with pivoted wings that again failed to fly. Subsequently he designed wings, fitted with rudimentary ailerons, but they were flat wings.

After another six years of independent study, he developed a parabolic curve that worked well. To Montgomery, it seemed the curved surface deflected the air downward, so that the wing in effect rode the crest of a wave, like a surfboard.

What amazed Chanute was how he developed the curve. With no knowledge of how to construct a wind tunnel, he borrowed a feather pillow from his mother's linen closet, set the wing up on a hilltop in a high wind, and watched the way the feathers blew over and around it.

Next he built small tin wing sections and mounted them inside an open box, with a damper at one end. He set up a mirror to reflect the sun's rays at right angles to the airflow, then opened the damper and sifted in smoke and dust particles. The crude heliostat enabled him to see both laminar and turbulent airflow patterns, and so he designed a curve that gave the best L/D ratio—the most efficient lift for the least drag.

In Cairo, Egypt, Mouillard worked along different lines, studying the flight of great African vultures to determine how they achieved controlled flight. He designed a pair of ailerons for a rigid wing glider that worked the way the vulture's feathers worked. To turn left, the left aileron was depressed into the airstream, creating drag that effected a turn. In 1892 Mouillard applied for a United

Prof. John J. Montgomery (third from left) poses with his tandem hang glider Santa Clara. Pilot Dan Maloney (far right) was killed attempting aerobatic maneuver after a balloon launch.

65

Replica of Montgomery's tandem glider flown for movie "Gallant Journey" proved design was successful.

States Patent for his aileron control system. It was duly granted May 18, 1897.

Interestingly, the secret of the ultimate success of Dr. Paul MacCready's Gossamer Condor lay in just this principle, of using wingtip drag to assist in a turn, at the same time providing extra lift by increasing the relative angle of attack of the inner wing.

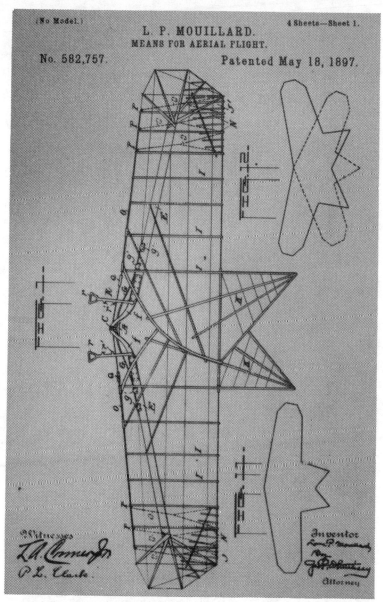

L. P. MOUILLARD.
MEANS FOR AERIAL FLIGHT.

4 Sheets—Sheet 1.

No. 582,757.

Patented May 18, 1897.

Witnesses

Inventor

Attorney

In 1897 French designer Louis P. Mouillard patented glider design featuring wingtip "dragerons" used today in modern hang gliders and Gossamer Condor MPA.

As stability became more important in aircraft design, legal problems arose. Orville and Wilbur Wright fought bitterly through the courts to establish priority for their claim to have invented the

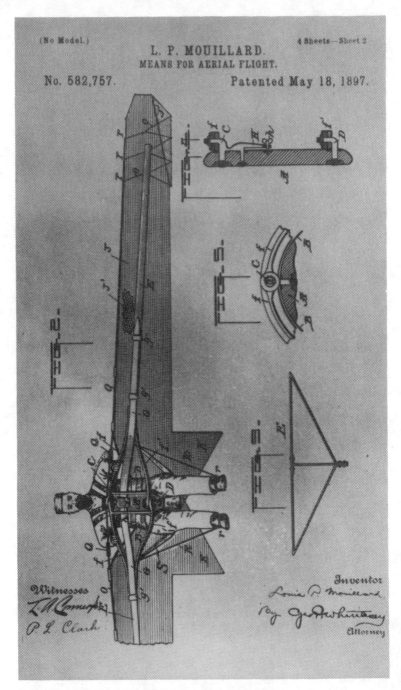

(No Model.)

4 Sheets—Sheet 2

L. P. MOUILLARD.
MEANS FOR AERIAL FLIGHT.

No. 582,757.

Patented May 18, 1897.

FIG. 2.

FIG. 4.

FIG. 5.

FIG. 6.

Witnesses

Inventor
Louis P. Mouillard
By Geo. H. Whittaker
Attorney

Patent drawing of Mouillard's "Drageron" control system.

"three-torque" system of control of an aircraft, using a combination of wing-warping, elevator, and rudder surfaces.

Injunctions were filed to prevent other birdmen like Louis Paulhan from flying in this country, but the chief "enemy" of the Wrights was the Aerial Experiment Association. Alexander Graham Bell, an AEA member, had invented and patented a three-torque control system that employed hinged ailerons, not wing warping. It was flown successfully by Glenn Curtiss and other AEA members.

But still earlier, according to Dr. Zahm, was a three-torque control system invented by the French experimenter Alexander Goupil in 1884, and flight tested in January, 1917, by the Curtiss Aeroplane and Motor Corporation, at the peak of the patent fight.

Even the Goupil system was antedated, Dr. Zahm pointed out, by a British patent issued in 1868 to Matthew Boulton.

Today, such developments in the history of mechanical flight serve only to remind us that man, over the centuries, has created a technical heritage that has taken us to the moon, and into hypersonic atmospheric flight. In the realm of low-velocity man powered flight, however, the search for new ideas goes on.

Chapter 5
Onward and Upward

Otto Lilienthal, killed in a glider crash in 1896, might have lived well beyond his 48 years had he followed his own advice and stuck with man powered aircraft, instead of trying to fly an ornithopter with movable wingtips and a carbonic acid gas motor. He had made more than 2,000 successful glides before the urge to switch to power sidetracked his amazing path of progress.

Some 30 years of research and preparation by Otto and his brother, Gustave, preceeded his first glider flight in 1891. Lilienthal's early gliders strongly resembled the onithopter batwing designs of Leonardo da Vinci, his first one weighing 40 pounds, with a wing area of 107 square feet, made from waxed cotton cloth stretched over a framework of peeled willow wands.

From the outset he was aware that controllability was the big problem in man powered aircraft. He once cried: "To fly is everything! To contrive a Flying Machine is nothing; to construct one is something; to control it in flight is to reach the heights."

For starters, Lilienthal practiced flight control with a machine of Multiple sets of wings, operated by foot power, and suspended from a boom projecting from the roof of a house. His wings were gracefully curved, and when flapped raised him 30 feet off the ground, assisted by counterweights at the end of a rope run over a pulley.

Otto Lilienthal, famed German glider pilot, died in his crash on August 9, 1896.

In 1889 Lilienthal came to a number of conclusions, published in his *Der Vogelflug als Grundlage der Fliegekunst* (Bird Flight as the Basis of the Flying Art):

- Practical flying machines in nowise depend upon the discovery of light and powerful motors.
- An ordinary man's strength is sufficient to work efficiently an appropriate flying apparatus.
- The wings of large, high-flying birds should be used as models.
- Experiments must determine whether to use the broad wings with spread-out primary feathers of waders, or narrow, tapered wings of sea birds.
- Wings must be curved, concave on the bottom side.
- Depth of the curve should be one twelfth its chord.
- Wing spars should be located as far forward as possible.
- In flapping flight, the widest portion of the wing must cooperate in the upstroke to sustain weight.
- The wingtips only need oscillate, the rest remaining rigid for soaring flight.

Lilienthal had workmen build a gliding hill, from dirt removed for a canal near his home at Gross Lichterfelde, near Berlin, with a launch platform constucted on top and a cave dug below to store his gliders.

To test his ornithopter wings, he also installed a springboard in his garden. After a sprint of 26 feet, he bounced into the air, learning how to flap. "Dexterity alone," he once wrote, "invests the native inhabitant of the air with superiority over man in that element."

On August 9, 1896, Lilienthal made one final glide from his artificial hill, to test a new rudder control, a line that ran to a head band. It was to be used next day in a powered glider, that had proved to be unstable. On that flight Lilienthal's machine stalled and crashed. He died the next day of a broken back.

If Lilienthal had given his life in an effort to wrest the secret of muscle-powered flight from the birds, it was not in vain. He would become the inspiration for future experimenters, including the Wright Brothers, and in a sense proved that earlier ornithopter advocates like da Vinci had not been altogether wrong.

Over the centuries since da Vinci dreamed of flying from Swan Mountain, the subject of human flight became an important part of

Lilienthal, like da Vinci, used batwing design, with a cruxiform tail.

Cabane struts and wires supported batwings of Lilienthal glider.

Lilienthal flies biplane glider to base of hill.

English literature. A common theme was based on efforts of a shipwrecked mariner to escape from an island, a plot immortalized by Daniel Defoe's *The Life and Strange Surprizing Adventures of Robinson Crusoe*, which appeared in 1719.

Robinson Crusoe, based upon the real-life survival story of the shipwrecked Scottish sailor Alexander Selkirk, was preceded by 81 years with the publication in 1638 of Francis Godwin's *The Man in the Moone*, another island adventure tale. In this story the hero, Domingo Gonsales, a Spaniard, is abandoned (by reason of sickness) during a sea voyage, on the then uninhabited island of St. Helena.

The escape theme is not so mundane as Crusoe's efforts at building a raft. Instead, Gonsales occupies his time training a number of wild swans to obey his call, and eventually to fly with small burdens.

Eventually he trains a flock of seven "Gansas or Large Geese" to fly in harness carrying a small lamb, which he envies as "the first living creature to take possession of such a device." (Prophetically, this reference was followed on September 19, 1783, 65 years later, by the ascension of a sheep, a cock, and a duck, in a hot-air Montgolfier balloon basket, as history's first living creatures to ascend in a manmade aerial vehicle.)

The story gets a bit wilder as Gonsales hooks up 25 Gansas and goes aloft himself. Later, when he is shipwrecked returning to Spain, Gonsales is rescued by his Gansas, who head for the moon—their real home—and carry him thence in 11 days, on a migratory flight. On the journey, the birds encounter gravitational equilibrium and remain stationary for a while, resting, before continuing their space flight.

The next author to combine the shipwreck theme with human flight escape was Robert Paltock, in 1751, in a book whose title page tells the whole plot: *The Life and Adventures of Peter Wilkins, a Cornish Man: Relating particularly, His Shipwreck, near the South Pole, his wonderful Passage thro' a subterraneous Cavern, into a kind of New World: his there meeting with a Gawry or flying woman, whose Life he preserv'd, and afterwards married her; his extraordinary Conveyance to the Country of Glums and Gawrys, or Men and Women that fly...Taken from his own Mouth, in his Passage to England from off Cape Horn in Africa, in the Ship Hector.*

There is more to the story, of course—Peter Wilkins, defending the kingdom of Doorpt Swangeanti (the Land of Flight) against a

Lilienthal launching from platform atop his flying hill.

rebel invasion by 5,000 winged men flying in five layers, opens fire and shoots down 300. "They fell so thick about me," he relates, "that I had enough to do to escape being crushed to death by them."

In the same year that *Peter Wilkins* appeared, the Rev. Ralph Morris brought out another shipwreck flying story entitled "The narrative of the Life and astonishing adventures of John Daniel, a smith, at Royston in Hertfordshire."

Here, the hero's son, also mechanically minded, builds an ornithopter with several ribbed wings "cloathed with callicoe dipt in wax" and operated by pump handles. He took his father for a ride and "away we went," the narrator says.

We now come to Dr. Samuel Johnson, the noted British writer and lexicographer, who reportedly became interested in man-powered flight when he once roomed in the same lodging house with a man who broke his legs in a fall while attempting to fly. In a ficticious letter to a British periodical, The Rambler, in 1752, Dr. Johnson, signing himself "Hermeticus," reports that he had twice dislocated his limbs and once fractured his skull trying to fly.

Seven years later he devoted a full chapter to the subject of man-powered flight in a hastily written book, *Rasselas*, which he turned out in a single week and sold for 100 pounds to defray the costs of his mother's funeral. Rasselas is an Abyssinian prince of eloquent speech, who discourses on flight with a young artist building a flapping-wing flying machine.

The artist seems to have had a good grasp of the mechanical, if not the aerodynamic, requirements of heavier-than-air flight. He says: "You will be, necessarily, upborne by the air, if you can renew any impulse upon it, faster than the air can recede from the pressure." (In 1861, J. S. Phillips used these words almost verbatim in an abridgement of the patent specification for his invention of a Flying Machine).

When Rasselas complained that "every animal has his element assigned him; the birds have the air, and man and beasts the earth, the artist had a ready answer: "So, fishes have the water, yet beasts can swim by nature, and men by art. He that can swim need not despair to fly; to swim is to fly in a grosser fluid, and to fly is to swim in a subtler. We are only to proportion our power of resistance to the different density of matter through which we are to pass."

If the artist seems to have had a good grasp of fluid mechanics, his ideas on gravity and how to escape it were far-fetched: "The

Lilienthal perfected use of "Body English" for lateral balance.

labor of rising from the ground," he says, "will be great; but as we mount higher, the earth's attraction and the body's gravity will be gradually diminished, till we shall arrive at a region where a man will float in the air without any tendency to fall: no care will then be necessary, but to move forwards with the gentlest impulse.

"You, Sir," he tells Rasselas, "whose curiosity is so extensive, will easily conceive with what pleasure a philosopher furnished with wings, and hovering in the sky, would see the earth and all its inhabitants rolling beneath him, and presenting to him successively, by its diurnal motion, all the countries within the same parallel.

"How must it amuse the pendent spectator to see the moving scene of land, ocean, cities, and deserts! to survey, with equal security, the marts of trade, and the fields of battle; mountains infested by barbarians, and fruitful regions gladdened by plenty and lulled by peace! pass over distant regions, and examine the face of nature from one extremity to the other!"

When Rasselas complained that the upper atmosphere might be too thin to breathe, the artist volunteered to make the first test flight of the wings by himself. Rasselas agreed, and for a year dropped by from time to time to check on his progress.

Finally the wings were finished, Johnson wrote, "and on a morning appointed, the maker appeared furnished for flight on a promontory; he waved his pinions awhile to gather the air, then leaped from his stand, and in an instant dropped into the lake. His wings, which were of no use to him in the air, sustained him in the water, and the prince drew him to land half dead with terror and vexation."

If Dr. Johnson's vision of man-powered flight was futuristic, he did live to hear of man's conquest of the sky in 1783 by hot-air balloons, before his death in 1784. The word came in letters written to Sir Joseph Banks in London, from Benjamin Franklin in Paris. Franklin, the American Ambassador to France, was a serious supporter of aerostation. No doubt Franklin had read Francis Godwin's *The Man in the Moone* and Robert Paltock's *Life and Adventures of Peter Wilkins*, both of which employed harnessed birds to provide lift and propulsion, for among Franklin's papers, in the American Philisophical Library, is a curious drawing of a conical balloon to which 16 birds are harnessed.

Among the more amusing early references to the ornithopter principle of flight was an article which appeared in the Scientific

Flock of wild geese hooked to flying machine provided power for fictional flight to the moon, 17th Century.

American in 1851 on "A successful experiment with a new apparatus for flying."

"The flyer," according to the article, was a Miss Juanita Parez, who though rather fat and corpulent, moved through the air, by the help of wings, with the greatest of ease and rapidity. She was

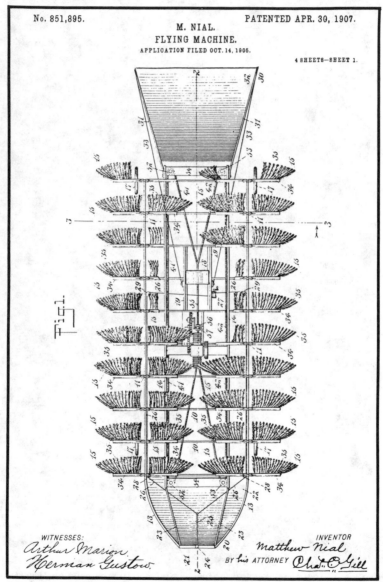

Patented flying machine by M. Nial in 1907 used feathers.

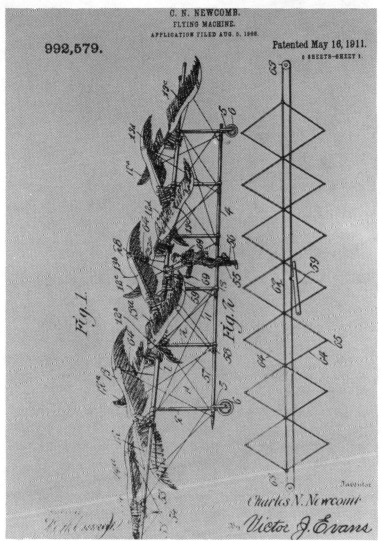

C. N. NEWCOMB.
FLYING MACHINE.
APPLICATION FILED AUG. 5, 1908.

992,579.

Patented May 16, 1911.
8 SHEETS—SHEET 1.

C. N. Newcomb's Flying Machine used man power to flap feathered wings.

advertised to fly a distance above 1200 feet, raising above 600 feet, but exceeded the program both in height and distance. No description of the wings is given. They have a spread of some fifteen feet, are fastened by ligaments of great flexibility, and arranged so as to move with great rapidity, and they make a noise like a windmill. The astonishment at Madrid was immense, and no wonder—just think of a corpulent damsel flying through the air and making a noise like a windmill!"

83

Chapter 6
The Westerners

"He regretted that he was not a bird, and could not be in two places at once."

— Sir Boyle Roche (1743-1807)

Reuben Jasper Spalding, a Colorado prospector, spent seventeen years of his hard life working on a lovely spread of feathered wings, which he dreamed of soaring amongst the great eagles near his cabin at Rosita.

Like others before him, Spalding saw no reason to believe that he could not fly with them, rising on the slope winds that carried the wheeling birds up the face of the eastern escarpment, sometimes even above the timberline and into snow country.

Built in secret, first word of the Spalding Flying Machine leaked out when William J. Orange, enterprising editor of the *Silver Cliff Russler*, sneaked into the miner's barn one day in 1890 and wrote up a feature story about what he saw.

Forty-six years old when he began work on his winged wonder, Spalding was 63 by the time it was ready to fly. Rather than being angered by Orange's story, he felt a measure of pride that he had been noticed.

"The machine is fashioned exactly like a bird's wings and tail," Orange had written. "The wings and tail and all the springs, hinges, cords and attachments to operate them are attached to a leather harness. The steel used is of the best quality, having cost 80 cents a pound."

In each wing, Orange counted, were 14 feathers made of silk and eagle quills. There was a head rest and leg rests and the "flapping, curving and folding of the wings is controlled by an easy forward arm motion."

The workmanship was, in fact, so gorgeous that the patent commissioner, in issuing Patent No. 398,984 to Spalding on March 5, 1889, called it "the only perfect duplicate of nature's flying apparatus ever made in the world," Orange wrote.

But would it fly?

H. F. Moore, a resident of nearby Florence, Colorado, told the author some years ago: "Spalding would get up on top of buildings and fly to the ground."

In the summer of 1888 the old miner went to Denver and took a train clear to Washington to arrange for his patent. He carried a model tucked under his arm, arousing much curiosity and considerable laughter. In the capital, he sat for the only portrait known to exist of him.

Back home, Spalding arranged to give a flight demonstration of his machine at Denver. Shops were closed. Cowhands and miners came to the city from miles around. Old Reuben strapped on his lovely wings and jogged up and down the street to limber up.

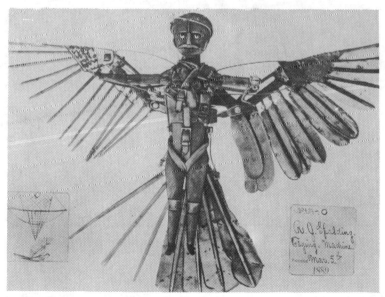

Patent model of Spalding's Flying Machine reposes in National Air & Space Museum.

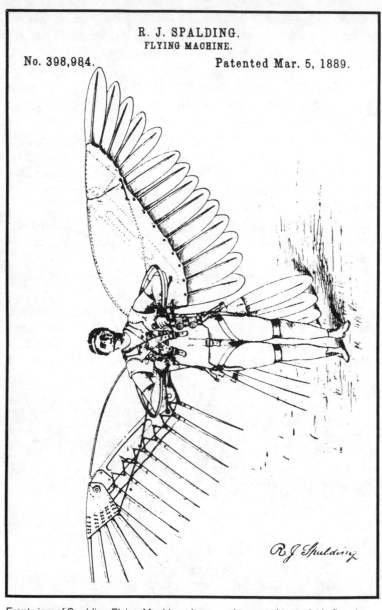

R. J. SPALDING.
FLYING MACHINE.

No. 398,984.

Patented Mar. 5, 1889.

R. J. Spalding

Front view of Spalding Flying Machine shows springs used to assist in flapping.

"Go ahead and fly!" someone shouted. A gun went off; dust exploded at his feet.

In alarm, Spalding sprinted for the courthouse, wings flapping as he ran. He didn't get off the ground. He hadn't meant to—not that way. He paused for breath, waiting for friends to show up with a hot-air circus balloon to lift him into the sky, so that he could cut loose and glide back to earth.

The crowd of cowhands ran after the old man, grabbed him from behind and tossed him roughly into the air, amid shouts of laughter.

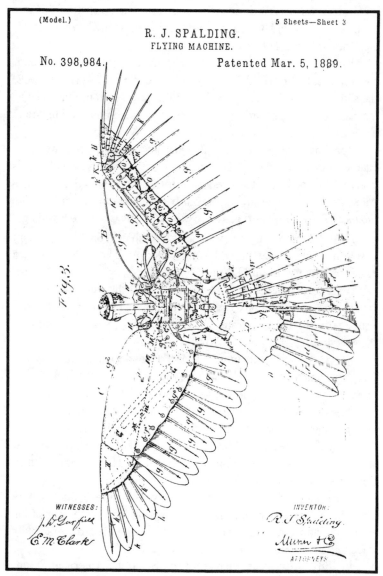

(Model.)

5 Sheets—Sheet 3

R. J. SPALDING.
FLYING MACHINE.

No. 398,984.

Patented Mar. 5, 1889.

Fig.3.

WITNESSES:
J. W. Garfield
E. M. Clark

INVENTOR:
R. J. Spalding.
Munn & Co.
ATTORNEYS

Rear view of Spalding Flying Machine shows coiled springs (j) and method of attaching feathers.

But Spalding was tough. Eyes flashing, he lit into the crowd like an avenging angel, kicking and punching.

When the street brawl ended, Spalding's lovely wings hung loosely, the parts broken. The leather body harness bore marks of sharp Bowie knives.

"I afterwards saw those knife cuts in the harness, after they had been neatly repaired by grandfather," his grandson, Clarence Spalding, once told the author.

Sadly the old man packed away his angel wings and forgot about his dream of flying. He died at Swallows, Colorado, April 19, 1902, the same year Wilbur and Orville Wright, two Dayton, Ohio bicycle mechanics, were preparing to make history with powered flights at Kitty Hawk, North Carolina.

Spalding's wings were destroyed in a fire in 1917, but two of his hand-crafted patent models remain to show what an old man's dreams are made of. One reposes in the National Air and Space Museum in Washington, an official tribute to a forgotten aviation pioneer. The other was donated to the author by Clarence Spalding.

A contemporary flying enthusiast who shared Spalding's dream of soaring high above the Old West was Sure Shot Bill Beeson, a familiar character around Dillon, Montana faro parlors in the 1880s.

A carpenter by trade, Beeson had joined the rush to the Montana mining country along the Beaverhead River, in the Bitterroot Range. He decided to pursue his trade building houses in booming Dillon.

For recreation, old timers recall, Beeson played faro by the hour, stroking his moustache and watching the cards with calculating shrewdness. Because the house seldom got the better of him, he won the sobriquet "Sure Shot Bill." George R. Metlen, a Dillon mining engineer and former highway commissioner, who knew Beeson well, recalled that "he would put a dollar on the faro layout. If he lost the dollar he quit, but if he won he stayed in the game until he began to lose, when he immediately cashed in."

Sure Shot Bill Beeson had another vice besides gambling—he was a born Darius Green. He kept a pigeon loft at the rear of his workshop, and would spend long hours watching the birds gracefully wheeling and dipping through the sky.

In 1881, with assistance from the Scientific American Patent Agency, which did a thriving business with independent inventors,

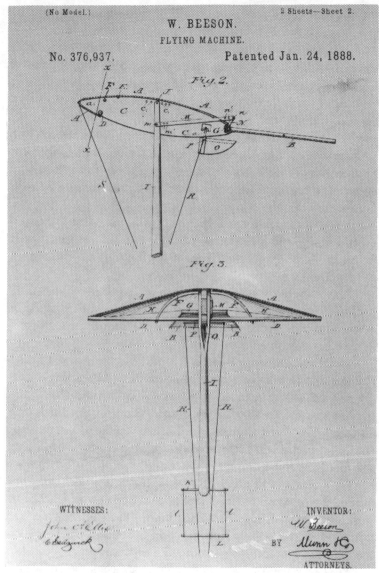

W. BEESON.

FLYING MACHINE.

No. 376,937.

Patented Jan. 24, 1888.

Fig. 2.

Fig. 3.

WITNESSES:

INVENTOR:

BY

ATTORNEYS.

In 1888 Beeson patented Flying Machine with tail operated by pilot riding on a trapeze.

Sure Shot Bill patented a Flying Ship that was just what its name implied. Utterly simple in concept, it consisted of a boat hull from which two masts protruded upward and outward. Sails hung from crossbars between the masts, like sheets on a clothesline. A system of ropes and pulleys permitted the set of the sails to be changed in flight to catch the wind at the proper angle. That was all.

"To start the ship," Beeson explained to the Patent Office, "it is carried up by a balloon, and is dropped at the proper time, or is raised like a kite, all the sails being set almost vertically—and when the ship is up high enough this rope is cut in the same manner as one would cut a kite string."

When he wasn't playing faro or pigeon-watching, Beeson was dreaming up new ideas. In 1887 he patented another new brainstorm for Aerial Navigation. It also consisted of a number of canvas planes, arranged to catch the wind from any quarter, suspended by rope from a supporting balloon.

Below his "four-winged sail" hung what he called a "winged propeller"—an enclosed canvas cell in which an aeronaut rocked from side to side, causing a pair of fabric wings to rise and fall alternately.

And below the winged propeller was his piece de resistance—a "sail suit"—two sheets of canvas sewn together with room for an aeronaut to crawl inside, where he could work arms and legs like a flying squirrel in an effort to fly.

Not one to give up, Beeson the next year patented a Flying Machine that resembled a huge cambered kite with a hinged tail, from which was suspended a trapeze. The aeronaut rode the trapeze, swinging back and forth and so working the tail up and down for propulsion. As an afterthought, he added in the patent description: "The machine may also be made and used as a toy, and as such will afford amusement to many persons."

Typical of the lone inventor who stumbled blindly along un-marked trails toward realization of an idea he knew simply *had* to work, Beeson plunged ahead. Early in the 1890's he took a closer look at his pigeons, and decided that perhaps Reuben Jasper Spalding had the right approach—a set of mechanical wings.

"His machine was a rather ingeniously constructed affair," George Metlen wrote to the author years ago. "It was shaped as near the form of the pigeon's wings as he was able to build it out of thin strips of pine wood. The wings were about six feet in length by 18 inches in width at their widest part."

Early in 1892 Beeson felt the wings were properly adjusted and braced for an actual flight test. For an assistant he called on his

Author's father, cartoonist Clare Victor Dwiggins, did this sketch of Sure Shot Bill Beeson's famous flight from Opera House roof in 1880s.

favorite faro dealer, a person known as Billy the Dick. Together they carried the wings to the roof of Dillon's two-story opera house, some forty-five feet above the street. The whole town turned out to watch.

Billy the Dick strapped Sure Shot Bill into his flying machine, and after a few experimental wingflaps, Beeson tensed his muscles for the leap that would bring him fame or misfortune. Metlen, who was there, describes the great Dillon flight:

"After the straps were all securely fastened, Bill took off into space. The results were not wholly satisfactory; however, he was on the right track.

"The wings acted like a glider and he planed to the ground about two hundred feet from the take-off. The air resistance was so great that he could not flop his wings, and had it not been for the tie-down, he would have fell directly to the ground; but instead, he made a gliding, sliding landing, the buck stay on his belly landing first and with enough force to about wreck old Bill and knock all the air out of him. One wing was reduced to splinters. Notwithstanding the jibes old Bill was subjected to by the crowd that gathered to witness the flight, he did actually glide from a height of 45 feet a distance of 200 feet from the take-off to the ground."

Beeson still would not give up, Metlen recalled, for "After his unsuccessful flight he built another machine along the same lines as the first, but tried to operate it by pedaling the wings from crank pedals like a bicycle. He was able to get up enough speed on his wings to make the contraption jump from the floor of his shop, but she lacked the necessary horsepower to raise off the ground."

Chapter 7
The Tunnel Men

"They have sown the wind, and they shall reap the whirlwind."
—Hosea viii: 7.

Introduction of the wind tunnel as an aerodynamic research tool was an important step toward understanding basic laws governing not only the flight of birds, but of all heavier-than-air craft which depend upon the atmosphere for support. As Mouillard put it, observing bird flight was one thing; understanding it was something else.

Whereas the 1893 Chicago Conference on Aerial Navigation convinced the scientific community that they were on the right track to achieving mechanical flight, little was understood of the basic principles of aerodynamics involved. It was well and good to watch birds fly, but there had to be some way to simulate flight in a controlled laboratory environment, before accurate measurements of lift, drag, and other forces could be achieved.

Oddly, many of the foremost researchers involved in aerodynamic studies continued their bird-watching in hope of learning the secret of flight.

Professor Samuel Pierpont Langley observed: "Nature has made her flying machine in the bird, which is nearly a thousand times as heavy as the air its bulk displaces, and only those who have tried to rival it know how inimitable her work is, 'for the way of a bird in the air' remains as wonderful to us as it was to Solomon."

Sir Hiram Maxim said: "Man is essentially a land animal. It is quite possible if Nature had not placed before him numerous examples of birds and insects that are able to fly, he would never have thought of attempting it himself."

Both Langley and Sir Hiram, however, eventually put aside their bird-watching and turned to the laboratory to understand the dynamics of flight. The old empirical laws of mechanics somehow didn't work.

As early as 1808, Sir George Cayley in England had come remarkably close to grasping the mechanical action of a bird's wing, in a sketch of an ornithopter that clearly shows the bird-like action of a wing's leading-edge spar and its flexible area behind, in creating a propelling action on both the upstroke and downstroke.

The British aeronautical historian Charles H. Gibbs-Smith, in his book: *Sir George Cayley's Aeronautics 1796-1855*, (Her Majesty's Stationery Office, London, 1962), described this action with the interesting explanation:

"All birds are propelled by the airscrew action of the outer parts of their wings, which provide all the thrust and some of the lift: in some birds the emarginated outer primary feathers of each wing twist into four or five airscrew blades; in some high-aspect-ratio birds the outer primaries twist collectively into a single blade; and in birds with wings of large area, and medium aspect-ratio, nearly half the wing is twisted in this way. As all the movement of a wing is communicated by the equivalent of a leading-edge spar, the outer hind portion heels up on the down-stroke, and down on the up-stroke; but owing to the camber of the wing construction as a whole, there is less heeling down on the up-stroke—hence less thrust—than there is on the down-stroke."

Gibbs-Smith thus disagreed with other bird-watchers, like B. Baden Powell, who in 1894 observed that a bird, seen from below, appears alternately to extend and flex his wings, "and it is therefore probable that the wing during the down stroke is well spread out to take advantage of the greatest area for compressing the air beneath, while during the up stroke the wing is flexed."

He concluded: "It seems extraordinary that, after all the careful observations of scientists during many centuries, we cannot say that we thoroughly understand the exact action of a bird's wing during flight."

Simon Newcomb, the 19th Century mathematician, observed: "The desire to fly like a bird is inborn in our race. We can no more be expected to abandon the idea than the ancient mathematician could be expected to give up the problem of squaring the circle!"

Professor Joseph Le Conte, the eminent naturalist, said frankly: "I am one of those who thinks that a flying machine is impossible, in spite of testimony of the birds!"

This was the attitude held by most of the scientific community before the advent of the tunnel men, who would point the way toward conquest of the sky through laboratory observation and analysis of the winds.

In California, John J. Montgomery almost stumbled onto the secret of aerodynamic lift, with his crude wind tunnel observations of dust particles blowing over cambered airfoils. Montgomery mistook their curving path for the crest of a wave, and missed the whole point—the lifting force of the lower pressure area above the wing, identified mathematically by Daniel Bernoulli.

The world's first wind tunnel was built by Francis Herbert Wenham, founder of the Aeronautical Society of Great Britain. With straightforward British logic, the Society in 1871 raised a subscription for Wenham to undertake systematic aerodynamic experiments to obtain "data on which a true science of aeronautics can be founded."

Wenham's tunnel, which he described in a paper read at the Chicago Conference of 1893, was a wooden trunk 18 inches square and 10 feet long, through which a steam-powered fan blew a 40-mph wind. Wenham went ahead blindly, experimenting with flat plates, inclined at angles from 15 to 60 degrees to the airflow. Despite their crudeness and unexpected turbulence, these experiments were encouraging. Wenham found that lift, at small angles of incidence, exceeded drag by a much greater extent than had previously been suspected.

Recognizing the need for varying the speed of the air through his tunnel, Wenham told the Society he hoped to build a larger apparatus with a wind velocity "from a gentle breeze up to a tornado that could rip the clothes off your back, or blow you away like a feather; but no flying man should mind this effect," he added.

In 1900, then 76, Wenham actually succeeded in building a tunnel that produced a 25-mph wind with a hand-driven fan spun at

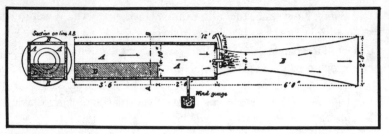

Horatio Phillips' 1884 wind tunnel was first to use narrow-throat Venturi tube design.

1700 rpm. "I could not get beyond this, as it absorbed all my strength to work it," he complained.

The first tunnel man to identify the area of lower pressure formed above a cambered airfoil was Horatio Phillips, using a homemade wind tunnel built in 1884. It was a novel device which produced a controlled air current by means of a steam jet that eliminated much of the turbulence Wenham encountered.

Far more sophisticated than Wenham's, Phillips' tunnel employed a little known principle discovered by an Italian physicist, G. B. Venturi (1742-1822) while studying the flow of fluids through narrowed channels. This was the first "Venturi tube" which Phillips described as "an expanding delivery tube of sheet iron" into which steam was sprayed through fine nozzles under a pressure of 70 psi. Rushing through the throat of the Venturi tube, the mixture of steam and air created a suction that gave a wind velocity of 60 feet per second.

In his experiments, Phillips developed his famous series of patented, cambered airfoils, some of which featured a drooping leading edge, later adopted by Louis Bleriot and other pioneer aircraft designers in 1908-1910. In May, 1893, Phillips built and successfully flew a large, powered model craft that resembled a Venetian blind, with twenty long, narrow, cambered airfoils stacked one above the other. Mounted on a tricycle gear and powered with a steam engine, it reached a speed of 40 mph flying in sweeping circles, at the end of a control line.

In patenting one of his airfoils, in 1891, which he used in the Venetian blind machine, Phillips first described his discovery of low-pressure lift: "The particles of air struck by the convex upper surface are deflected upward...thereby causing a partial vacuum over the greater portion of the upper surface..."

First to run wind tunnel measurements of pressure distribution over a wing was H. C. Vogt, of Copenhagen, in 1894. A marine engineer, he was inspired not by bird flight but by the mysterious action of the wind blowing over the spreading sails of yachts plying the North Sea. Vogt discovered that it was this action of the wind which gave the sails their graceful curves, but he was puzzled as to why the sails obtained much of their forward thrust from the leeward side, where a low-pressure area formed.

To learn more about this phenomenon, Vogt built an ingenious wind tunnel powered by the strong updraft inside the 100-foot tall smokestack of the Copenhagen Gas Works. With the help of the firm's director, Johan Irminger, he knocked a hole in one side of the chimney and inserted one end of his 40-inch tunnel.

Inside this tunnel Vogt inserted hollow airfoils that had been drilled with a number of small holes. These were opened one at a time, and the resulting pressure readings were taken from a common water gauge connected to the inside of the airfoil.

Vogt is credited with first discovering that the region of greatest lift along a wing occurs toward the leading edge where the upward deflection of air is more pronounced.

Dr. Albert F. Zahm, the scientist who helped Chanute organize the 1893 Chicago Conference on Aerial Navigation, in 1901 built history's first complete wind tunnel laboratory on the grounds of the Catholic University of America. It was financed by a New York inventor of a giant flying boat, Hugo Mattulath, who had hired Dr. Zahm as a consultant.

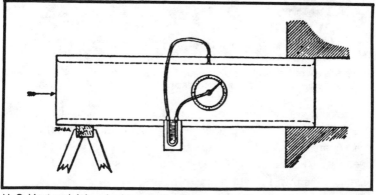

H. C. Vogt and Johan Irminger built wind tunnel inside a factory smokestack at Copenhagen Gas Works.

Multiplane aircraft, thought of by Horatio Phillips in 1890 and Octave Chanute about same time, were used in MPA designed in 1923 by W. F. Gerhardt.

Ironically, the true nature of induced drag, which accounts for the major portion of total drag, escaped him—his researches convinced him that skin friction was to blame. Inside a 40-foot tunnel 6 feet square blew a 27-mph wind from a 5-foot suction fan. Dr. Zahm invented his own measuring instruments.

His investigative methods were unusual, to say the least. Once he hung a 16-foot plank in the tunnel endwise, then sawed off one foot at a time, checking the drag reduction as he went. He did not doubt that skin friction was heavily involved.

To measure accurately the speed of his manmade wind, he floated a toy balloon down the tunnel. On its way it interrupted two thin pencils of light focussed on a moving plate of film. It worked well.

In 1902 Dr. Zahm's tunnel work was interrupted by the death of Mattulath, who suffered a stroke. The flying boat project was abandoned, but grants from the Smithsonian and Carnegie Institutions permitted him to resume his work. In February, 1904, he revealed his conclusions about viscosity, or skin friction, in a paper on "Atmospheric Friction" which he read before the Philosophical Society of Washington.

Dr. Zahm was to occupy a niche in the hall of aviation fame because of his intense laboratory investigations. He is remembered today as America's Father of Flight Theory. Not one to hog the spotlight, Dr. Zahm permitted other researchers to use his wind tunnel for their own studies. Chanute once sent him a stuffed buzzard, to check its lift and drag coefficients, and a rocketship designer, Emile Berliner, also used the facility.

Among other early wind tunnels was one built by Dr. Ernst Mach of Vienna, in 1893. First to use a wind tunnel to photograph air flow, through a glass window, Dr. Mach used a piece of wire mesh over the opening to align the current, sucked through the tunnel by a centrifugal fan at a rate of 10 meters per second. Visualization was achieved with silken threads, cigarette smoke, and particles of glowing iron. Streams of heated air, invisible to the eye, also were recorded on a photographic plate. Dr. Mach's name is used today to describe the ratio of a flow velocity to the speed of sound—called the Mach number.

Gustave Eiffel, the French engineer best remembered for the 1,000-foot tower in Paris which bears his name, and for the Statue of Liberty in New York, devoted his later years to studying aerodynamics of aircraft. He built his first tunnel on the Champ de Mars in 1909, and in 1911 built a larger one at Auteuil, later donating it to the French Government. Eiffel developed a series of airfoils which also bear his name, and which were widely used in early powered aircraft.

Two other early wind tunnels deserve mention for the contributions of their designers to a fuller understanding of the true nature of aerodynamics—Nikolai E. Zhukovski in Russia, and Ludwig Prandtl at Gottingen in Germany.

Zhukovski's tunnel, 40 feet long and 4 feet in diameter, was built in 1905 at the Koutschino Aerodynamic Laboratory near Moscow and was financed by a Czarist capitalist, M. D. Riabouchinsky. A low-velocity tunnel (14.5 mph), it was used by Zhukovski for pioneer studies of the thrust of helicopter blades, with wool tufts glued to them for flow visualization.

Zkukovski and a German scientist, M. Wilhelm Kutta, came independently to the idea of the circulation hypothesis of lift and produced the mathematical theory that for the first time fully explained how a wing flies. Their work, however, was preceded by that of Frederick W. Lanchester in England, who is credited with first suggesting the idea of total circulation of an airfoil of infinite span, and the vortex theory of lift of a wing of finite span.

Many researchers today credit Prandtl's mathematical formulation of the circulation theory of lift as one of the most useful contributions ever made in the field of aeronautics. It was Prandtl who also

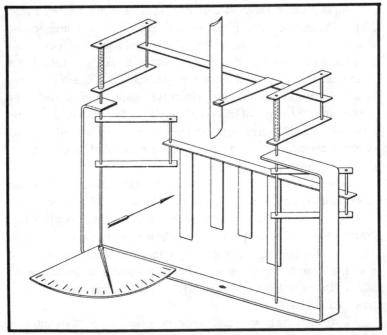

Mechanism of measuring apparatus designed for wind tunnel studies of airfoils by the Wright brothers.

first recognized that the total resistance of an aircraft is composed of three parts—skin friction (viscosity), form or pressure drag, and that produced by lift (induced drag).

Many airfoils developed by Prandtl at Gottingen are in use today, and are known as Gottingen curves.

Attention must be paid to the tunnel experiments of Orville and Wilbur Wright in October, 1901. About 6 feet long with an interior of 16 square inches, their tunnel had a glass top. A blower fan forced air through honeycomb windstraighteners at 40 feet per second.

The Wrights tested some 200 wing models of sheet metal, each set at 14 different angles of attack from 0 to 45 degrees. Other tests were run on various aspect ratio wings, and on superposed surfaces. The curved airfoils were balanced against plane surfaces, to provide a series of aerodynamic tables, after the Dayton brothers found that Lilienthal's tables were highly inaccurate. Their tunnel work was a chief factor leading to their success at Kitty Hawk in achieving powered flight in 1903.

Chapter 8
You'll Never
Get Off the Ground

"I said it to Orville, and I said it to Wilbur—"

T. W. Mather, writing in *The Popular Science Monthly* in November, 1885, came to the conclusion that, despite the examples of the birds, inventors of flying machines "as a rule belong rather in a lower class" than balloonists.

"The perpetual-motion man," he sneered, "is likely also to know just how to make a successful flying machine. The pathway has been strewn with wrecks, and I fear there is a feeling that, after all, it leads nowhere in particular, unless it be to the almshouse or lunatic asylum."

But still, he added, "there are the birds."

"One cannot help thinking," Mather concluded, "that we are about as likely to make a practicable flying-machine by copying the motions of the bird as we are to make a steam road-wagon by imitating the action of a horse."

If history proved him right, the dream of imitating bird and/or insect flight is ageless and continues today, although man-powered ornithopters still appear to be beyond the reach of aircraft designers and builders.

"Nature cannot always be trusted," Mather warned. "Why should we try to copy the motions of a bird's wing any more than those of a fish's tail? Our machine, in imitating them, would be complex and liable to get out of order. The desired results can probably be obtained in a much more simple and effective way. There has been a strong current of misguided thought and invention, particularly to be noticed in our Patent Office reports."

Truly, flying machine inventors were considered rather mad in the last century. Reuben Jasper Spalding nearly lost his life when drunken cowhands attacked him, when he attempted to fly on his patented wings. Scorn, or at least amusement, greeted others who succeeded in patenting their updated da Vinci devices, such as Watson F. Quinby's batlike Flying Apparatus of 1872.

Dr. Watson Fell Quinby's secret interest in flying was typical of ingenious American back-country folk, who shunned public attention because of the ridicule of "authorities" like T. W. Mather, who lumped them with "perpetual-motion men." An adventurous, mechanically-minded descendant of English Quakers who migrated to America in the 17th century, Dr. Quinby was born in 1826 in Mill Creek Hundred, near Brandywine Springs, Delaware.

As an admirer of Oliver Evans, a pioneer investigator of steam power who lived nearby, Dr. Quinby's first attempt to design a flying machine was to be a steam-powered aircraft which also could be manually-powered. Patented in 1861, it featured screw propellers at the stern and above, with wings consisting of curious oiled-silk valves that opened on the upstroke and closed on the downstroke, reminiscent of one of da Vinci's early designs. Lack of a suitable steam engine caused him to put the idea aside.

A country doctor by profession, Dr. Quinby had gone to Mobile, Alabama, to practice medicine, but in 1849 was lured to the California gold fields. He returned to Delaware in 1852, married, and set up a new practice. In 1853 he was inspired to develop his steam-powered aircraft when the showman P. T. Barnum posted a $5,000 prize for the first person to fly across the Atlantic to Europe.

Although his 1861 flying machine was a failure, the idea of flying stayed with him through the better years of the Civil War, and in 1867, when he had more time for his own projects, he patented a new "Improved Flying Apparatus," this one a truly man-powered aircraft design. It consisted of oiled silk wings and a tail, strapped to the operator's back in a manner to keep the arms and legs free.

"In using this invention," he explained, "a motion is given to the arms and legs almost precisely like that in swimming, and the effect is nearly the same, the difference being in the density between water and air being compensated for by the greater extent of surface

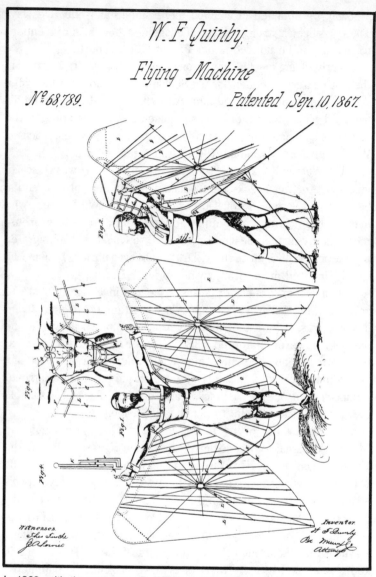

W. F. Quinby,

Flying Machine

No. 68,789. Patented Sep. 10, 1867.

Fig. 2.

Fig. 3.

Fig. 1.

Fig. 4.

Witnesses.
Thos Smith
J. A. Lennel

Inventor.
W. F. Quinby
By Mun & Co.
Attorneys

In 1869, with the war over, Dr. Watson Fell Quinby designed and patented winged MPA for operator to use by swimming motions.

presented by the wings. The wings are brought up to their full height, and then suddenly pushed forward, and by a pronation of the hands thrown outward, and then brought down by a full force or power of both arms and legs. By this method, every muscle of the body is brought into action to the best advantage."

The Scientific American, reporting on the device, felt that the use of all body muscles really *was* an improvement on earlier Darius Green machines, but warned: "We hardly think he will be able to compete with the swallows in this harness, and would advise him to start from some low point at first, so that, if he should fall down, it would not hurt him much."

Dr. Quinby apparently took the well-meant advice, according to an elderly Wilmingtonian who in 1927 recalled an attempt the doctor made to fly from the roof of a low farm building, where he had secretly built his device:

"Dr. Quinby expected in the hop-off from his elevation to get his machine 'carrying on' before he alighted on the ground fifteen feet below. But being so close to the ground, Dr. Quinby and his flying machine had a rough fall, violent enough to lay the physician up for a day or two, while his machine, badly damaged by the drop, was hidden away and never again given the opportunity to demonstrate that it could be made to fly."

For a time the good doctor, stung by ridicule, forgot flying and devoted his spare hours to writing pamphlets, one presenting arguments for and against adopting the metric system in this country: *"The Yard or the Metre, Which Will Ye Choose?"*

The lure of the sky was too strong, however, and in 1869 he patented still another flying machine, this one a set of wings whose spars served as oars, with a foot-actuated tail surface behind. Abandoning that design, in 1872 Dr. Quinby patented a new set of wings which, like da Vinci's favorite design, resembled those of a bat.

"The weight of the whole machine need not exceed 15 pounds," he said. "It is constructed inside a semicircle, all the points touching the periphery. I describe a semicircle on the floor 10 or 12 feet in diameter, and bisect this figure with a radius."

In operation, he wrote, "It is intended to start from the ground." (no more rooftop launches!) "One foot is disengaged from the stirrup, when, by raising the other foot and pushing the hands upward and forward, as in swimming, the wings are raised. Then by suddenly depressing the wings, by means of the elevated leg, the body is elevated. This alternate elevation and depression of the wings is continued as long as flight is desired. After rising from the ground the other foot may be inserted in its stirrup and both legs used."

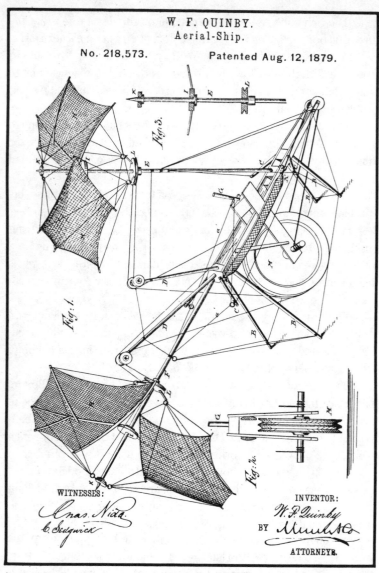

In 1879 Dr. Quinby's last patented Aerial Ship used sailwings for lift and propulsion.

In a last fling at flying, Dr. Quinby in 1879 patented his final "Aerial-Ship", returning to his original idea of providing a boat to ride in, and sets of winged sails that served for both lift and propulsion, adjustable in pitch, a crude forerunner of the modern variable pitch propeller.

After a full life, Dr. Quinby died in 1918 at the age of 92, having lived to see the conquest of the sky become an actuality, albeit with rigid-wing aircraft, not ornithopters.

Indeed, the success of the Wright Brothers in flying a rigid wing machine at Kitty Hawk in 1903 in no way deterred dreamers from their pursuit of the age-old goal of imitating bird flight with mechanical wings. Even today, serious study is again being given to the problem, from both the aerodynamic and mechanical viewpoint.

Far ahead of his time in this respect was Professor Harry LaVerne Twining, a physics instructor at Los Angeles Polytechnic High School, who in the early 1900's studied the action of a buzzard's wing in an unusual manner—he waved the wing of a dead buzzard, in imitation of its natural vibration, close to a piece of silken cloth, 2 by 3 feet, hanging from a support.

"Whenever the concave or convex surface of the wing was brought close to the cloth," he said, "it was attracted to the wing and stuck to it as though glued there."

He traced the airflow pattern in this crude fashion and concluded that "the air comes in toward a vibrating wing from above, from below, from the whole front, and from the rear for two-thirds of its length. This air is gathered into two streams, one above the wing and one below the wing, and is discharged at the rear tip of the wing for one-third of its distance. At this place the air is driven violently away from the wing, backward and downward, forming a large cone of moving air with the apex at one-third of the rear edge of the wing."

Twining, who thus came remarkably close to grasping the hypothesis of total circulation and wingtip vortex flow, set about building a set of canvas wings, went alone into the hills, and tried to fly with them. A gust of wind caught him up and roughly tossed him into a mesquite bush. He decided the matter needed more careful thought.

"The flying of soaring of birds," he concluded, "can be explained upon well-known mechanical principles, and it is surprising that these feats of winged creatures have remained so much a mystery." He pointed out that the resultant of all forces acting on a bird's wing, whether moving upward or downward, is forward in the plane of the wing. It was his belief that "the machine is held firmly between two planes of resistance, between which it glides smoothly forward."

After publishing these conclusions, Professor Twining turned for a while from flying machines to a far more subtle mystery of nature—the weight of a mouse's soul. In 1907 he busied himself in his high school laboratory, weighing mice just before and after killing them. He repeated his experiments on grasshoppers and kittens.

It was his snap conclusion that an apparent loss of weight before and after expiration proved the existence of a soul, but later he retracted that view—he concluded the weight loss was due to the loss of body gases and moisture, not ectoplasm.

Two years later Professor Twining was back at flying machine work, as secretary of the Aero Club of California, which was sponsoring an air meet at Dominquez Field near Long Beach. He revealed in 1909 what he had been up to: "Some five years ago," he reported, "I made a machine with wings and took it into the hills of San Pedro, in the darkness of early morning hours. There for two days, like a condor with a full stomach, I tried to get off the ground, but it would not work—the first machine that a man makes never does. But I learned a great deal by experiment, and with the added knowledge I propose in the near future to build another machine. My first machine weighed 35 pounds. The wings had a spread of 24 feet from tip to tip and a width of 2 ½ feet."

Professor Twining spent the summer of 1909 working on his second wing flapper, whose mechanism he described in a patent, issued to the inventor August 20, 1912. Completed in the fall of 1909, the machine was wheeled from Twining's workshop for its initial test hop. The appearance of the ornithopter in the streets of Los Angeles prompted considerable interest. A story in the *Los Angeles Daily Times* on August 13 reported:

HIS FLIP-FLOP
TWINING'S BIRD
ABOUT TO FLY

Professor Believes He Has
The Real Airship

"Professor H. LaV. Twining...has almost completed a machine with which he believes he will fly. In the workshop of J. H. Klassen is a frail aircraft, equipped with two great wings that suggest some monstrous bird of prehistoric time. The wings, carefully modeled after those of an eagle, measure 27 feet from tip to tip, the operator's station being three feet wide.

"Professor Twining does not intend to rise far from the ground at first, and is confident that when it does get into the air there will be

Professor Harry LaVerne Twining of Los Angeles built an ornithopter reporters called the "Flip-Flop." It barely got off the ground.

"His ground runs were one of the highlights of amusement," says Lippisch. "Oskar Ursinus (who later formed the Muskelflug-Institut, or Institute of Man-Powered Flight), running in front with a handkerchief to determine the wind direction and Brustmann high on the wheels flapping the wings like a newly hatched chicken."

Dr. Brustmann's machine was a flop, but he had something more important to contribute to the MPA program. As a sports physician who trained athletes for Olympic competitions, he had experimented on how to reach a man's highest power output, although his figures were quite optimistic.

What intigued Lippisch was the trend of Dr. Brustmann's figures, which showed the relation between human-power output and its duration to be a kind of hyperbolic function. "This relation," he recalls, "showed that the human body stored a certain amount of energy which could be expended over a short period, and high-power output could be expended for a period of less than one minute. At least, I knew that for a short time it seemed actually possible to fly by one's own power, since a lightly built glider plus man would not need more than one horsepower to be flown horizontally."

The upshot was that Lippisch decided to build a very light test craft, as a flapping-wing MPA. "The reasoning was based primarily on the physiology of the function of muscles designed for intermittent use," says Lippisch. Besides, he felt that wing flapping would have better efficiency and would cause less additional structural weight for the required power-delivery mechanism. He still held this view in 1960. Dr. Brustmann suggested utilizing arm and chest muscles in addition to the leg muscles for propulsion power.

Lippisch's man-powered ornithopter was built by Alex Schleicher in Poppenhausen as a high-winger with an open pilot seat and a covered fuselage behind it. The wings were moved by leg action, as in rowing from a sliding oarsman's seat.

Each wing was supported by a triangular strut, the end of which slid along a guide rail on the fuselage, controlled by cables. Shock-cord rubber tension springs in the rear fuselage were adjusted to provide wing dihedral in normal gliding flight.

The wing was built around a single spar, with thin veneer on the leading edge and fabric behind. The root section was highly cambered, and the tip almost symmetrical. The craft's empty weight was around 50 kg, or 110 pounds, higher than anticipated, due to the wing-flapping mechanism.

Professor Harry LaVerne Twining's ornithopter of 1909-10.

no danger...He intends to conduct his first experiments in private, and will begin today to endeavor to operate the machine."

Many years later, Professor Twining, interviewed by the author, recalled what happened: "I flapped the wings furiously, but was only able to get the front of the machine off the ground. I was on the point of making alterations in the machine's design, when it became apparent that the rigid wing type aircraft was vastly superior for any commercial purposes. I still believe, however, that my ornithopter can be made to fly with only slight modifications to the original design."

As President of the Aero Club of California, Professor Twining on January 10, 1910, assisted in getting America's first aviation meet rolling. The Professor's Flip-Flop, as the newspapers dubbed his ornithopter, went on exhibition, but no attempt was made to fly it.

That summer Professor Twining, with the help of his physics students, completed construction of a conventional monoplane. It did manage to get into the air for a few feet, but its Model-T engine was underpowered.

A noted German sailplane designer, Alexander Lippisch, holds the honor of developing the world's first ornithopter man-powered aircraft to perform with any success, in the year 1929. Lippisch first came into prominence in the post-World War I period from 1920 to the mid-thirties, as Technical Director of the Rhoen Rossiten Gesellschaft at the Wasserkuppe. Among his outstanding designs was the *Professor*, *Wien*, *Falke*, and *Fafnir I* and *II* sailplanes. Work on a tailless Delta-wing glider led to his design of the Me-163 rocket interceptor, the Komet, in which Heini Dittman becave the first man to fly at 1,000 km/h (620 mph) in level flight.

Lippisch later was spirited to the United States, at the end of World War II, and continued his man-powered aircraft researches well into the 1960s. At that time, he recalled in the Journal of the Royal Aeronautical Society his early MPA work on ornithopters.

During the 1920s at the Wasserkuppe, a time when he was designing airfoils and calculating induced drag according to Prandtl's newly discovered wing theory, he was frequently called upon to evaluate MPA's built by others. Seen from a distance, he recalled, they "resembled more one of those prehistoric bird petrifacts." He called them *Pteroptodons*.

Lippisch felt it would be helpful and inspirational to invite these inventors to attend the soaring competitions at the Wasserkuppe, and among them was a medical doctor, Martin Brustmann, who arrived with a kind of ornithopter constructed around and above a bicycle.

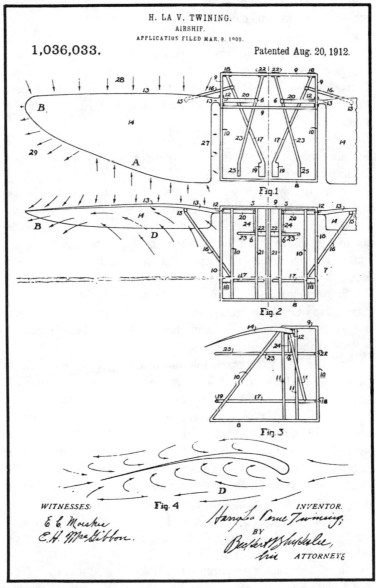

Patent granted to Professor Harry LaVerne Twining in 1912 reveals his ideas on wing aerodynamics.

A young athlete, Hans Werner Krause, was selected to test fly the machine, early in 1929. A single control stick operated both rudder and elevator. There were no ailerons, because Lippisch believed lateral control could be obtained by flapping one wing harder than the other. Wing twist on the downstroke, he believed, would be achieved by aerodynamic forces bending the thin veneer leading edge.

The machine was launched by shock cord, and after a few flights as a pure glider Krause began the flapping tests. Results were disappointing—the glide angle did not improve at all. Lippisch then went to a flexible trailing edge, adding Taube-like flexible wingtips of bamboo.

The result was now startling—on one flight Krause flew a distance estimated at 600 feet, according to Lippisch, although this distance has been disputed.

Later on, when Krause complained that it was hard work pumping the wings, Lippisch appealed to his romantic instincts to encourage him to try harder. If he could reach a small water puddle 300 meters distant from the launch point, Lippisch suggested, he could have the weekend off to visit his girl friend in Berlin. He made it on the first try.

Subsequently, the machine was shipped off to Berlin for an air show, and a welded steel tube undercarriage was added, "making it a truly earthbound machine," Lippisch says. Krause died shortly afterward in the crash of a sport plane.

In later years, Lippisch felt the machine could be modified somewhat, and built with modern lightweight materials in a manner that could make it even more successful than it was back in 1929.

An admirer of Lippisch's work, Douglas Kruse, of Long Beach, Calif., in 1977 built a model of a similar high-aspect ratio ornithopter (40:1) to test a new design for a flapping mechanism, the Golden Eagle. His goal was to build a machine with a span of from 74 to 90 feet, and wing area of from 160 to 190 sq/ft., all cantilever construction, with a metal spar and fiberglass and polyurethane covering.

And in Morgan, Utah, Klaus Hill, designer of a number of ultralight powered aircraft, was working on an ornithopter at this writing.

In 1973 Hill built an experimental MPA with a 28-foot span, 5' 3" chord, and a 5-foot propeller to be driven by pedal-power. The wing was built around an aluminum U-channel spar shaped with foam and

Klaus Hill of Morgan, Utah, designed all-metal MPA for ground-run evaluation of design, in effort to win the Kremer Award.

fabric covered. Fuselage was beautifully worked sheet metal, highly polished. The airfoil was symmetrical, of 12 percent thickness, with a drooping leading edge. It weighed 90 pounds empty.

"It was strictly an experimental craft," says Hill. "I built it to run taxi tests to check certain aerodynamic and mechanical design features, hoping to go from there toward winning the Kremer Award."

Other inventors around the country still hold to the idea of flying with flapping wings. In Inglewood, Calif., Rex Pagett went to the concept of using the powerful back muscles to power his wings, which attached to the shoulders of the pilot.

But if any wing-flapper finally succeeds in achieving controlled flight over a period of time, it might well be the Orni-Plane, a design of Percival H. Spencer, of Sun Valley, Calif. Designer of the Republic SeaBee, the Spencer Amphibian Air Car, and numerous other aircraft, Spencer in 1977 celebrated his 80th birthday flight testing a thing he calls the Hydro-Glider.

Spencer also made a small fortune with a patented commercial toy called the Wham-O Bird—625,000 were sold in the late 1950s. Rubber-band powered, it flaps its way around the sky with the greatest of ease. His patented toy features a link between the wing flap and the tail feathers, to permit it to glide properly regardless of the wing position when the power runs down.

Earlier in his career, Spencer had designed numerous other ornithopter models, but his most successful one, he claims, is an 8-foot wingspan model of the Orni-Plane that hangs in his bedroom.

His dream is to secure financing to build a man-sized Orni-Plane, fly it once, then retire it to the Smithsonian Institution.

One other machine bears attention here—a patented flapper called the Orniplane, developed by three Russian inventors, I. N.

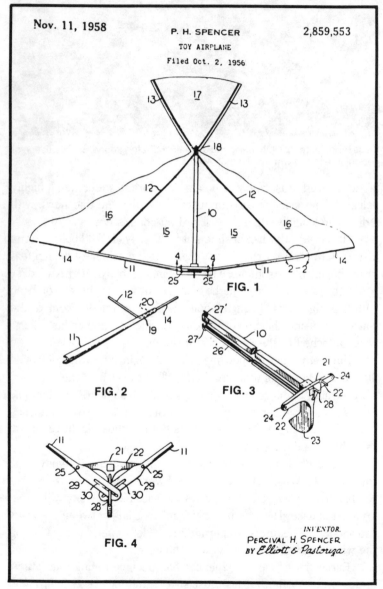

P.H. Spencer in 1958 patented a Toy Airplane that flew well as a wing-flapper. It was sold commercially as the Wham-O Bird.

P. H. Spencer's Wham-O Bird in flight.

and R. I. Vinogradov and V. M. Andreyev, whose secret lies in its feathered wingtips. The patent description explains:

"For the purpose of increasing thrust and lift, at the wingtips are used propelling tips (manus) consisting of feather-like vanes, made of synthetic material, with metal longerons. The vanes are arranged in fan-shape in one block executing reversive-torsional oscillations, transmitted by a helicoidal automat, consisting of hinge-jointed telescopic wing section longerons and power cylinders with supports on telescopic longerons and spring-blocking in the hoops of the cylinders."

Their machine also included a boundary layer control system, and a hydraulically-operated flywheel system (elastic-plastic) for automatically changing the wing profile. At least, that's what a translator at the Air Force Systems Command made of it.

Any why, after all, would anybody really want to fly like a bird, with flapping wings? "The best reason is simply that it hasn't been done successfully yet," says Walter H. Carnahan, who in 1975 conducted a forum on ornithopters at the Experimental Aircraft Association's summer convention at Oshkosh, Wisc.

Carnahan adds: "Have we forgotten that flying can also be fun? The birds haven't forgotten. On a day that is so gusty that old, bold human pilots are sitting on the ground reading about flying, the seagulls take to the air and cruise in turbulence, having a ball!"

Chapter 9

Bugsville

Two hundred sixty million years ago, in the Paleozoic epoch of the world's history, there lived a species of gigantic dragonflies called Protodonata. They flew on two pairs of graceful wings, with a span of two feet. The wings were formed of tough membranes stretched over an elaborate framework of veins.

The Protodonta were strange creatures with a thousand eyes, who pursued their loved ones relentlessly and mated in mid-flight. They could fly from dawn til dusk on warm, sunny days—hovering, darting forward or backward, with amazing precision.

Today, scientists marvel at the fossilized remains of these fantastic flyers, preserved in the Carboniferous strata at Commentry, France. They were the largest of some 4,870 species of Odonata, commonly called the Dragonfly. This is not a large figure, considering that the total number of living forms of insects runs between 2,000,000 and 4,000,000, dominating by sheer number all other forms of life. Of this huge number, roughly 750,000 species can fly.

One man who became fascinated by the darting flight of a dragonfly, catching mosquitos on the wing, hovering, backing up or rising vertically, was William Bushnell Stout, the noted designer of the Ford Trimotor all-metal transport. Once asked whether he was a descendant of David Bushnell, designer of a famous Civil War sub-

William Bushnell Stout, designer of Ford Tri-Motor transport, built experimental models of mechanical dragonflies.

marine, he shook his head and smiled: "All the world knows he died a bachelor!"

Stout was a man of typical Yankee ingenuity. Among his contributions, besides the Ford Trimotor, forerunner of toay's airliners, were the Sky Car, a family flivver plane with a tricycle landing gear; the first light, streamlined railroad car, and the 1932 Scarab, a streamlined, rear-engined autombile of the future.

Hence, his interest in the flight of the dragonfly was no passing fancy. He put other things aside and researched the subject at the

Congressional Library in Washington, D. C. There was not a single reference to the mechanics of insect flight!

Next Stout looked up Professor Leigh Chadwick, who had taken movies of insects flapping while held by forceps, using a stroboscopic light. Dragonflies, he discovered, flapped their wings 30 times a second, while common house flies and bumble bees flapped at more than 300 beats a second!

He recalled reading in Scientific American, in 1884, that a scientist named Paul Mazo, in Lausanne, Switzerland, had calculated that a fly's wings beat at 330 strokes a second, and mosquitos at 2,000 strokes a second. "Therefore," Mazo had concluded, "a number of common flies weighing 20 tons, and 130 tons of mosquitos, would require one horsepower to sustain themselves in the air."

That wasn't good enough for Bill Stout. He looked up a beekeeper, who told him that by putting a landing board at a 60 degree slope in front of the hive, instead of a flat landing board, his bees flew in with 30 per cent more honey on each flight. "The bee is flying close to a stall with his load of honey," Stout was told. "If he lands on a flat board, his hind legs land first and his front legs slap down and break off. If he lands on a slanting board, all six feet land at once; hence, 30 per cent more payload."

All this sounded like more folklore, so Stout decided to set up an experimental laboratory to learn first hand all about insect flight. Using a common music stand and a pivoted arm, he mounted an electric motor at one end and attached insect models at the other, so that the artificial wings were flapped by electric power. He called his device a "Geflopigus Giganticus".

From microscopic studies of actual insects Stout concluded their wings all had one common design feature—a stiff leading edge spar, getting more and more flexible from root to tip, with a flexible membrane behind the spar. "As the spar flaps up and down with some kind of motion," he said, "simple, harmonic, or otherwise, the trailing membrane takes various shapes and thrusts the air backward."

Consequently, Stout began building his model bug wings around a curved leading edge spar, tapering from the hinge point to the tip, where it curved around to the rear. He glued a sheet of tissue paper to the spar, so that its springing action held it in tension.

How to flap the wing was the next problem. A simple up-and-down stroke in a fanning action wouldn't do—others had tried that and failed. But on his "Geflopigator" the darned thing did work—to his surprise the crude wing flew around and around at some 20 mph.

To Stout, the whole exercise was simply one he hoped youngsters would follow up on. It was educational rather than demonstrative of any particular design for a practical "bug machine." He said: "I claim no results—only the beginnings of a new interest in the oldest and most efficient flight method of all."

In 1953, when the author was a reporter on the *Los Angeles Daily News*, he interviewed Bill Stout in his laboratory in Phoenix, Arizona. At that time, Stout firmly believed that a research and engineering group could carry on his work and come up with a one-man ornithopter you could fly to work and back, over all that freeway traffic.

He likened the action of flapping flight to that of a helicopter blade, which must change its angle of attack as it swings from the forward to the backward stroke. "In our flapping wing airplane," he

Stout launches rubber-band powered toy flapper.

said, we have to do the same thing, to get a constant lift at all times, and no bobbing up and down."

Early experiments on his whirling arm "Geflopigus" convinced him that the fly-type wing wouldn't work, as it produced more lift than thrust, and much of the wing area was simply parasite surface. Then he got the bright idea to study dragonfly wings.

"I photographed dragonfly wings to check on their structure," he explained. "There was the complex nature of the joints, the possibilities of effects of changes of blood pressure in the tubular spars, the structure of the hinge joint, and its angle at various points of flight."

Further study of the dragonfly wing convinced Stout he needed to know more about its intricate flapping action. An idea struck him—"what is the difference between whirling a single helicopter blade through a complete circle, or two blades in a half circle?"

The problem of reversing the blades every 180 degrees a couple of hundred times a minute "gives a structural man the jitters," he grinned. "However, the problem is not so bad as it seems. The two blades from opposite sides come together at the end of the stroke if you want to make a complete half circle, so that between these two wings can be built up an air pressure, an impact for an extra amount of strength at the end of each stroke, using up the inertia and taking it off at the end of each stroke. This is what you hear when birds take off suddenly in a steep climb, and the wings hit each other at the top of each stroke."

Further study of different insects revealed something important to Stout—their wings were pivoted in such a way that the trailing edge moves around the leading edge as a pivot, as the wings flap up and down. Through large arcs the wing actually acts like a helicopter blade, in effect, two full, connecting half circles of thrust.

"Then," he pointed out," after the insect is off the ground and in flight, amplitude decreases, the wingtips do more of the thrust work, the wing does more of the lift from the speed of progress, and we have a machine very efficient in horizontal speed—impossible in a helicopter."

Put another way, Stout maintained that with flapping wings you have the potential of helicopter-type takeoffs and landings, with better-than-airplane forward speeds. "Also," he explained, "full engine power and flywheel effort can be used for hovering and for vertical descents, after we learn more about what a wind does. The principle is there, and all the rest is accomplished except the engineering."

Stout built a second, improved "gefioppter" using a discarded vacuum-cleaner motor for a powerplant, and the first wing tried on it was constructed of pine, string, and tissue paper, with some liquid glue and thread. "It lasted about a minute," Stout said. He was impressed by the huge stresses involved.

Later designs were made with spars of split pine, with bamboo tips, and membranes of tissue paper, gold beaters skin, Saran, Cellophane, and other materials. The big problem was eliminating wrinkles.

Stout was astonished at the success of his new whirling arm machine and what it revealed, and immediately made plans to develop models of the dragonfly, nature's perfect flying machine.

Stout poses with mechanical dragonfly prototype MPA.

On my visit to Stout's laboratory, I witnessed one amazing flight of his mechanical dragonfly. It began with the whirring of the electric motor and the fluttering of the four wings as they beat up and down in a sort of figure-8 motion. Slowly the arm began to rotate. Stout stepped up the rheostat. Faster and faster the dragon-fly wings flapped. The noise rose to a high scream and the dragonfly model became a blur. He switched off the power, and the wings slowed to a stop.

I felt that I had looked into the future, as Stout showed me a model aircraft with a balsa-wood fuselage, with a tiny figure in the cockpit. He linked it to the rotating arm, beneath the wings, and as it began traveling in circles I believed that someday such a machine could be built and flown.

Bill Stout did not live to see a full-size model of his dragonfly machine fly, but others since have carried on his research work on insect flight, with more sophisticated equipment. At the University of Cambridge, Torkel Weis-Fogh discovered something overlooked by earlier aerodynamicists.

Reporting on his studies in *Scientific American*, Weis-Fogh explained: "The lift and propulsion of aircraft depend on the action of airfoils that move through the air steadily. In contrast, the muscle-powered flight of birds, bats, and insects depends on the flapping of wings, which introduces a degree of nonsteady airflow. Nonsteady aerodynamics is thus inherent in natural flapping flight."

Weis-Fogh recalled the work of Otto Lilienthal in 1889 in his classic analysis of the flying stork: on the downstroke, the wing's leading edge twists increasingly downward moving outward from base to tip. This twisting does two things. It adjusts the angle of attack to the direction of flight, and tilts the resulting force forward to provide both propulsion and lift. Conversely, on the upstroke the leading edge twists upward to keep the angle of attack small, providing some lift but no propulsion.

(This conclusion is in direct opposition to that of Professor Harry LaVerne Twining, who stated: "The upstroke of the wing drives the bird forward in the plane of the wing just as surely as the downstroke does.")

Weis-Fogh's conclusion was that two non-standard aerodynamic principles are involved in hovering flight—mechanisms he calls the *Clap-Fling* and the *Flip*. It is the Clap-Fling that pro-

A Pop-Art MPA not designed actually to fly, built in 1977 by Belgian artist PANAMARENKO. He calls it the UMBILLY II.

duces the noise of some birds in vertical takeoff flight, when their wings clap overhead, as Stout reported.

In high-speed photography of the wasp *Encarsia formosa*, Weis-Fogh discovered that the insect's two interlocked wings on each side clap together behind its back, rest for a half millisecond, then suddenly fling open to oscillate on the downstroke to a position short of clapping underneath.

At this point the wings "flip" or twist suddenly through 120 degrees, to begin the upbeat.

By this mechanism, he explains, after the clap, when the wings open, air rushes in to fill the partial vacuum created between them, a

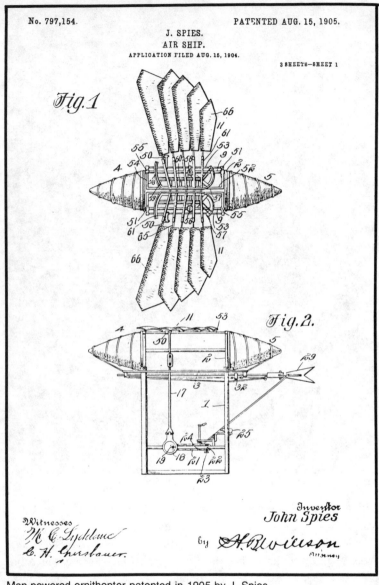

Man-powered ornithopter patented in 1905 by J. Spies.

potential flow that creates two symmetrical vortices of equal and opposite action.

Historically, says Weis-Fogh, as early as 19 B.C. Virgil observed that the rock dove claps its wings once or twice at the start of a steep climbing takeoff. Etienne-Jules Marey in France in 1890 demonstrated that the noise was produced by the wings clapping together behind its back.

Weis-Fogh admits that much research lies ahead before a full understanding of air circulation, lift, drag, and other aspects of nonsteady aerodynamic effects can be attained.

It remains doubtful, however, whether flapping-wing flight can ever be adapted to man-powered aircraft, except to extend glides, as Lippisch accomplished in 1929. P. H. Spencer, designer of the world's only really successful ornithopters, says the requirement for MPA flight by ornithopter propulsion would lie between 5 and 10 horsepower, far above the ability of the strongest athlete.

Spencer's engine-powered ornithopters, on the other hand, have been amazing. One gull-like machine, now in the Smithsonian Institution, built in 1959, with an 8-foot wing-span, performed beautifully. "It used to fly up into a clear sky so high it would disappear from sight," he says. "You could hear it flapping away, but you couldn't see it!"

A really "outa-sight" performance!

Chapter 10
The First MPA Race

Ever since Dr. Watson Fell Quinby was inspired to design a man-powered aircraft by the great showman Phineas T. Barnum, who in 1853 posted a $5,000 prize for the first man to fly across the Atlantic, the promotional value of man-flight projects has been a big factor in their development. With no obvious commercial or social value, they did offer excitement and adventure, and were sure-fire attention getters.

When Wilbur Wright made his first powered flight from the plain of Auvors, near Le Mans, in France on August 8, 1908, and in the following month amazed Europe by flying 52 miles in 1 hour 32 minutes 25 seconds for the world'd endurance record, the feats were headlined around the world. Wilbur ended his year of triumph by flying his biplane 77 miles in an amazing 2 hours 20 minutes 23 seconds, to win the 20,000-franc Michelin Trophy.

Officials of France's firm of Peugeot, makers of popular motor cars, did not miss the point—the flying craze had a tremendous advertising potential. But after the achievements of Wilbur Wright, how could they top them? The answer, they decided, lay in man-powered aircraft, which they called "Aviettes." Thus on February 1, 1912, Peugeot posted a 10,000-franc prize to stimulate interest in an MPA competition.

Flying Magazine, in its July 1912 issue, commented: "Why it should have suddenly been deemed easy to fly without a motor when it is precisely the motor, coming after thousands of years of fruitless yearning, which make flight possible, it is hard to say. But after the Peugeot firm had offered 10,000 francs for the first man who would traverse ten meters in the air without the aid of a motor, and had stated the hour at which entries would be received for the contest, twelve competitors were standing in line at that hour, apparently imbued with the idea that the first one to attempt the feat would succeed in it.

"When the entries for the first trials on June 2 closed they numbered exactly 198, and included such familiar names as Gabriel Voisin, Colliex, Ladougne, Duthiel, Poulain, de Kergarion, and Goupy; but as the various competitors practised for the event it became evident that the prize would not be so easily won after all and, seized with misgivings, the organizers offered a preliminary prize of 1,000 francs for a 'flight' of 40 inches at a minimum 'altitude' of 4 inches for 'winged' propellerless bicycles.

"When on the morning of June 2 this prize, which at first seems (and probably is) within the capability of some bicycle acrobats, it was realized that the Peugeot prize would not be won, only 23 of the 198 entires showed up and, notwithstanding countless attempts, not one of them got off the ground for the fraction of a second.

"It is evident that the problem is not being approached in the proper manner, but the experiment is nonetheless interesting and may lead to more fruitful ones along this line. There are two radically different kinds of Aviettes, the man-propelled aeroplanes in which propellers are driven by man power, and the 'winged' bicycle which has no propeller and merely depends on its speed to make the required jump.

"Two weeks ago Lavalaed, the middle-distance bicycle racer, is claimed to have 'flown' 44 inches at 8 inches elevation on his winged bicycle. From motion pictures of this feat the contrivance certainly appears to make little hops which take it completely off the ground, but there is not the slightest impression of a flying machine, and the wings seem more of a hinderance to getting up speed than a help when Lavalade makes his wheel hop."

Lavalade cheated a bit on his performance of May, 1912— although the Peugeot rules did not cover a ramp-assisted takeoff, he pedaled his machine up a short incline before plopping back to earth less than four feet distant.

Baron Fredericks's pedal-powered MPA of 1910, Germany.

Some of the Aviettes entered in the Peugeot—competition were quite novel. Mons. Didier's sported a pair of butterfly wings on the handlebars. Mons. Vincent's carried tandem fabric wings fore and aft. Mons. Malby's Bleriot-type wings were attached to a specially designed tricycle with the third wheel behind, not in front.

Didier decided to modify his flapping wings late in 1912, substituting two small front wings and a pair of surfaces over the rear wheel. With this arrangement he succeeded in winning a 2,000-franc prize, posted by the Michelin tire firm for a five-meter flight, on December 21, 1912, in Paris.

The Peugeot prize remained the big one for nine years, and in 1920 the rules were revised to include a flight in opposite directions to compensate for any favoring wind. On July 9, 1921, a favorite competitor, Gabriel Poulain, wheeled out his machine, built at the Nieuport factory, at the Longchamps race track.

It was long before sunup, and more than a hundred spectators were on hand when Poulain's "aerocycle," sporting a pair of staggered wings, made its first "flight."

As Dr. Paul MacCready had learned in later years with his Gossamer Condor, the winds were lighter and the air pressure heavier in the cool predawn hours. Poulain made several attempts, in both directions, before finally succeeding, shortly after 6 o'clock, in completing two flights at an altitude above one meter and roughly 35 feet in distance. In winning the 10,00 franc Peugeot prize, Poulain had one big advantage—he was a qualified power pilot as well as an experienced bicycle racer.

Another Peugeot prize of 20,000 francs was posted for the first Aviette to fly 50 meters, but it went unclaimed. Poulain felt that it was not sporting, because it required a flight in both directions for a considerable distance. "Do they want to destroy the spirit of the inventors and also their enterprise?" he demanded.

Detailed accounts of the Aviette competitions are given in D. A. Reay's reference: *The History of Man-Powered Flight* (Pergamon Press, 1977).

The Peugeot contests brought considerable favorable publicity to the auto makers, and inspired others throughout Europe and the rest of the world to attempt Aviette flights as a simple sport. One enthusiast, Baron Fredericks, of Germany, built an Aviette with a tractor propeller that spun quite close to his nose as he furiously pedaled his two-wheeler. A second drive chain turned the rear wheel, and lift was provided with a spread of monoplane wings and a tail.

With powered flight banned in Germany by the Treaty of Versailles after World War I, MPA competitions there in the 1920s took their place beside sailplane contests at the Wasserkuppe. Consider the situation at that time, an important moment in aviation's march of progress:

In the German heartland of Hesse, nestled between the Fulda River and the Iron Curtain, lie the historic and lovely forested Rhon Mountains, a volcanic upthrusting where slope winds blow steadily over the highest peak, 3,117 Mt. Wasserkuppe. Here the right man and the right machine appeared at the right place at the right time.

Wolfgang B. Klemperer, born in Dresden in 1893, flew with the German Air Force in World War I, and in 1920, again a civilian, graduated from Dresden's Institut of Technology to become an assistant to the distinguished aeronautical engineer Professor Theodore von Karman, with whom he worked on wind tunnel designs of light planes and soaring craft.

Forbidden by the International Allied Commission of Control to build high-powered aircraft, von Karman's group sought other means to keep Germany's highly-developed aeronautical technology alive. Klemperer was well aware of the rich potential of the Wasserkuppe for slope soaring; as early as 1910, two Darmstadt high school boys, Hans Gutermuth and Berthold Fischer, had made long glides there in Lilenthal-type machines. Gutermuth in October, 1912, stretched a glide to more than 2700 feet.

In 1920 Oskar Ursinius, editor of the German flying magazine *Flugsport*, organized the first glider meet at the Wasserkuppe,

Wolfgang Klemperer was pioneer in man-powered flight studies.

urging German youth to bring their bedrolls and their machines for a two-month campout. A total of 24 showed up. Performances were not up to expectations, however, and one youth, Eugene von Loessl, was killed when his glider broke up in severe turbulence.

Enthusiasm was dampened by the accident, and the meet would have ended then and there had not Klemperer shown up with a mystery glider, his *Black Devil*. Built by a group of students who called themselves the Aachen Aeronautical Society, the Aachen machine had thick, swept wings with a slight reverse camber and non-balanced ailerons. Wing loading was a mere .32 lb/sq. ft.

On its first flight, launched by shock cord, the *Black Devil* soared effortlessly for more than a mile—6006 feet, a new world's record. The effect of the Aachen glider's appearance was electric, and similar types were begun for the second Wasserkuppe meet of 1921. Two distinct glider types emerged. In one, the goal was to achieve a flatter glide ratio by reducing resistance to a minimum through careful streamlining. In the other, they sought to reduce the wing loading and achieve a better L/D (lift to drag) ratio and hence a better glide angle by making the wings longer and narrower.

Of 34 machines that showed up in 1921, three held special interest—Klemperer's *Blue Mouse*, a refinement of his *Black Devil*; an open primary type, the Munchen glider flown by Karl Koller; and another mystery ship, the *Vampyr*.

Oskar Ursinius in 1920s sponsored German youth glider meets that led to MPA development.

Wolfgang's historic Blue Mouse glider.

The latter craft, designed and built by members of the Hanover Institut of Technology, was a well-streamlined, high cantivered monoplane similar to the wartime Fokker F3. The pilot was almost completely enclosed in its small cockpit, and rubber footballs were used for landing shock absorbers.

Assigned to the design group on the *Vampyr* project were some of Germany's top aerodyanmicists, including Walter Blume, a former jadgstafel commander who had served on the Western Front. They could devote full time to the project, as German aircraft production was at a standstill. To Blume, this was the best thing that could have happened: "We could forget the inefficient relics of wartime," he

Famous Vampyr sailplane of the 1920s was breakthrough in aerodynamic design.

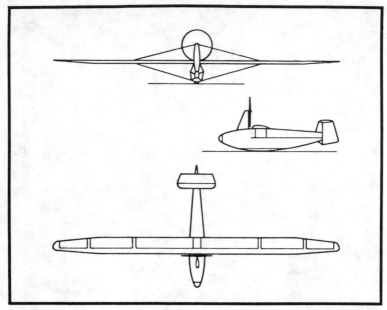

Haessler-Villinger MUFLI competed for 500-mark prize posted by German magazine Flugsport for first MPA flight of one kilometer.

said. "The designer was free to make complete use of recent experience, to devise radical improvements."

The wind tunnels of Gottingen came to life, not to produce warplanes, but to refine a strange-looking craft that carried the wing on top and had no landing gear underneath. The fuselage was swept upward to support a high tail with no stabilizer, only a rudder and balanced elevator. In the *Vampyr*, the Wasserkuppe airmen saw the shape of the future—the sleek Hanover glider had increased the 5:1 glide ratio of the old Wright biplane to 16:1!

If the *Vampyr* proved to be a revolutionary design, a brand new flying technique was born at the Wasserkuppe a few days later when Frederic Harth, flying a homebuilt machine constructed with the help of the famous Willi Messerschmitt, soared for 21-½ minutes along the ridges near Hildenstein, following the graceful seabirds in sweeping figure eights, and finally landing less than 200 yards from his launch point. Harth had introduced the art of slope soaring, and the era of simple downwill skysliding was over.

For those who would pursue adventure in the high sky, the Wasserkuppe experiments of the 1920s would lead to a better understanding of how to harness the winds and thermals for both lift and propulsion in slender sailplanes that had to be launched with shock cords, winch, or auto or plane tow. The MPA spinoff would be the secondary serendipity.

On one unforgettable afternoon, when a towering, anvil-shaped cloud boiled and throbbed above the Wasserkuppe, a group of sailplane pilots launched into the wild sky to probe the storm's interior on a daring research project. One by one they were sucked inside the seething vapors to vanish in a churning blackness, where energies greater than that of a hundred atomic bombs were being unleashed by nature.

Stabbing lightning glowed eerily around the sailplanes and the heavens thundered. Violent updrafts hurtled them higher and higher, through stinging raindrops and pelting hailstones.

The pilots suffered from anoxia; their controls stiffened with ice. Most of the pilots managed to escape the raging thunderhead, but in his anger, Zeus, the thunder god, exacted a terrible toll for this invasion of his domain—by snapping the wings from three sailplanes. The birdmen, Lemm, Schultz, and Bleh, kicked free from their wrecked gliders and dove into the darkness, tugging on their parachute ripcords. For nearly an hour they rose and fell helplessly on the winds, inside the electrically-charged arena of death, then one by one dropped finally to earth. Their bodies were found later—one was charred by lightning, the others had frozen to death.

Said Professor Walter Georgii, director of the Rhon Rossiten Gesellschaft Research Institut at the Wasserkuppe: "Such experiences will give a new generation of flying men a body of weather wisdom by which they may safely meet and even turn to useful purpose the atmospheric disturbances so frequently met in air transport today. The true meaning of 'air sense' lies in this conquest of the variable atmosphere by the soaring pilot."

Atop the Wasserkuppe today stands a rocky cairn topped by a bronze condor, intently facing the winds from the west. The monument is a tribute to the heroic birdmen of Hesse, who gave their lives probing the unknown frontiers of the sky.

There is a close link between pure soaring craft and MPA's—both must be built with a sufficiently small wing loading to fly, the former on nature's updrafts, and the latter, in still air, on muscle power. Later on we will discuss the future of MPA's as a sport, which surely will result in combination machines wherein man-power can be utilized to stretch the glide of soaring craft when the thermals run out.

Thus in the 1920s, two different types of flying machines developed in Germany, where aerial engines were outlawed by the Treaty of Versailles—the true soarers, and the MPA's. The Peugeot Aviette activities in France only barely preceded a similar competition at Rhon, Germany, in the mid-1920s.

One interesting MPA developed at this time was a craft with odd rotating airfoils designed by a Silesian named Porella in 1925. Reay describes the machine as resembling a ship with paddle-wheels, which produced both lift and thrust on their forward and downstrokes. A fixed wing of some 30 feet span and a conventional empennage were added. The pilot lay in a prone position and drove the paddlewheels with his feet. There is no record that it ever flew.

About 1935, Oskar Ursinus formed an MPA study group known as the *Muskelflug-Institut* at Frankfurt to assist independent researchers in the field with basic studies of such problems as power-train links with rotating (pedaling), reciprocating, and rudder-flutter motions. Herr Gropp, a young athlete, was the principal test pilot.

Already Ursinus's magazine *Flugsport* had posted a prize of 500 marks for the first MPA flight of one kilometer around two pylons 400 meters apart. No one claimed the prize, but a consolation prize

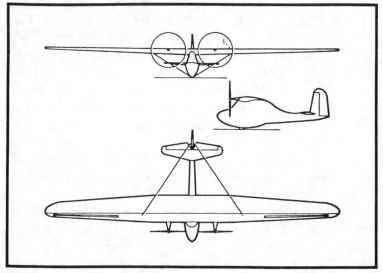

Bossi-Bonomi PEDALIANTE failed to complete one-kilometer MPA flight to win prize posted by Italian government.

went to a pair of Junkers engineers, Helmut Haessler and Franz Villinger.

The Haessler-Villinger machine, called the *Mufli*, was a single-seat monoplane resembling a typical sailplane, with a wingspan of 13.5 meters. The pilot flew in a reclining position, pedalling a foot-crank geared to a propeller, of 1.5 meters diameter, mounted on a pylon, by means of a twisted belt drive.

Mufli's cockpit was exceedingly cramped, and the pilot assumed an almost fetal position, clutching a joystick for lateral and pitch control. The wingspan was 44 feet, with a thick Gottingen 535 airfoil. Launched by shock cord, the machine once traveled 790 yards to win the *Flugsport* consolation prize.

In Italy in 1936, an Italian-born American, Enea Bossi, designed a glider-like MPA with two contra-rotating propellers to compete for a prize posted by the Italian government for the first MPA flight of one kilometer.

Bossi, following preliminary tests with various machines in America and in Italy, contracted with Vittorio Bonomi to construct a competition machine with a wingspan of 58 feet and a low aspect ratio of 13.4. Unfortunately, the Italian government insisted on their meeting rigid airworthiness standards, which resulted in an excessively heavy craft, estimated by D. A. Reay at nearly 100 kg.

Bossi favored large-diameter propellers and tried unsuccessfully to utilize an energy-storage device, consisting of twisted lengths of rubber shock cord. The pilot, Emilio Casco, flew the machine, called the Pedaliante, on numerous flights of considerable distance. The longest, according to Keith Sherwin, was a distance of 980 yards, from a shock cord launch, mostly downhill.

Chapter 11
The Kremer Prize

Wars have a strange way of changing the course of events in unexpected directions. At the close of World War I Germany's aerial might was emasculated by the Treaty of Versailles, yet that instrument was responsible for the rise of technological development of both soaring craft and man-powered airplanes.

World War II, which cut off the supply of rubber from the Dutch East Indies, opened the way to development of synthetic materials and the giant petro-plastic industry. This, together with new breakthroughs in aerodynamic designs, finally provided the technology for development of ultralight flying machines that would have been impossible to construct earlier.

There remains one forgotten page of history in the man-powered aircraft story that was interrupted by the second World War—the *Colditz Cock*. In the waning months of the war, a group of British war prisoners, confined to Colditz Castle in Germany, resorted to a desperate means of escape, using an engineless glider with stored energy.

Working in shifts, four hours a day for ten months, they constructed a two-place "escape" machine in a concealed attic workshop. There they secretly fashioned a craft they nicknamed the Colditz Cock, from any materials they could scrounge. Wings were covered with bed sheets, doped with boiled milk; control surfaces were attached with cupboard hinges. A 60-foot catapult launch track made from mess tables was to straddle the ridge of the tiled roof, and a two-ton bag of rocks, tied to a rope, was to be dropped to provide launch power. Amazed Yankee invasion troops were shown the strange bird by the proud POW's, who never got the chance to see if she really could fly. The story came to light after the war in an article in *Air Review*, authored by the project's leader, Flight Lieutenant L. J. E. Finch.

In 1948 man-powered flight was discussed in the periodical *Aeronautics* by Brian Worley, who stressed the importance of minimum weight, and of low induced drag to be achieved by using a high aspect ratio wing.

Shortly thereafter the center of MPA activity shifted to the United States, where August Raspet, a noted aeronautical engineer at Mississippi State College, applied to the problem his extensive research work on sailplane design. Like Worley, Dr. Raspet recognized that flying close to the ground offered an opportunity to reduce the induced drag of the wing by some 50 percent. He further studied the laminar flow characteristics of birds' wings and applied that to a boundary layer control design, for adaptation to MPA's flying at low Reynolds Numbers.

Also interested in boundary layer control by means of wing suction devices was T. R. F. Nonweiler at Glasgow University, who in 1956 published his views on the potentials of man-powered flight. A key point was his careful determination of power required, through wind tunnel studies of the drag produced by a racing cyclist suspended inside the tunnel. He concluded that sustained power output of 0.40 kW was a reasonable figure for a cyclist in good condition.

About this time an unusual inflatable MPA was built and flown by Dan Perkins at the Royal Aircraft Establishment at Cardington, England, as a hobby. The delta-shaped single wing had a span of 27 feet and area of 250 square feet, and weighed 38 pounds. Dubbed the *Reluctant Phoenix*, it was made from one-ounce plain-weave nylon, proofed with 2 oz. of polyurethane for a total weight of 3 oz/yard.

The craft could be rolled up for easy transport, and in the field was inflated with a vacuum cleaner. Although its wing loading was suitably low, its low aspect ratio of 4.4 gave it a very high induced drag. Perkins made short flights a few inches off the floor of the Cardington airship hangar. He sat like a cyclist and drove the pusher propeller via a series of pulleys and a polyurethane-covered rope belt.

Considerably more interest in man-powered flight was generated at this time by the lectures and writings of Beverly B. Shenstone, an MPA enthusiast and chief engineer of British European Airways. To Shenstone, the problem was age-old—the ridicule heaped on MPA inventors made the subject difficult to be taken seriously.

What Shenstone proposed was to start from scratch and first establish just what the limitations of human power available were; second, draw a set of power-required and power-available curves for flights of required duration; and third, design the MPA to fit the curves. It was his belief that a tandem two-seater would work best, as it would have more than twice the power available—the second man could devote full energy to propulsion, while the first divided his energies between propulsion and control.

Another consideration was the relative inefficiency of the propeller (80%) and drive chain (90%), giving an overall efficiency of 72%. The wing design he said, should have as much laminar flow as possible at a requisite Reynolds Number, on the order of 0.7×10^6, and have the bottom of the laminac flow bucket at a lift coefficient of the order of 0.9. Two possible airfoils, he suggested, were the NACA 65A (10)12 and the German Section FX05-H-126.

Unlike the Italian Government, the British Air Registration Board was more lenient on MPA ultimate load factors required for safety—a ULF of 2.5 would do well, thank you. That meant the design could have a quite flexible wing to save weight, while still avoiding flutter or control reversal at operating speeds.

Shenstone felt that the power train was the biggest problem to be solved—the best route to go, he suggested, would be to use pedals, sprockets, and chains, and a propeller of at least 6 feet diameter, possibly of balsa wood. As to overall design, he felt the tail-first (canard) type was more attractive than tailless or conventional types "because it is an easy job from the aerodynamic and control point of view and fits in well mechanically."

Bit by bit, Shenstone was outlining the basic requirements for a successful MPA that would become an integral part of the Kremer Competition regulations. "At present," he wrote in 1959, "there is no liklihood of the man-powered aircraft rising more than a few feet above the ground, because the power required within the ground cushion is so much less than the power required at about 15 or 20 feet. In fact, at about 10 feet altitude the ground effect doubles the effective aspect ratio of the wing, which has a large effect on the power required, because the wing incidence is quite high."

Shenstone concluded that "real interest in this problem is increasing because it is gradually being realized that the problem is one which is very close to solution, and the technical background is almost all available."

On January 10, 1957, a meeting of interested parties was held at the College of Aeronautics at Oranfield, at which was formed a Man-Powered Aircraft Committee (MAPAC) chaired by H. B. Irving. Committee members came from universities, the aerospace industry, and other groups such as the Royal Aeronautical Society and the British Gliding Association. MAPAC subsequently became a part of the Royal Aeronautical Society.

Without funds, MAPAC was kept busy making available MPA information to interested parties, but in November, 1959 their enthusiasm was backed by an offer of £5,000 from Henry Kremer, a British industrialist, for the first MPA to fly around a course specified by the Sociey's Group in consultation with the Royal Aero Club.

The Kremer Competition was laid out as a figure-eight course around two markers half a mile apart. Power for takeoff and during flight had to be muscle-power alone, without use of stored energy, or lighter-than-air gases. The aircraft had to cross the start and finish lines at a height of at least ten feet.

Limited to citizens of the British Commonwealth, the Kremer Competition had no takers, hence in March, 1967 Kremer added another £10,000 in prize money and the affair became international. As the goal seemed almost unattainable, early in 1973 Kremer raised the ante to £50,000.

In addition to the prize money posted, a fund was formed to assist in the development of the more promising designs, which appeared to be attainable only through costly research and development by team effort. In 1960 Air Commodore J. G. Weir donated £1,000. Kremer added to that, as did three leading UK aircraft firms, bringing the fund total to £5,000.

In March, 1967 another contest, the Kremer £5,000 Competition, was devised, consisting of two slalom runs in opposite direc-

British industrialist and health enthusiast Henry Kremer posted huge prizes for MPA competitive flights.

tions around three markers, and in 1976 Kremer also posted a prize of £1,000 for the first UK three-minute flight. Finally, there was the Robert Graham Undergraduate Project Competition, with an annual prize of £200, on any subject appropriate to man-powered flight.

Impetus of the Kremer Competition gave tremendous push to the MPA efforts around the world, and in England in November, 1961, two machines actually did achieve flight solely by their pilots' physical efforts. One was *Sumpac*, designed and built by research students at Southampton University, and now on permanent display in the Shuttleworth Collection. The other was *Puffin*, a product of the Hatfield Club at Hawker Siddeley's Airfield, which flew for 993 yards in 1962. *Puffin* was later redesigned and rebuilt at Liverpool University, where it flew briefly as the *Liverpuffin*.

PUFFIN Mark I flew 993 yards in 1962.

By 1970, a second generation of man-powered aircraft was beginning to appear. In November, 1971 the Weybridge Group's machine *Dumbo* flew, and in December 1972 the Hertfordshire Pedal Aeronauts' *Toucan* became the world's first two-man-

PUFFIN Mark I had pusher propeller behind tail.

The 1930's saw rise of "Batmen" like Jimmie Goodwin who "flew" during parachute freefalls.

powered aircraft to fly. Then in 1972 Lt. John Potter flew another British MPA, the *Jupiter*, for a distance of 1171 yards for an observed world record.

Potter's record was surpassed in January, 1977 by a machine built by students of Professor Hidemasa Kimura of Nihon University in Japan, with a flight of 2290 yards in 4-½ minutes.

These competition machines and others, described in the following chapters, all contributed something to the state of the art of flying by muscle power, culminating with the amazing flights of Dr. Paul MacCready's *Gossamer Condor* in California in August 1977, to capture the big Kremer Award. Beyond that, an exciting future awaits designers of both competition machines and MPA's to be flown purely for sport.

The *Gossamer Condor's* great flight prompted Kremer to post a still more generous award—a £100,000 prize for the first MPA to

Batman Clem Sohn was killed in jump at Vincennes, France, in 1937 when his parachute cords became tangled with fabric wings.

Leo Valentin in freefall with wooden wings.

cross the English Channel, from England to France. The Kremer International Competition prize of £10,000 for the first figure-eight course MPA flight was limited to non-US citizens. And the Kremer Double Slalom prize money of £5,000 was limited to the first three British Commonwealth entrants to complete the double slalom around three markers.

Other Man-Powered aircraft grants, it was announced, would be available, at the discretion of the Royal Aeronautical Socity, MPA Group, to individuals or organizations who submit promising projects designed to further the achievement of man-powered flight.

Chapter 12
The Kremer Race Begins

British sporting blood was stirred by Henry Kremer's challenge. All over the United Kingdom aeronautical talk turned to the problem of man-powered flight, and the chances of winning the Kremer Award were hotly debated. Two MPA groups were immediately formed, each receiving a £1,500 grant from the MPA Group of the R. Ae. S.

Of these, one had the technical and financial backing of a giant of England's aerospace industry, the de Havilland Aircraft Company at Hatfield. The other consisted of a number of graduate aeronautical engineering students at the University of Southampton.

Where the Hatfield group had at their disposal de Havilland's giant wind tunnels and other facilities, the Southampton group was on its own. They had alrady begun MPA studies as a sort of hobby when the Kremer Award was posted. Their first step was to gather data on power output from all available sources.

A leader of the student group was a female—Anne J. W. Marsden, whose enthusiasm and inspiration gave impetus to their difficult research task. Writing in *Sport Aviation*, she recalls:

"We had teams of undergraduates running up and down stairs while we timed them with stopwatches, and finally we made a rig to simulate what we thought was a favorable position for the pilot, and measured the power output of a number of cyclists pedalling in the reclining position. The power was absorbed by electrical resistances from a pedal-driven generator and measured with a wattmeter.

"As a result of this work it was found that an average cyclist in the reclining position could provide about ½ hp for nearly ten minutes with his hands completely free to work any controls. This was made the basic of all our subsequent design work, although we allowed some good margins for error."

Head of the Hatfield MPA Club was a talented aerodynamicist, John Wimpenny, who in 1946 had already built a model MPA, which formed the basis for the "HMPAC" design.

Both MPA groups were limited in their design work by lack of availability of airfoil sections designed for performance at the low Reynolds Numbers appropriate to manpowered flight. Compared to current airfoil designs with lift coefficients of 1.2, with correspondingly low airfoil profile drag, the C_1 values in 1961 were on the order of 0.85 at Southampton and 0.8 at Hatfield.

Thus the trend was toward conservative wing design with emphasis on low weight values. The Southampton machine, called *Sumpac* (Southampton University Man Powered Aircraft), had a span of 80 feet and a wing area of 300 sq/ft., and the Hatfield *Puffin I* a span of 84 feet and 330 sq/ft. of wing area.

Two other major differences were apparent—*Sumpac* carried its propeller mounted on a pylon, to avoid the long driveshaft required if the prop were carried at the tail, and the limiting effect on size by being lower to the ground.

The *Puffin* builders, on the other hand, favored the rear-mounted propeller to avoid the extra drag of the pylon. A balsa wood drive shaft broke, and was replaced by a metal tube. The entire transmission and drive linkage, which powered both the propeller and ground wheel, was developed by engineers of the Dunlop Company's Aviation Division.

For pilot training, the Hatfield group developed a flight simulator to solve a sticky problem—recovering from a bank was so sluggish that large ailerons and aileron deflections were found necessary, thus producing unwanted large aileron drag and yaw forces.

Meanwhile back at the *Sumpac* group, design limits were placed at 80 feet of wingspan, says Marsden, "because we didn't think our pilot would be able to manage to handle much more", flying in ground effect to cut induced drag. Further, they avoided assiduously using flying wires, struts, and exposed undercarriage, calling for a fully cantilevered monoplane wing, similar to the *Puffin's*.

Southampton University's SUMPAC had 80-foot wingspan, with inset ailerons and washout wingtips. Propeller was mounted on pylon to avoid long driveshaft to tail.

Wooden construction was decided on, with doped parachute nylon for covering. The *Sumpac* airfoil was the NACA 65₃818, a heavily cambered section which depends on maintaining laminar flow back to 60 or 70 percent chord. Tested at Southampton University's wind tunnel, it was modified by trial and error. *Sumpac's* biggest aerodynamic design problem was discovered in tunnel studies of a

1/6-scale model of the complete machine, at full scale Reynolds Numbers. At the root of the pylon, interference drag caused by breakaway flow was unacceptably high. A unique fairing was designed to correct the matter.

The propeller was shaped with built-up ribs over tubular metal spars, designed to produce 7 lb. thrust at 20 mph cruise speed. Tested in a slow-sped wind tunnel, it achieved 89 percent efficiency by using a turbulator strip glued to the top surface of the blades.

The propeller was shaped with built-up ribs over tubular metal spars, designed to produce 7 lb. thrust at 20 mph cruise speed. Tested in a slow-speed wind tunnel, it achieved 89 percent efficiency by using a turbulator strip glued to the top surface of the blades.

To get an elliptical spanwise loading on a tapered wing, severe washout of ten degrees was used, achieved by a twist of the double spars. The pilot sat inside a tubular framework, which supported the pylon and landing gear. A thin steel belt drive from the rear wheel to the propeller, twisted through 90 degrees, was found to slip badly, so a compound called *Belt Stick* was applied.

For a pilot, the *Sumpac* students wanted to use a well-known long-distance runner, Martin Hyman, but as he was not a pilot they substituted Derek Piggott, an experienced sailplane pilot. Piggott suggested that the first trials be held at Lasham Airfield in Hampshire, a glider port.

On a number of trial runs, Piggott found the control linkup confusing as it required "bobsledding"—use of right rudder to turn left. The linkage subsequently was reversed to standard aircraft practice. The first few trials were small disasters, with many breakages. The machine was stored in a war surplus Nissen hut that leaked badly, hence rerigging was required for each flight. By this time the morning winds were up.

Piggott also found the rudder area too small, so its size was doubled, but even then pedaling inside the enclosed cockpit was hard work, producing half a horsepower. The uniform of the day was shorts and singlet.

Rumors came that *Puffin I* was ready to fly, and had a far better chance of approaching the Kremer course rules than *Sumpac*—they had a closely guarded secret; their machine was covered with transparent Melinex plastic film, that could be shrunk to a smooth cover with a hot iron. The entire covering weighed only 2 pounds. Further,

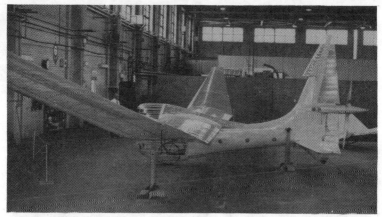

PUFFIN II, redesigned from PUFFIN I, had 90-foot span with stong dihedral. Only fuselage was used from PUFFIN I in redesign.

their pilots had been rigorously training on a tight schedule, fed on Spencer steaks!

Piggott recalls the day when all was ready with *Sumpac*, and *Puffin I* had yet to fly:

"It was late in the evening of 9 November 1961, one of the most thrilling moments of my life. We had asked a cameraman to record what happened, we were that confident. It was damp and cold when I climbed into the seat and strapped myself in. The nose was bolted on...there was scarcely a breath of wind as I accelerated slowly down the main runway trying to keep straight, and watching the green pellet of the Cosim variometer, my airspeed indicator, which was slowly rising to the 18 feet per second mark at which I could ease back, and perhaps fly.

"Pedalling the machine was rather like riding a tandem bicycle up a gradual slope with the girl friend not bothering to pedal. Then I eased back on the stick...the pedals began to slip a little and it all became easier. Tremendous excitement! I pedalled harder trying to make it stay up for as long as possible.

"One wing began to drop and we turned slowly off the line of the runway. My reactions were slow, as I thought out the required aileron and rudder movements to stop the turn. Gradually she responded and the wings came level again. The elevator control was very sensitive and the aircraft pitched up and down as I overcontrolled. This caused extra drag and suddenly there was the rumble of the wheel on the grass. I stopped pedalling and concentrated on keeping it straight as I slowed down. I was puffed-out with trying so hard to keep up, but by no means exhausted. Anne rushed up to congratulate me, and my reaction was to congratulate her. Their machine had really flown at last, and we had film to prove it!"

Less than a week later, on November 15, 1961, the *Puffin I* was rolled out of the hangar at 10:15 p.m. and Wimpenney made the first taxi runs. The next day another pilot, Jimmy Phillips, made the first flight down the main Hatfield runway. Within another two days flights of up to one minute duration were accomplished.

Minor problems were discovered and corrected with *Puffin I*—oxygen deficiency was caused by a too-small air inlet in the cockpit area...forward vision was inadequate on hazy days, and in one crash, blamed on the lost horizon, half a wing was broken off.

A bike racer named Chris Church made several flights until one day early in April, 1963, a wind shear blew the machine off the runway. It crashed and collapsed in a heap of splinters. Rather than being discouraged, the Hatfield group took the opportunity to completely redesign *Puffin I* into *Puffin II*, which featured a wider wingspan of 93 feet and 60 square feet extra wing area, with 6 pounds more empty weight. From August 27, 1965, until retired two years later, *Puffin II* made several flights of more than half a mile. Its pilots learned something important on these flights—rudder alone served in making small turns or heading corrections. Perhaps ailerons were unessential after all!

Sumpac also made many good flights, one of more than 1,800 feet, and following graduation of the student-designers, it was moved to London by one of the group. It finally crashed for the last time on November 12, 1965, and was retired to the Shuttleworth Aircraft Museum at Old Warden Field near Bedford.

During their brief careers, both *Sumpac* and *Puffins I & II* were frequently flown with auxilary power supplied by model aircraft engines, to give the pilots more time to practice turns. Straightaway MPA flight was a proven success, but the Kremer course around a figure-8 had not even been attempted.

Although *Sumpac* and the *Puffins* were the first British MPA's to take advantage of the funds made available by the Man-Powered Aircraft Group of the RAeS, four other fixed-wing MPA projects were similarly funded, with grants ranging from £500 to £1,500. Of these, the Southend *Mayfly* two-place MPA never got off the ground. Built of spruce spars, balsa ribs and modellers' tissue, it

Southend MAYFLY never flew—it was damaged in hangar collapse.

encountered a series of mishaps, including a hangar collapse that did it in.

The single-place Woodford MPA, later to become the *Jupiter*, was nearly completed by its designer, S. Hodges-Roper, when it was badly damaged in a fire, but it was later rebuilt in the early 1970s to become a highly successful Kremer contender. The other two funded MPA'a were the Hertfordshire Pedal Aeronauts' *Toucan* and the Weybridge MPA.

Both the latter craft benefitted largely from lessons learned from the earlier Southampton and Hatfield efforts, according to John H. McMasters, an MPA designer and historian. The *Toucan* (Two Can Fly if One Cannot) had an impressive wing span of 123 feet and 600 sq/ft of wing area. It was designed by a group of employees of the Handley-Page Company led by Martyn Pressnell.

An interesting feature of *Toucan* was its midwing design, intended to make the most of ground effect, together with slotted ailerons and wingtip spoilers for faster control response. First flight took place in December 1972. Its longest flight was more than 1,000 feet.

The Weybridge MPA was constructed by a group headed by P. K. Green and included a number of employees of the British Aircraft Coporation. Like the *Toucan* it had a huge wingspan, of 120.3 feet, its extreme aspect ratio meant to lower induced drag. It featured a low wing and pusher propeller at the tail.

Initially formed in 1967, the Weybridge MPA Group eventually nicknamed their machine *Dumbo*. Its light weight proved a problem in gusty air, and first flight date was postponed until September 18, 1971. After a few more flights *Dumbo* was moved to Cranwell, where Squadron Leader John Potter's MPA took over the project, renaming it the *Mercury*.

WEYBRIDGE MPA airborne for first flight, flown by Chris Lovell, September 18, 1971.

All these efforts were lumped by McMasters into an initial design effort, Phase I (1958-1964), in which the designers were strongly influenced by the early opinions of Shenstone and Nonweiler, which led to development of the Kremer rules. Limited data on low-Reynolds-Number aerodynamics and model-airplane type materials were used.

Dumbo and *Toucan*, however, were also to be identified in a Phase II effort (1965-1971) overlapping the earlier work, and including four design goals within the Kremer Competition Rules, says McMasters. These were:

1. Reduce speed and lower wing loading.
2. Extend wings to gain a better L/D in ground effect.
3. Cruise at conditions closer to minimum power required.
4. Stress ingenious structural design to hold the weight of larger wings in check.

In addition to *Dumbo* and *Toucan*, another two huge MPAs were developed—the French Hurel *Aviette* and the amazing seven-place Canadian *Cochkanoff*, which was never completed. *Aviette* did cover a distance of some 1,000 yards before it was broken in a crash.

The results of Phase II were disappointing, says McMasters, proving that "big is not necessarily beautiful." The success of any MPA in competing for the Kremer prize would follow from a fresh approach to the problem taken by Flt. Lieut. John Potter's group of Royal Air Force apprentices.

Among their goals was development of better stability and control characteristics of MPAs, and a flight program that involved "jump" takeoffs out of ground effect and climbs to altitudes of 20 to

TOUCAN's midwing design took advantage of ground effect.

TOUCAN used auxiliary model airplane engine under right wing during trial flights. It once flew 1000 feet.

30 feet. In *Jupiter*, built at Halton RAF College in 4,000 man-hours by some 100 persons, they had what looked like a real winner.

Jupiter, with a span of 80 feet using the NACA 653618 airfoil, made a flight in 1972 of 1.23 kilometers with Potter as pilot. Flying

TOUCAN in 1975 during modification.

French MPA AVIETTE had 138-foot span, flew at Le Bourget Airport. Aspect ratio was 30:1.

high, Potter felt more comfortable than flying in ground effect, but flying figure eights remained the elusive goal, and for five years the Kremer Award would be safe.

Two men in England had quite similar views on the subject of man-powered flight—Henry Kremer and Dr. Keith Sherwin, of the Liverpool University's Department of Engineering. Dr. Sherwin was primarily interested in basic research, as was Kremer, chairman of the engineering firm of White & Riches Ltd. (another interest of Kremer was weight-lifting, which no doubt contributed to his interest in MPA's).

In September, 1969, the remains of *Puffin II* were donated to Dr. Sherwin after it was demolished in a crash into airfield equipment on its final flight. Rather than rebuild it to compete for the Kremer Prize, Dr. Sherwin used it as an undergraduate project to teach engineering design.

Renamed *Liverpuffin*, the machine was rebuilt with definite goals in mind—it had to be easy to build, manageable on the ground and in flight, able to fly up to 300 yards at 3 to 5 feet altitude, and easily transportable. The smashed balsa ribs of *Puffin II* were replaced with styrofoam formed with a hot wire, the first MPA in the UK to use this modern material, common today in ultralight sport aircraft.

No lateral controls were provided; instead, a 20 degree dihedral was built into the 64-foot wing. Wing area was 305 sq/ft., all-up weight 300 lb., for a wing loading at gross weight of 1.10 lb/sq. ft. The airfoil chosen was the Wortmann FX-63137, same as in *Puffin II*.

TOUCAN on 700-yard flight in 1973.

Fourth MPA built by Paul Stephaan Masschelein and Eric Verstraete, flew 820 feet at Calaid-Dunkirk Airport July 24, 1974.

Halton RAF College's JUPITER MPA had 80-foot span, was flown out of ground effect by John Potter. In 1972 it covered a distance of 1.23 kilometers.

JUPITER MPA during press demonstration flight.

Liverpool University's LIVERPUFFIN was rebuilt from wreckage of PUFFIN II by students of Professor Keith Sherwin in effort to win Kremer Prize. Note foam leading edge at end of center section, where outer wing panels attach.

Liverpuffin made her first flight March 18, 1972, with Dr. Sherwin as pilot, covering 20 yards at an altitude of 9 inches above the runway at Woodvale Airfield, Formby, Lancashire, proving to his satisfaction that styrofoam construction and rudder-only control near the ground was workable.

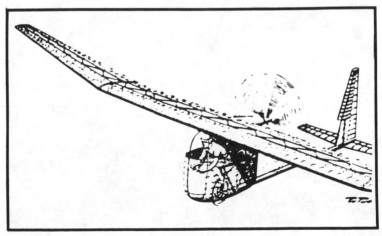

Cutaway view of LIVERPUFFIN shows pilot position.

Chapter 13
Yankee Doodlers

As had been expected, the Kremer Prize attracted its share of MPA designers we may kindly call unconventional, both in the UK and abroad.

Among the early contestants was a would-be birdman aptly named Donald Partridge. At 6 o'clock one foggy morning Partridge, wearing only slim trunks and a sweater, poised atop Hammersmith Bridge in London, vigorously flapping a pair of homemade wings. He stepped off into space and flew 50 feet—straight down into the muddy Thames.

Emiel Hartmann, a Chelsea sculptor fascinated with bird flight, did better on November 2, 1959, when his ornithopter reached an altitude of 50 feet above the jet strip at Cranfield, in tow behind an auto.

Alan Stewart, a Sheffield engineer, built a flapper with a wingspan of 14 feet, to be powered with both arms and legs. Nowhere.

Nick Walton, 23, sprinted down Creech Barrow Hill near Taunton in the West Country, with mighty flaps of his 22-foot wings, but failed to become an eagle.

Bob Wilson, at 39 the father of eight children, had energy left to pump away on his gyro-bike, a sort of autogyro with wheels within wheels, until a gust of wind toppled him. "We shall carry on," he announced.

Emil Hartman's MPA was towed aloft 50 feet.

E. Winter was improving steadily on takeoffs with his Air Screw Propeller Bike, the Glastonbury Zodiac (he scorned wings).

In Italy, Vincent Carnevali, the Roman Fly-Man, fluttered along the runway at Erbe Airport every morning for weeks to prove that da Vinci was right after all; in vain.

In Moscow, Dmitri Vladimitovich Ilyin, a Soviet test pilot, used a 3-horsepower engine to supplement his muscles in flapping a pair of wings, with no success.

Across the Atlantic, Britishers looked with some amusement at "Colonials" in the United States, who felt that good old Yankee ingenuity could achieve what solid British logic had failed to accomplish, when Kremer doubled his prize to £10,000 and opened the competition to all comers on February 19, 1967.

Alexander Lippisch, who left Germany and the Wasserkuppe for America after World War II, held to the belief that MPA's should be flown purely as a sport, and not for prize money. He suggested a small single-seater of balsa wood with a delta-shaped wing, but it was never completed.

A dozen other American projects were begun as feasability studies, reported one investigator, Robert Graham. These included groups at Purdue University, Massachusetts Institute of Technology, Georgia Technical University, Michigan State College, the Bell Telephone Laboratories, Grumman Aircraft Co. and the Philco Ford Corporation.

MIT's BURD II MPA was built of balsa and Mylar, featured end plates to increase effective span. Topsail and canard elevator was included.

165

At Purdue, Curtis Cole and John McMasters became fascinated with the subject. McMasters saw a great future in MPAs, but more as a sport than as a Kremer contest affair.

Of more than ordinary interest was the work at MIT, where Professor Eugene E. Covert supervised a student MPA project from its inception in January, 1970, when it began as a study of the current state of the art. The study convinced the group that an entirely new type aircraft was needed to improve performance.

With an eye to capturing the Kremer Prize, they developed a two-man biplane-canard configuration which was tunnel-tested at full Reynolds Numbers. For control, spoilers were chosen for roll and yaw, with the canard providing pitch control. Originally the MIT group called themselves *Bumpas* (Biplane Ultralight Man-Powered Aircraft Systms) but later the project was renamed *Burd*.

After six months' study of low-speed aerodynamics, high-efficiency propulsion systems, and low-density materials, a decision was made to pick the crew size. Four legs were better than two for propulsion, they decided.

A pusher propeller was adopted to minimize prop-wash interference on the aircraft, while the canard surface provided an effective visual reference for pitch and bank. Effort on drag reduction was geared to improving induced drag control rather than streamlining. *Burd* I was designed to fly at the speed for least power required rather than best L/D, to be compatible with the pilot's ability to maintain a steady low-power output. Preliminary design called for a wing area of 625 sq/ft., an aspect ratio of 25:1, and a gross weight of 450 lb. for a wing loading of 1.38 lb/sq. ft.

The Wortmann FX 61-163 was finally chosen and the wing loading reduced to .66 lb/sq. ft. Wire bracing between the top and bottom wings was considered acceptable in view of the emphasis on reducing induced drag. Tip deflections of only 4 inches were achieved, compared to 12 feet in monoplane designs like the Weybridge machine.

Disadvantage of the biplane configuration was its low aspect ratio of 13.6, hence tip plates were added to increase the effective aspect ratio. The canard was all-moving for pitch control, and wing spoilers on the top surface of the lower wings gave good roll and yaw control at once. As Wilbur and Orville Wright learned in 1903, the canard stalls first and drops, preventing main wing stall, a design feature also in current use in Burt Rutan's stall-proof VariViggen canard design, a light sport plane. It also was found that tip vortices from the canard at high angles of attack blanketed the spoilers when placed behind the canard, hence they were repositioned further outboard.

While the wing spar was built of balsa wood, aluminum tubing was used for the fuselage truss system. The Schwinn Bicycle Company provided the design for the two-man cycling positions. Nylon skin was used for covering.

The first flight resulted in nearly complete structural collapse, and the machine was rebuilt as *Burd II*. The primary changes were internal, to reduce weight. An accident to *Burd II* in the late fall of 1977 put the craft back in the shop, and although the *Gossamer Condar* had already flown the Kremer course successfully, the students decided to go ahead, regardless.

James M. McAvoy of Georgia Technical University in 1962 came up with a novel departure in design, for a low-wing monoplane featuring a 10-foot diameter, four-bladed ducted-fan propeller at the rear of its triangular cross-section fuselage. Enclosing the propeller in a shroud was intended to increase the propeller efficiency by reducing blade-tip loss, and the shroud also served as a rudder and

Prof. Eugene E. Covert of MIT checks two-man BURD II MPA.

James P. McAvoy of Gerogia Technical University designed this MPA in 1962, with four-bladed ducted fan propeller.

tailplane. Elevators were mounted at the top and bottom of the annulus. Differential wing flaps were added to control banking. A single stick and hand lever in front of the open cockpit provided control input. Robert Ritchie, the pilot, sprinted the machine down the main runway at Fulton Airport—and crashed.

In Southern California, where Professor Twining's "Flip Flop" ornithopter had been ridiculed in 1910, students at the Northrop Institute of Technology (now Northrop University) in the early 1970s designed an unusual channel-wing MPA with two counter-rotating, four-bladed propellers turning inside shrouds, similar to the McAvoy design. The students—Thurman Elliott, Jeffrey Kildow, Malcolm Smith, and William Sutherlen—proposed to construct the wing with Kraft paper honeycomb, paper Nomex honeycomb, both hexagonal and expanded cell, and thin vinyl, covered with 0.00035 inch Melinex. Two pilots were to pedal their *Flycycle* in tandem.

Like others before them, the NIT students had been turned onto MPA design work by the Kremer Competition, and in January,

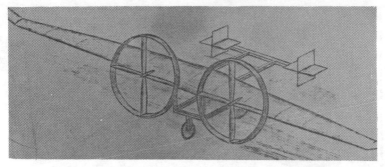

Early Northrop Institute of Technology MPA design featured counter-rotating propellers, twin tails, two-man propulsion.

1971, the project was transferred from Kildow's home to the NIT Aerodynamics Laboratory. A group of 20 other students joined them, with faculty guidance from Dr. Takashi Sugimura, assistant professor of aerospace engineering.

Eleven designs were tried before they settled on the final *Flycycle* design, a tandem two-place monoplane with a single pusher propeller. While the design work progressed, two two-man teams were chosen. Lead pilots were Steve Slaughter, a 17-year-old glider pilot, and Mrs. Rosemary Lichter, a sailplane pilot and wife of Lloyd Lichter, executive director of the Soaring Society of America.

Flycycle's wing spanned 80 feet on paper and would weigh only 15 pounds completed. Plans were made to flight test the NIT MPA at El Toro Marine Station, then move it to the Salton Sea area for a shot at the Kremer Prize in the dense, below-sea-level sky.

Later NIT MPA design was two-seater with pusher prop. It never flew.

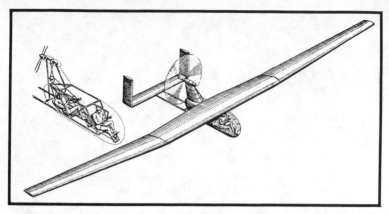

Melville M. Murrell switched MPA design to glider and made flights in 1877 at Panther Springs, Tenn.

Graduation of the Northrop students ended the project temporarily, but in 1973 it was briefly reviewed by a new student group working under Professor Johann Arbocz. A complete computer analysis of the Wortmann airfoil was run before interest lagged again. The project was never revitalized before the *Gossamer Condor* flights.

"Yankee Doodlers" in fact were busy long before the Kremer Competition got under way. Historically, one of the first American MPA's ever to get off the ground was Melville M. Murrell's *Aerial Navigator* of more than a century ago. In 1877 he patented an ornithopter in which the operator pushed on a crossbar with his feet to make the wings flap. The wings consisted of a number of hinged slats, normally kept closed by springs, which opened only on the up-stroke by air pressure from above. A pivoted tail was so rigged that a "wriggling or partially-rotary motion" could be imparted by the pilot.

Born in 1855, young Melville enjoyed tinkering with tools in the barn of his father's big home at Panther Springs, Tennessee, on the Knoxville-Bristol post road. Only 22 when he won his United States Patent, Melville altered his MPA design somewhat before flying it. The slats were mounted to provide foreward propulsion rather than lift, and the wing was a cloth-coverd rectangle. The pilot rod underneath the wing in a tubular framework. A cannard surface was mounted forward of the main plane.

In this machine the young inventor made several flights, launched at the end of a tow rope, and frequently covered several

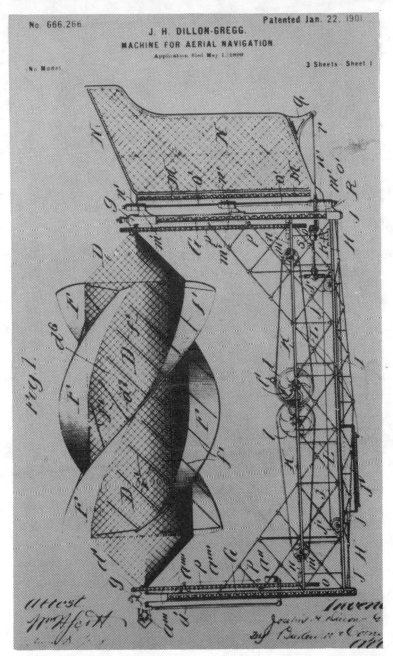

Archimedian screw principle was used in Jean Lassie's 1856 "Navigable Balloon" design, Craft was 900 feet long, designed to carry 300 men inside cylinder, with 150 men running on a treadmill to provide power. Trim weight is suspended below. (Hatfield Aeronautical Library)

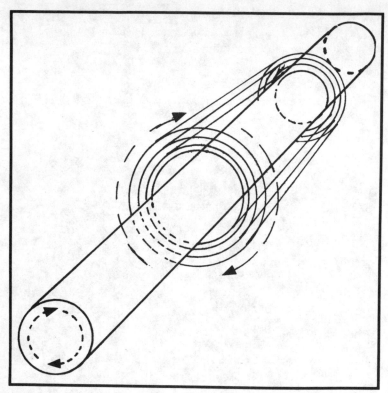

Magnus Effect.

hundred yards, according to family records. Historically they stand as the first recorded man-carrying glides in a heavier-than-air machine in the United States, and in fact preceded Lilienthal by more than a decade.

His goal was to achieve true powered flight, but lack of an adequate engine frustrated him, and soon he turned to religion, riding circuit as a backwoods preacher for the next 45 years. Many times the Reverend Murrell prayed that he might fly over Panther Springs in an aerial machine, his son recalls. In all, he did fly his device over the family apple orchard three times, no mean feat at the time. Murrell dies in 1932, satisfied to know that powered flight was no idle dream.

A quite different approach to man-powered flight has occupied the minds of researchers since the turn of the century—the Magnus Effect, in which a cylinder rotating around its spanwise axis in an air flow sets up a circulation and generates lift. D. A. Reay, a British engineer and author of *The History of Man-Powered Flight* (Pergamon Press, 1977), in 1965 undertook a research program at Bristol University in unconventional lifting-devices including Magnus Effect cylinders.

In 1969 in the United States, William F. Foshag and Gabriel D. Boehler of Aerophysics Company in Washington, D. C. published a paper on "HARWAS"—Horizontal-Axis Rotating-Wing Aeronautical Systems—listing some 1200 references to this subject, concluding that "promising new aeronautical systems" exist in this design.

Among the HARWAS devices tested was a wing rotor glider demonstrated by Koppen in 1903, and a Navy-Assisted Magnus Effect Aircraft by Ames in 1910. The Zaparka Magnus Rotor Aircraft possibly flew briefly in full size in 1930, they state, and an eight-foot wing rotor sailplane showed good flight performance and stability about all axes.

The Magnus Effect is basic to an understanding of the Kutta-Zhukovski theory of total circulation (see Chapter 4). It works this way: A cylinder spinning in a fluid at rest with respect to the cylinder sets up a circular and purely rotational flow, due to viscous forces in the fluid. If the cylinder is set in motion, the airflow assumes a streamline pattern with compression of the streamlines above the cylinder, a widening below it, and a downward component behind it, thus producing a vertical lifting force, or Magnus Effect.

An airfoil moving through still air produces a rotational flow in a similar manner to that around a cylinder, with a bound vortex around the wing and a starting vortex at the trailing edge, developing a downward momentum corresponding to the lift generated, as with the spinning cylinder.

Clyde D. (Daring) Goehring of Oceanside, Calif., experimented with MPA's at 72.

Third Archimedian screw propulsion idea for a MPA was used in the FLY WORM built in 1929 by Paul Maiwaru of San Diego, Calif.

Almost every day, new and unusual MPA's appeared in the public press, and too often were subjected to ridicule. Some progress was made, however, in various parts of the country. Wayne Bliesner of the University of Washington succeeded in making a towed flight in his winged machine before the hanger roof fell in and destroyed it. He was rebuilding it at last report.

In Oceanside, California, 72-year-old Clyde D. "Daring" Goehring in 1977 was at work on a pedal pusher tractor monoplane MPA with a huge propeller up front. Goehring drew on past experience as a wind tunnel technician at Douglas Aircraft Co., but he was still ground-bound when *Gossamer Condor* took off to make history.

And then there was Nick Dee of Los Angeles, who in 1972 was working on a secret MPA design that included a sort of slotted parachute that let him jump four feet off the garage floor and come down nice and easy. Later he changed the design so he could lie flat under the wings and drive a propeller with both hands and feet. It worked—too well. He flew smack into the wall and busted the prop.

Chapter 14
The Winner!

July, 1977, passed quickly at Shafter-Kern County Airport. The *Gossamer Condor* had by now made more than 430 flights since its conception just a year before. It had accumulated more flight time and traveled a greater distance than all previous MPA's combined, and yet the Kremer Award was still intact.

Time was running out. It was now or never, Dr. Paul Mac-Cready realized. The secret was out — the world knew how the giant flying machine crept around corners, with its reverse-action wing-warping mechanism. In mid-August, *Gossamer Condor* was rebuilt for the last time, following the crash that occurred when a trailing vortex from a landing Ag Cat snapped its frail wing.

The fuselage was reworked and the crank mechanism lightened by drilling holes through the wheels, and now the craft stood seven pounds lighter. Jack Lambie estimated that meant a reduction in power-required by 0.2 horsepower.

Then came news from overseas—Professor Kimura's Stork was warming up for a final shot at the Kremer Prize! The chief pilot, 5' 7" T. Kato, had been in training by riding his bike 50 kilometers a day, and already had made a remarkable flight of 6,807 feet at Shimofusa Airfield; he might have done still better, had the runway been longer.

That flight was an official world record, observed by officials of the Japan Aeronautic Association as covering 2074.9 meters in 4 minutes 43 seconds, nearly doubling the former world distance MPA flight of 1071 meters held by John Potter in England. Dr. MacCready felt uneasy—would the Japanese learn his secret and be able to fly the figure-eight Kremer course?

When I visited Dr. MacCready earlier that year, covering the *Gossamer Condor* flights for Homebuilt Aircraft Magazine, I was sworn to secrecy about certain tehnical aspects of the design, and adhered to my promise. But now the full story can be told.

Professor Emeritus Hidemasa Kimura of Nihon University had encouraged his engineering students to develop a man-powered aircraft, soon after word arrived in 1961 of the flights of Britain's *Sumpac* and *Puffin* machines.

As a first step, in 1963 an experimental testing device was designed to measure the power exerted when a man pushes against a bicycle pedal. The second year was devoted to operations research into optimum airframe dimensions, weight, aerodynamics, and other factors. And in February 1966 Japan's first MPA rolled out—the *Linnet*, named for a tiny bird whose flight performance, in Professor Kimura's words, "is rather unimpressive."

Japanese MPA Linnet first flew in February, 1966.

He reported: "On February 25, 1966, our dear *Linnet*, with Munetaka Okamiya at the controls, lifted wheels off the gound for the first time. The following day the bird flew some 15 meters, marking Japan's first successful steady flight of a man-powered aircraft."

Because of his aerial feat, says the professor, "Mr. Okamiya became the first Japanese who was able to walk on the ground, swim at sea, and fly in the air using his own power."

In all, five *Linnets* were built, mainly as a research project for the students, not to compete for the Kremer Award. Secrets of the *Linnet* design were light-weight construction and use of styrene paper for covering, superior to the Melinex used in England. A student got the idea when he spotted some sashimi (raw fish) being sold wrapped in styrene.

A design drawback was the requirement for a long transmission shaft to turn the propeller at the tail, which resulted in considerable vibration. Pilots chosen to fly the *Linnets* were all licensed private pilots.

A new design series called *Egret* was launched in 1972, and the tail propeller position was abandoned for a pylon mount and a belt drive, similar to the British *Sumpac* and *Jupiter* machines. The rear fuselage was lengthened to provide greater longitudinal stability. Of three *Egrets* built and flown, the first was destroyed by turbulence, but the others flew quite well.

By 1975, the Nihon freshmen class had become seniors, with considerable design experience behind them. One student, Junji Ishii, was an expert designer, and Professor Kimura left him in charge of the new MPA, called the *Stork*.

Aerodynamically improved over *Egret*, the *Stork* featured detachable wings for easy transport. Its overall weight was amazingly low—36.0 kg—and yet it was quite rigid. Parts of the machine were covered with a Japanese paper called *ganpi-shi*. Every ounce of excess weight was removed, and a chain drive replaced the troublesome belt drive, linked to both the propeller and a ground wheel.

The initial *Stork*, called Model A, first flew on March 12, 1976 and in all made 45 flights including 11 over 400 meters (1312.33 feet). On June 4, 1976, unknown to the *Gossamer Condor* team in California, a student pilot, K. Churei, succeeded in making a 180-degree turn, at a 10-degree bank flying 9 feet above the ground.

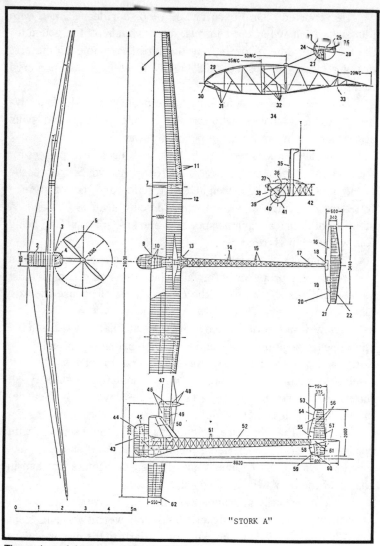

Three-view of Japanese MPA STORK A.

The turn wound up into a spiral dive, however, and the machine struck the ground. Professor Kimura was elated, nevertheless, and was convinced *Stork* could fly the figure-eight course at a smaller bank angle. *Stork*, he believed, had reached the level of the British MPA performances.

Rebuilt as *Stork B*, the Japanese MPA's wing was waxed to cut friction drag, the fuselage reinforced with balsa bulkheads, and the

Nihon U. student works on STORK's propulsion system.

cockpit canopy reshaped to fit their top pilot, T. Kato. The elevator movement also was decreased, against the amount of the twist of the control lever.

Officially designated the NM-75 *Stork*, the cantilever shoulder-wing monoplane used the Wortmann FX61-184 airfoil at the root, and FX-63-137 at the tips.

Nihon U. students assembling wing of STORK MPA.

Nihon U. students work on STORK's wing.

With a wingspan of 68 feet 11 inches and wing area of 233.6 sq/ft., STORK's wing loading was only 0.89 lb/sq. ft. Its optimum speed was 19.2 mph with a C_l of 0.94, and the power required in ground effect was computed at 0.33 hp, or 0.35 hp at 3 meters altitude.

Professor Kimura had other plans for *Stork* than simply shooting for the Kremer Award—it served well as a student engineering project, and plans were made to install solar panels along the wing's upper surface, to power an electric motor with solar energy.

Closer to home, Dr. MacCready kept a weather eye on conditions at El Mirage Dry Lake on the Mojave Desert of Southern California, where Taras Kiceniuk was flight-testing his *Icarus* ground effect MPA, designed to skid through its turns rather than bank.

Icarus' fuselage was built from aluminum and styrofoam, with an aluminum tail boom sticking out behind. The empennage was built up from foam sheeting, with the control cables running forward through the tail boom to the control handle-bars. The tail boom also served as the propeller shaft. The propeller blades had variable pitch, to maintain a constant rpm.

The wing construction was unusual, consisting of 56 individual styrofoam blocks cut out with a hot wire. Each block was hollowed for lightness, then all were glued together over the full 41-foot span.

Flight of STORK B at Shimofusa Naval Air Base, Japan.

	AIRCRAFT	LINNET I	LINNET II	LINNET III
	DATE OF FIRST FLIGHT	26 Feb.'66	19 Feb.'67	26 Mar.'70
	MAXIMUM DISTANCE FLOWN (m)	43	91	31
DIMENSIONS (m)	WING SPAN (m)	22.30	22.30	25.30
	LENGTH O.A.(m)	5.60	5.80	5.86
	HEIGHT O.A.(m)	4.185	3.52	4.14
	TAIL PLANE SPAN (m)	5.40	5.40	5.80
AREAS (m^2)	WING, GROSS (m^2)	26.0	26.0	30.2
	AILERONS, TOTAL (m^2)	2.20	2.20	— (1)
	FIN (m^2)	0.97	0.97	1.53
	RUDDER (m^2)	0.46	0.46	0.45
	STABILIZER (m^2)	2.18	2.18	— (2)
	ELEVATORS (m^2)	1.46	1.46	3.40
WING	AEROFOIL SECTION	NACA63$_3$-1218	NACA63$_3$-1218	NACA8418-8415
	WING THICKNESS(%)	18.0	18.0	18.0∿15.0
	ASPECT RATIO	18.5	18.5	21.2
	TAPER RATIO	3:1	3:1	3:1
	DIHEDRAL	3°	3°	6°
PROPELLER	DIAMETER (m)	2.70	2.70	3.00
	r.p.m.	160	200	125
	SPEED OF AIRCRAFT (m/s)	8.2	8.0	7.6
WEIGHTS	WEIGHT EMPTY (kg)	50.6	44.7	49.8
	FLYING WEIGHT (kg)	108.6 (3)	102.7 (3)	107.8 (3)
	WING LOADING (kg/m^2)	4.18	3.95	3.57
WEIGHT BREAKDOWN (kg)	WING	22.83	19.23	22.0
	TAIL UNIT	4.03	3.23	3.1
	CONTROL SYSTEM	0.86	0.96	1.0
	FUSELAGE	11.90	12.68	12.0
	UNDERCARRIAGE	2.55	2.55	3.5
	PROPELLER	} 4.78	1.03	1.3
	TRANSMISSION		3.66	5.5
	MISCELLANEOUS	3.65	1.36	1.4

(1) no aileron   (2) flying tail   (3) weight of pilot = 58 kg.
O.W. outer wing   N.A. no data available

	LINNET IV	EGRET I	EGRET II	EGRET III	Stork A	Stork B
	13 Mar.'71	28 Feb.'73	30 Oct.'73	16 Nov.'74	12 Mar.'76	24 Nov.'76
	60	34	154	203	595	2093.9
	25.30	22.70	22.70	23.00	21.00	
	5.80	7.40	7.71	7.70	8.85	
	4.14	2.29	3.66	3.70	2.40	
	5.91	4.00	5.00	4.70	3.44	
	30.2	28.5	28.5	28.5	21.7	
	— (1)	1.90	3.11	2.40	2.52	
	1.55	0.75	1.04	1.01	0.81	
	0.45	0.50	0.56	0.76	0.35	
	2.33	— (2)	1.98	2.13	— (2)	
	1.55	3.30	1.32	0.70	1.71	
	NACA8418	FX61-184	FX61-184	FX61-184	FX61-184 ∿FX63-137	
	18.0	18.4	18.4	18.4	18.4∿13.7	
	21.2	18.1	18.1	18.6	20.3	
	3:1	2.5:1 (O.W.)	2.5:1 (O.W.)	2:1 (O.W.)	2.36:1 (O.W.)	
	6°	6° (O.W.)	6° (O.W.)	6° (O.W.)	7° (O.W.)	
	3.00	2.70	2.70	2.70	2.50	
	125	180	180	120	210	
	7.7	8.5	9.6	9.8	8.6	
	55.0	57.0	55.7	61.1	35.9	
	113.0[3]	115.0[3]	113.7[3]	119.1[3]	93.9[3]	
	3.74	4.04	3.99	4.18	4.33	
	N.A.	25.3	24.0	33.0	19.9	
		3.0	3.0	2.8	1.0	
		5.0	4.7	2.9	7.4	
		11.5	15.0	} 15.0	}	
		3.0	3.0		1.0	
		1.2	1.0	1.4	1.0	
		5.0	5.0	6.0	5.6	
		3.0	—	—	—	

Taras Kiceniuk (left) and assistants Bill Watson and Dave Sachs with ICARUS ground effect machine, canopy removed at El Mirage Dry Lake.

A small wheel was built into each wingtip, and the wing spar was carved from a piece of 1″ by ½″ Douglas fir, tapering to ⅛″ at the tips. Wings and fuselage were covered with a total of 60 rolls of red and blue translucent solar film, donated by a commercial firm, Pactra.

On August 1, 1977, Taras Kiceniuk took *Icarus* out to El Mirage Dry Lake for its initial flight test, but its high-aspect ratio wooden propeller stalled at about 1/3 its anticipated thrust. A foam propeller was substituted and worked better.

Three different pilots flew *Icarus* — Kiceniuk, Bill Watson, and Dave Sacks, the latter a glider pilot and bicyclist. On each flight the machine was towed aloft behind a small motorbike at about 20 mph, to let the pilot get the feel of the control system. As beautiful and graceful as she looked, skimming over the alkali lake bed, *Icarus* was still far from attaining anything like the ungainly *Gossamer Condor's* performance.

But there was still another MPA for Dr. MacCready to worry about — Joe Zinno's *Olympian* ZB-1, which became the first MPA to fly in the United States on April 21, 1976, from a runway at Quonset Point, North Kingstown, R. I. A retired Air Force Lieutenant Colonel, Joseph A. Zinno lifted off at 8:10 a.m. in a quartering wind of 8 knots, rose a foot, and covered 77 feet before touching down.

Zinno was tracked by Navy radar at 15.4 fps for 5 seconds, at a ground speed computed at 9.77 mph following a liftoff speed of 17.77 mph. Average ground speed was timed at 10.5 mph.

"The most important thing," Zinno told the author, "is to solve the problem, not win the Kremer Award, no matter how long it takes. The problem is definitely solvable, and with the growing number of people interested in MPA flight, each with his own approach, somewhere along the line, if we could find a clearing house for all these ideas, we might find the making of a solution."

Working alone with limited resources, Zinno, an ex-USAF pilot with 8,000 logged hours, had flown every type aircraft there was, "and it got so that one airplane was just like any other. There was no challenge left!" The next thing he knew, "There I was with this crazy model airplane on my hands!"

Bill Watson pumps air with cardboard box pump into ICARUS cockpit to keep it cool.

Taras Kiceniuk's ICARUS MPA flies in tow behind motorcycle.

Zinno's *Olympian* ZBl-1 was basically a midwing cantilever pusher with a 78-½ foot span, conventional tail and a flying stabilator attached to a 4-inch diameter aluminum boom. Propeller diameter was 8.7 feet, the wing built up around a box spar. Empty weight was 150 pounds, design gross weight 290 pounds. Wing area was 312 sq. ft., optimum loading under 1 lb/sq. ft.

Controlled conventionally from an enclosed cockpit, the Zinno MPA used bike-type hand grips, for rudder control on one side and for the elevator on the other. He used a treadle-type propeller drive system. He went to the Wortmann 150B airfoil near the wing root, with a tremendous camber to generate high lift at low speed, and a Wortmann 137 airfoil outboard "to compensate for a hellatious diving moment."

So that was the main known competition on August 23, 1977, when Bryan Allen eased into the cockpit of the 70-pound *Gossamer Condor*, at Shafter-Kern County Airport, for the 223rd time. All systems were go. Smoothly he accelerated into a shifting, 2-knot zephyr that drifted him slightly off course. He sailed easily over the ten-foot hurdle to enter the first turn to the right, around the first pylon.

Cries of encouragement spurred him on as he pedaled rhythmically toward the next pylon. Rounding that, to the left, he saw Jack Lambie holding the hurdle bar in the distance—the finish line! He later related:

"I was busy pedaling and flying the *Condor*, judging the turns to make sure I was outside the markers and correcting for the wind

Col. Joe Zinno, USAF (ret.) poses with his MPA, the Olympian ZB-1, that flew 77 feet.

which kept trying to move us off course. Then I saw the T bar ahead of me and suddenly, almost shocked, I realized that this flight would be it!

Prize-winning flight of GOSSAMER CONDOR on August 23, 1977, that won coveted Kremer Award of $50,000. (Photo by Judy MacCready).

Bryan Allen, who flew Gossamer Condor to victory.

"I speeded up my pedaling a bit and topped it with three feet to spare. I was tired but not exhausted so I slowed but flew another 400 feet before landing. Dr. MacCready came over, with a smile as wide as his face."

To Paul MacCready, success of the 7½-minute flight belonged to the full team, not to any one individual. His MPA had finally won the coveted Kremer Award, but the future lay ahead. What good was it? The *Gossamer Condor* had become a docile behemoth, so easy to fly that a number of men, women, and children who had never flown before, successfully flew it on short hops. He observed:

"The Kremer Prize flight represented an aviation milestone, in the sense of reaching one form of man's oldest aviation dream. Unlike some other aviation milestones, there does not seem to be any direct practical or commercial application which can follow.

"Human powered flight may help man's spirit, may raise his appreciation for his physical potential, and serve as an incentive for people on physical development programs, and may give him a better understanding of the flight challenges of soaring birds, but he will not pedal to the market or to work."